Y0-DWZ-509

The Legacy of the French Revolutionary Wars

A major contribution to the study of collective identity and memory in France, this book examines a French republican myth: the belief that the nation can be adequately defended only by its own citizens, in the manner of the French revolutionaries of 1793. Alan Forrest examines the image of the citizen army reflected in political speeches, school textbooks, art and literature across the nineteenth century. He reveals that the image appealed to notions of equality and social justice, and with time it expanded to incorporate Napoleon's victorious legions, the partisans who repelled the German invader in 1814 and the people of Paris who rose in arms to defend the republic in 1870. More recently it has risked being marginalised by military technology and by the realities of colonial warfare, but its influence can still be seen in the propaganda of the Great War and of the French Resistance under Vichy.

ALAN FORREST is Professor of Modern History at the University of York. His previous books include *Paris, the Provinces and the French Revolution* (2004), *Napoleon's Men: The Soldiers of the Revolution and Empire* (2002) and *The Revolution in Provincial France: Aquitaine, 1789–1799* (1996).

Studies in the Social and Cultural History of Modern Warfare

General Editor
Jay Winter, *Yale University*

Advisory Editors
Omer Bartov, *Brown University*
Carol Gluck, *Columbia University*
David M. Kennedy, *Stanford University*
Paul Kennedy, *Yale University*
Antoine Prost, *Université de Paris-Sorbonne*
Emmanuel Sivan, *Hebrew University of Jerusalem*
Robert Wohl, *University of California, Los Angeles*

In recent years the field of modern history has been enriched by the exploration of two parallel histories. These are the social and cultural history of armed conflict, and the impact of military events on social and cultural history.

Studies in the Social and Cultural History of Modern Warfare presents the fruits of this growing area of research, reflecting both the colonization of military history by cultural historians and the reciprocal interest of military historians in social and cultural history, to the benefit of both. The series offers the latest scholarship in European and non-European events from the 1850s to the present day.

For a list of titles in the series, please see end of book.

The Legacy of the French Revolutionary Wars

The Nation-in-Arms in French Republican Memory

Alan Forrest

WITHDRAWN

CAMBRIDGE UNIVERSITY PRESS
Cambridge, New York, Melbourne, Madrid, Cape Town, Singapore, São Paulo, Delhi

Cambridge University Press
The Edinburgh Building, Cambridge CB2 8RU, UK

Published in the United States of America by Cambridge University Press, New York

www.cambridge.org
Information on this title: www.cambridge.org/9780521810623

© Alan Forrest 2009

This publication is in copyright. Subject to statutory exception
and to the provisions of relevant collective licensing agreements,
no reproduction of any part may take place without
the written permission of Cambridge University Press.

First published 2009

Printed in the United Kingdom at the University Press, Cambridge

A catalogue record for this publication is available from the British Library

Library of Congress Cataloguing in Publication data
Forrest, Alan I.
The legacy of the French Revolutionary Wars : the nation-in-arms in French republican memory / Alan Forrest.
p. cm.
Includes bibliographical references and index.
ISBN 978-0-521-81062-3 (hbk.) 1. France–History–Revolution, 1789–1799–Influence. 2. France–History, Military. 3. France. Armie–History. 4. War and society–France–History. 5. Civil-military relations–France–History. 6. Collective memory–France–History. 7. Political culture–France–History. 8. Republicanism–France–History. 9. Nationalism–France–History. 10. France–Intellectual life. I. Title.
DC151.F675 2009
355.020944–dc22
2009011445

ISBN 978-0-521-81062-3 hardback

Cambridge University Press has no responsibility for the persistence or
accuracy of URLs for external or third-party internet websites referred to
in this publication, and does not guarantee that any content on such
websites is, or will remain, accurate or appropriate.

Contents

Acknowledgements

My interest in the legacy of the Revolutionary armies began some years ago when I was principally concerned with the armies themselves and the young men who served in them. I was curious to know more about what motivated them and about the real as well as the rhetorical construct of citizenship; and I quickly became fascinated by the legend they created, a legend of commitment and enthusiasm as well as of republican equality that stretched into the nineteenth century and beyond to become a central strand of French republican identity. The idea of tracing that legend across the period from the eighteenth to the twentieth century took root in the years from 1997 to 1999 when I took part in a three-year research seminar at the Institute for Advanced Study in Princeton, convened by Daniel Moran and Arthur Waldron, which brought together historians from Europe, America and Australia to discuss the legacy of the French *levée en masse* throughout the modern world. This collection was published in 2003 by Cambridge University Press under the title *The People in Arms. Military Myth and Political Legitimacy since the French Revolution*. It was the experience of participating in that seminar which persuaded me to work on the myth in the context of France itself.

As a historian of the late eighteenth century I have leant heavily on approaches and insights of historians from later periods of French history and must acknowledge the debt which this book owes to others. I have enjoyed long and fruitful exchanges with a wide array of friends and colleagues, most notably Michael Broers, Charles Esdaile, Robert Gildea, Sudhir Hazareesingh, Holger Hoock, David Hopkin, John Horne, Annie Jourdan, Matthias Middell and Kevin Morgan, who all, in very different ways, have fed ideas and insight into the project. I have found inspiration in the work of French specialists on the Great War and in the rich historiography that has come out of the *Historial de la Grande Guerre* at Péronne. And since 2005 I have benefited enormously from working with an international research group on the experience and memory of the Revolutionary and Napoleonic Wars, based here in

York and in Berlin. To Richard Bessel, Etienne François, Karen Hagemann, Leighton James, Catriona Kennedy, Jane Rendall and Marie-Cecile Thoral I owe a special debt of thanks. At Cambridge University Press I received support and encouragement from my editor, Michael Watson, and valuable advice from two anonymous readers. Various parts of the text have also been submitted to the criticism of conference and seminar audiences, both in this country and abroad. The role of school textbooks was the subject of a colloquium held by Anna-Maria Rao in Naples in 2003, while I discussed the central argument of the book in a seminar in 2004 at the Ecole des Hautes Etudes en Sciences Sociales (EHESS) in Paris, thanks to a generous invitation from Patrice Gueniffey to spend a month there as a *directeur d'études*. Other sections have been exposed to the constructive criticism of seminar audiences in Cambridge, Liverpool, Dublin, Minneapolis and New York, and here in York in the congenial interdisciplinary atmosphere of the Centre for Eighteenth Century Studies.

As always, my greatest debt lies closer to home, to Rosemary and Marianne, to whom this book is gratefully dedicated.

Alan Forrest
York, March 2008

1 Introduction

It was during the nineteenth century that the legend of the nation-in-arms achieved its fullest expression, presenting an idealised image of the citizen-soldier to which republicans, in France and in many other parts of Europe, remained firmly wedded right up to the Great War of 1914–18. The legend was rooted in notions of civic equality and citizenship, emphasising the courage and resolution of young men who believed in their cause and fought for their people and their nation, selflessly and without regret. In a spirit of willing sacrifice that was reminiscent of the virtue of Athens or Sparta, they were depicted as heroes defending right against the massed forces of darkness, as the Gallic embodiment of an enduring Classical myth. And if in the twentieth century this image lost much of its potency, that had less to do with the popular appeal of the legend – the demand that all should serve the nation in moments of great danger, that rich and poor alike should share in acts of collective sacrifice, continued to be persuasive – than with the more specialist nature of warfare and the technological needs of modern armies. The imposition of mass conscription or the call to popular insurrection against an invader made sense when wars were fought by huge infantry regiments or when fighting meant sniper-fire from the roofs of Paris; they become less relevant in an age when armies have specialist tank regiments and rely on missile technology. This may explain why, in the twentieth century, the myth of the nation-in-arms proved more popular in the emergent nations of the developing world – China, Algeria or Vietnam – than on the European continent.[1] In sub-Saharan Africa, for instance, conscription and forced recruitment remain almost universal; indeed, recruitment is not always limited to adult males as it was in France. Many African societies regard those thirteen-year-old boys who have participated in cultural rites of

[1] See the chapters by Arthur Waldron, Greg Lockhart and Douglas Porch in Daniel Moran and Arthur Waldron (eds.), *The People in Arms. Military Myth and National Mobilization since the French Revolution* (Cambridge, 2003), pp. 189–255.

passage as having already attained adulthood; while the Constitution of South Africa specifically permits the recruitment in times of emergency of boys over fifteen years of age. Even children are part of the nation-in-arms.[2]

In 1996 France finally gave up its commitment to a conscript army and to the principle of universal military service, President Jacques Chirac accepting that modern warfare required a smaller, and above all a professional, army in which the ideal of the nation-in-arms no longer had a place. But the principle of universal service was not given up without a struggle; to many it seemed that it was part of the nation's culture that was being discarded, part of the republican identity of France.[3] For large sections of the Left, in particular, conscription was not just a fair and equitable basis on which to raise troops for the nation's defence. It was the debt owed by every young Frenchman to his country, and part of what Annie Crépin has identified as a 'triple apprenticeship' – for membership of the nation, for full citizenship and as an induction into the traditions of the French republic.[4] It was therefore seen as a central part of state pedagogy, and this was not something that could be lightly discarded. The issue of conscription had been discussed in a highly political – even an ideological – language. It had been a recurrent theme of the defence debates of the 1970s and 1980s, in which the Left had shown great reluctance to depart from the principle of universal service and from the ideal of civic equality. This stemmed in part from their deep-seated distrust of the officer class in the army, whom they were always prone to suspect of harbouring political ambitions and of plotting to seize power as they had done with Bonaparte in 1800, or Louis Napoleon in 1851, or – most recently – General de Gaulle in 1958. They were especially fearful of creating a separate military class of men divorced from the needs and ambitions of civil society. As recently as 1973 the Communist Party insisted that 'military service, equal for everyone, will be of a length of six months', adding that the equation of the soldier and the citizen must be safeguarded at all costs. 'A democratic statute for soldiers and officers will be adopted', while, to ensure their integration into

[2] Michael Wessells, 'Recruitment of children as soldiers in sub-Saharan Africa: an ecological analysis', in Lars Mjøset and Stephen Van Holde (eds.), *The Comparative Study of Conscription in the Armed Forces (Comparative Social Research,* vol. 20) (Amsterdam, 2002), pp. 239–40.

[3] The continued relevance of the ideal is reflected in correspondence in the columns of *Le Monde* during 1996.

[4] Annie Crépin, *La conscription en débat, ou le triple apprentissage de la nation, de la citoyenneté, de la République, 1798–1889* (Arras, 1998), p. 13.

society, 'military personnel will be able to receive freely newspapers and periodicals of their choice'.[5] Increasingly, however, theirs was a political rather than a military argument, until, at the time of the Gulf War, the emptiness of this rhetoric became patent to all. Armed with a force of young conscripts, France had neither the highly skilled troops needed to operate the most advanced tanks, nor the capacity – since they were largely manned by conscript sailors – to take their aircraft-carriers out of port.[6] From this moment the principle of conscription, like the ideal of universal citizen service, was surely doomed.

With it died the last embers of the legend of the nation-in-arms. The legend had its origins, of course, in the French Revolutionary Wars of the 1790s and in the fiercely patriotic discourse of revolutionary politics, when the *patrie* was in danger of invasion, and when France's soldiers were transformed into 'volunteers', fighting with republican commitment and ferocity to save their country from invasion and defend their new-won freedoms against the paid hirelings of tyrants.[7] The nation-in-arms was the force that turned the war around and repulsed the enemy from French soil. It was composed of men who were deeply committed to the cause of the people, patriotic, idealistic men, the cream of their generation, rushing to the frontiers and fighting selflessly to defend their homes, their womenfolk, their villages. The phrase was central to the revolutionaries' identity, and was rather indiscriminately used to describe whatever army the Revolution chose to place in the field. It was applied to the army of 1792, composed of an uneasy mixture of young volunteers and veterans of the line; the mass army of three-quarters of a million men that saved the Jacobin republic in the campaigns of 1793 and 1794; and even the men who set out to Italy and Egypt under the Directory to fight campaigns that were more imperialistic than revolutionary. All were described in ideological terms by their generals and their political leaders. And all, basking in the roseate glow of memory, took their place in the national narrative as patriots, republicans and idealists, fighting with courage and exuberance – a bravura that was itself specifically revolutionary – to defend a cause in which they profoundly believed.

This image necessarily gained new inflections over time, with the violent swings that marked French political life in the nineteenth

[5] Parti Communiste Français, *Programme commun de gouvernement du Parti Communiste Français et du Parti Socialiste* (Paris, 1972), p. 173, quoted in R.E. Utley, *The French Defence Debate. Consensus and Continuity in the Mitterrand Era* (London, 2000), p. 32.

[6] Utley, *The French Defence Debate*, pp. 185–6.

[7] Moran and Waldron, *The People in Arms*, pp. 1–5.

century, the Revolution giving way to the Empire, then to legitimism, to the July Monarchy, a second republic and a second empire, before finally establishing some kind of institutional stability after 1870 in the shadow of the Paris Commune. But the basic image, and with it the essence of the legend, remained largely unchanged. Indeed, the legend, what some preferred to call the 'myth', of the nation-in-arms gained in strength and in romantic appeal with the passage of time, as France appeared increasingly urban and materialistic – the France of Decazes and Royer-Collard, the Paris of Rambuteau and Haussmann. There was little in the values of political life which they could identify with honour and idealism, *élan* and derring-do; so many looked to the past, to the colour and drama of a very different age. Some continued to identify with the First Republic, and for those committed republicans the legend of the nation-in-arms acquired greater precision; it was the army of the Year II that continued to inspire their loyalty and admiration, the mass army constructed on the basis of a universal call to arms. But for many others the legend was almost infinitely flexible, with the consequence that little distinction was drawn between the Revolutionary and Napoleonic Wars, between Valmy and Austerlitz, Campo Formio and Friedland. These were the high points of a golden generation, and of an era when France was the unquestioned master of Continental Europe. It was an adaptable, elastic image that appealed to many on the Right as well as on the Left of the political spectrum, and which was endorsed by such widely different writers as Balzac and Victor Hugo, Jaurès and Déroulède.[8]

This book is about that legend – its construction and adaptation over succeeding generations, its renewed vitality in moments of revolutionary insurgency like 1848 and 1871, and the manifold uses that were made of it in preparing the young men of the Third Republic – another generation whose lives would be scarred and dominated by war – for the trenches of 1914. If I have preferred to use the word 'legend' rather than 'myth', it is not because there was no mythologising, amongst French republicans in particular, but rather because in the images devoted to the republican armies – whether in art, sculpture, poetry or novels – there was also more than a grain of truth. The democratic image of the citizen-soldier, the potent emblem that was the nation-in-arms, these are the stuff of both myth and legend, developing over time to construct a powerful narrative that would be one of the foundation myths of the French republic. In this it shares much of the potency of another

[8] Alan Forrest, 'L'armée de l'an II: la levée en masse et la création d'un mythe républicain', *Annales historiques de la Révolution Française* 335 (2004), pp. 111–30.

national legend, that of the Anzac forces at Gallipoli, which did so much to provide twentieth-century Australians with a national identity, free from the constraints of the British Empire. It was at Gallipoli in 1915 – rather as at Valmy in 1792 – that the courage and fighting qualities of her soldiers gave Australia the 'baptism of fire' which helped forge her nationhood. The ingredients are so strikingly similar, and the national characteristics which they supposedly revealed were ones with which generations of Australians would be happy to identify and which everyone, from newspaper editors and war correspondents to the writers of war memoirs and regimental histories, reinforced.[9] Australians, it was emphasised, were not like the British troops alongside whom they fought against the Turks. They were self-reliant, loyal to their mates, egalitarian. And they had a hint of a wild streak which their countrymen recognised and admired. 'They seemed to belong', wrote George Johnson in one of the countless tributes to Australia's young heroes, 'not to the standard conceptions of military prowess and discipline, but to some other, younger, more exuberant world of the spirit'; they were 'activated by simple codes of loyalty and comradeship'; they respected their opponents 'far more than they ever admired or respected their own leaders'.[10] At Gallipoli, a heroic-romantic myth was born that would help shape a nation's identity.

The myth of the French citizen-soldier, like its Australian counterpart, had a basis in historical reality, or at least in a selective reading of that reality. There were volunteers and idealists among the soldiers of the Republic, young men who did dream of a new age that was dawning and wished to play their part in the betterment of mankind. There were selfless sons who bade their families a tearful farewell – the trope of so many a painting and popular print[11] – before sacrificing their lives in defence of the rights of others. There were young soldiers in the armies of Italy or the Rhine who wrote home from the front in 1794 to urge still greater sacrifices and more radical laws against hoarders or refractory priests.[12] Such men looked to their local clubs and popular societies for support, and they often saw the Jacobins as

[9] Alistair Thomson, 'A past you can live with: digger memories and the Anzac legend', in Alan Seymour and Richard Nile (eds.), *Anzac: Meaning, Memory and Myth* (London, 1991), pp. 21–31.

[10] George Johnson, 'Anzac: a myth for all mankind' (1965), quoted in Jenny Macleod, *Reconsidering Gallipoli* (Manchester, 2004), p. 6.

[11] For examples of these images see Michel Vovelle, *La Révolution Française: images et récit* (5 vols., Paris, 1986), vol. III, pp. 50–5.

[12] Alan Forrest, *The Soldiers of the French Revolution* (Durham, N.C., 1990), pp. 159–60.

their strongest supporters in civil society.[13] And among their officers there were increasing numbers of committed Jacobins who, after the fall of Robespierre on 9 Thermidor, sought careers in the army so that they could continue to pursue their dreams once the political stage had been denied them. Such men existed. They were not mere figments of the nineteenth-century mind, however furiously their royalist opponents cast scorn on their naivety or their bloodthirsty devotion to terror. But they were relatively few in number and hardly typical of the army at large – except perhaps during that brief Jacobin interlude when the armies were subjected to intense political propaganda and egalitarian values were spread by deputies on mission from the Convention and by *sans-culotte* militants within the ranks. Of all the forces revolutionary France put into the field, it was the army of the Year II that came closest to the patriotic ideal, closest to the army of republican dreams and to the revolutionary legend for future generations. In the words of the socialist Jean Jaurès, the revolutionaries had in 1794 created something new and rather special, an army that was close to the people and ready to fight in its name.[14]

It was also, the legend maintains, an army which, because of the strength of its beliefs and the sincerity of its patriotism, fought better and with greater commitment than other armies, with a courage and bravura unparalleled across Europe. Because they were citizens defending their homes and fighting for their rights, so the argument ran, they suffered none of the self-doubt and low morale that bedevilled the traditional armies of the day. And because they were truly representative of the French people, they shared the virtues and qualities of the population at large – their bravery (self-esteem dictated that every nation considered itself without equal in courage and strength of character), their reckless energy, their gallantry towards women. In keeping with more traditional French self-representations, they took pride in their sociability, their *légèreté*, their penchant for seeking out pleasure.[15] According to the republicans of the 1870s and 1880s, it was only to such an army, an army that identified with the cause and the character of France, that the people could entrust their defence. After the humiliating collapse of the army of the Second Empire in the Franco-Prussian War, it was perhaps unsurprising that the politicians should look to a moral solution rather than a tactical or strategic one. Like Jaurès they believed that

[13] Isser Woloch, *Jacobin Legacy. The Democratic Movement under the Directory* (Princeton, N.J., 1970), p. 195.

[14] Jean Jaurès, *L'armée nouvelle* (2 vols., Paris, 1992), vol. II, p. 248.

[15] David Bell, *The Cult of the Nation in France. Inventing Nationalism, 1680–1800* (Cambridge, Mass., 2001), pp. 147–9.

it was imperative for the army to rediscover the moral force that had characterised the men of the Year II, and they did not hesitate to draw the obvious parallel between the army of 1871 and its predecessor of 1793. 'On this very day 78 years ago', thundered Léon Gambetta on 21 September 1871, 'our fathers founded the Republic and swore, in the face of foreign forces which defiled the sacred soil of the motherland, to live free or to die in combat. They kept their word; they were victorious, and the Republic of 1792 has remained in the memory of men as a symbol of national grandeur'.[16] For Gambetta and the leaders of the Third Republic, identification of these values with republican virtue was self-evident. In a speech commemorating the revolutionary general Hoche, delivered in his home town of Versailles in 1872, Gambetta did not hesitate to link Hoche's military qualities with his devotion to the revolutionary cause. He was a paragon of republicanism, 'the son of the Revolution, and the child of the people created by the Revolution', who led the life of an exemplary patriot; and if he was a great general, it was because he was 'respectful of the rights of each and every individual, understanding the value of his men'.[17] The soldiers of the Year II were not just gentle knights in war; they were commemorated both as citizens and as republicans.

They had, in other words, become incorporated into a specifically republican legend of France's military past, a myth that was at once patriotic and revolutionary. In the process, the soldier of the Year II entered France's public history and took his place in popular memory. He would prove an enduring and largely uncontested figure, the most acceptable form of memorial to an age which was brutally divisive and which continued to conjure up contrasting memories in different regions and different communities within France. The soldier as man of the people, as citizen, lost much of his ideological force, to be integrated into that vague 'religion of liberty' which Raoul Girardet characterises as 'revolutionary sentimentality'.[18] He was remembered more for what he had achieved on the battlefield – his qualities, his patriotism, his professionalism in the face of the enemy – than for his supposed belief in the Jacobin cause. He could be represented as being both the defender of the nation and the representative of the nation as no political leader of the period could hope to do. He became, in other words, depoliticised in the eyes of posterity, one of the few figures emanating

[16] Léon Gambetta, speech of 21 September 1871, quoted in André Rossel, *1870. La première guerre, par l'affiche et l'image* (Paris, 1970).

[17] Léon Gambetta, *Le Général Hoche. Discours prononcé à Versailles le 24 juin 1872* (Paris, 1872), pp. 7, 11.

[18] Raoul Girardet, *La société militaire de 1815 à nos jours* (Paris, 1998), p. 25.

from the revolutionary years who was held blameless for the spread of political violence and with whom all might seek to identify. In this sense, rather like the image of Napoleon during the July Monarchy, the soldier of the Year II could act as a point of reference for both supporters and opponents of the regime, a figure aloof from party politics, whose historical legacy could be – and was – claimed by men of every political persuasion.[19] Bonapartists, radicals, conservative republicans and nationalists, all except the most legitimist of monarchists, might identify with the legacy of the revolutionary armies, using them to rally support and unify the people behind them. Even those republicans who aligned themselves with the extreme Right during the 1880s and 1890s – most notably the supporters of Paul Déroulède's *Ligue des Patriotes* – took obvious pride in donning the cloak of revolutionary patriotism, seeing themselves as the natural heirs of the soldiers of the Year II.[20]

Public history is, by its very nature, highly selective, an exercise in collective amnesia as much as in national commemoration, providing present generations with justificatory readings of their past. The French path from subject to citizen, as Pierre Rosanvallon has demonstrated,[21] would never be smooth or uncontroversial, and many saw in the French Revolution the germs of so much future antipathy, not least among those communities – royalists, Catholics, moderate republicans, opponents of terror and state violence – who counted themselves among the Revolution's victims and whose future identities had been largely moulded by a chastening experience of the First Republic.[22] For these communities – and locally, they were numerous – the legacy of bitter months of dechristianisation and denunciation, faction-fighting and settling old scores, conjured up memories of terror and counter-terror at town and village level. But if politics divided the people against one another, and continued to do so across the nineteenth century, the memory of military triumphs and the call of *la Grande Nation* elicited a much warmer response. In recalling the

19 Robert Alexander, 'The hero as Houdini: Napoleon and nineteenth-century Bonapartism', *Modern and Contemporary France* 8 (2000), p. 457.

20 Christian Amalvi, 'Nationalist responses to the Revolution', in Robert Tombs (ed.), *Nationhood and Nationalism in France from Boulangism to the Great War, 1889–1918* (London, 1991), p. 39.

21 Pierre Rosanvallon has traced the development of French democracy in the period since the Revolution in a trilogy of volumes – *Le sacre du citoyen* (Paris, 1992); *Le peuple introuvable* (Paris, 1998); and *La démocratie inachevée* (Paris, 2000).

22 The Vendée provides what is almost certainly the most glaring instance of a region whose entire identity was constructed upon its experience of martyrdom during the Jacobin republic. See Jean-Clément Martin, *La Vendée de la mémoire, 1800–1980* (Paris, 1989).

Revolutionary period for posterity the armies offered an acceptable face, an image of patriotic zeal and heroic sacrifice for a regime whose ideology was, in the eyes of many, sullied by bloodletting, vengeance and needless violence.

The presence in so many villages of old soldiers, veterans of the Revolutionary and Napoleonic Wars who had returned home after years of campaigning to resume their civilian lives and – in surprisingly many cases – to assume responsibilities in the lives of local communities, ensured that the memory of war did not fade once military adventure ceased to have political appeal. They could not forget their adventures in the name of liberty and equality, or those – more frequent among the survivors of 1815 – in the armies of Napoleon. Military glories of the past seemed all the more resonant when they were contrasted with the decline in France's ambitions after Napoleon's exile, and their image was further burnished by the parsimonious treatment which the Bourbons reserved for those who had served the republic or the Empire and who now faced an 'impossible reinsertion' into civilian life.[23] Old soldiers looked back with pride, and asked only that their sacrifices be recognised by their compatriots. But how did the wider public, and in particular the public authorities, celebrate and reflect on the wars and the men who had fought in them? That would be an altogether harder question to resolve, as successive regimes sought to position themselves in respect to France's revolutionary tradition. In the process they selected their own myths, and constructed their own versions of the national narrative.

Some, like the Restoration monarchy, shunned any association with those who had fought for what it persisted in calling an illegitimate regime. Others, like the July Monarchy, made huge efforts to associate themselves and their public rhetoric with the military legacy of Bonaparte and of the Year II. All, of course, chose with care what part of that legacy to identify with, which heroes to elevate on national pedestals, and which values to incorporate in the mythology of the nation. Victories were hailed more often than defeats lamented – national galleries and army museums almost invariably bear witness to moments of triumph, skirting lightly over reverses and losses – while the cult of military leaders focussed on those who were tragic as well as heroic figures. Sites of memory in the nineteenth century shunned controversy, and the revolutionary army lent itself to this role, producing its quota of much-sung heroes – men like Hoche, Kléber and Marceau – who

[23] Natalie Petiteau, *Lendemains d'Empire. Les soldats de Napoléon dans la France du dix-neuvième siècle* (Paris, 2003), p. 141.

had died noble deaths, falling on the battlefield or in the line of duty, and who in death encapsulated chivalric values that were eternal and stripped of republican specificity.[24] Like Horatio Nelson in England, an equally compelling icon for a maritime nation, they were presented first and foremost as martyrs, their cult founded in the manner of their dying.[25] The fashion flourished particularly during the last quarter of the nineteenth century in France, in public sculpture, art, literature and theatre, largely in response to the popularity of the earlier cult of another revolutionary general, Napoleon Bonaparte.[26] One could praise the exploits of the Army of the Nord or of Napoleon in Italy without taking a public position on such domestic matters as the Terror, the Supreme Being, or the execution of Louis XVI.

The attention lavished during the nineteenth century on the revolutionary armies and their glorious achievements does, of course, beg the most central question of all. For supporters of the legend it was important to present the soldiers of the republic as a new and different kind of army, since, they insisted, it was its novelty and its egalitarian spirit that enabled them to turn a war of defence in 1793 into a great war of European conquest a year later. An army composed of citizens was necessarily, they believed – and here they were following the teachings of Clausewitz as much as their own political rhetoric – better motivated, driven by desire born of their status as full members of civil society: the 'elemental violence' of the people had been unleashed by the armed uprising of an entire nation.[27] But was it? Was the concept of an army of citizens as novel or as effective as apologists for the French Revolution liked to claim? Did the reality of army life in the 1790s reflect the political rhetoric of the age? Did the citizen-soldier succeed in giving the military a new and more respectable public image, effacing centuries of prejudice and contempt which had been heaped on the men who served the Ancien Régime?[28] In order to understand the power of the legend, we must first explore the army reforms that lie at its root, reforms which veered dramatically over the ten years of the Revolution before annual

[24] Michel Vovelle, 'Fortunes et infortunes de Marceau', in *Le Général Marceau. Figure emblématique du héros révolutionnaire* (exhibition catalogue, Chartres, 1996), p. 28.

[25] N.A.M. Rodger, 'Nelson and Napoleon: an Introduction', in Margarette Lincoln (ed.), *Nelson and Napoléon* (London, 2005), pp. 3–7.

[26] Venita Datta, '"L'appel au soldat": visions of the Napoleonic legend in popular culture of the Belle Epoque', *French Historical Studies* 28 (2005), pp. 1–4.

[27] Karl von Clausewitz, *On War*, trans. Michael Howard and Peter Paret (Princeton, 1976), p. 479.

[28] E.G. Léonard, *L'armée et ses problèmes au dix-huitième siècle* (Paris, 1958), pp. 47–50.

conscription was finally introduced in 1799. It will become clear that, for all the apparent simplicity of the legend, it, too, had very different faces – obedience to the state and equality of obligation on the one hand, voluntarism and enthusiasm on the other, civil duty and spontaneity marching hand-in-hand against the enemy in defence of the nation and its people.

2 Creating the legend

It did not take the revolutionaries long to recognise that they had a problem with the line army that they inherited from the Bourbon monarchy, a problem which, even in 1789, manifested itself in a number of very different ways. The new regime could not assume the loyalty and commitment of its troops, and desertion rates soared, especially amongst officers who had taken a personal oath of fealty to the King and thought that their oath had been rendered irrelevant by the dramatic change in the polity. Many of the men in the ranks, too, became suspect in the eyes of the new government, since the authorities could not feel sure that they would obey orders when faced with a stream of countermanding political currents. Some were felt to be easily led and might follow their officers into counter-revolution or emigration; others could be intoxicated by the language of liberty and equality and lured into acts of indiscipline and mutiny. It could not be assumed, in other words, that the soldiers would remain obedient, carrying out without question the will of the new government, or that generals who had obeyed the orders of a sovereign king would now transfer their loyalty to the sovereign nation. The large number of resignations from high-ranking officers and the departure of many prominent military figures into emigration in Turin, Mainz and Coblenz added to the distrust which the revolutionaries felt for the officer class, while the violent mutinies at Nancy, Perpignan and elsewhere during 1790 fuelled fears that the line army could disintegrate, leaving Paris open to attack and the Revolution perilously vulnerable. The King's flight to Varennes the following summer was almost an incitement to noble emigration.[1] Regiments were left with gaping holes in their command, and there were fears that France did not have sufficient numbers of trained officers to put a credible army in the field. If the Revolution introduced dramatic measures to change the culture of the army, it

[1] Samuel F. Scott, *The Response of the Royal Army to the French Revolution. The Role and Development of the Line Army, 1787–93* (Oxford, 1978), pp. 108–9.

did so as much out of necessity – the perception that the existing structures were incapable of providing the new nation with adequate defence – as out of any ideological considerations. By 1792 France was at war with Austria and Prussia. And by then the emergency was both immediate and threatening, as over one-third of the officer class had resigned their commissions, many passing into emigration or offering their swords to the Emperor. Soldiers were short of supplies; uniforms and boots, rifles and ammunition were unobtainable while the contractors to whom the revolutionaries turned included unscrupulous profiteers and speculators, men like Bidermann and the Abbé d'Espagnac, who turned to their political allies to seal lucrative contracts.[2] It did not take the publicity surrounding Dumouriez's high-profile defection to ram the message home. The *patrie* was, indeed, *en danger.*

But that is not how politicians presented their reforms, nor yet how posterity has remembered them. The revolutionaries tended to the view that, in war as in everything else, they were breaking new ground, fighting a new kind of war for liberty and social justice and fighting it with a new kind of army. To the leaders of the Republic, in particular, this seemed self-evident. Theirs was a just war, fought in the cause of the people, and to fight it the nation needed an army of citizens, since only those who enjoyed the full rights of citizenship were capable or worthy of the task of national defence. Even the Girondin group in the Assembly, whom successive historians have suspected of favouring war for purely factional reasons and who may even have been conspiring to start a war that France would lose, argued the case in 1791 and 1792 in ideological and moral terms.[3] By declaring that the French nation was sovereign, argued Carra, the Convention was implicitly recognising the sovereignty of others; the deputies responded by granting fraternity and aid to all peoples who sought help from France to recover their liberty.[4] For this they required an army of committed republicans. As for the Jacobins – even those who, like Robespierre, had argued passionately in 1792 against involvement in unnecessary foreign adventures – they were eager to ensure that France's army was both national and patriotic, an army fit for the task of defending the people against their enemies at home as well as abroad. In this context, the refusal

[2] Jean-Paul Bertaud, *Guerre et société en France de Louis XIV à Napoléon Ier* (Paris, 1998), pp. 87–9.

[3] François Furet, 'Les Girondins et la guerre: les débuts de l'Assemblée législative', in François Furet and Mona Ozouf (eds.), *La Gironde et les Girondins* (Paris, 1991), pp. 189–205.

[4] Speeches by Carra and Lépeaux to the Convention, 19 November 1792.

of obedience to noble officers could itself be construed as a positive political gesture, as an act of revolutionary commitment. Soldiers, as Mirabeau had reminded the deputies, could never be persuaded to abandon their intellectual faculties because they were an integral part of the community, of the nation itself.[5]

Robespierre talked at length about the *patrie* and the need for all to be involved in its defence; indeed, in his corpus of speeches and published works,[6] a recent study has shown that he used the word *patrie* more often than he used *nation* (219 mentions as against 178), though by far his preferred form of collective reference was the more popular, democratic *peuple*.[7] He was largely uninterested in tactical questions, but fervent about the ideological context of the war, preaching incessantly about the justice of France's cause, arguing that it was a contest between the forces of good and evil. And if he shared the Jacobins' distrust of the officer class, he repeatedly proclaimed his belief in the integrity of the ordinary soldier, who, he argued, shared the fundamental goodness of the people from whom he had sprung, the people who were themselves trustworthy and patriotic, moral and virtuous, though necessarily also naive and often credulous.[8] 'Carefully avoid', he urged the deputies, 'everything that could ignite in the souls of the *citoyens-soldats* such military spirit as cuts off soldiers from citizens and which yokes glory and self-interest to things that make for the ruin of citizens'.[9] In a republic, he believed, army and civil society were as one, and any sense that the army formed a separate estate was inherently dangerous.

Historians of the Revolutionary Wars, especially those close to the classical French tradition of revolutionary historiography, have shown a marked reluctance to deviate from Robespierre's vision or to interpret the innovations of the early Revolution in other than ideological terms, preferring to present the army as a truly national force which could be relied upon to represent the new nation in war with the enthusiasm

[5] Marcel Reinhard, 'Observations sur le rôle révolutionnaire de l'armée dans la Révolution française', *Annales historiques de la Révolution française*, (1962), p. 170.

[6] Marc Bouloiseau, Georges Lefebvre, Jean Dautry and Albert Soboul (eds.), *Oeuvres de Maximilien Robespierre* (10 vols., Paris, 1950–67).

[7] Annie Geffroy, 'Le mot *nation* chez Robespierre', in Jean-Pierre Jessenne, Gilles Deregnaucourt, Jean-Pierre Hirsch and Hervé Leuwers (eds.), *Robespierre: De la Nation artésienne à la République et aux Nations* (Lille, 1994), p. 95.

[8] Annie Jourdan, 'Robespierre and revolutionary heroism', in Colin Haydon and William Doyle (eds.), *Robespierre* (Cambridge, 1999), p. 60.

[9] Robespierre, *Oeuvres*, vol. 7, p. 263, quoted in Alan Forrest, 'Robespierre, the war and its organisation', in Colin Haydon and William Doyle (eds.), *Robespierre* (Cambridge, 1999), p. 135.

that only citizenship could confer.[10] From Albert Mathiez to Albert Soboul – who devoted an entire book to *Les soldats de l'an II*[11] – they present an image of the nation-in-arms in which the soldiers fight less for themselves or for their officers than for a political ideal, until, in Soboul's phrase, 'in the ranks of the Army of the Year II, national fervour and revolutionary spirit were one and the same'.[12] It is an image that owes much to Jules Michelet and the romantic imagination of the nineteenth century. Michelet set the tone of much subsequent writing when he depicted the revolutionary armies as the people of France, arguing that in the 'heroic battles' of 1793 'our soldiers caught the spirit of an entire nation that had risen to support them; they did not have the people with them, but they had their force, their soul, the divinity of France'.[13] By inference, if not explicitly, the contrast is continually drawn between an army of citizens and an army hired by their ruler like the line armies of the Ancien Régime. These are often derided in the manner of Voltaire and so many of the *philosophes*, who dismissed eighteenth-century soldiers as men with no roots in society and no interest in the cause in which they were engaged, concerned only to accumulate loot and booty, men prone to violence and crime, whose enlistment owed more to poverty than to any sense of commitment, to family quarrels, to a desire to escape parental control, or to a simple sense of adventure. Some were recruited from the King's prisons; many were foreign mercenaries whose only loyalty was to their current paymaster. They had, argued the *philosophes*, no sense of their responsibility towards civil society, with the result that they were feared and treated as common criminals, as 'bands of murderers' across the whole European continent.[14] Revolutionary historians have tended to agree, emphasising the contrast between old and new, and suggesting that by 1789 the spirit of the armies of Louis XVI was being sapped by what Soboul calls 'an internal sickness', their dependence on the structures and social assumptions of the Ancien Régime at a time when officers

[10] This tendency is much less marked in English-language historiography. See especially T.C.W. Blanning, *The French Revolutionary Wars, 1787–1802* (London, 1996).

[11] Albert Soboul, *Les soldats de l'an II* (Paris, 1959). Soboul quotes with evident approval Clausewitz's dictum that 'in all circumstances war must be considered as an instrument of politics and not as an independent entity' (p. 7).

[12] Albert Soboul, *Comprendre la Révolution. Problèmes politiques de la Révolution Française, 1789–99* (Paris, 1981), p. 276.

[13] Owen Connelly, 'The historiography of the *levée en masse* of 1793', in Daniel Moran and Arthur Waldron (eds.), *The People in Arms. Military Myth and National Mobilization since the French Revolution* (Cambridge, 2003), p. 38. The republican writing of Jules Michelet is discussed in greater detail in Chapter 9.

[14] The phrase is from Voltaire's *Dictionnaire Philosophique*, quoted in E.-G. Léonard, *L'armée et ses problèmes au dix-huitième siècle* (Paris, 1958), p. 225.

and men alike were exposed to the patriotic spirit unleashed by the Enlightenment. 1789 would demonstrate that for army morale and discipline this was an intolerable tension.[15]

Instead of the underclass who served in the armies of kings and emperors, they imply, the French now had an army that represented all parts of the nation and was not limited to any single social grouping or section of society. For the first time the people of France accepted collective responsibility for their defence, and this not only gave moral force to what the armies were required to do but also helped provide legitimation for the state itself. Voices among the Jacobins, in particular, identified France's goals in the war with saving the revolution and securing the republic, which could be achieved only if the army was itself republican, since conquering the British and ending counter-revolution were two aspects of the same military campaign.[16] Hence revolutionising the army came to be seen as one part – an essential one – in the wider project of revolutionising society. In the process, of course, they constructed an idealised representation, of a young man whose patriotism was equalled only by his virtue. They also demonised the other, both the men who fought for the Holy Roman Emperor and the King of Prussia and those who had sold their services to Louis XIV or Louis XV. This demonising process was never wholly convincing, however, especially in areas like the East which had traditionally sent large numbers of men to the armies, and popular media like woodprints and folktales tell a significantly different story, expressing society's fear of soldiers and representing them as armed bands living on the margins of civil society, but also showing sympathy for the painful separation of soldiers from their families, the curious induction rites that marked out soldiers from others, and the harsh demands made on the young farmhand who was forced by poverty to sign away his life for seven years. Soldiering might be a violent and dangerous way of life, but it was not an unfamiliar one; nor was it without a trace of a glamour born of images of banditry and tales of derring-do.[17]

If presenting a damning indictment of professional armies came fairly naturally to the revolutionaries – were they not all the slaves of tyrants, fighting wars in which they had no stake or interest? – finding a coherent image of the revolutionary soldier was rather more difficult. Under the constitutional monarchy, when reforms took the form of responses

[15] Soboul, *Les soldats de l'an II*, p. 9.

[16] Olivier Le Cour Grandmaison, *Les citoyennetés en révolution, 1789–94* (Paris, 1992), p. 170.

[17] David Hopkin, *Soldier and Peasant in French Popular Culture, 1766–1870* (London, 2003), pp. 215–39.

to crises rather than to any consistent ideology, the image of the army was especially confused. The revolutionaries had set their store by the abolition of privilege, yet the line regiments they had inherited continued to field the same officers and the same troops as in the 1770s and 1780s, despite the cycle of mutinies that had characterised the first year of the Revolution and the brutal repression that had followed. Twice they had recourse to volunteers – in 1791 and 1792 – but on the second occasion it became clear that the voluntary principle was incapable of raising the large numbers of soldiers they required. With the *levée des 300,000* in the spring of 1793 they abandoned the notion of a volunteer army (though they stubbornly refused to stop describing their troops as *volontaires*), moving instead to a system of local quotas proportionate to levels of population. This seemed for the first time to imply that citizens were expected to give military service to the nation, but there was no obligation: local quotas could be selected by whatever mechanism was most acceptable, and local communities were not obliged to resort to balloting or the drawing of lots. Some called for volunteers; others asked for nominations for what they flatteringly described as 'the most patriotic' men of military age; some brazenly selected paupers from their poorhouses or migrant workers who chanced to be passing through, or those – like shepherds and goatherds – who led isolated, marginal lives on the edge of village society. There were even communes, especially in agricultural regions, which organised collections so that they could seek out apprentices from nearby towns to fight in their stead. As for the rich and respectable, they could still find a way out of personal service by the simple expedient of buying a substitute to serve in their place.[18] The *levée* produced men for the army, without doubt; but it also raised charges of inequity and even of widespread corruption by those seeking exemption for their sons or their workers, charges which left large numbers of young Frenchmen feeling angry and disaffected. Jacobins and egalitarians were scandalised by the inequities that were tolerated, arguing that any system that permitted replacements was unacceptable to public opinion and damaging to the army. In Carnot's words, 'men get used to selling themselves like cattle', with the consequence that 'they make a business of deserting so that they can sell themselves to different battalions five or six times over', while strong men, good physical specimens, were being replaced by the lame, the alienated and men devoid of morality.[19] It was hardly the stuff of which legends are made.

18 Alan Forrest, *Conscripts and Deserters. The Army and French Society during the Revolution and Empire* (Oxford, 1989), esp. pp. 26–32.

19 Jean-Paul Bertaud, *La révolution armée. Les soldats-citoyens et la Révolution Française* (Paris, 1979), p. 101.

Until the extension of the war in the spring of 1793 to include Britain and Spain there had been talk of equality before the recruitment law, and of the duty to defend the nation that was incumbent on the young; but there had been little talk of conscription, and when there was, it was only to reject it out of hand. When, for instance, one of the foremost military reformers of the 1780s, Joseph Servan, author of a famous pamphlet on *Le soldat-citoyen*, proposed to the military committee of the Constituent Assembly that it introduce universal, compulsory military service, the idea found little support among the deputies.[20] Indeed, in these early months the issue was scarcely debated: one of its few supporters was Dubois-Crancé, who would go on to become War Minister in the Jacobin republic, who spoke out for a national system of recruitment that would fall, as he phrased it, on everyone alike, from 'the second person in the state' to 'the last active citizen'.[21] He argued against tolerating any form of replacement or of exemption on the basis of conscience; for, he said, quoting Servan, 'in France, every citizen must be a soldier and every soldier a citizen'. On examination, of course, this service was less than universal, since Dubois-Crancé was proposing to arm only active citizens, those of a certain social standing or owners of property, in defence of the state. But even this seemed far too radical for most of the deputies. Many were convinced that any form of compulsion should be avoided as a retrograde step, one that recalled the worst abuses of the Ancien Régime. The conscript, they argued, would make an unwilling soldier who was dragged against his wishes from the fields or the workshop; and there were those in the military who added that he would therefore make a bad soldier, a malingerer, lacking the passion and idealism which these wars required. They saw the patriotic enthusiasm and the vitality which they associated with the volunteer as the qualities that most clearly epitomised a revolutionary army, not the bureaucratically enforced equality of regular, annual conscription.

Even the Jacobins resisted conscription, though their response to the chronic manpower shortage which by the summer of 1793 was again threatening the country's military capability had moved a long way in that direction. This was the *levée en masse*, decreed on 23 August, a call to arms to the population at large that was intended to produce a mass army three-quarters of a million strong and repel foreign troops from French soil. This time the government took care not to repeat the mistakes of earlier levies by making it clear that military service must be

[20] For an account of the revolutionary career of Servan, see Jean-François Lanier, *Le général Joseph Servan de Gerbey (Romans, 1741 – Paris, 1808). Pour une armée au service de l'homme* (Valence, 2001).

[21] Annie Crépin, *La conscription en débat, ou le triple apprentissage de la Nation, de la citoyenneté, de la République, 1798–1889* (Arras, 1998), p. 19.

regarded as an integral aspect of citizenship, an obligation which fell on all equally, and by quite specifically excluding the possibility of *remplacement*. There was to be no distinction based on income or property-ownership; the poor as well as the well-to-do would be entrusted with the civic duty of national defence, and wealth brought no dispensation. Recruitment was to be organised on the simple egalitarian principle that the nation was the sovereign authority in the republic and that the nation was therefore entitled to demand, as of right, that all citizens of military age perform their military service as one of the fundamental duties which citizenship implied. All were put in a state of requisition, even if all could not be called upon to serve: the armies did not need to be submerged in raw recruits, while the republic recognised that civic and economic life must go on – the fields had to be tilled, taxes collected, administration and justice guaranteed. But the gesture was powerful, and the words of the decree were weighty, emphasising the principle of inclusion, a moment when civil equality and equality of obligation coincided and when the law recognised only one single form of citizenship.[22] All had discrete duties to perform, since all were part of the nation. Young men of military age were to serve in the armies, while the rest of the population were assigned a variety of support roles in the country's war effort – women through nursing or by sewing clothes for the warriors, children by making lint for use in hospitals, and old men by preaching the values of the Revolution in public places and exhorting the young to perform their patriotic duty.[23] The *levée en masse* was nothing less than the mobilisation of an entire nation in defence of its territory, its rights and its people. It appealed to the heart as well as to the head, and would be central to the legend of the revolutionary armies during the nineteenth century. Moreover, it imposed clearly gendered divisions, with men and women ascribed different roles in the military, the women limited to supporting professions like nurses, cooks and laundresses.[24] Yet small numbers of women, in this army as in most European armies of the day, did take up arms alongside their brothers and husbands, often cross-dressing to conceal their identity, and gaining a somewhat iconic status in the annals of revolutionary warfare.[25] They too would help fuel the nineteenth-century

[22] Pierre Rosanvallon, *Le modèle politique français. La société civile contre le jacobinisme de 1789 à nos jours* (Paris, 2004), pp. 25–55.

[23] For the text of the decree of 23 August 1793, see John Hall Stewart, *A Documentary Survey of the French Revolution* (New York, 1951), pp. 472–4.

[24] Patrick Bouhet, 'Les femmes et les armées de la Révolution à l'Empire', *Guerres mondiales et conflits contemporains* 198 (2000), p. 14.

[25] Jean-Clément Martin, 'Travestissements, impostures, et la communauté historienne. A propos des femmes soldats de la Révolution et de l'Empire', *Politix* 74 (2006), pp. 31–48.

legend of the *levée en masse*. An image of sacrifice and enthusiasm as well as a symbol of civic equality, the *levée* would have a much greater resonance than the annual conscriptions that followed, remorselessly, year on year, after 1799, turning military service into an accepted rite of passage for young Frenchmen as they approached adulthood.[26] It had greater resonance for another reason, too, since there would be no further large-scale recruitment until that first conscription six years later. The men who were raised by the *levée en masse* would remain in the armies year after year, defeating the Prussians, fighting a civil war in the Vendée, before following Bonaparte into Italy and Egypt. They were, to a degree unparalleled by any other cohort, the men who fought for revolutionary France.

So, for posterity, the soldiers of the French Revolution would remain the men of the Year II. This was an army of idealists without precedent in history. Neither in the city-states of antiquity nor in earlier European revolutions, in England or Geneva, nor, indeed, in the infant United States had young men offered themselves for sacrifice in such a cause, a cause in which they believed. Future generations of Frenchmen would be attracted by their valour and by the generosity of their sacrifice. They found excitement in the revolutionaries' ambition, in the belief that France could be defended by volunteers alone, in their boldness in ordering the amalgamation of these volunteers with the old line units to form the *demi-brigades* of the Year II. They were dazzled by the scale of their achievement, as near-defeat in 1793 was turned into victory and successive coalitions were destroyed. They marvelled at the map of Europe with France's boundaries extended to the Rhine and the Republic surrounded by a reassuring assembly of sister-republics in Holland, northern Italy and Switzerland. For the armies that entered legend were, above all, victorious armies, led by young and dynamic generals who owed their promotion to their own intrinsic merit. For all these reasons, the soldiers of the Revolution would continue to command the admiration of generations to come, even from many who had but scant sympathy for their political goals. In the process they acquired characteristics and values which may not have been theirs, as the soldier's image became confused and distorted through the lens of memory. The successive phases of the Revolution were merged into a single image as very different military experiences were jumbled into one – the *patrie en danger* with wars of conquest, the call for volunteers with the

[26] The working of the system of conscription introduced under the Loi Jourdan is discussed in detail for one department by J.-A. Castel, 'L'application de la Loi Jourdan dans l'Hérault' (mémoire de maîtrise, Université de Montpellier, 1970).

levée en masse and the first conscriptions, the men on the frontiers with the National Guard at home. All their qualities became wrapped into one – enthusiasm with equality, youth with a sense of duty, professionalism with republican ideology. A military legend that would endure throughout the nineteenth century emerged not from any single image of war, but from a kaleidoscope of contrasting images that were born and widely publicised during the French Revolutionary years.

Just as the nature of the war in which they fought became confused with the passage of time, so the soldier of the Year II became a kind of republican shorthand for all those who fought in the name of revolutionary France. Distinctions that were real enough at the time became blurred with the passage of the years, and the soldier became in his turn a political ideal, devoted, patriotic and loyal, rolling into one memorable image several distinct revolutionary identities. The *masse* played a large role in that image, the notion that the armies which defended France were drawn from the people at large, the youth of a nation united in a common cause regardless of their social and economic lot. Difference was forgotten, subsumed in their shared identity as Frenchmen, as citizens of the new republic. Equality was paramount, the equality of all in the service which they owed their country, the equality of a *classe*, a military generation called upon, together, to draw numbers in the ballot or to submit to the cursory medical examination that would decide whether they were 'bons pour le service'. But it was not equality alone that characterised the young men of the revolutionary levies. As the nineteenth century remembered them, they were also committed republicans, men who understood the cause in which they were called to fight and who offered themselves in that cause because that cause was theirs. They were in uniform because they chose to be; their service was marked by its spontaneous character. It was voluntary and unforced in a way that does not quite reflect modern notions of conscript armies, and which harks back more to the first volunteers of 1791 and 1792, those who came forward of their own accord, and whose youth and idealism would contribute so powerfully to the legend of Valmy. Already two generations of warriors, two discrete revolutionary ideals, were being merged into a common image. The idealised soldier of the 1790s also became a thinking man and a committed revolutionary – incarnating not only the volunteer of 1791 and the *requis* of 1793, but something, too, of the sturdy, dependable revolutionary *notable* who found his way into the ranks of the National Guard. All served the Revolution in one way or another, whether on the frontiers or in the streets of Paris. All were recognisably republican. All continued to be described in official speeches and republican eulogies as 'volontaires', even if during 1793 the official language of the Convention betrayed an uneasy sense of ambiguity by resorting to the somewhat illogical notion of 'volontaires requis'.[27] And all were perceived as gallant, selfless and unerringly patriotic; enmeshed together, they helped to burnish the patriotic image of the republic-in-arms which nineteenth-century republican opinion continued to cherish.

The myth of the revolutionary volunteer was a consistent theme in that wider revolutionary myth, that of Valmy, of the victory of the nation-in-arms over the slaves of tyrants, the paid mercenaries of foreign kings. On the one side stood the sons of France, who had stepped forward to defend their frontiers and fight for liberty; they were faced by mercenary troops, paid to defend the hierarchical values of kings and emperors. And if they won, it was because theirs was a necessary victory, made possible by their spirit and their heroism, but also by the justice of their cause. In reality, Valmy was an unlikely and unemphatic victory, a triumph snatched by Dumouriez's forces through superior artillery fire against an enemy unable to dislodge them from the higher ground. It was a victory, however, that was based on good intelligence and the use of patrols to reveal the enemy's positions; it was a tribute, too, to Dumouriez's insistence that men at every level should show initiative and take responsibility on the battlefield.[28] What made Valmy so important, however, were its consequences, in that it gave the French a new self-belief and became a revolutionary paradigm that would remain a key point of reference for students of French battle tactics. For Charles de Gaulle it would be the very epitome of revolutionary commitment: how, he asked rhetorically, could one hope to understand the Revolution without Valmy?[29] The fact that the Duke of Brunswick withdrew and that France was saved continued to reverberate long after the detail of an insubstantial battle had been forgotten. 'From this place and this date', the French agreed with the German poet Goethe, 'was born a new epoch in the history of the world', one where armies were reflections of popular sovereignty.[30] Valmy provided the model that others would follow, the ideal of the nation-in-arms that would inspire military reforms across the continent and lie at the heart of nationalist myths, not least in Prussia itself, where the *Erhebung*, the supposedly popular uprising that fuelled the War of Liberation in 1813, was greatly

[27] Crépin, *La conscription en débat*, p. 22.
[28] Jean-Paul Bertaud and Daniel Reichel, *Atlas de la Révolution Française. 3: L'armée et la guerre* (Paris, 1989), pp. 50–1.
[29] Charles de Gaulle, *Le fil de l'épée* (Paris, 1932), avant-propos.
[30] Jean Planchais, *Adieu Valmy. La fin de la nation en armes* (Paris, 2003), p. 7.

inspired by the French example.[31] Opinion, of course, varies on just how popular this war really was; David Gates is scathing about those young men from the middle classes who chose to volunteer before they were conscripted, pointing out that in August 1813, when some 300,000 young Germans had been mobilised, the volunteer *Jäger* accounted for fewer than 10,000 of them. The idea of a people's war he sees as an elite view and as a product of the romantic imagination.[32] 'Like the levée of 1793', argues Daniel Moran, 'Prussia's mobilisation turned upon the interaction of official coercion and popular emotions, and gave rise to a retrospective mythology that was, if anything, even more complex than that engendered by the French experience'.[33]

The sense that they were taking part in a historic battle did not escape those who were present on the battlefield.[34] Valmy assumed great importance not because of the scale of the battle or the level of their losses – in all, no more than 300 Frenchmen and 180 Prussians were killed or wounded in the fighting – but because of the simple fact that they had engaged with the enemy, young and inexperienced as so many of them were, and had emerged victorious. One man who left a personal record of Valmy was *dragon* Marquant, whose words go far to recapture the bravura of the moment. The French, he recalls, had taunted the Austrians and tried to lure them from their strong defensive position on the higher ground. 'Cowards!', the French troops jeered at the soldiers who faced them,

> come on down from your mountain; we are here ready to receive you; but no, you vile slaves of tyranny, you want to have victories that are free of all danger. If there were still among you traitors capable of buying us into captivity, you would not blush to do so; those are the sorts of victories you win; you have no place for those that are crowned by gallantry; they seem too deadly for your taste.[35]

To French eyes, Prussian discipline was met with French dash and daring, Prussian obedience with belief and fervour. Valmy was not just a victory in the field, by one army over another. It was far more

[31] Karen Hagemann, 'German heroes: the cult of the death for the fatherland in nineteenth-century Germany', in Stefan Dudink, Karen Hagemenn and John Tosh (eds.), *Masculinities in Politics and War. Gendering Modern History* (Manchester, 2004), pp. 124–7.

[32] David Gates, *The Napoleonic Wars, 1803–1815* (London, 1997), p. 229.

[33] Daniel Moran, 'Arms and the concert: the nation-in-arms and the dilemmas of German liberalism', in Moran and Waldron (eds.), *The People in Arms*, p. 52.

[34] Emmanuel Hublot, *Valmy ou la défense de la nation par les armes* (Paris, 1987), p. 399.

[35] Jean-Paul Bertaud (ed.), *Valmy, la démocratie en armes* (Paris, 1970), p. 36.

significantly the triumph of a people, and of a revolutionary ideal. That was why it would live on so long in popular memory.

And with the notion of French *élan* – that sense of daring and bravura in which the French republic liked to envelope its soldiers, that carefree spirit which distinguished the French from the armies of other nations – went a sense of commitment, a self-belief that had its roots in the fact that they were revolutionaries, men who believed in their cause and who were devoted to the defence of France and of their fellow citizens. Deputies on mission with the armies never tired of assuring the Convention that the troops in the field were devoted to the republic, that they treasured the freedoms which the Revolution had bestowed on them, and that they were not automatons in the service of the regime, but thinking men who were prepared to die in the name of liberty. They listened to political speeches on the eve of battle, and they cheered the leaders of the Republic; they attended political clubs in their regiments or in the towns where they were garrisoned; above all, they sang patriotic songs like the *Marseillaise* and the *Chant du départ*, anthems that exuded enthusiasm and bravado and helped to steady nerves on the eve of battle. As early as April 1792, the Girondin press, papers like the *Chronique de Paris* and the *Courrier*, helped to arouse a passion for singing both among civilians and among soldiers, and thus 'drafted song culture to the cause by generating enthusiasm for war songs'.[36] Some wrote from the armies to their clubs and sections, providing evidence of their patriotism that would be quoted and re-quoted by Jacobin leaders back home. Others recorded their hatred for counter-revolution, or for organised religion, or they expressed their anger when their own republicanism was called into doubt.[37] And it was not only committed Jacobins who declared their love of revolutionary principles or expressed their loyalty to the republic. When, for example, Robespierre told the Convention that the men of the Gironde made lukewarm republicans and implied that serious political differences pitted them against the soldiers from the Paris sections, one volunteer could not hold back his irritation. He wrote in protest to the President of the Convention himself, insisting that Robespierre was seriously misinformed. His battalion had been deployed with one from Paris, he declared, and they spent all their time together, day and night. They had come to know one another well, and 'the only difference we have had is disputing the honour of

[36] Laura Mason, *Singing the French Revolution. Popular Culture and Politics, 1787–99* (Ithaca, N.Y., 1996), p. 93.

[37] Alan Forrest, *Napoleon's Men. The Soldiers of the Revolution and Empire* (London, 2002), pp. 79–94.

being the first to fly to engage the enemy'. He added that, since they were serving in the front line, this was something they did every day, and something they looked on with a deep sense of pride.[38]

If the image of the army of the Year II would be strongly coloured by that of the volunteer, enthusiasm merging with duty and equality of sacrifice, so, too, it would owe something to another force of the 1790s that became synonymous with the Revolution, the National Guard. Its function was more to police the community than to fight on the frontiers, but clear parallels were there for those who sought to make them. General Custine, indeed, expressed the view that the idea of a citizen-army in 1789 was most accurately reflected in the 'force territoriale' that was the National Guard. It was not a ridiculous notion, for the guardsmen were among the very first Frenchmen to volunteer for some form of armed service, albeit one aimed principally at defending their homes against criminal gangs and popular violence. They were recruited locally, and often they were representative of the younger, more idealistic citizens, those who paraded on the Champ de Mars and who fraternised with the Parisians who launched their attack on the Bastille. Not all were solidly bourgeois: in rural communities, in particular, where the number of active citizens was low, a high percentage of *passifs* were to be found in local *garde* units.[39] What distinguished them was their commitment: within a town or *bourg*, the guardsmen often constituted what Roger Dupuy has termed 'the dynamic elements of patriot power'.[40] Membership of the Guard even came to be equated with citizenship, especially in Paris, where revolutionary committees of surveillance turned *garde* service into a precondition for issuing *cartes de civisme* during the Terror. Besides, guardsmen were present at the key moments of the Revolution, when their influence could be seen as positive in advancing the cause of the sovereign people. They came to Paris from all over France to celebrate the Fête de la Fédération in July 1792, and their intervention proved crucial in the events of 10 August that overturned the monarchy. Again in the summer of 1793, it was men of the Paris National Guard who arrested the Girondin deputies in the Convention. Battalions of the Guard were quick to capitalise on their patriotic reputation, reminding their fellow citizens of their revolutionary involvement every time they turned out for a municipal celebration or festival. The men of the Faubourg Saint-Marcel, for example, chose

[38] *Archives Parlementaires*, 12 July 1793; the letter was written on the 10th, from Lille.

[39] Roger Dupuy, *La Garde Nationale et les débuts de la Révolution en Ille-et-Vilaine, 1789 – mars 1793* (Paris, 1972), p. 253.

[40] Roger Dupuy, *De la Révolution à la chouannerie. Paysans en Bretagne, 1788–94* (Paris, 1988), p. 190.

a design for their banner that symbolised their most famous triumph, their involvement in the assault on the Bastille in 1789 – the image of a peasant leaving his cottage to attack a local 'bastille' to cries of 'Liberty or Death'.[41] Resplendent in their blue uniforms and carrying muskets or pikes, the guards were the most visible defenders of the Revolution both in the Paris sections and in the towns and villages of provincial France. They, too, would contribute to the Revolution's military legend.

This was the revolutionary image which the Guard liked to present, the image of a force that was directly linked to the people it defended, and a force that understood the goals of the Revolution and was not afraid to assume its own role in defending them. For if the army was seen as subject to military discipline, and hence entitled to hold no views of its own, the Guard presented itself rather differently, as volunteers who were first and foremost revolutionaries rather than soldiers. For posterity they, too, came to reflect the qualities of the citizen-soldier. The guards talked politics and offered their opinions on the major issues of the day. In Limoges, for instance, they claimed the right to discuss the decrees of the National Assembly. 'Our task', they declared, 'is not limited to the subordinate role of executing the decrees of others'. They went on to say that

> it is not just to provide assistance to the authorities that we are armed. We must, in concert with the municipal councils, watch over the enemies of the Revolution and uncover the treacherous methods used by evil citizens to achieve their sinister ends. What they plot and what they do, what they say and what they think, all justify our curiosity and investigation.[42]

Much of what they did, of course, consisted of policing the community, and closely resembled the work of the gendarmerie. But the image they presented was far more complex, a mixture of the idealistic and the repressive, men who were there to enforce the law and protect property – unquestionably their principal task – but also to protect the regime from the manoeuvres of counter-revolutionaries and, if the external crisis warranted it, leave for the frontiers and defend the fatherland. In moments of crisis they, too, became soldiers, fighting alongside the men of the line and the volunteers of 1792. The *garde nationale* was then transformed into the *garde du peuple* of republican legend.

But if it is possible to offer a radical view of their activities, especially in the capital, there is another, more conservative reading. Especially

[41] Hans-Jürgen Lüsebrink and Rolf Reichardt, *The Bastille. A History of a Symbol of Despotism and Freedom* (Durham, N.C., 1997), p. 170.

[42] Paul d'Hollander, 'Les gardes nationales en Limousin, juillet 1789 – juillet 1790', *Annales historiques de la Révolution Française* 190 (1992), p. 487.

during the early years of the Revolution, and again after Thermidor, the Guard played the part which it had been assigned in 1789, that of a bourgeois militia, created to defend property and guarantee order. It was the Guard, after all, that had defended towns and villages against the Great Fear in 1789, and which, in Paris, tried to stop the rioters attacking Réveillon's wallpaper factory. The law of 14 October 1791 makes it clear that the Assembly's intention was not to open its ranks to all: Guard service was made obligatory for active citizens, as it was for their sons when they reached the age of eighteen, whereas those of humble origins were expressly excluded. Its duty was to oversee and maintain 'order and public tranquillity'; it was not a military corps and could act only when requisitioned or provided with legal authorisation; in short, the deputies took every step they could to minimise its power and its autonomy.[43] Nor did they wish it to be perceived as either popular or national. They preferred that it should remain a bourgeois force, representative of the local social elites, and restricted to a well-defined role in maintaining public order. This is the Guard that is represented in some of the most famous pictures of the period – notably in Bellier's oil portrait of citizen Nau-Deville, standing proudly in his guard uniform, and displaying all the self-confidence of his class and his rank.[44] Its archetypal representative is probably La Fayette himself, commander of the Paris National Guard and a man of increasingly conservative political instincts. With time La Fayette's unpopularity grew, and he was represented by pamphleteers and caricaturists as arrogant, corrupt, an ally of aristocrats and counter-revolutionaries. He was 'the man on the white horse' who had given the order to fire on the crowd at the Champ de Mars. 'The most adroit of tyrants', sneered one pamphlet, followed by that most damning of revolutionary insults, 'a Cromwell'.[45]

La Fayette did not, of course, come to symbolise the 'revolutionary' aspect of the National Guard, any more than the aristocratic officers of the line were allowed to symbolise the spirit of the military in Year II. The revolutionaries took great care to present their soldiers as heroes symbolising their values and loyal to a republican ideal that had its roots in classical antiquity. They emphasised, too, the originality of the army, insisting again on their central tenet that citizenship

[43] Georges Carrot, *La Garde Nationale, 1789–1871. Une force publique ambiguë* (Paris, 2001), pp. 118–20.

[44] 'Portrait du citoyen Nau-Deville en uniforme de garde national', reproduced in Michel Vovelle, *La Révolution Française: images et récit* (5 vols., Paris, 1986), vol. II, p. 167.

[45] Roger Barny, 'L'image de Cromwell dans la Révolution Française', *Dix-huitième siècle* 25 (1993), pp. 387–97.

was indivisible, and imposing on all the imperative of inclusion that was central to their ideology.[46] This idea, which had been expressed by many local communities in the *cahiers de doléances*, was taken up in revolutionary rhetoric. 'Let all the people of France arise and march as a man!': the idea of this mass, of this joyous expression of the unity of the French people, marching towards the frontiers to defend their nation without a second thought for their personal safety, was itself intoxicating. In Year II the mass was also taken to define a community of thought, a collective undertaking by the French to sustain the Revolution. One grenadier declared on 24 July, when he heard of the assassination of Marat, that 'a mass departure to avenge Marat should result across the whole country'.[47] Indeed, it is arguable that the main power of the mass was rhetorical, an idea stronger in speeches and public eulogies than it could ever be in the armies on the ground.

One favoured means of propagating a heroic image of the soldier was the habit of the republicans – with the Jacobins to the fore – of praising the courage of individuals and of bringing 'heroic actions' to the notice of the people. Both the Convention and the public at large were regularly regaled with tales of exceptional bravery and selflessness, instances where individuals had tried to rescue others with no thought to their own safety. Collections of these tales of bravery were periodically printed on the orders of the Committee of Instruction, which deemed them useful for instilling a sense of civic responsibility in the young, and schoolmasters found them a ready source of inspiring anecdotes for their charges. The pamphlet presented by Léonard Bourdon in Year II, for instance, was 'to be read out in the popular assemblies every *décadi*, and in the schools', since it had 'the quality that should be looked for in elementary school books, an insistence on the value of heroism'. It also had the merit of telling a good story with which the young, especially young boys, could immediately identify. Unsurprisingly in a period of war, many of the heroes were soldiers, young volunteers who selflessly put their own lives in danger to save their comrades. Bourdon cites, for instance, one brave young man who had leapt into the enemy entrenchment and seized the bridles of their artillery horses, pulling them off with one hand while he slashed with his sabre with the other. He was attacked from all sides and seriously wounded, whereupon he cried out to his comrades to carry him behind French lines; then, dying, he

[46] Pierre Rosanvallon, *Le monde politique français. La société civile contre le jacobinisme de 1789 à nos jours* (Paris, 2004), pp. 117–21.

[47] Bertaud, p. 113.

asked his friends to leave him in the shelter of a wood, passing over his wallet so that they could share what money he had left. His last words typified the republican idealism which the pamphlet sought to propagate: 'Leave me here; go and fight. I can feel that I am going to die; your care will be to no avail. Long live the Republic.'[48]

The image was not confined to the spoken or written word. The soldiers of the French Revolution were familiar figures in the France of the 1790s, along the frontiers and on the main roads leading towards the Rhine and the Alps, in garrison towns in the north and east, and in the villages of *la France profonde* during the recruiting season. For the most part they could, as the sons and brothers of civilians, hope and expect to be better received and better understood than their predecessors in the royal armies of the eighteenth century, whose presence had aroused fears and suspicions rather than fellow-feeling. And this in turn meant that they provided an appropriate subject for artists and playwrights, for those in the creative arts who felt the pull of patriotism or the need to express their revolutionary ardour. For a country at war – and one that was defending its frontiers against tyranny and counter-revolution as much as enemy action – valour and military values aroused fascination among civilians almost as much as in the ranks of the military themselves, and under the Directory, especially, the army was prominent among the themes chosen for painting and drama. This may be explained by renewed public appreciation for history painting as a genre. Or it may reflect the increasingly military culture of the later Revolution as public interest veered from the tribunes of the National Assembly to the armies in Italy or Egypt. Soldiers evoked sympathy and admiration from audiences and among onlookers, even from men and women who did not agree with the cause in which they had fought or died. They stood for the cohesive values of patriotism and the nation, whereas works that attempted to summon up admiration for politicians always risked falling on deaf ears or even of attracting accusations of counter-revolution. The soldiers were a much safer subject for creativity.[49]

And yet, the development of military subjects in the painting of the 1790s was to be a slow process, with artists unwilling to abandon the more allegorical classical themes which so dominated the early *salons*. Distrust of army officers and suspicion of their political motives may

[48] Léonard Bourdon, *Recueil des actions héroïques et civiques des républicains français, présenté à la Convention Nationale au nom de son Comité d'Instruction Publique* (Paris, an II), vol. V, pp. 18–19.

[49] Vovelle, *La Révolution Française*, vol. IV, pp. 108–9.

have discouraged artists – as it certainly discouraged their patrons in government – from favouring battle scenes or portraits of victorious generals returning from campaigns. Under both the constitutional monarchy and the republic revolutionaries feared a military coup d'état, or what they termed 'Caesarism', the rise through the army ranks of a 'new Cromwell', a potential military dictator. They therefore discouraged any art form that glorified military violence and ideas of military honour. Rather, in the Paris Salon of 1793, there were good sales for portraits, especially portraits of France's new political leaders, while one painting in four was a landscape, betraying a new spirit of romanticism and a departure from the classical themes of the recent past.[50] Military scenes were almost wholly absent, although, as France declared war on all the major powers of Europe, the theme of patriotism soon blended with republican virtue to produce a rash of militaristic caricatures, many of them devoted to denigrating France's enemies. Cartoonists, inspired by the work of English artists like Gillray and Cruikshank, which circulated widely in Paris, lampooned the languorous, aristocratic leadership of the Austrians and the British, portraying their armies as the butt of *sans-culotte* mirth. But their greatest contempt was reserved for fellow-Frenchmen, for the émigré armies which were, it was widely rumoured, forming along the Rhine to invade France and destroy the Revolution. The series of caricatures devoted to the *Grande Armée du ci-devant Prince de Condé*, presenting the prince as a modern-day Don Quixote and his army as the most improbable of military threats, are among the most vitriolic and the best executed of the early years of the Revolution.[51]

When French artists did portray their own soldiers, it is interesting how much they emphasised their youth and their civic qualities rather than more traditional military values. In particular, artists conveyed the sense of sacrifice, of the young men themselves but also of the families they left behind, in a series of prints and paintings on the theme of *Le départ du volontaire*.[52] Here the mixed feelings of their mothers and loved ones are often sensitively expressed, that mixture of fear and sadness on the one hand, pride and responsibility on the other, that captures the essence of the choice that was made by each volunteer who set off for the front in 1792 or 1793. Less ambiguous were the various depictions, often engraved, of the *Patrie en danger*, which showed the

[50] Jean-François Heim, Claire Béraud and Philippe Heim, *Les salons de peinture de la Révolution Française, 1789–99* (Paris, 1989), pp. 47–9.

[51] Antoine de Baecque, *La caricature révolutionnaire* (Paris, 1988), pp. 195–207.

[52] See, for example, the images of Guyard and Coqueret reproduced by Vovelle, *La Révolution Française*, vol. III, pp. 52–3.

enthusiasm of the young as they rushed to answer the call-to-arms, most memorably, perhaps, on the Pont-Neuf in Paris, presenting themselves for service on the frontiers without a second thought for their personal safety.[53] Some depictions, more thoughtfully, linked the spirit of the volunteer with the imposition of the state, the demand that all had a duty to perform. In Guillaume Guillon-Lethière's oil painting of *La patrie en danger* (1799), for instance, a response to a new military crisis towards the end of the decade, the artist unashamedly revives the iconography of 1793 and shows a united society, in which women and girls are urging their young warriors to sign on for the army in what John Horne has termed 'an act of generalised civic virtue'. Here, in idealised form, is the essence of the *levée en masse*, the coming together of society – albeit a strictly gendered society where fighting is a role restricted to men – in an emotionally-charged spirit of patriotism and sacrifice.[54]

During the revolutionary years, depictions of battle scenes would be rare – as indeed would coins or medals struck to celebrate victories, a gesture of triumph that was much more common in Britain, Austria and Prussia than in France. The *soldats-citoyens* of the National Guard were celebrated in this way after their intervention on 10 August at the Tuileries, but no commemorative medals were struck for the army itself until 1794, when we find two medals, one celebrating victory at Fleurus, the other praising the bravery of the sailors during the sinking of the *Vengeur*, a tragic incident which had come to characterise republican courage and was in no sense a victory.[55] Indeed, as Bertrand Barère described to the Convention the last minutes of the doomed crew of the stricken ship, holed and surrounded by the Royal Navy, who nonetheless dragged themselves on deck to shout their defiance, he could talk of 'the touching and spirited spectacle of a civic festival rather than the dreadful moment of a shipwreck'. And so it was represented in David's etching of *La Mort des marins du 'Vengeur'*, which shows the sailors singing their patriotic anthem as the battle raged around them.[56] It would

[53] 'Les enrôlements volontaires au Pont-Neuf, 22 juillet 1792', engraving by Berthaut, reproduced in Vovelle, *La Révolution Française*, vol. III, p. 50.

[54] Guillaume Guillon-Lethière, *La patrie en danger* (1799), hangs in the Musée de la Révolution Française, Vizille (MRF 1985–14). The painting is discussed in a paragraph by John Horne in Moran and Waldron (eds.), *The People in Arms*, p. 23.

[55] Jean-Charles Benzaken, 'Des soldats-citoyens au général en chef de l'armée d'Italie, 1792–99: étude numismatique', in Monique Cubells (ed.), *La Révolution Française: la guerre et la frontière* (Paris, 2000), p. 417.

[56] Philippe Bordes and Régis Michel (eds.), *Aux Armes et aux Arts! Les arts de la Révolution, 1789–99* (Paris, 1988), pp. 118–19.

be after Brumaire, during the years of the Consulate, when Napoleon finally sought to unite the army and art in the cause of national glory, returning to a tradition that had been prominent under the Ancien Régime, and most especially during the reign of Louis XIV. Then artists like Gros, Géricault and Lejeune would portray the military in the most gloriously heroic and romantic light, until *L'Arlequin au Muséum* in 1801 could remark that 'this year you might say that all the artists have agreed to offer us only battlefields covered with the bodies of the dead and dying'.[57]

The war effort also finds a strong echo in the theatre, an art form which throughout the eighteenth century provided an accurate barometer of public taste and manners, and which, in the revolutionary years, became a veritable battleground for political faction as theatregoers took advantage of the anonymity provided by the stalls or the gallery to cheer for their heroes and to jeer and hiss at actors representing characters they disliked. Feuding reached its pinnacle in the theatre wars after Thermidor, when the parterre was turned into a stage for the *jeunesse dorée*, but even at the height of the Terror the Paris theatres were closely policed lest opponents of the regime used them to pursue their own political ends. The more radical actors who worked with Talma at the Théâtre de la Nation found themselves proscribed and banned from performing, while staging a play deemed too moderate by the censors led to the closure of the Comédie Française after 113 years of continuous production.[58] Military themes could be less contentious, more innocent outlets for republican patriotism – although even lines celebrating French triumphs over the Austrians could lead to outbursts of sardonic whistling from émigré sympathisers. And there were particular events – French victories, for instance, or the defeat of counterrevolution, or the triumphal return of local regiments – which called out for public celebration. In Bordeaux, the return of the city's troops from their tour of duty in the Vendée was greeted at the Théâtre de la Nation with performances of two unambiguously patriotic dramas, *L'Hymne des Marseillais* and *Guillaume Tell*.[59]

But such instances were not typical: they were the product of the immediate political context of the Year II, fortified by Jacobin censorship. It was more common for images of military valour and patriotic

[57] Eric Boullenger, 'L'image de l'armée à travers la peinture du Consulat et du Premier Empire' (mémoire de maîtrise, Université de Paris-I, 1988), p. 8.

[58] François Gendron, *La Jeunesse dorée. Episodes de la Révolution Française* (Montréal, 1979), p. 110.

[59] Henri Lagrave, Charles Mazouer and Marc Regaldo, *Le théâtre à Bordeaux des origines à nos jours* (Paris, 1985), vol. I, p. 397.

devotion to be presented within a traditional dramatic setting, as part of a comedy of manners or a play about human sensibility, for even during the revolutionary decade the success of the theatre rested much more on appealing to human emotions than it did to politics or political correctness. Plays about human frailties, the victory of virtue over weakness, or – the most traditional theme of all – unrequited love still dominated the playbills, both in Paris and the provinces. The theatre was concerned with the broadest range of human emotions, and the backcloth of war provided playwrights with the opportunity to spice their dramas with both patriotic excitement and a sense of danger. Plays emphasised the heroism of the soldier, the sense of self-sacrifice, the ever-present threat of death. They talked of his patriotism and hatred of aristocrats, but these were seldom the crucial themes. Their concern was with the soldier as a private individual – his gallant demeanour, his humour in the face of war, his companionable nature, his love of wine and song, his affairs with girls he met along his route, and the heartbreak he caused for wives and sweethearts left at home in France. The play was seldom set on the battlefield or close to the front line; rather, it dealt with the soldier's domestic concerns, the tension between his duty to the state and his affection for his family. Play after play evoked the ambivalence of the *citoyen-soldat*, the tension implicit in his double existence as soldier and citizen, as son, lover, *père de famille*. It was this tension – often evoked through the female characters – that gave these plays their dramatic quality, that element of human drama that was necessary to their artistic enjoyment and commercial success.[60]

It took skill to integrate a simple political message into a play of this kind without it reading – to our ears at least – like propaganda for the war effort. But we must bear in mind that everyday language was seeped in patriotism. Joseph Lavallée, in *Le départ des volontaires villageois pour les frontières*, chose to set his village love-story against the backcloth of those divisions between wealth and poverty which had counted for so much in the Ancien Régime. The hero, Alexis, is a soldier who has been driven by poverty to borrow money when he set off for the army; now back in his village and seeking his sweetheart's hand in marriage, he feels honour-bound to repay his debt. But he is helped by the village mayor, who recognises his goodness of heart and offers to pay the money that will save Alexis's honour and reward him with the hand of

[60] Erica Joy Mannucci, 'Le militaire dans le théâtre de la Révolution Française', in Philippe Bourdin and Gérard Loubinoux (eds.), *Les arts de la scène et la Révolution Française* (Clermont-Ferrand, 2004), pp. 379–80.

the girl he loves.[61] Joigny's *Le siège de Lille, ou Cécile et Julien*, performed at the Opéra-Comique in Paris in 1792, is on one level a simple love-story, a comedy of the kind all too familiar to eighteenth-century theatre audiences: Cécile falls in love with Julien, but is being importuned by Julien's uncle, who treats his own nephew as a rival in love. The backdrop to their affair is the city of Lille, under siege by the Austrians, and their conversation soon turns to their own duty as citizens of the city. It is at this point that the customary give-and-take of lovers' banter gives way to more serious conversation, as both are drawn to consider their own obligations as citizens. Asked by Cécile if he would be prepared to lose his life in the defence of the walls of their town, Julien does not hesitate: 'That sacrifice is a duty. By surrendering like cowards through fear of dying, we would incur eternal opprobrium from the whole of France, indeed of the whole world. If any among us dare to propose such infamy, let him perish on the spot.' Less predictable, perhaps, is Cécile's response, though he need not have worried, since, like so much of revolutionary theatre, this is an essentially moral tale. Far from thinking about herself or lamenting his departure, she responds like a good republican, expressing admiration for his sentiments and saying that they make her proud to love him. His reward is not long in coming. Her father, inspired by Julien's patriotism, scorns the uncle's request for her hand in marriage, dismissing him as a shameful *égoïste* with no sense of public duty. Julien goes to the defence of Lille and falls into Austrian hands, where his bravery impresses his captors; while his rival in love is the object of almost universal ridicule. The story, of course, has a happy ending, as Julien breaks free of his guards, seizes a sword, captures an Austrian flag and returns, heaped with military honours, to claim the hand of his beloved Cécile.[62]

Not all plots ended so joyously; indeed, many of the dramas of these years were tragedies, leading to the heroic death of the citizen-soldier and to the inconsolable grief of his loved ones. These plays provided the opportunity to explore the nature of grief in the face of heroic death – a theme reminiscent of the drama of ancient Greece and Rome – and to analyse the reactions of parents to the deaths of their sons in war. Philipon chose the famous tale of *Agricol Viala, ou le Jeune Héros de la Durance* to talk of republican bravery and enemy treachery, relating the story of the boy-soldier from the Vaucluse mercilessly shot by his

[61] Joseph de Lavallée, *Le départ des volontaires villageois pour les frontières: comédie en un acte et en prose* (Paris, 1793), pp. 6–9 [Bibliothèque de l'Arsénal, Rf.18.473].

[62] Joigny, *Le siège de Lille, ou Cécile et Julien* (Paris, 1793) [Bibliothèque de l'Arsénal, Rf.18.426].

captors when he refused to renege on his republican principles. His mother is smitten with grief as Agricol bids her farewell, offering the reassurance that his death is a fine and beautiful thing in such a noble cause. In the final scene, the republican aide-de-camp comforts the grieving mother, reminding her that the country owes its salvation to her son's sacrifice.[63] The text plays on Agricol's youth, the pathos of a young boy mown down for his beliefs. Just as poignant is the choice that faces Wimpfen, the commander charged with the defence of Thionville against the Austrians in the lyrical drama written by Saulnier and Butilh, *Le Siège de Thionville*, performed on the Paris stage in 1793. Wimpfen's son is a young French officer who has been captured by the Austrians, who try to use him as a pawn in the surrender of the city. As battle is joined and the French fall on the Austrian army that is approaching Thionville, the Austrian general, Waldeck, brings young Wimpfen into full view of the French defences, with 'a hundred bayonets at his breast', threatening to kill him unless the French surrender. The young man indignantly refuses any dishonourable barter, preferring to die than to sacrifice his virtue, and shouts to his fellow countrymen to attack. The play ends with a terrible slaughter, and Wimpfen's final words, a plea to God to allow him one last glimpse of the French victory before he dies, demonstrate his patriotism and his selflessness. His father, in a scene worthy of Brutus, gives thanks for the victory while lamenting his own terrible loss.[64]

Revolutionary theatre was not confined to the stage, and increasingly the work of artists and choreographers was turned to political festivals and public ceremonial – which themselves became more military in their themes and their staging. The early festivals to celebrate unity and the sovereignty of the nation were militarised by the onset of war, and from 1793 the place of the military in *fêtes civiques* and *patriotiques* was increasingly central, until, as Marvin Carlson phrased it, 'we find a troupe of actors setting off to war in stage chariots and presenting battle recreations on fields where the blood was scarcely dry'.[65] Soldiers had traditionally played a role in state ceremonial, of course, though kings had used them very differently from a revolution that was intent on presenting the army as an integral part of civil society, and for whom the festival was a means of communicating the message of social harmony

[63] Philipon, *Agricol Viala, ou le Jeune Héros de la Durance* (Paris, an II), performed for the first time at the Théâtre des Amis de la Patrie, 13 messidor II [Bibliothèque de l'Arsénal, MF 12/270].

[64] Saulnier et Butilh, *Le siège de Thionville: drame lyrique en deux actes* (Paris, 1793) [Bibliothèque de l'Arsénal, Rf.15.246].

[65] Marvin Carlson, *The Theatre of the French Revolution* (Ithaca, N.Y., 1966), p. vi.

and national unity. Louis XIV, most famously, had made effective use of military triumphs to burnish his image of absolutism and to add colour and vibrancy to court ceremonial: the bright uniforms and cheering music, fireworks, statues, the formal gardens planned by André Le Nôtre at Versailles – all had combined to sing the praises of the monarch and to draw the common people to him.[66] But under the Revolution the army helped to forge an image of a very different sort, that of a new sovereign body, the French people themselves. Men and women of all social classes and all walks of life were there to celebrate this unity, and with it their commitment to a shared cause which united them as friends – the words *amis* and *amitié* recur frequently in the discourse of the festival – and positively glowed with harmony and fraternity. The army and civilian society were as one, part of the idyllic harmony of the nation, as the festival performed its most essential function, that of dramatising national unity.[67] For those who were present, the festival, and the celebrations that accompanied it, should be indistinguishable from the Revolution itself.

The content of these festivals tended to become more military, and the presence of soldiers more prominent, as the Directory and Consulate made ever-greater play of their military successes in order to win public approval at home. In Nantes, for instance, military and diplomatic successes were among the most common occasions for public celebration after 1793: there were festivals to celebrate the triumph of the Republic in the Vendée (1794), the capture of Trieste (1797), the Peace of Campo-Formio (1798), the seizure of Naples (1798), and the peace treaties of 1801, both on land and at sea. All were presented as triumphs, as the serene progress of the nation-in-arms against its sworn enemies across Europe.[68] Military themes, it might appear, had taken centre stage after a flurry of earlier festivals to celebrate the constitution, or the federation, or the planting of liberty trees. The desire to celebrate triumphs in war is unquestionably present, and under the Directory public attention was increasingly focussed on the Italian campaign. But it should not be assumed that the military was ignored in earlier festivals, or that the fusion of civil and military authority was

[66] For a discussion of the creation of Louis' monarchical image, see Peter Burke, *The Fabrication of Louis XIV* (New Haven, 1992); an excellent discussion of the propaganda value of the royal gardens is Chandra Mukerji, *Territorial Ambitions and the Gardens of Versailles* (Cambridge, 1997). Mukerji specifically makes the point that military ambitions – and military engineering – played their part in the layout of Versailles.

[67] Mona Ozouf, *La fête révolutionnaire* (Paris, 1976), p. 152.

[68] Archives Municipales de Nantes, series I-1, Cérémonies et fêtes publiques officielles, 1790–1815.

not a constant source of concern throughout the 1790s. A glance at the festival programmes from the early years of the Revolution shows clearly how in the celebration of the Federation in 1790, in the *Fête de la Réunion* in 1793 , and in the Festival of the Supreme Being later that year, soldiers were always involved, their marching carefully choreographed, the impact ensured by a mix of regiments and the interplay of uniforms, the presence of cavalry units with their majestic horses, of army veterans grown old in campaigning, and – always – the rousing sound of military music.[69] Drummer-boys were a fixture of every revolutionary festival, their youth and innocence adding to the power of the music-making. And there was no doubting that the soldiers were there as heroes, the defenders on whom the future of the country, the Revolution, and all its citizens depended. As an example one might cite David's programme for the Festival of Unity and Indivisibility, presented to the Convention on 11 July 1793, which gives the troops, returning from the front, a place of honour in the procession:

> A group of soldiers will come next, triumphantly leading a chariot drawn by white horses; it will contain an urn which will hold the ashes of those heroes who have died gloriously for the motherland; the chariot, decorated with garlands and civic wreaths, will be surrounded by the relatives of the men whose virtues and courage we are celebrating.[70]

They were there to be commended, to be cheered on by an appreciative crowd, a crowd whose purpose – at this as at any other revolutionary *fête* – was to admire and learn. The message they were soaking up was a message of national unity, the idea that soldiers and civilians were as one, each as essential as the other in propagating revolutionary values and defending the infant republic.

[69] Marie-Louise Biver, *Fêtes révolutionnaires à Paris* (Paris, 1979), pp. 175–8, 183–7, 192–6, and 199–201.

[70] *Ibid.*, pp. 184–5.

3 Napoleon and the blurring of memory

Among the innumerable images created to celebrate the revolutionary nation-in-arms, none is better known, and none more influential, than François Rude's sculpture, *Le départ des volontaires en 1792*, engraved on one of the great panels that decorate the Arc de Triomphe in Paris. Here are portrayed, in the high romantic style of the early nineteenth century, all the central themes of the revolutionary legend – the voluntarism of the recruits, their selflessness, their burning patriotism and devotion to the cause of the French republic. It is a heroic image, destined to achieve iconic status and to be reproduced many times on posters, etchings and patriotic prints; we find it serving as a recruitment tool in the early months of the Great War, and as an encouragement to French civilians to invest in war loans in 1915 and 1916.[1] And yet this republican icon conceals a crucial ambivalence. It may seem to celebrate voluntarism; yet 1792 was the last time the French felt confident enough to rely on the voluntary ideal, and their armies, as we have seen, were recruited largely by imposing quotas, drawing lots, resorting to some form of compulsion. And the tablet depicting the departure of the first volunteers does not stand alone, however much its fame now surpasses that of the other sculptures that accompany it. For Rude's commission was not to celebrate republicanism. It was to commemorate, jointly with two other sculptors, the glory and the sacrifice of French troops across the twenty years of war from 1792 to 1815. This was achieved through a series of four panels spanning the war years, the departure of the volunteers in 1792 being complemented by three images that were in no sense republican: Napoleon's military triumph, shown through a winged Victory (and sculpted by Cortot); the heroic resistance of the French people when their country faced invasion in 1814; and the signing of the peace treaty in 1815 that finally delivered the respite so many longed to see (the last

[1] Daniel Moran and Arthur Waldron (eds.), *The People in Arms. Military Myth and National Mobilization since the French Revolution* (Cambridge, 2003), pp. 34–5.

two panels the work of Etex).[2] The message was not, therefore, intended as a plea for the cause of revolution, though it was highly suggestive of the anger and ferocity of a revolutionary war. Like the Arc itself, it must be seen as a memorial to the success of French arms, to military glory and human sacrifice, to the seamless unity of France's military effort between the early revolution and the final days of the Empire. Above all – and it was an uncomfortable reminder for republicans – it was a monument to the genius of Napoleon Bonaparte.

At first sight, given the bitterness of French factional divisions during the post-revolutionary years, this confusion may seem difficult to comprehend. Republicans were little inclined to compromise with supporters of the Emperor, whom they saw, not without reason, as their natural opponents in a battle for the hearts and minds of the people, a battle on whose outcome the future of republicanism would depend. They increasingly demanded violent action, calling for a just war that would be fought in the name of the people and against the enemies of the people; indeed, from the earliest years of the July Monarchy republican secret societies were already expressing their belief in the need for action in order to establish republics throughout Europe. They chanted songs of insurrection, among them the *Chant du départ* and other battle hymns of the First Republic.[3] There was, in short, a new vibrancy and a renewed militancy about the republican movement, and with it a rejection of political compromise. Louis-Philippe's government, of course, had no such qualms, going out of its way to remind French voters of the new King's revolutionary past at the same time as it consciously milked the last dregs of sympathy for Napoleon in order to expand support for the new regime. In 1833 a statue of Napoleon was restored to the Vendôme Column as a mark of public respect, but it was a popular image of Napoleon that was created, a Napoleon of legend in greatcoat and *tricorne* hat.[4] It is no accident that the panels for the Arc de Triomphe were sculpted in the early 1830s, in the period immediately after the creation of the Orleans monarchy when Louis-Philippe's crusade was at its most intense; the monument itself was ready for its public unveiling, amidst the most lavish ceremonial, in 1836.

The blurring of the distinction between the revolutionary and imperial army was not, of course, entirely the work of governments or of future

[2] Maurice Agulhon, *Marianne into Battle. Republican Imagery and Symbolism in France, 1789–1880* (Cambridge, 1981), p. 45.

[3] Karma Nabulsi, 'La Guerre Sainte: debates about just war among republicans in the nineteenth century', in Sudhir Hazareesingh (ed.), *The Jacobin Legacy in Modern France. Essays in Honour of Vincent Wright* (Oxford, 2002), pp. 23–4.

[4] Robert Gildea, *The Past in French History* (New Haven, 1994), p. 96.

generations. Wars do not religiously follow the rigid contours laid down by their political leaders, and it is at least arguable that Napoleon's *coup d'état* on 18 Brumaire was less of a natural caesura in the history of European warfare than it was in the internal politics of France. Men who had begun their military careers fighting for the republic seldom laid down their arms or threatened mutiny; they continued to serve the First Consul as they had the Directory and the Jacobin republic, as loyal to their corps and their comrades as they were to any political regime. In 1804, they would marvel at the sumptuousness of the coronation ceremony and would hail Napoleon as their emperor. Some – those strong and lucky enough to survive two decades of war – would still be there, fighting on behind the imperial eagles, in the last futile months of the war in 1814. In part, of course, that is in the nature of armies; they are engaged to serve, to obey orders, to support whatever regime is in power. Not even the Jacobins had sought to transform the revolutionary soldier into a political animal who could take political decisions or challenge authority; the army, they were clear, should in no circumstances be *délibérante*, capable of independent thought and action. But it also reflects the fact that for the serving soldier little of substance changed with the overthrow of the Directory. The political speeches they had listened to in the heady days of Valmy and Jemappes had long given way to the more prosaic lessons of the drill-book, and it would be fanciful to see in the long marches across the Alps or the exoticism of the Egyptian campaign anything that was especially redolent of revolutionary ideals. Tactics and military drill had not changed radically; for much of the revolutionary decade, indeed, the French continued to use the drill-books of the Ancien Régime. Men who had either volunteered in 1791 or been recruited under the *levée en masse* of 1793 were by 1800 inured to the hardships and routine exercises that marked military life; they were unlikely to feel any strong ideological attachments or to be moved by the justice of their cause. Indeed, what signified the greatest change for the troops at the turn of the century was less the change of regime than the introduction of annual conscription and the routinisation of military service which it implied. And if there was a key moment which in their eyes offered the hope of a new dawn, it was less the coup of Brumaire – which not even contemporary painters thought to commemorate[5] – than the prospect of peace held out, briefly, by the Peace of Amiens in 1801.[6]

[5] Barthélemy Jobert, 'Les représentations contemporaines du Dix-huit août dans les arts', in Jacques-Olivier Boudon (ed.), *Brumaire. La prise de pouvoir de Bonaparte* (Paris, 2001), pp. 116–17.

[6] The announcement of the peace was greeted with joy and public celebration throughout France. See Alan Forrest, 'La perspective de la paix dans l'opinion publique

Nor should we be induced by the glowing accounts of generals and political leaders into believing that the vast majority of the soldiers shared their ideals or enjoyed their experience of army life. Only briefly, during the early Revolution, did the French succeed in inspiring their men to heroism by appealing to their idealism, their love of liberty, their belief in their nation and their cause. Increasingly they appealed to more traditional military instincts – emphasising their patriotism, loyalty to comrades and regiments, the joys of victory, the lure of honours, tangible rewards for what for many were real and painful sufferings. For whatever the dreams of the young men who had left home to fight for republic or empire, most would soon discover that soldiering was not fun, a liberating moment that would serve as a rite of passage to manhood. They spent long weeks on forced marches, were struck down with debilitating fevers, lost limbs in battle, suffered from shell-shock and depression. Some suffered agonising and lingering deaths in field ambulances and hastily-converted military hospitals. Others – many others – preferred the uncertain perils of desertion to the certain miseries of war. There was exhilaration, of course, in moments of victory, a general joy when their efforts were finally rewarded and when success could be celebrated with friends in wayside inns. These were the moments they talked about in their letters, and which would provide the basis for the nineteenth-century legend. But they were necessarily rare; most of the time there was little exciting about soldiering. Indeed, if there is a single theme that recurs in the personal accounts of the soldiers who fought in these wars, it is boredom – the sheer dullness of waiting, the frustration of inactivity. The reality of this war, as with others in the modern period, was far removed from the glamour of the myth.

Boredom was often accompanied by a degree of disillusionment. The young men who set out for the front often looked to the army, as young men have done from time immemorial, to inject excitement into their lives, to provide an escape from a rather humdrum, predictable civilian existence. Instead, they were catapulted into a world where boredom was endemic, whether the boredom of doing nothing, or the boredom of endless hours of drill and military exercise. 'When we are on campaign', wrote a young cavalryman, Jean-Michel Chevalier, 'it is another matter; but when we are on garrison duty we die of boredom'.[7] Those who had joined the battalions filled with youthful confidence soon learned the numbing effects of tedium. The experience of Jean-Baptiste

et la société militaire', *Bulletin de la Société des Antiquaires de Picardie* 166 (2002), pp. 251–62.

[7] Jean-Michel Chevalier, *Souvenirs des guerres napoléoniennes* (Paris, 1970), p. 43.

Barrès, at nineteen a private in the Imperial Guard, was unexceptional in this respect. He explains in his memoirs how, when he left Paris, 'war was the one thing I wanted. I was young, full of health and courage; and I thought one could wish for nothing better than to fight against all possible odds'. He wanted, he explains, to share in the adventure of war, 'to see the country, the siege of a fortress, a battlefield'. But, he goes on, that optimistic spirit would soon be broken as he came to understand the reality of the soldier's lot. Now 'the boredom which is consuming me in cantonments and four months of marching about, months of fatigue and wretchedness, have proved to me that nothing is more hideous, more miserable, than war'.[8] His disillusionment was widely shared among troops on all sides in what seemed an unending war, in which the desire for peace at least equalled the desire for victory. For those who survived, the campaigns they had taken part in and the long years they had spent in the army had something of a generic quality. It was a period marked by moments of fear and excitement, the end of campaign seasons, the opening of new fronts, and forced marches to new destinations. These were military moments, quite distinct from governments and regimes.

It was not only the troops who failed to make any clear distinction between the Revolutionary and Napoleonic Wars. The iconography of the Directorial period had become increasingly dominated by images of French military success and courage on the battlefield, as the Directory sought to deflect attention from its domestic failings. From the *sacre du philosophe*, in Annie Jourdan's felicitous phrase, the country passed rapidly to the *sacre du militaire*.[9] The majestic backdrop of the Alps and the sheer exoticism of the Egyptian Campaign made these natural subjects for the artists of the day, especially those attracted by the challenge of a large canvas and the theme of France's destiny. Besides, Bonaparte's natural gift for self-publicity – shown most spectacularly in Egypt – helped to ensure that his victories would be recorded for posterity by France's greatest artists. A study of the *Cabinet des estampes* at the Bibliothèque Nationale for a single year, 1798, illustrates the degree to which pictures with a military flavour appealed to French taste, as well as showing the extent of Bonaparte's personal domination of the

[8] Rory Muir, *Tactics and the Experience of Battle in the Age of Napoleon* (New Haven, 1998), p. 4.

[9] Annie Jourdan, 'Les monuments de la Révolution française. Le discours des images dans l'espace parisien, 1789–1804' (doctoral thesis, University of Amsterdam, 1993), p. 85; Annie Jourdan, 'Du sacre du philosophe au sacre du militaire', *Revue d'histoire moderne et contemporaine* 34 (1992), pp. 403–22.

market in prints and etchings.[10] There are colourful images of the army on campaign in Egypt, and of operations against the Mamelukes: one shows the British fleet in flames; another, the entry of the French army into the gates of Cairo; yet another, in splendid classical style, a regiment mounted on dromedaries, painted against an exotic desert landscape. Napoleon himself appears in many of the prints. He is depicted leaving Toulon for North Africa, directing the capture of Malta, camped beneath the Pyramids, and crowned with the fruits of victory; there is the triumph of the return of Egyptian antiquities to France when the campaign is over, and the sash, resplendent in its republican red-white-and-blue, which the French general had given to an Egyptian bey. Every step that Bonaparte took, it would seem, is recorded for posterity, even his less-than-successful plan to invade England at the end of the year. Uncritical praise was heaped upon him, with Cossia coming close to hero-worship in a print of 5 September which portrays the republican general in the manner of a romantic idyll.[11]

None of this happened by chance. Napoleon was highly adept at exploiting his military successes during the 1790s, and he used every form of propagandist flourish to establish his reputation with the French people. He was a master publicist who, from his first campaigns in Italy through to the years of exile on Saint Helena, demonstrated an unshakable self-belief and a quite exceptional capacity to control and manipulate public opinion. In this, his close association with the ideals of the French Revolution played an essential part. His military bulletins were only partly about the day-to-day news from the front; they were also clarion calls to the troops, summoning up their energies and sympathising with their sufferings, galvanising them into one final effort that would bring victory and peace.[12] He used his military successes both to exalt the achievements of the army and to establish his place as a hero in the classical republican tradition. But he was careful not to concentrate exclusively on his own role and that of the high command, in a way that risked arousing jealousy or antagonising the men in the ranks. In his earlier campaigns, indeed, it is notable how often it was the heroism of ordinary soldiers that was emphasised in his bulletins and

[10] The images described are to be found in the *Cabinet des estampes* at the Bibliothèque Nationale (site Richelieu), in series Qb and Qb1 for 1798, and in the Collection De Vinck.

[11] Bibliothèque Nationale, *Cabinet des estampes*, De Vinck 6842.

[12] The language used in the *Bulletins* changed over time, becoming less militant, more serene and paternal, as Napoleon evolved from revolutionary general to emperor. See Didier Le Gall, 'Etude léximétrique de la prose napoléonienne à travers les proclamations, les allocutions et les ordres du jour' (mémoire de maîtrise, Université de Paris-I, 1991).

despatches, and in the pages of the military press which he established and subsidised in Milan (most notably the *Courrier de l'Armée d'Italie* and *La France vue de l'Armée d'Italie*, aimed at subtly different – but particularly Parisian – readerships). There was, of course, nothing novel in producing newspapers in the armies; it had become almost a standard practice during the revolutionary campaigns.[13] But Napoleon used the medium to particularly potent effect. In 1797 he launched a third paper, the highly partisan *Journal de Bonaparte et des Hommes Vertueux*, which emphasised his ambition for France and served to burnish still further his heroic image. And, with the help of the ever-loyal Berthier, he regularly placed news stories written by sympathetic journalists in the mainstream Paris press, and published letters from the war, including a number in the *Moniteur*. In these letters Napoleon was omnipresent, the exclusive focus of Berthier's interest: he pointed to Napoleon's role as the organiser of French victories as well as his courage under fire, his involvement in every stage of the battle.[14] Together, these initiatives formed the basis for a highly professional campaign of news and misinformation that was targeted principally at Paris and the civilian population.[15]

Little was left to chance. To edit his papers he turned to seasoned journalists and polished writers who had already served their apprenticeships in revolutionary politics or political journalism[16] – men like Regnault de Saint-Jean d'Angély and the former Jacobin and right-hand man of Robespierre, Marc-Antoine Jullien.[17] The papers were cleverly directed at specific audiences – officers and men in the armies, the troops in northern Italy, but especially the civil population back in France. And the young General Bonaparte was always ready with a memorable phrase, a soundbite from the front line, that could capture the colour of the moment and impress itself on the minds of his readers. In his youth he wrote in the language of the Revolution, replete with ideals and abstractions, using and abusing the terminology of the times to drive home his point. Like any other republican orator, he

[13] The phenomenon of the military press in France is analysed in Marc Martin, *Les origines de la presse militaire en France à la fin de l'Ancien Régime et sous la Révolution, 1770–99* (Vincennes, 1975).

[14] Jean-Yves Leclercq, 'Le mythe de Bonaparte sous le Directoire, 1796–1799' (mémoire de maîtrise, Université de Paris-I, 1991), pp. 32–5.

[15] This theme is developed in Alan Forrest, 'Propaganda and the legitimation of power in Napoleonic France', *French History* 18 (2004), p. 432.

[16] Jean-Paul Bertaud, *La presse et le pouvoir de Louis XIII à Napoléon* (Paris, 2000), p. 204.

[17] Robert R. Palmer, *From Jacobin to Liberal. Marc-Antoine Jullien, 1775–1848* (Princeton, N.J., 1993), pp. 76–92.

made constant reference to notions of liberty and patriotism, though his speeches and bulletins were notable, by the standards of the time, for their clarity and directness. As Nada Tomiche has acutely observed, his preference was for short, succinct words that made immediate impact, replacing the long, rather tired adjectives of standard revolutionary rhetoric – words like 'indivisible', 'inaltérable', or 'incorruptible', which had become near-obligatory in the political speeches of the 1790s – with crisper, punchier words of his own, like 'grand', or 'sage', or 'sévère'. They had more impact for their directness, but they were still recognisably revolutionary.[18] With the passage of time, and aided by the desire of the Directory to exploit its triumphs on the frontiers, these papers came to place greater emphasis on individual exploits and personal glory; it became respectable to praise great men, not least generals and military leaders, and this gave Bonaparte the opportunity he needed to represent himself as a hero, and to embellish his existing reputation as a loyal republican, established during the siege of Toulon in 1793. In the process, without seeming to break with the revolutionary tradition, he was able to metamorphose from republican general to all-conquering hero, patriot and saviour of the French people, although, throughout this exercise in self-reinvention, he was careful to emphasise his continued loyalty to the government, to underline his humble origins, to stress his claims to be a son of the Enlightenment. He would save the Revolution, and his people, by rooting out the threat of anarchy, by destroying the corruption of political factions, by giving France the order she craved and a government based on virtue and principle. Even in presenting his own image, the future emperor was careful not to rupture his ties with the past or his claim to a share of the revolutionary heritage.

The Napoleonic image was carefully nurtured and meticulously constructed, the product not just of his writings but of the depictions made of him by others. In particular the Napoleonic legend was created during the Directorial years by painters and artists eager to capture the great moments of the Italian campaign. He was helped, as Philip Dwyer has noted, by the revolutionary tendency to dramatise the heroism of Jacobin militants and deputies-on-mission, especially in the face of enemy fire; it was the revolutionaries, rather than Napoleon himself, who first publicised the image of the victorious revolutionary general sweeping aside all who stood in his path, urging on his compatriots in the cause of the Republic. This proved an enduring image, one that fed upon Napoleon's youth and fiery appearance, and which he himself would embellish over the years. It was popularised by artists seeking

[18] Nada Tomiche, *Napoléon écrivain* (Paris, 1952), p. 210.

to exploit the two most familiar images to emerge from the Italian Campaign, the largely fictional scenes depicting the battles of Lodi (in June 1796) and Arcola (in November of the same year). Indeed, in all there would be fifteen different paintings of Lodi alone, ranging from imaginative scenes of the battle, dramatically set on the bridge over the River Adda, to images of Bonaparte as the hero of the hour.[19] Arcola, another battle with a bridge as its centrepiece, would be made famous by the stunning portrait of Napoleon by Antoine-Jean Gros, one of the foremost history painters of his day and a major contributor to the Napoleonic myth.[20] The image, notes Christopher Prendergast in a telling phrase, is 'of the hero in a force-field of action, all dynamic flows and forward movement'. It is a dramatic and memorable public statement, and one on which Napoleon himself would draw in analysing his military successes. 'The hair, wind-swept in proto-romantic style, merges with the flag, both specked with reddish gold, further rhyming with the gold braid of the uniform. Flag, face, colour and light thus meet, as a golden identification of symbol and actor: Bonaparte does not just lead the army; he *is* the army'.[21] In this way the Revolution and its general fused into a single, heroic figure.

He was aided by the Directory's desire to play down political divisions and minimise ideological commitments, which resulted in a clampdown on political faction in France and an increasing reliance on the support of the army. It was always a rather uneasy relationship: the Directors were apprehensive about the possibility of a military coup, and had done their best to discourage the generals from dreaming of political careers (Augereau, in particular, had twice been a candidate for a position as Director, though twice he had failed to get elected). But in Fructidor Year V the army had become involved in politics in a sudden and decisive way, when, with the elections returning a royalist majority, it was called in by the government to disperse the deputies after it had annulled the results in forty-nine departments.[22] The Directory had used military force to overturn the expressed will of the electorate, and, whether the Directors liked it or not, they were now dependent – and, more damagingly, were seen to be dependent – on the

[19] Philip Dwyer, 'Napoleon Bonaparte as hero and saviour: image, rhetoric and behaviour in the construction of a legend', *French History* 18 (2004), pp. 381–2.

[20] David O'Brien, 'Antoine-Jean Gros in Italy', *Burlington Magazine* 137 (1995), pp. 651–60.

[21] Christopher Prendergast, *Napoleon and History Painting. Antoine-Jean Gros's 'La Bataille d'Eylau'* (Oxford, 1997), p. 146.

[22] Martyn Lyons, *Napoleon Bonaparte and the Legacy of the French Revolution* (London, 1994), p. 16.

military for their continued enjoyment of office. In the process the state became more identified with the military, and the influence of the more powerful generals inevitably increased. They were now public figures to a quite unprecedented degree, part of the polity and, whether in the West, in Italy or in Egypt, the most dashing and glamorous part, winning victories and suppressing the opponents of revolutionary France. Increasingly, too, it was the triumphs of the military that were celebrated in public festivals, glorified in caricature and popular prints, and praised in the new plays that opened in the Paris theatre. Even revolutionary songs came to focus on the one non-divisive element in public affairs, the army and the nation's military effort abroad. Bonaparte was the particular beneficiary of this interest, until, celebrated as 'the model for our warriors' and compared to 'the heroes of antiquity', he became the central figure of the Directory's political anthems.[23] Indeed, there is little doubting that for Napoleon these years were crucial, constituting the first act in the construction of a personal legend, years of triumph and cultural aggrandisement that turned him into a popular hero.

The legend was primarily made in Italy and consecrated in Egypt. It was during the Italian Campaign that the quality of invincibility passed from the army to its young general, the *homme miraculeux* who could be compared to Hannibal in the Alps, then with Alexander the Great and Julius Caesar. No military metaphor seemed too absurd for a man who was portrayed, and who portrayed himself, as a conquering warrior, as a bringer of peace, as a soldier-philosopher worthy of the Age of Enlightenment.[24] In Egypt, too, his role was multi-faceted, as he led an expedition that was at once military, naval and scientific into one of the most exotic landscapes on earth. Both the military failings and the naval disaster were predictably elided from the narrative as the French people turned their attention away from domestic shortcomings to be dazzled by tales of the Orient. Bonaparte, declared the *Décade Philosophique*, worked wonders in Egypt, to the point where he came near to being talked of as a successor to Mahomet.[25] As for the army, its failures were played down; its image was of a civilising force, a patriotic army of French citizens battling gallantly against a backdrop of camels and Pyramids. They came not as simple conquerors, but as heralds of Enlightenment, bringing to Egypt the benefits of rationalism,

[23] Laura Mason, *Singing the French Revolution. Popular Culture and Politics, 1787–1799* (Ithaca, N.Y., 1996), p. 193.

[24] Leclercq, 'Le mythe de Bonaparte sous le Directoire', pp. 165–6.

[25] Frédéric Régent, 'L'expédition d'Égypte de Bonaparte vue par la presse parisienne, 1798–99' (mémoire de maîtrise, Université de Paris-I, 1992), p. 40.

humanism and revolutionary liberty.[26] Once more the soldiers fighting under Napoleon were clearly identified with the values of progress, of liberalism and of civilisation; the Revolution and Bonaparte were as one, and the country was fascinated, unable to consume enough pictures, exhibitions and Islamic artefacts. The contrast with Brumaire, the military coup which brought him to power, could not be starker. Few artists appear to have been interested in recording the event; such images as were produced – and there are no more than thirty in the Bibliothèque Nationale – were limited to popular prints and occasional caricatures. The first major painting to celebrate the event would not be produced until a generation later, when it was commissioned by Louis-Philippe for the Musée de Versailles.[27]

Though as First Consul and later as Emperor, Napoleon sought to replace his youthful image with that of a more sober, reflective and statesman-like ruler, working for the benefit of his people, he could not entirely cast off his revolutionary past. Nor, in truth, did he want to, given how central military success remained to the image of his empire. The continuities were, in any case, clear to see. The armies of the Napoleonic Wars were built on a firm foundation laid down during the French Revolution. They were, of course, much larger, and for most of the Empire they were fighting a war of foreign conquest rather than one of national defence; they were composed of conscripts drawn from across the continent rather than from France alone; and there was no longer any pretence that their cause was that of the people, far less that they were fighting for the betterment of mankind. They fought, more traditionally, for honours and rewards rather than the plaudits of a grateful nation.[28] But the manner of their fighting was little changed. If the artillery played a more important role than previously, this was still recognisably an eighteenth-century army where soldiers armed with muskets and bayonets fought with the enemy face-to-face. And just as, during the Italian campaign or in Egypt, Napoleon had been a soldiers' general, knowing how to talk to his troops and inspire them with the belief that he was sharing in their sufferings, so in government he continued to rely heavily on the army's support, both to intervene at moments of crisis and for more routine tasks of public order and

[26] André Raymond, 'Les Égyptiens et les Lumières pendant l'expédition française', in Patrice Bret (ed.), *L'Expédition d'Égypte, une entreprise des Lumières, 1798–1801* (Paris, 1999), p. 104.

[27] Jobert, 'Les représentations contemporaines, pp. 116–17.

[28] John Lynn, 'Toward an army of honor: the moral evolution of the French army, 1789–1815', *French Historical Studies* 16 (1989), pp. 152–73.

the repression of crime. Those on whom he relied most, his generals and marshals, were lavishly honoured and richly rewarded for their services. The fact that so many of them had served the revolutionary state before transferring their loyalty to the Emperor only emphasised the degree of continuity across the period of the wars, the lack of any real break – other than the short truce provided by Amiens – before 1815, when Napoleon was finally forced to sue for peace after Waterloo.

Napoleonic France continued the Directory's practice of glorying in military victories and praising the triumphs of great men. The Empire was not only a state at war; in many ways it was a state whose centralised institutions had been designed for waging war, ensuring the systematic collection of intelligence, providing mandatory and well-defined lines of reporting and communication, and codifying a single system of law for the entire country. And, in contrast to the early Revolution, Napoleonic France had a sufficiently strong state apparatus, with functionaries and gendarmes working in its service, to be able to enforce the often unpopular laws and impositions which war on this scale demanded. It had in place the means of raising soldiers, imposing garrisons, extracting requisitions and seizing horses and other draught-animals from a reluctant peasantry, and with the expansion of the Empire beyond France's boundaries, there were satellite kingdoms from whom tribute could be demanded and where the troops might be supplied. Security was the paramount consideration, and to ensure national security Napoleon was prepared to impose new limitations on freedom, to authorise arbitrary arrests and to hold prisoners without trial, to sacrifice even the most basic of civil liberties.[29] In all, between two and three million men were mobilised for active service. Indeed, it has been calculated that for the *Grande Armée* alone, Napoleon mobilised more than two million men, of whom 1,660,000 were French, and that the losses sustained – estimated at around 900,000 men for the years between 1800 and 1815 – represented a death rate of nearly 40 per cent, a rate of loss that had not previously been sustained and would not be again until the butchery of the Great War. The toll was highest, of course, in the desperate last years of the fighting: of those born between 1790 and 1795, nearly 42.5 per cent were called to the colours.[30] And though these troops were overwhelmingly engaged in pursuing wars of

[29] Michael Sibalis, 'Arbitrary detention, human rights and the Napoleonic senate', in Howard G. Brown and Judith A. Miller (eds.), *Taking Liberties. Problems of a New Order from the French Revolution to Napoleon* (Manchester, 2002), p. 169.

[30] Jacques Houdaille, 'Pertes de l'armée de terre sous le Premier Empire, d'après les registres matricules', *Population* 27 (1972), pp. 49–50.

conquest and European colonisation, they still fought against the same enemies using similar weapons and an equally nationalistic ideology. The Republic might have given place to the Empire, and the Revolution to the *Grande Nation*. But little else seemed to have changed, and it was easy to believe that they were still, as in 1792, Frenchmen fighting for the future and the glory of the nation, even once, patently, the *patrie* was no longer directly threatened by defeat or invasion.

Above all, there was continuity in the experience of war – by soldiers, most notably, cut off from their families and discovering a new lifestyle and a new sociability in the army. Many who volunteered in the early 1790s or were conscripted under the Loi Jourdan never found their way back to civilian life. Some appreciated the freedom the army offered, or enjoyed the responsibility that came with promotion; others grew old in the service of the Emperor and, knowing no other skills, stayed on. Many of the men who finally dispersed when the army was driven back across the eastern frontier in 1814 on to French soil had spent years, some even decades, in their battalions, having become professionalised into the army, and regarding a return to the fields or the workshop with more bewilderment than pleasure. But it was not just those who fought who had been changed by their experience. Wives had become widows or had been worn down by the hard manual labour of maintaining the farm; children grew up who had never known their fathers. Gender roles changed, too, as did authority structures and traditional assumptions about the father's place within the family; this was true of all countries involved in these long and draining years of conflict.[31] Petty jealousies and resentments were opened up between those who had gone to the war and those who had stayed behind; in many rural communities a certain communal spirit was destroyed for ever. And as the government sent in gendarmes and garrisoned troops on villagers in an attempt to flush out conscripts and deserters, so relations between the local community and the state were seriously damaged. The government was seen to be oppressing local people, using line troops to round up draft-dodgers and arrest those who were hiding them, and imposing on French villages the same repressive measures they used in occupied territory.[32] Civilians as well as soldiers found their lives changed

[31] For a comparative perspective see Karen Hagemann, 'A valorous *Volk* family: the nation, the military and the gender order in Prussia in the time of the anti-Napoleonic wars, 1806–15', in Ida Blom, Karen Hagemann and Catherine Hall (eds.), *Gendered Nations. Nationalisms and Gender Order in the Long Nineteenth Century* (Oxford, 2000), pp. 179–205.

[32] Louis Bergès, *Résister à la conscription, 1798–1814. Le cas des départements aquitains* (Paris, 2002), p. 439.

utterly by the experience of war, their domestic economies enriched or imperilled, their very identities challenged. When the soldiers returned to their homes – if they returned – after 1815, and when some kind of normality was at last restored to people's everyday lives, the experience which they most vividly remembered was simply that of war.

Yet across the generation that separated the young men who left home in 1793 to fight for the First Republic and those who followed in their footsteps to serve the Emperor in Russia or in the Peninsula there was surely one very real difference, and a difference which crucially altered their image of patriotic service. Many still fought with passion and commitment; but they fought for a more prosaic cause, for their unit or their regiment, for pride and promotion, or for the fruits which the promise of victory would bring. They might find a family in the army, a society where they felt valued and to which they dedicated themselves, commanders and especially comrades with whom they shared bonds of common experience and terrible suffering and to whom they felt a correspondingly deep loyalty. But they could not repeat the experience of the young men who volunteered in 1791 or who marched off to war as part of the *levée en masse*. They no longer thought of themselves as fighting in an ideological crusade for liberty and the rights of man, as the revolutionary *commissaires* and deputies on mission had repeatedly assured their fathers that they were. And they could no longer believe, after a decade of territorial expansion, that they would be greeted as liberators and not simply as occupiers – especially since all Europe knew that in France Napoleon had destroyed liberty and sought to eliminate many of the benefits of the republic.[33] Behind the rhetoric of glory and honour that characterised the Napoleonic years, these were armies of conscripts, of men who served for the simple reason that they had no choice. Annual levies had become a familiar part of the process of growing up, the day of the *tirage* becoming a rite of passage for adolescent boys. They might still be a tribute to the revolutionary ideal of equality; but the urgency, the sense of necessity and bravura that had marked the first calls to arms during the early Revolution had long since vanished. This was especially true in the final years of the Empire, when the army was taking men from all five *classes* and was incorporating even sixteen- and seventeen-year-olds in the regiments. Most marched off doggedly, even fatalistically, the product of a country exhausted by years of heavy recruitment and cowed by threats of arrest and punishment.[34]

[33] Paolo Viola, 'Napoléon, chef de la révolution patriotique', in Jean-Clément Martin (ed.), *Napoléon et l'Europe* (Rennes, 2002), p. 36.

[34] Charles Esdaile, *The Wars of Napoleon* (London, 1995), p. 260.

The Emperor, of course, acknowledged none of this, as Napoleonic propaganda pressed the absolute priority of war, honouring heroism and sacrifice, praising the ideal of service to the nation, and lauding the masculine qualities of courage, virility and physical strength. He lavished praise on his *braves*, praise and flattery, while reserving the highest honours of state – including the newly created Legion of Honour – for his officers and marshals. Napoleon recognised, as, indeed, the Directory had begun to do, how deeply the system of honours accorded with the aspirations of the army, and the new elite which he created at the apex of French society was strongly biased in favour of the military. Soldiers responded to grandiose ceremonies like the one at Boulogne in 1804 where, with 100,000 men lined up before him, he distributed the coveted eagles to the new members of the Legion. The Legion remained an overwhelmingly military honour. Of the 35,000 legionnaires alive in 1815, only one in fifteen had been rewarded for service in the civil sphere; the others were soldiers.[35] He in return was rewarded with superhuman effort and – from many of the *grognards* whom he had led across a continent – with levels of personal loyalty that came close to adulation, even to affection for a man they had come to regard as their 'avenger, protector and father'.[36] Even those who had previously served the Revolution – and they were still many in the armies of 1805 and 1806 – seemed to respond to the honours and gongs that were bestowed upon them, and they fought as bravely and with as great patriotic commitment for the cause of the Emperor. The new value system in no way diminished their fighting powers or diluted their motivation; their achievements on the battlefield are well-known to all, and their loyalty to Napoleon and to the imperial cause was legendary.[37] When Captain Coignet referred to Napoleon in his journal, the reference was always effusive, the memory warm and seemingly personal: he was 'mon Napoléon', 'notre cher Empereur', a man to be loved and venerated; and there were so many Coignets in post-Restoration France![38] Many, of course, were summarily paid off by the Bourbons, their military adventures brought to a peremptory close. But even those who remained in the army showed little affection for the Bourbon cause. For men like Captain Bertrand, seasoned soldiers who had served in long campaigns, Napoleon was an idol and an inspiration.

[35] Claude Ducourtial, 'Introduction' to a special issue of *La Cohorte* to mark the exhibition at the Musée National de la Légion d'Honneur in Paris on 'Napoléon et la Légion d'Honneur' (Paris, 1968).

[36] Steven Englund, *Napoleon. A Political Life* (New York, 2004), p. 271.

[37] J. Lucas-Dubreton, *Le culte de Napoléon, 1815–48* (Paris, 1960), pp. 11–14.

[38] Jean-Roch Coignet, *Les Cahiers du Capitaine Coignet* (Paris, 1968).

He remained, said Bertrand, 'notre Drapeau', and though military discipline forced him after 1815 to march behind the white flag of the monarchy, 'we felt that our hearts, and all our souls, went out to him'.[39] For many, like Bertrand, the Revolution was only a distant memory, the *levée en masse* part of a vanishing tradition that meant little to them. In the years after 1815 they would form one of the principal vectors of a rival, imperial legend.

Because the Napoleonic polity was so dominated by the fact of war, by the need for ever greater armies and for the resources to sustain them, the image of the soldier and the symbolic representation of military values became more and more prominent in the public sphere. Especially in the early years of his reign, when so much of his prestige depended upon his reputation as a military leader and a victorious general, Napoleon made sure that the French people were kept constantly aware of the extent of their debt to the army and of the degree to which France's well-being was linked to the success of her troops. The very identity of the nation was increasingly expressed in terms of glory and military conquest, and these in turn were epitomised in the person of Napoleon; as he himself insisted, the French people saw themselves in the person of 'a leader made famous by military glory', an image that gave them pride and self-belief, in contrast to the 'speeches of ideologues' which they did not understand.[40] Artists were encouraged to contribute to this image both through direct commissions and through the themes chosen for the competitions that were sponsored by the Academy. The biennial Salons gave a privileged position to the large history paintings so beloved of the period, presenting voluptuous images of massed armies and of victories on the battlefield, and never hesitating to trumpet the military glories of Napoleon's soldiers in the field. His artists were discouraged from expressing doubt or regret, or allowing themselves the luxury of sadness or pathos.[41] Only in the piled-up corpses that form the foreground to his *La Bataille d'Eylau*, presented to the 1808 Salon and highly controversial at the time, do we find any expression of regret or outrage at the scale of the losses which Napoleon's victories had entailed. More typical were images of the hero, Napoleon crossing the Alps, or his troops triumphant on the battlefield of Marengo. Painters recognised that they had a mission in the service

[39] Natalie Petiteau, *Lendemains d'Empire. Les soldats de Napoléon dans la France du dix-neuvième siècle* (Paris, 2003), p. 131.

[40] Letter of Napoleon to Miot de Melito, quoted in André Palluel-Guillard, 'L'idée de nation en France entre 1800 et 1815', in Natalie Petiteau (ed.), *Voies nouvelles pour l'histoire du Premier Empire. Territoires, Pouvoirs, Identités* (Paris, 2003), p. 29.

[41] Timothy Wilson-Smith, *Napoleon and his Artists* (London, 1996), p. 150.

of the Empire almost as soldiers did; indeed, Meynier's painting at the 1804 Salon, *La France triomphante encourageant les sciences et les arts au milieu de la guerre*, is one artist's acknowledgement of that mission. It was, in Christopher Prendergast's words, 'a celebration not only of war by painting but of war *for* painting'.[42]

There was, of course, a constant danger that the propagandist tone of the history paintings that were produced for Napoleon – and which Vivant Denon ensured were given a prominent place on the walls of the Louvre – would destroy their impact with the public and thus undermine their primary purpose. The painters themselves, from the established like David to the young and up-and-coming, could resent Denon's constant interventions in their art and comment disparagingly on the historical purpose of some of his commissions.[43] They knew that they were painting for a new imperial establishment, and that fact alone – when added to the habitual rancour and jealousies between artists – aroused resentment. The consumers of these great tableaux were, in any case, largely restricted to those with the leisure and education to visit galleries and art exhibitions. Those of more modest means were dependent on cheap reproductions, on prints and woodcuts that could be printed in newspapers or sold in print shops. For the great moments of the Napoleonic legend these prints abound in great profusion. A good example is the depiction of Napoleon's triumphant progress in the Egyptian campaign, as it was recorded by the engravers of 1798. The titles of their works are indicative of their central theme, the mingling of glory with exoticism in the greatest of all *missions civilisatrices*. Napoleon is shown advancing steadily from triumph to improbable triumph, the impact made all the greater by the repeated contrast between France and Africa as he uncovered to an admiring gaze the wonders of an exotic world. Contemporaries were invited to follow his – and France's – greatest military adventure in a series of sumptuous images – Bonaparte crowned by victory in Egypt; the Regiment of *Dromadaires*; Napoleon before the Pyramids; the entry of the army into Cairo; the triumphal return of the scientific and artistic monuments to France.[44]

What David, Gros and Ingres did for the salons, Jean-Claude Pellerin achieved for ordinary Frenchmen, the peasants and tradesmen for whom the local fair or market was their principal interface

[42] Christopher Prendergast, *Napoleon and History Painting. Antoine-Jean Gros's 'La Bataille d'Eylau'* (Oxford, 1997), p. 80.

[43] Bruno Foucart, 'La grande alliance de Napoléon et des peintres de son histoire', in *Napoléon, images et histoires. Peintures du Château de Versailles, 1789–1815* (Paris, 2001), p. 15.

[44] The prints are located in B.N., *Cabinet des estampes*, Iconographie, June–July 1798.

with culture, and, very frequently, with those strangers, like pedlars and soldiers, who could bring news of the outside world.[45] Pedlars, in particular, were respected as sources of information – unlike soldiers, they were not handicapped by a reputation for boasting and telling tall tales – and this gave the merchandise they purveyed added authority in rural society. It should be stressed that Pellerin and the other *imagistes* from Epinal were only peripherally interested in political and military images at the beginning of the Empire. Their main effort lay in the production of religious pictures and in printing books and cheap tracts for a popular readership: fairytales and popular fiction, devotional tracts, catechisms and saints' lives were still their stock-in-trade. And the great flourishing of the trade in Napoleonic *images d'Epinal* did not come before the 1820s and 1830s; as a loyal Bonapartist, Pellerin's principal contribution would be to the memory of his Emperor and to the creation of his legend.[46] But already in Napoleon's lifetime their catalogues were beginning to contain images of his military victories and to reflect the sumptuousness of Napoleonic court life, subjects which would be greatly in vogue in the years after 1820. They also reflected the growing popular taste for bright military uniforms, which came out especially well in the bold dyes used by the colourists; so that by the end of the Empire, Pellerin's production regularly included engravings of soldiers, resplendent in their regimental uniforms, whole sheets of images that could appeal as much to the peasant family whose son had left for the war as to old soldiers nostalgic for the comradeship of their unit. The 1814 catalogue lists them in detail: 'musique française, garde impériale, chasseurs de la garde impériale, grenadiers de la garde impériale, chasseurs français, cavaliers français, cuirassiers français, hussards français, hussards à pied'. And, as a reminder that these had been no ordinary wars, the catalogue added 'cavalerie turque', and 'mamelukes et tartares'.[47]

In prints and caricatures, the French soldier was portrayed showing many of the traits and characteristics which he himself valued and with which he increasingly came to be identified. These were far from the morally upright, virtuous qualities that were supposedly the hallmark of the revolutionary soldier. Napoleonic soldiers were shown as being rather vain, proud of their military rank, pleased to be distinguished

[45] The identification of soldiers and pedlars in popular imagery is noted by David Hopkin, *Soldier and Peasant in French Popular Culture, 1766–1870* (London, 2003), pp. 71–3.

[46] Jean-Marie Dumont, *Les maîtres-graveurs populaires, 1800–50* (Epinal, 1965), p. vii.

[47] Jean-Marie Dumont, *La vie et l'oeuvre de Jean-Charles Pellerin, 1756–1836* (Epinal, 1956), pp. 50–1.

from their civilian fellows by their bright uniforms and military bearing. Officers, in the traditions of the Ancien Régime, wore their swords and medals with pride, identified with their regiments, even strutted with a certain arrogance that emphasised their status. The troops also cut dashing figures in bright, well-cut uniforms; in contrast to their revolutionary counterparts, Napoleonic troops were elegantly attired, and every soldier on joining his regiment was completely outfitted and provided with an allowance to ensure that he would remain smartly kitted out. The smart appearance of the army was integral to its morale, and if the everyday reality, especially during long, hot marches, fell badly short of what military regulations demanded, there is little doubt that soldiers, and especially officers, took their appearance seriously. The Garde Impériale might be especially elegantly dressed to defend the person of their Emperor, but they were not alone. Every regiment had its full dress uniform (*grande tenue*) for parades and battle, distinguished by its collars and cuffs, waistcoats and epaulettes. Bandsmen and musicians wore braided coats and sumptuous plumes.[48] Off-duty French troops took an obvious pride in their image, their lightness of touch and ease of social grace, their gallantry, their elegance, their appeal to women. French soldiers were sociable and polite, sharing with their fellow countrymen that quality of *légèreté* which eighteenth-century writers had so openly praised.[49] There was something jaunty about their gait, a pride and a sense of representing a proud and elegant civilisation – an almost narcissistic delight that was expressed in languid gestures and epitomised by waxed moustaches.

These images were, of course, the stuff of future memories – crisply-drawn, brightly-coloured images that would achieve renewed popularity during the nineteenth century and which presented the Napoleonic soldier as he liked to be remembered and as his fellow countrymen would prefer to think of him. They played an important part in establishing in the public mind the image of the imperial soldier, an image that was different in significant ways from the joyful volunteer of 1792, or the young husband dragging himself from his wife's arms to defend the *patrie en danger*. The Napoleonic army, forged through annual conscription, attracted few who were genuine volunteers, few whom poverty or family quarrels or a youthful taste for adventure had not pushed in the direction of the army. It is no accident, for instance, that

[48] John R. Elting, *Swords around a Throne. Napoleon's Grande Armée* (London, 1989), pp. 440–1.

[49] David Bell, *The Cult of the Nation in France. Inventing Nationalism, 1680–1800* (Cambridge, Mass., 2001), pp. 148–9.

a large proportion of the recruits raised in Paris were the sons of recent immigrants from the rural hinterland or came from the poorest areas of the city. And many of the youngest – those aged between twelve and fifteen who signed on as boy soldiers – came from the most disadvantaged groups of all: boys whose mothers had been abandoned, or who had lost both their parents, or whose fathers had only the most marginal employment. It was poverty, not patriotism, that had driven them to enlist, whatever the imperial propaganda machine tried to pretend, a poverty reminiscent of the traditional recruiting grounds of the Ancien Régime.[50]

There was, of course, another reason to cast doubt on the patriotic idealism of Napoleon's army – the stark fact that his army was no longer French, no longer an army of citizens, but was raised across the European mainland, with men recruited in all the lands France conquered as well as from those traditional nurseries of soldiers like Hesse and Saxony, Scandinavia and Ireland. They could not share in that identification with the nation that had characterised the *levée en masse*. That did not necessarily reduce their fighting qualities, of course, but it made them a very different kind of army from the young men who had marched off to defend the *patrie* in 1793. Napoleon's troops had gained in professionalism and in military pride, showing dedication to both the cause of the Emperor and to the imperial order, loyalty to their officers, a new sense of commitment to their regiments and an awareness of past battle honours. The Irish Legion established after the breakdown of the Treaty of Amiens was just one of many foreign units to be incorporated into Napoleon's army, consisting originally of those officers and men who had joined up in the wake of Wolfe Tone's rebellion, many of them believing that they would be given the chance to liberate Ireland, whereas in fact they found that they were increasingly used as regular units in the *Grande Armée*, their Irish complement diluted through the recruitment of other, mainly French, troops.[51] The result was perhaps predictable – that disillusionment affected some of the Irishmen and that desertion and indiscipline posed problems for the Legion. But increasingly those who remained were respected for

[50] Louis Bergeron, 'Recrutements et engagements volontaires à Paris (Ier, VIIIe et Xe arrondissements) sous le Consulat et l'Empire', in Marcel Reinhard (ed.), *Contributions à l'histoire démographique de la Révolution Française, 3e série – Etudes sur la population parisienne* (Paris, 1970), pp. 233–51.

[51] In 1814, at the end of the war, the Third Foreign Regiment (which incorporated a large part of the Legion) contained 36 per cent of Irish officers as against 54 per cent of Frenchmen. The remaining officers were Swiss, Poles, Swedes, an Italian and a Bohemian. See John G. Gallaher, *Napoleon's Irish Legion* (Carbondale, Ill., 1993), p. 200.

their professionalism: they fought bravely for the imperial cause, were rewarded with promotions and decorations, and tried to emulate the glory of the old Irish Brigade which had served the Bourbons for a century from 1690 and had fought so memorably at Fontenoy. In short, they shared with their French counterparts a pride in their regimental history and they responded like them to the lure of military medals and battle honours.[52] What they could not share was the experience of the French Revolution, an understanding of French citizenship, or any real grasp of what it had been like to serve in the battalions of the First Republic.

This revitalised sense of pride in soldiering and identification with the service of the state was exactly what Napoleon wanted; he had little interest in stirring memories of revolutionary idealism. Rather, he insisted that his army should be well-drilled and disciplined, obedient to orders and ready to sacrifice itself in the cause of glory. He was ready to reward his soldiers and honour their courage; he would allow them a customary degree of licence when circumstances favoured it; but above all, he expected them to behave professionally and to conduct themselves in a manner that reflected the majesty of the imperial state. Consider the words of his proclamation to the army in December 1805, following the defeat of Austria and the signature of the peace treaty at Pressburg. He congratulated his men on what they had achieved, and thanked them for the sacrifices of two arduous campaigns. He had decorated and promoted those whose conduct had been particularly meritorious, and he now promised them a part in the celebrations that were to follow: 'You have seen that your Emperor has shared with you all dangers and fatigues; I wish also that you come to see him surrounded with all that grandeur and splendour which becomes the sovereign of the first nation in the universe. I will give a great festival at Paris in the first days of May; you shall all be there.' But there was another side to this bargain. Napoleon was insistent that during the months ahead, while they would be returning to their homes, they must behave well towards civilians and conduct themselves with the correctness that would be expected of true professionals. The proclamation continues with a veiled warning.

> Soldiers, during the three months which are necessary for your return to France, be the model of all armies; you have now to give examples, not of courage and intrepidity, but of strict discipline. May my allies have nothing to complain of in your passage, and on arriving on the sacred territory, conduct yourselves like children in the middle of their family; my people will

[52] Gallaher, *Napoleon's Irish Legion*, p. 222.

conduct themselves towards you as they must do towards their heroes and their defenders.[53]

Soldiers were more than warriors; they were servants and representatives of the Empire.

Napoleonic power was, of course, constructed on the success of the military, and the Emperor never forgot his dependence on the power of the army. Even the *sacre*, the sumptuous coronation ceremony choreographed by David in 1804 to crown the 'hero' as Emperor, was resonant with military order. The huge procession of judges, court officials, departmental administrators and civic and religious leaders who were called to Paris for the ceremony was headed by those at the very top of the Napoleonic hierarchy: the twenty-two 'grand officers of the Legion of Honour', all army generals, took precedence, closely followed by the commanders of the *divisions militaires* and the *généraux de division*.[54] There was little mistaking where power lay, or what message Napoleon was sending to his new empire. As Marshal Marmont pertinently recorded, the ceremony was intended to be august and to inspire awe both inside France and across Europe. Nothing, he remarked, was omitted in a ceremony which embraced 'the glory of arms, the triumph of civilisation, and the interest of humanity'.[55] But it was not just the great affairs of state that emphasised the link between the Empire and its army, as increasingly it was military exploits which were publicly celebrated and the colour and splendour of the army which set the tone of official festivals. All *fêtes* now routinely began with repeated salvos from the artillery, and involved marching, drill and military music; some, in an attempt to appeal to a wider and younger audience, staged firework displays or introduced military games. The themes of festivals, too, became increasingly martial – like the *fête du 1er vendémiaire* which in Year VIII celebrated France's past military heroes and focussed on the transfer of the ashes of Turenne to the Invalides.[56] Following the Concordat, the clergy could once more be involved in public festivals and asked to conduct services of thanksgiving for Napoleon's victories: bishops would demand that their clergy sing *Te Deums* in churches

[53] Proclamation of the Emperor Napoleon to the Army, 27 December 1805, in J. David Markham (ed.), *Imperial Glory. The Bulletins of Napoleon's Grande Armée, 1805–14* (London, 2003), pp. 72–3.

[54] 'Liste nominative des fonctionnaires appelés à la cérémonie du sacre et du couronnement de Leurs Majestés Impériales', in Jean Tulard (ed.), *Napoléon: Le Sacre* (Paris, 1993), p. 63.

[55] Tulard, *Napoléon: Le Sacre*, p. xxxix.

[56] This was celebrated throughout France. The document cited here was consulted in the Archives Départementales of the Puy-de-Dôme (A.D. Puy-de-Dôme, M122).

throughout their dioceses, or would participate in festivals alongside civic officials to add religious solemnity to the impression of power provided by a strong military presence.[57]

Even the Festival of Saint-Napoléon, instituted in 1806, involved the military authorities in what was in essence a religious celebration.[58] For many Catholics this was going far beyond the realms of decency, and its introduction proved a test of political loyalties as much as of religious faith. In Italy, indeed, Michael Broers dismisses it as 'an accident waiting to happen'.[59] In those parishes where the festival was respected – and the choice of 15 August, the date of Assumption, for the new public holiday ensured that, through habit at least, it did not pass in total silence – the faithful learned that Napoleon was a military saint in the tradition of the medieval Church. At Rueil, where a bust of Napoleon was placed on a pedestal at the church entrance, a board proclaimed to the faithful just what had earned Napoleon his sanctification, and many must have found the explanation curiously secular. 'May homage and glory be offered', it read, 'to the victor of Austerlitz, Napoleon the Great, who has brought peace to the world'.[60] Here, close to the Empress's palace and secure in the military environment of Versailles, the service passed without incident. But in general the festival generated little enthusiasm, and did little beyond encouraging effusions of public rhetoric in praise of the Emperor and his successive conquests.[61]

The festivals, in common with painting, theatre, popular prints and other forms of visual representation, helped to change civilian perceptions of the military, and to redefine the soldier as a disciplined, professional and highly efficient state official – an impression which the use of troops to police public disturbances and impose requisitions only served to reinforce.[62] But this should not be taken to imply that no vestige of the enthusiastic and patriotic volunteer of 1791 survived, or that

[57] A.D. Puy-de-Dôme, M122, letter from the Minister of the Interior to the prefects of France, 12 thermidor X.

[58] A.D. Somme, 99M283, Fête du 15 août 1806, *affiche* which printed the instructions of the *secrétairerie d'Etat*.

[59] Michael Broers, *The Politics of Religion in Napoleonic Italy. The War against God, 1801–14* (London, 2002), p. 82.

[60] L. Bigard, 'Le Saint-Napoléon à Rueil et les évènements de 1814, *Revue Historique de Versailles* 27 (1925), p. 153. For a fuller account of this ceremony at Rueil, see Alan Forrest, 'Propaganda and the legitimation of power in Napoleonic France', *French History* 18 (2004), pp. 437–8.

[61] Sudhir Hazareesingh, *The Saint-Napoléon. Celebrations of Sovereignty in Nineteenth-century France* (Cambridge, Mass., 2004), p. 16.

[62] This theme is developed in a number of national contexts by the contributors to Michael Rowe (ed.), *Collaboration and Resistance in Napoleonic Europe. State-Formation in an Age of Upheaval, c.1800–1815* (London, 2003).

the Napoleonic army had turned its back totally on the spirit of insurgency that is associated with the *levée en masse* and the call-to-arms in defence of the nation. Napoleon still talked of his annual conscriptions as a call to the youth of France to support him in destroying the nation's enemies. The *garde nationale* was not wholly disbanded and, though Napoleon had little faith in their ability to perform a civil function, preferring the *soldats-gendarmes* of the new Gendarmerie Nationale to the *citoyens-gardes*, he was quite prepared to give them a role in national defence, at least in times of danger. By 1810, four battalions of *gardes nationaux* had been incorporated into the Garde Impériale.[63] Here Napoleon was building on the revolutionary tradition of the *levée en masse*, and in the last failing years of the war even the hallowed words *levée en masse* make a renewed appearance as the Emperor called for a last supreme effort to save his regime. The decree of 6 January 1814 called for armies of reserve composed of national guardsmen, in all 121 battalions each 840 strong who would rush to the defence of Paris and Lyon as foreign armies advanced on to French soil. It was, the decree spelt out, an emergency measure for national defence, a new call, like that of 1793, to save the *patrie en danger*, 'to stop the enemy's advance, to preserve our fields and our cities from pillage and devastation, to protect our families, to preserve unsullied the name and the honour of France, in the final analysis to maintain our existence and our national independence'. Here, as French resistance crumbled, was the true cry of 1793, a cry to the heart, to the people of France, to perform an exceptional civic duty. The service that was being asked for, the law insisted, was utterly exceptional; it would involve only a short period away from home and family; and it was an appeal to the spirit and sentiment of the people as well as to the self-interest of all.[64]

There was a spontaneity about the public response, too, which distinguished the new recruits of 1814 from their elders, from the serried ranks of young conscripts who, year on year, had been herded past the medical orderlies and signed fit for service. Napoleon was desperate for fresh troops, and he was forced to abandon the structured order of annual conscriptions and fill the ranks as he could, playing on the fears of frontier towns and cities, on the abilities and ambitions of local power brokers, on the hatreds stirred by experience of invasion. And just as the revolutionaries had allowed local units of *miquelets* and *chasseurs des montagnes* to provide for the local defence of Alpine and Pyrenean

63 Georges Carrot, 'Une institution de la nation: la Garde Nationale, 1789–1871' (thèse de doctorat de 3e cycle, Université de Nice, 1979), p. 123.

64 A.N., F9 357, decree of 6 January 1814.

valleys, so the Emperor now condoned the recruitment of *corps francs* and other informal groupings of partisans – often local militias raised by private adventurers in response to the threat of invasion in their own communities, recruited and commanded privately, with the stamp of official approval but with no call on the public purse.[65] Clearly this could only be acceptable in moments of acute danger, and the government sought to restrict it to frontier areas and to eastern departments facing enemy incursion. Prefects, indeed, often expressed reluctance to approve what were essentially private armies at a time when they were also trying to fill depleted regular units, seeing this, not without reason, both as an added tax on the community and as a challenge to the authority of the state. Was there not a danger that men would desert from the regular battalions in favour of the good pay and lax discipline of the partisans? Thus the Prefect of the Gironde tried to lay down strict constraints on recruitment. The *partisans de la Gironde* were to recruit only from men who had already retired from army service, he declared, and the names of all partisans were to be presented to the Prefect for approval.[66] The Minister of War, too, was cautious in his welcome of this military manna from heaven. He noted that the *corps francs* were often unruly and disorderly; that there was no clear chain of command; and that there were unacceptable delays in putting the corps into active service because there were no weapons or ammunition, or because their leaders were unable to find the necessary sponsorship.[67] The resort to partisans might create the image of a spontaneous popular insurrection, but the reality they concealed was often anarchic and faction-ridden.

For posterity, however, it was the image that would be most enduring. When France was invaded, when their own homes and communities were threatened, the partisans responded to the call to defend the *patrie*, often poorly trained and armed, other than with their courage and their patriotic fervour. Fired by claims that this would be a war to the last man – what the Minister of the Interior, Montalivet, described as a 'war of extermination' in a circular to his prefects – they rose in defence of their homes, of their Emperor, and of their pride in the French nation. It was an image that transcended the long years of continental war, the years of glory, of obedience, of suffering, to recall the spontaneity of the first great *levée en masse* in 1793. And, though

65 A.N., F9 357, letter from Minister of War to Minister of Interior, 22 March 1814.

66 A.N., F9 522, Affaires militaires (Gironde), letter from Prefect of the Gironde to Minister of Interior, 27 January 1814.

67 A.N., F9 357, letter from Minister of Interior to the Minister of War, 29 February 1814.

the numbers who joined the army in these desperate months were disappointingly low, though the prefects were repeatedly reporting that the population was tired and that there was little appetite for further fighting, it is this image of a popular uprising, of a people's war against the British, Austrian, Prussian and Russian troops who would occupy French territory after the Hundred Days, that helped give Napoleon his reputation with the ordinary people of France as a democrat, the *petit caporal* who had maintained his bond with the population. Once again, as in 1793, wall posters urged people to rise in defence of their liberties, to take up arms for the cause of the nation. The war was declared to be a 'national' crusade, in the sense that it was a war for the entire French people. Consciously and repeatedly, the public utterances of 1814 recalled the sacrifice of 1793 and reminded the people of that previous moment when the country had faced defeat and invasion. The people, it was inferred, were again in arms, with everyone – men, women and children – called on to make a personal contribution to defend the soil of France.[68]

[68] Jacques Hantraye, *Les Cosaques aux Champs-Élysées. L'occupation de la France après la chute de Napoléon* (Paris, 2005), pp. 46–8.

4 Voices from the past

Warfare on the scale which France had experienced between 1792 and 1814 remained firmly embedded in public consciousness. Too many men had seen their adolescence interrupted and their ambitions cut short; too many, whether they were volunteers or conscripts, had suffered and died in the pursuit of revolutionary liberty or Napoleonic glory. The impact of war was not confined to those who served in the armies. Civilians, too, had seen their livelihoods destroyed, their homes turned into emergency billets, their farmhands and apprentices called to the colours, their crops and livestock requisitioned for the war effort. Gender roles had been challenged as women were forced to take over the farm or supplement the family income in the absence of the principal breadwinner, while land risked falling out of production through a shortage of young, able-bodied labourers. The natural tenor of the generations was interrupted, as sons died before their fathers, and mothers were left to the chill reality of widowhood and a lonely old age. War left France both economically weakened and facing serious demographic consequences that would not magically disappear with the return of peace. Alone of the great powers France had been involved in an almost unbroken land war since the early 1790s. French losses and suffering over a whole generation – there were men conscripted in 1812 and 1813 whose fathers had volunteered in 1791 or been caught up in the *levée en masse* two years later – can be quite realistically compared to those of the First World War, even if they occurred more gradually, over twenty years rather than four.[1] The challenge after 1815 was at once economic, social and political: how to reconstruct the nation for peace after the material and cultural destruction of a generation at war.

[1] See Jacques Dupâquier, 'Problèmes démographiques de la France napoléonienne', *Revue d'histoire moderne et contemporaine* 17 (1970); the more general problem of France's rates of mortality is discussed in Alain Bideau, Jacques Dupâquier and Jean-Noël Biraben, 'La mortalité de 1800 à 1914', in Jacques Dupâquier (ed.), *Histoire de la population française* (4 vols., Paris, 1988), vol. III, pp. 279–98.

For the men who returned – those who did return – the world they came back to would be dominated by political and economic uncertainty. They faced problems of reinsertion into civilian life and, for many, the misery of unemployment and of seeing themselves condemned to exist on the margins of society.[2] The army which provided them with food, shelter and at least a modicum of security during their years of service rapidly disintegrated in the face of defeat, with thousands of soldiers gratefully accepting what they saw as their traditional right to scatter and return home once their units had been driven back on to French soil. And since a peacetime government had little need for the massive Napoleonic army, swollen by annual conscription and by levies imposed on the countries France had conquered, the widespread desertions and unexplained absences may even have been helpful in the task of reducing the military to a force more suited to peacetime defence. On 12 May 1814 the government ordered the suppression of nearly a hundred infantry regiments and of thirty-eight cavalry regiments, with similar levels of troop reduction throughout the army. No one was spared in the cull. Artillery regiments were cut from eighteen to twelve, the number of engineers halved from sixty companies to thirty. Officers and non-commissioned officers were removed from active service and placed on reserve, on *demi-solde*, their number further swollen by the reconstitution of the old *Maison du roi* and the return of royalist officers from emigration; the suspicion was well-founded that the officer corps was being purged of all those who had advanced their careers under Napoleon. And the Hundred Days, by presenting the officers with such clear temptation and compelling them to declare their loyalty for or against the monarchy, only worsened the dilemma facing the old imperial army. Did they remain in inactivity, their freedom of movement curtailed and their pensions barely adequate to keep them alive, waiting for the day when the Bourbons would decide their fate? Or did they rally once again to the cause of the Empire, and to the *tricolor* flag for which they all, republicans and Bonapartists alike, felt a certain nostalgic regard? Those who did, and who were again seduced by the call to glory, risked paying a heavy price for their mistake during the Second Restoration. Most of the generals of the Hundred Days chose to leave the country rather than face investigation: Soult to the Rhineland, Rapp to Switzerland, Sébastiani to England, Grouchy to the United States. Those who stayed were summoned to appear before a commission set up to 'examine the conduct of officers of all grades

[2] Natalie Petiteau, *Lendemains d'Empire. Les soldats de Napoléon dans la France du dix-neuvième siècle* (Paris, 2003), p. 142.

who had served the usurper'.[3] Only the continued influence in government of Gouvion Saint-Cyr and MacDonald prevented the wholesale dissolution of the Napoleonic army which the more extreme royalists were demanding.[4]

Royal *ordonnances* issued in late July and early August 1815 made it clear that for those judged loyal to Napoleon there would be no turning back, and certainly no forgiveness. First the government proscribed those it identified as the Napoleonic political and military elite; it then went on to order the dismissal of all those officers and soldiers who had served under Napoleon and his marshals, ordering them to return to their homes at once. Further steps were taken to reduce the size of the army by forcibly retiring those who had passed the age of fifty or who had performed twenty-five years of service, thus ridding the army at a stroke of many of the men who had served under the Revolution. Those who had been seriously wounded in the service of the Emperor were likewise forced to retire, on the grounds that they could no longer carry out the duties required of them. As a result, large numbers of veterans, many ill or wounded, returned to their homes within a few months of the peace, condemned to probable unemployment and only parsimonious assistance from a bankrupt War Ministry and a state that felt it owed them little. Thousands of men were released in this way, left to face an uncertain future in their home communities. Others, who had no homes to return to or who had no means of support, were kept in the army, though not in active service. They were to be placed in provisional companies, while those soldiers who had not yet earned their discharge were ordered to serve in the newly-created *légions départementales*. It was hardly a satisfying outcome for men whose lives had often been dominated by military values and imperial dreams, and it was made worse by the fact that their numbers were so dauntingly large. For if 600,000 troops died during the Revolutionary and Napoleonic Wars, around a million returned in 1815. Men who had fought valiantly to defend their country were now reduced to a state of inactivity, left waiting for further orders, often without pay and condemned to near-indigence. It was an unenviable plight.[5]

During 1816, in the vengeful climate created by the *Chambre Introuvable*, a clear majority of officers who had served the Emperor were withdrawn from active service – Jean Vidalenc estimates the figure

[3] Bruno Colson, *Le général Rogniat ingénieur et critique de Napoléon* (Paris, 2006), pp. 645–6.

[4] Isser Woloch, *The French Veteran from the Revolution to the Restoration* (Chapel Hill, 1979), p. 297.

[5] Petiteau, *Lendemains d'Empire*, p. 86.

at around 20,000, compared to only around 5,000 who were retained[6] – with many of them left to face uncertainty and relative poverty. The amounts of their pensions were decided by a military commission, whose task was to place each man in a category that would determine his pension and against whose decision he had no right of appeal. But there was worse. They were not allowed to leave their homes, were banished to their villages of birth, and refused permission to live in Paris or in any significant town; they were forbidden to travel freely without obtaining permission from the mayor of the commune where they lived. They did not enjoy any of the benefits of military life, yet they were permanently on call for possible army service, a call that never came. For that reason during the early months of the Restoration they were also forbidden to search for work, a fact which further alienated them from local people and made it more difficult for them to be reinserted into civil society. The Bourbon monarchy, it was apparent, had little use for their talents or their military experience, while the new royalist chamber was more than happy to humiliate them and spy on them as enemies of the state. The law of 9 November 1815 even instructed the courts to deprive of all or part of his pension any Napoleonic officer convicted of 'invoking the name of the usurper'.[7] It is scarcely surprising if many became depressed and resentful, looking back on their years in the army with an unashamed sense of nostalgia.

Money, it might seem, was less of a problem than boredom, a sense of rejection, and the problems of reinsertion that were unavoidable after a quarter of a century of war, since the royalist government was keenly aware of the danger of creating a vast pool of discontent among the former troops. Towards veterans who had retired after years of active service, the pensioners of the *armée morte*, the new government quite deliberately showed a degree of indulgence, promising that it would maintain their existing pension levels and that it would pay them the arrears that had accumulated during the last months of the Empire. Benefits due for retirement and for the loss of limbs in service remained similarly unchanged, though – like the Directory and the Empire before – the Restoration monarchy did fall behind with pension payments in 1816 as a result of the heavy costs incurred through military occupation and of the need to pay reparations to the Allies. Not all, however, were satisfied with their lot. Those who lost out most were those – largely ordinary infantrymen and non-commissioned officers – who had suffered lesser injuries and who now found themselves denied

[6] Jean Vidalenc, *Les demi-solde. Etude d'une catégorie sociale* (Paris, 1955), pp. 20–2.
[7] Petiteau, *Lendemains d'Empire*, p. 93.

the pensions they would previously have claimed, and compensated only with relatively small one-off payments on discharge. And officers forced into retirement found their accustomed style of living dramatically undermined. Their pensions compared unfavourably with those in other European armies, and many saw the conditions in which they were forced to live as demeaning, their income levels humiliating.[8] As the years passed, pensioners and *demi-soldes* merged to form a single mass of former soldiers, increasingly discontented as they faced the ravages of time and the pain of old age.

The former Napoleonic officers adjusted with wildly contrasting degrees of success to the challenge of civilian life. There are plenty of individual success stories of men who accepted that their military career was over and turned to another, in trade and industry, in the professions, or in farming, finding without difficulty new roles in civil society.[9] The fact that to be an army officer demanded a degree of education, a basic literacy and command of language, also provided them with opportunities in the liberal professions and in civil administration, where the demands of the long years of war had resulted in severe shortages of suitably qualified staff. Among retired officers it is perhaps not surprising to find a clutch of teachers and clerks, notaries and small-town lawyers. The less educated men of the lower ranks were more likely to find jobs with the *gendarmerie* – for whom veterans were always a solid source of recruitment[10] – or as *gardes-champêtres* and gamekeepers. More disturbing for the Restoration authorities, though, was the number of *demi-soldes* who found their way into public administration, holding office in town halls and village *mairies* or finding an outlet for their energies in elected positions, as mayors or *juges de paix*. As former soldiers they had travelled, seen different countries and been exposed to their cultures, broken down the relative autarchy of village life, qualities which won the admiration of many of their peers and made them natural notables in the post-war years. They also enjoyed that particular prestige that came from having shared in the nation's military adventures, from having played their part in history, in the glory of the Revolutionary and Napoleonic Wars, making them seem natural choices for positions of local dignity and responsibility. As early as 1816 the reports from prefects throughout France drew attention to the large number of former Napoleonic officers who had found employment

[8] Douglas Porch, *Army and Revolution in France, 1815–1848* (London, 1974), pp. 26–7.
[9] Vidalenc, *Les demi-solde*, pp. 63–114.
[10] See Clive Emsley, *Gendarmes and the State in Nineteenth-Century Europe* (Oxford, 1999).

with local authorities; in a circular of April 1822 the Minister of War expressed his indignation that 'a great number of officers on half pay' were now manning the civil administration, that so many enemies of the new order had infiltrated the public domain.[11]

The Bourbons did more than voice their distrust of returned soldiers who had served their enemies; they also played on feelings of fear and rejection in the local population, so that veterans often found the process of reinsertion more painful than it might otherwise have been. Returning soldiers who expected to be welcomed as heroes found their status undermined by the new regime, which added to the natural unease that was caused by the rapid release of so many men without jobs or means of support into the local economy. In regions where the Revolution had left bitter scars on local society – where religious fault lines ran deep or where memories of terror and counter-terror still divided families and communities – veterans might find themselves ostracised by their neighbours and blamed for the sins of their fathers. The Vendée, the south-east and the Rhône valley were all areas prone to such acts of political revenge, areas where local people had not forgotten or forgiven the excesses of the *colonnes infernales* and where the process of terror and counter-terror had never completely been put to rest. In the West the restoration of the Bourbons unleashed a further wave of anti-republican violence, its brutality veiled in the sentimentality of remembrance as the heroes of the Vendeans' struggle were recreated as Christian martyrs, each marked by his humane or chivalric qualities – the rural simplicity of Cathelineau, the spirituality of Charette, the generosity of Bonchamps.[12] In the Cevennes men who had fought in the name of the Revolution and Empire risked being caught up in the recurrent cycle of sectarian conflict between Protestants and Catholics.[13] To be a victim it was sufficient to be a Protestant. In this orgy of revenge killings little attempt was made to distinguish those who had fought for the Revolution and those who had followed in their footsteps under the Empire, since, for committed royalists, support for the Emperor could seem an even greater crime against their legitimist ideals. In July 1815, for instance, among the first targets of looters in Nîmes were a café that had been known during the Hundred Days as the 'Isle d'Elbe' and the country-house of the notoriously Bonapartist General Merle.[14] All were merged into a single undifferentiated category

[11] Vidalenc, *Les demi-solde*, p. 105.

[12] Jean-Clément Martin, *La Vendée de la mémoire, 1800–1980* (Paris, 1989), p. 71.

[13] See Gwynne Lewis, *The Second Vendée. The Continuity of Counter-revolution in the Department of the Gard, 1789–1815* (Oxford, 1978), pp. 187–218.

[14] *Ibid.*, p. 194.

of public enemy – outlaws, disturbers of the peace, men of blood, in short the *brigands de la Loire* of popular stereotype.

Vilification was not the only factor that militated against an easy reintegration into society. Many former soldiers found it difficult to settle or to accept that their days of glory and adventure were now over. They remained footloose, poorly adapted to the needs of village or small-town France, irked by the petty irritants that the government set in their path or simply unable to adjust to the constraints of civilian life. Long years in the army had made them impatient with the slow pace of village life, or had left them temperamentally unsuited to a repetitive daily routine. They craved further adventures and longed to move on. They missed the excitement of battle and the intense camaraderie of the regiment. Or, as former revolutionary militants who had sought both a career and a refuge in the armies after Thermidor, they now found themselves compromised by their radical republicanism and their *sans-culotte* sympathies in the period before Fructidor, making reconciliation with the restored monarchy well-nigh impossible.[15] The most recalcitrant had little choice but to leave France altogether and seek the safety of exile, joining the sad little groups of ageing Jacobins and unrepentant regicides who huddled in the cafes of Liège and Brussels and Geneva, seeking solace in one another's company and dreaming of the day when they could return to France.[16] Some felt pangs of regret for a military lifestyle they had lost when Napoleon left for Saint Helena, an army that had assumed the role of home and family for men too long removed from civilian life. They were deeply hurt by the rejection they had suffered at the hands of the Bourbons, the dismissal of their long years of service as unworthy and somehow dishonourable, seen as a testament to their fickleness and unreliability. Some sold their services as mercenaries, travelling abroad and offering their swords to rulers who would appreciate them more. A number ended their careers serving the Austrian Emperor, with whom the French regiments who had fought for Napoleon enjoyed an understandably high reputation. Others served in Persia, or retraced their steps to Egypt, still an eternal source of fascination for many whose loyalty to Napoleon remained intact and who were too compromised during the Hundred Days to dream of being granted pardons at home. A few even served in the

[15] Isser Woloch, *Jacobin Legacy. The Democratic Movement under the Directory* (Princeton, N.J., 1970), p. 76.

[16] Their lot is memorably – and sympathetically – captured by Sergio Luzzatto in his emotive study of the years spent in foreign exile by former deputies to the Convention, *Mémoire de la Terreur* (Lyon, 1991), pp. 13–19.

armies of the Ottoman Empire or onboard ships of the Turkish fleet.[17] They had criss-crossed Europe, and at times the world, in the service of France, and the lust for travel, for exoticism and adventure proved impossible to cast off. They now sought out new wars through which to pursue their dreams.

Among the officers rejected by France after 1815 were men who were not just committed soldiers but also proven adventurers, men incapable of settling down to marriage and civilian careers, attracted by the promise of conquering new lands and opening up new frontiers. They had made a revolution that promised to liberate mankind, or had followed their Emperor to the ends of the earth, and their ambition and sense of adventure were not dimmed. We find them in the years after 1815 scattered across the Atlantic world, exiles and refugees from France who now congregated in identifiable French colonies in Philadelphia and New Orleans, in Mexico and Peru. Some were given land grants by the United States government on newly conquered Indian territories in Louisiana and Alabama, in the colonies of the Vine and the Olive, lands that were shared between refugees from Saint-Domingue and fleeing veterans of the revolutionary and Napoleonic campaigns. Among the most prominent French exiles who came to the Gulf Coast after 1815 were those the Bourbons could not forgive – Napoleonic officers who had rallied to the Empire under the Hundred Days, along with a smattering of unrepentant regicides, members of the National Convention of 1792. Others were simply young officers, deprived of their living back in Restoration France, seeking further adventure overseas, and angry with the Bourbon regime for insulting their military pedigree.[18] Some had been offered promotions during the Hundred Days, only to lose their rank and what they saw as their due when the Bourbons returned. Defeat and inactivity had dealt them a terrible blow, sufficient to alienate them from the new elites in France and drive them to seek their fortunes on the other side of the Atlantic. 'I had no homes ties, no interest even, to keep me in France', reported one exile, 'and my first idea was to leave a country which, according to my political opinions, I could no longer serve and from which I could not expect any consideration'.[19]

But many of them never settled. Their thirst for adventure was unquenchable, and the challenge of turning the unyielding soil of the Tombigbee and Black Warrior river valleys into vineyards and olive

[17] Vidalenc, *Les demi-solde*, pp. 115–17.

[18] Rafe Blaufarb, *Bonapartists in the Borderlands. French Exiles and Refugees of the Gulf Coast, 1815–1835* (Tuscaloosa, Ala., 2006), pp. 18–19.

[19] The words are from an officer who went on to publish his account of his adventures, Just-Jean-Etienne Roy cited in Blaufarb, *Bonapartists*, p. 18.

groves – never a terribly promising proposition – held little charm for them. Some who had been soldiers all their professional lives saw little reason to exchange their swords for ploughshares, and it was not long before they were being recruited for new, ever more implausible causes. They dreamed of further glory, and did not hesitate to join forces with insurgent groups in Latin America or pirates in the Gulf. Some of them, indeed, would end their days along the Gulf of Mexico, improbable colonists following Charles Lallemand in a bid to set up an independent French state in Texas and establish their cherished *Champ d'asile* in Spanish America. Lallemand was a natural leader for the idealistic dreamers of the Bonapartist cause, a man who was unable to settle down and content only when he was stirring insurrection or claiming territory for France. Despite the vigorous publicity campaign they mounted in Alabama and among the various clusters of French and Domingan exiles, especially in New Orleans and Philadephia, the expedition was doomed to abysmal failure that rapidly turned to farce. Neither Spain nor the United States had any interest in encouraging a French claim to land which was still disputed territory, or in welcoming the intrusion of Bonapartist exiles in the borderlands of the American south-east.[20] Fetid water, plague and disease often did the rest.

If some found active roles in the civil society of the 1820s, for others the end of the wars ushered in long years of enforced idleness that invited comparison with the past they had lived through and helped to shape. The contrast was made all the more striking in that, for most of the *demi-soldes*, their years of service had also been the years of their youth, years that were marked, in retrospect at least, by acts of daring and memories of comradeship. The majority had been born some time between 1760 and the end of the Ancien Régime, so that they were still in their forties and fifties when peace was signed. From retirement in their native village or exile in Liège or Brussels they looked back on the lives they had led and the adventures they had shared, and it was difficult not to see the present as a terrible anti-climax to a wonderful career, not to look to memories of the past as consolation for the tedium of the present. They had lived through exciting times – they were not alone in remarking that the years of the Revolution and Empire had been the most thrilling and the most life-enhancing of their age – and they often felt the need to write about them, to remind themselves of the historic events they had lived through, or to share their experiences with others, whether with their wives and brothers or their grandchildren, or, more generally, with posterity. In the words of Gouvion Saint-Cyr, justifying

[20] Blaufarb, *Bonapartists*, pp. 86–116.

his decision towards the end of his life to write about the war in his memoirs, retirement had provided an opportunity, and going back over such a glorious past was a way of giving him and those like him a new life, a second life once his active career was over. 'We had fallen into such a flat state of calm', he wrote, 'that if we were not to die of boredom we had to transport our spirit back into our past experience'.[21] For some old soldiers writing could act as a form of therapy.

The passage of time did, of course, affect their memory and their mood, the degree to which they were able to distinguish between fact and fiction, the extent of their willingness to overlook unpleasant memories, their investment in the nineteenth-century legend of Napoleon. Almost miraculously, it seemed, a new Napoleon was born, an emperor who was recreated in the face of all evidence as the champion of the Revolution, the legitimate heir to 1789 and the liberties of the French people. Every action of the Bourbons intensified the popular equation of Revolution and Empire – the destruction of liberty trees, the encouragement of Catholic missions, the removal of the *tricolor* from public buildings and the systematic rooting out of known republicans from positions of trust, all helped to forge new unity between those whose sympathies were with the Republic and those who harked back to the military glory of the Empire. Napoleon had been transformed into a man of the people, the little corporal who valued his men's lives and welfare above all else and who struggled to defend the interests of ordinary citizens. Amidst the hostile counter-propaganda of the Restoration years, and as a consequence of his opposition to the Bourbons during the Hundred Days, Napoleon was reborn as a liberal, an enemy of monarchy, a champion of individualism and progressive values.[22] As such he was feted not just by his former soldiers but by a new generation of artisans and workers, who associated him with their cause, the cause of the French people. In their eyes there was a fundamental difference between the wars of the Revolution and Empire and the imperial wars of the restored Bourbons. 'We were defending our country', veterans in Le Mans shouted at the troops heading for war in Spain in 1823; 'you are brigands and thieves'.[23] For such men Napoleon was at once an all-conquering hero and a liberal reformer – the very stuff of a patriotic legend that could appeal to the mass of the people, a legend ideally suited to the romantic spirit of the age.

[21] Gouvion Saint-Cyr, *Mémoires* (Paris, 1829), quoted in Jean Tulard, *Nouvelle bibliographie critique des mémoires sur l'époque napoléonienne écrits ou traduits en français* (Geneva, 1991), p. 7n.

[22] Sudhir Hazareesingh, *The Legend of Napoleon* (London, 2004), pp. 135–6.

[23] Bernard Ménager, *Les Napoléon du peuple* (Paris, 1988), p. 57.

The Napoleonic legend would grow steadily more powerful – and more radical – after 1830, as the July Monarchy appealed to the romance and reputation of the Empire in order to bolster its own flagging prestige. That romance was largely military, marked by the presence of four Napoleonic marshals at Louis-Philippe's coronation in 1831, by the inauguration of the Arc de Triomphe in 1836, or – most vibrantly of all – by the decision to repatriate Napoleon's body from Saint Helena amidst the most lavish ceremonial in 1840. The Return of the Ashes was a masterpiece of myth-making, an attempt by the state to present Napoleon as both a conquering hero who had saved France from invasion and as a son of the Revolution, true to the principles of the republic. Crowds turned out on the banks of the Seine and lined the Champs-Elysées as the Emperor's body passed before them, their patriotic chauvinism stoked by the rhetoric of empire and the emergent Eastern Question. Significantly, it was as much the chauvinism of old revolutionaries as that of dedicated Bonapartists. The liberal novelist Frédéric Soulié, himself an admirer of the military triumphs of the Empire, gave memorable expression to the idea of Napoleon as Father of Equality, a man who had succeeded in making permanent the gains of 1789. 'Remember also', he wrote in a popular pamphlet of 1840, 'that equality was the law under his reign. It is because of this that he is our hero; it is for this reason that he has remained so great and revered in our memories'.[24] The same theme was expressed in the prints of Pellerin and the couplets of Béranger as well as in hundreds of pamphlets and song-sheets sold in the streets of Paris. The Return of the Ashes was a state occasion, with Louis-Philippe himself receiving the coffin back on the soil of France. But it was also a moment of great military pomp, as General Bertrand placed below the catafalque Napoleon's sword from Austerlitz, and General Gourgaud – another of his faithful *compagnons de route* – his three-cornered hat from Eylau.[25] It also rapidly turned into a popular celebration, the celebration by Paris and its people of the return of a hero. The day belonged to the people, linked for all time to the army and the memory of the soldiers who had fought so long and so bravely in the cause of the *patrie*.

Many veterans were aroused from their retirement to respond to these new levels of public interest, to a new literary marketplace for memories of the Revolution and Empire that had grown up and which

[24] Frédéric Soulié, *Le Tombeau de Napoléon* (Paris, 1840), quoted in Michael Paul Driskel, *As Befits a Legend. Building a Tomb for Napoleon, 1840–61* (Kent, Ohio, 1993), p. 39.

[25] Jean-Marcel Humbert, *Napoléon aux Invalides. 1840, le Retour des Cendres* (Paris, 1990), p. 66.

would peak at various moments during the early nineteenth century. There was a ready readership for memoirs – especially memoirs of army life – and there was always the temptation to tell the story their audience wanted to hear, to invent or fabricate, or at the very least to add colour and drama to what might otherwise be a bald tale. The death of Napoleon on Saint Helena in 1821 and the publication two years later of the *Mémorial de Sainte-Hélène* served only to whet the appetite of the French public, and the slow trickle of memoirs which had been published before that date was suddenly transformed into a torrent.[26] Some were soberly written, limiting themselves to what actually happened or explaining the author's role in the imperial adventure – such was the case of Marshal Suchet, for instance, in 1827 or of Gouvion Saint-Cyr himself in 1829. But others were liberally laced with invention, with the consequence that the French reading public was fed a highly romanticised view of these wars, a view which placed great emphasis on individual sacrifice, on the role of chivalry and courage, and on the pursuit of glory. Some generals and politicians hired writers to express their views by proxy, or sold their name to publishers eager to tell of new discoveries and insights. Others gave authors permission to use their notebooks as they saw fit. A few were composed with little reference to the supposed author. Where there were no personal papers to draw upon, then words, phrases, whole chapters could simply be forged and reactions and emotions imagined. Jean Tulard particularly points to the various works of Villemarest, one of the more prolific authors of false memoirs of the Napoleonic period, and Lamothe-Langon, whose *Mémoires et souvenirs d'une femme de qualité sous le Consulat et l'Empire* was a work of pure fabrication.[27] Military historians, of course, are dismissive of such accounts and rightly warn of the falsehoods they contain. But nineteenth-century readers had no such qualms; nor were they necessarily driven by a desire to establish the truth. False memoirs, or those lavishly embroidered in retirement by officers eager to set the record straight, served to corroborate the views they already held and to give further credence of an idealised vision of the war years.

These views were only partly derived from personal contacts – from fathers or brothers who returned from the army, former soldiers who served as village mayors or who were recruited by the gendarmerie, or the huddles of veterans who became a familiar sight in the bars and inns

[26] On the power and propagandist use of words in the *Mémorial*, especially words that had strong resonance for republicans, see Didier Le Gall, *Napoléon et le Mémorial de Sainte-Hélène. Analyse d'un discours* (Paris, 2003), esp. pp. 131–4.

[27] Tulard, *Nouvelle bibliographie critique*, p. 8.

of every small town. They were also formed by the writings that had been left behind by revolutionary officers and soldiers, those writings which found their way into the hands of civilians and which did so much to forge their perceptions of the army of the Year II. Memoirs formed an essential part in the process of constructing long-term memory, the memory that would be revived under the Third Republic and in the years of preparation for the Great War. But they were only one part, a final building block in a longer process. They seldom destroyed the stereotyped view of war that was already formed in nineteenth-century French minds. Rather they built on existing images, adding detail and a wealth of illustrative anecdote to popular impressions, and producing a convincing narrative of experience. Memoirs helped to bring that experience alive to new generations, to men and women whose forebears might have fought at Valmy or in Egypt but who had not lived through the events described and were therefore reading them as history. They were appreciated for their sense of adventure, for the exploits they related, and for the vicarious pleasure that here in their pages history was being made. More than most writings, they gave encouragement to feelings of nostalgia for a world that was now lost, a world, moreover, often tenderly evoked years, sometimes decades, after the events they described.[28]

So much might depend on the purpose of the writer, the quality of any notes or journals he had kept since his years of service, and the timing of his decision to consign his memories to paper. For with the passage of time – and more especially the succession of political orthodoxies from the Restoration to the July Monarchy, the Second Republic to the Second Empire – it became more and more difficult to cocoon oneself in the past or to write one's narrative without taking account of the discourses of the present. Besides, some had scores to settle, the bitterness of exile to expunge. Amidst the fierce polemical debates of the early nineteenth century it was increasingly difficult to be neutral in the depiction of the revolutionary decade, or of the Empire, or the wars fought in their name. Opinions were easily identified with current ideologies, legitimism or republicanism or Bonapartism, so that it became almost impossible to divorce views of the revolutionary past from those of the republican present. From the 1820s the image of the republic became humanised as the publication of new histories, and of collections of Girondin memoirs, helped to give renewed respectability to a

[28] A good if somewhat extreme example is that of Jean Marnier, whose memories of his first campaign, back in 1793, were not published until nearly three-quarters of a century later; see Jean Marnier, *Souvenirs de guerre en temps de paix, 1793–1806 – 1823–1862* (Paris, 1867).

revolution that had too readily been equated with terror and regicide.[29] Once again, former revolutionary militants were encouraged to emerge from hiding, while the officers and men who had served the nation-in-arms began to be better perceived by their fellow countrymen, less ostracised by public opinion or vilified by Bourbon propaganda.

Even memoirs written without any overt desire to deceive had to be read with a certain care. Military memoirs – like those of politicians and others in public life – were generally written with a purpose, whether it was to help the former soldier or officer to remember and make sense of his younger self; to recount colourful anecdotes of army life for his grandchildren; or to justify himself to posterity before he died. There was no reason for him to recall everything he had lived through, no obligation even to pretend at objectivity. So memoirs tend to concentrate on the exotic, on those encounters that had left the most lasting impression. And they reflect what the former soldier or retired officer had experienced, both at the time and since – which for memoirs written long after the event, following years of retirement or exile, meant experience of a series of conventions and reinterpretations with the passage of time. Above all, they often show a coherency and a narrative strength that individual experience could rarely rival. Indeed, memoirs must be read as narratives of personal experience rather than as experience itself, as narratives that had been titivated, polished, expunged or expanded in the cause of greater coherence as the author struggled to make sense of his long years at war. Particularly for older men, looking back on their lives and trying to make sense of what they had seen and suffered, it was important to be able to detect patterns, to revive memories of great events, to recall those moments when, as Samuel Hynes acutely observed in the context of another war, their lives had intersected with history and they had been present as history was made.[30] That coherence was, for the men who wrote them, an important part of the process of memory, and of coming to terms with their lost youth. For the reader, the nineteenth-century onlooker who had no personal experience of war, it helped provide a consistent and satisfying picture, a narrative given a greater illusion of authority by the fact that the writer spoke from personal experience, in a direct line of communication that stretched from the battlefields of Valmy and Neerwinden to the drawing rooms of nineteenth-century Paris. These writings were eagerly consumed by an audience that had never known

[29] See, in particular, the multi-volume set of Girondin memoirs published in Paris in 1823.

[30] Samuel Hynes, *The Soldiers' Tale. Bearing Witness to Modern War* (London, 1997), p. 2.

the reality of war and was eager to share, however vicariously, in the story of a glorious national adventure. Republicans and Bonapartists, old soldiers and their families, all, it seemed, had an insatiable appetite for memories of the 1790s and the heroic memory of war.

Not all memoirs, of course, chose to present that narrative in heroic terms. For some old soldiers, embittered by their experience or by their subsequent rejection, writing provided an opportunity to communicate their woes and disappointments to a civilian audience to whom they had never found communication easy. Perhaps these were more prone to come from the ranks than from the officers' mess, from the relatively small numbers of ordinary soldiers who had the capability or the interest to consign their experiences to writing after the war was over. Jacques-Etienne Bédé was a good example of a man who did not have any special love of soldiering, a man of the people, a carpenter – a *tourneur de chaises* – born in the valley of the Loire at the beginning of Louis XVI's reign, who had joined the Revolutionary army from traditional rather than ideological motives. He suffered no illusions about the army; indeed, his memoir, the story of his life, is more concerned with what he sees as its high point in the workshops and journeymen's associations of Paris during the Restoration. He longed to travel, he tells us, and to see the world; and he had volunteered for the army in pursuit of adventure as much as to find an escape from the precarious conditions of small-town France. But there was also a strong economic motive, in that he had heard that a law granted aid to the mothers of young men who served the Revolution, and he wanted his mother to have such assistance.[31] And after six years of service, in which he had been disappointed in his ambition to join Napoleon's army in Egypt, he ended his army career with neither glory nor ceremony, joining around forty of his comrades in an act of mass desertion that brought them home to their families. Back in Orleans, he was welcomed into the local community, finding protection from his family and work from local masters; he was lucky enough to be left unmolested by the authorities, living a semi-clandestine existence while making a decent living from his trade.[32] His view of his years in his country's service was not wholly negative, however, as he looked back on his lost youth. The army had provided him with a social framework, with friends, and with a level of nourishment that was scarcely worse than what he had been accustomed to in civilian life. It had provided the adventure that rescued him from the weariness and boredom of the

[31] Rémi Gossez (ed.), *Un ouvrier en 1820. Manuscrit inédit de Jacques-Etienne Bédé* (Paris, 1984), p. 83.
[32] *Ibid.*, pp. 116–22.

village. And twenty years on, he took pleasure in talking about his part in these great wars that had become, in Louis Girard's phrase, 'the common experience of so many Frenchmen during the Restoration, in what had become a nation of old soldiers'.[33]

If the desire to be associated with the experiences of those who had fought for the Revolution and the Empire guaranteed a loyal readership for the memoirs of former soldiers and officers – even those published many decades after the war was over – it also created a demand for the most immediate of responses, the testimonies they wrote before time had dampened their memory or blunted their reactions. Nineteenth-century readers craved to know more about the battlefield itself, before the sights and sounds faded; they wanted to know more about the courage of the warriors, their idealism, their legitimate fears and anxieties; they sought out evidence of what it had been like to fight for ideals of liberty and fraternity, to respond to the urgings of deputies from the Convention, or to follow great generals like Dumouriez, Hoche, Marceau or Bonaparte. Not all memoirs were the product of fading memories or jaded appetites: among them are substantial numbers that were written within months of the events they described, or which were composed from notes taken on campaign.[34] These were especially popular among the officers who accompanied Napoleon to Egypt in 1798, many of whom were fascinated by the culture and the antiquities they came across in North Africa and who shared their commander's curiosity about the smells, colours and dramatic landscapes of the Orient. They also included journals, *carnets de route* and – increasingly – collections of correspondence written to families and loved ones from the bivouac, the hospital bed or the edge of the battlefield. Alfred Fierro's catalogue of memoirs from the Revolutionary period shows that these were rich and varied sources which allowed the discriminating reader to follow the revolutionary armies across the European continent. He counts, for instance, over one hundred memoirs that discuss the French Wars as they affected Germany, sixty-nine that talk of experiences in Italy, and sixty-three that take the reader on the Egyptian Campaign.[35] Those from the Napoleonic

[33] Louis Girard, 'Avant-propos', in Gossez, *Un ouvrier en 1820*, p. 6.

[34] A surprisingly large number of memoirs were published within a decade of Waterloo, for instance, both in France and overseas. I am grateful for this insight to Chantal Lheureux-Prévot, librarian at the Fondation Napoléon in Paris, who has drawn up an impressive list of soldiers' *carnets de route*, letters and memoirs written and published before 1825.

[35] Alfred Fierro, *Bibliographie critique des mémoires sur la Révolution écrits ou traduits en français* (Paris, 1988), pp. 470–2.

period would be far more numerous, with many published decades later. This is largely explained by the longevity of Napoleonic veterans, itself a reflection of their relative youth in the last years of imperial conscription. The numbers of Napoleonic veterans who lived long into the nineteenth century were far higher than those of surviving revolutionary soldiers: in the 1850s, when Napoleon III asked his prefects to draw up lists of surviving *grognards* eligible to receive the newly-minted *Médaille de Sainte-Hélène* in honour of their service, he discovered that almost 400,000 veterans of the Napoleonic Wars were still living in metropolitan France.[36] As a result, Napoleonic journals and memoirs far outnumbered revolutionary ones, though the veterans of both wars, being more literate than soldiers in previous campaigns and having singular adventures to communicate, left personal accounts of their experience on a scale previously unmatched in the history of European warfare. These constituted a formidable arsenal of sources that would excite men of succeeding generations and provide at least something of the flavour of what it had been like to be there.

Most seductive among these accounts were the letters and journals of serving soldiers, the documents they penned during the years of their service describing their experiences and impressions of war. These, even more than memoirs and reflective writings from later periods, had the fascination of immediacy, holding out at least the illusion that the reader was sharing vicariously in the experience of war. The piece of paper had been there, with the officer or infantryman who wrote on it, in camps and on long, hot marches across Europe; the letter had been written around campfires or on the edge of battlefields, by candlelight in late-night bivouacs or at the table of a wayside inn. And it had survived – survived the mud and the weather, the vagaries of a shifting battle zone, the long journey back to France, the many readings and re-readings in a village or provincial town, passed from hand to hand or treasured by a relieved wife or mother as evidence that her husband or son was still alive. Some passed from private hands into the clutches of the administration, whether in 1794 to help gain a share in the distribution of national lands, or in later years as evidence that the man had reached his regiment, and that he had obeyed the conscription law. The effort that had gone into the writing and sending of the letter, the ordinariness of much of its content or the occasional glimpse of drama – the reference to a military victory, to the sighting of a general or to participation in one of the great moments of the war – all persuaded the reader

[36] Sudhir Hazareesingh, *The Saint-Napoleon. Celebrations of Sovereignty in Nineteenth-century France* (Cambridge, Mass., 2004), p. 82.

of the interest and value of the testimony before his eyes. Letters were proof that the writer had been there, had played a part in making the nation's history.[37]

That is not, of course, to infer that the letters written by French soldiers were necessarily more reliable as sources on the Revolutionary Wars than other forms of writing, or that they in any way aspired to objectivity. Soldiers' letters and diaries took a multiplicity of different forms and they related very different levels of experience. The letters sent by generals and other high-ranking officers – men for whom the war could be seen as strategy and as the implementation of a pre-determined military policy – could take a broad overview of events, comparing the performance of their troops with those of the enemy or with the results achieved on other fronts. They were steeped in a strongly military culture, an understanding of tactics and motivation, and they had some grasp of government policy as well as of the objectives of the overall war effort. They often had a sufficiently broad perspective of the campaign that they could discuss the contribution of France's allies or have opinions about the strength and character of the enemy. Many of them were themselves committed revolutionaries, chosen as much for their loyalty to the republic as for their record on the battlefield.[38] That did not always mean that they were uncritical of the orders they were given or of their army's priorities; even Napoleon came in for considerable criticism from the officers around him in moments of crisis or when his army suffered setbacks, as happened, for instance, during the Egyptian Campaign.[39] But it meant that their letters – especially those written to the high command or to the Directory – have much of the measured gravity and informed assessment of official reports on the progress of the war. They cannot be regarded as simple eyewitness accounts.[40]

[37] For a more detailed discussion of the contents of soldiers' letters from the Revolutionary Wars and the value that subsequent generations would place upon them, see Alan Forrest, *Napoleon's Men. The Soldiers of the Revolution and Empire* (London, 2002).

[38] This is especially true in the Year II, when the influence of Jacobin deputies-on-mission to the armies was at its height and when generals were selected as much for their political loyalties as for professional reasons. See in particular the authoritative biography by General Herlaut of *Le général rouge Ronsin, 1751–1894* (Paris, 1956), and the more speculative work by Pierre Dufay, *Les sociétés populaires et l'armée, 1791–1794* (Paris, 1913).

[39] J. Wright (ed.), *Copies of Original Letters from the Army of General Bonaparte in Egypt, Intercepted by the Fleet under the Command of Admiral Lord Nelson* (London, 1798). I am grateful to Julian Aronberg for drawing my attention to this source, which he discusses at some length in 'French soldiers on campaign in Egypt: a study of letters sent during the period 1798–1799' (BA dissertation, University of Leeds, 2006).

[40] Good examples are the reports sent back to France by generals and military *commissaires* from the campaigns in Italy and Egypt. See, for instance, the collection

Very different were the letters and journals that came from the ranks, those written by ordinary soldiers and *sous-officiers*, who had no access to policy documents and often very little overall grasp of the context in which they were fighting. Unlike their officers, they could say little about the balance of strategic advantage, little about the war front as a whole, little, indeed, beyond the limited perspective provided by their own narrow corner of the battlefield. They did not offer any profound analysis of tactics or manoeuvres, beyond telling their own story, often in simple, rather naive terms. They were largely restricted to their own day-to-day experience, to recounting what they had seen and heard. But for their readers – whether it be the members of their family who read them at the time, or their descendants in the course of the nineteenth century, or the historians and local *érudits* of the Third Republic who uncovered their long-forgotten letters in attics or had them published in local newspapers and journals[41] – their very simplicity and directness of expression were virtues to be cherished. For these letters, viewed by posterity, became imbued with profound nostalgia, as tokens of the role played by ordinary people in events that were wholly extraordinary, young men who set forth from their farms or villages to defend their country and spread liberty and fraternity to the peoples of Europe. For a new generation of republicans, who saw the roots of their own beliefs in the period of the First Republic, theirs was an inspiring and at times harrowing tale of idealism and commitment, made the more powerful by the very ordinariness of the men to whom fell the duty of defending their fellow citizens.

Their letters, with a few notable exceptions, told such ordinary stories, too, tales of ordinary Frenchmen like themselves, driven to join the army by idealism or a sense of adventure, by poverty, or family problems, or a general sense of obligation. The needs and fears they expressed in their writing were ones to which the young of 1840 or 1870 could immediately relate; while the tone they used to express their ambitions and aspirations was that which they too would use when addressing mothers or brothers or village mayors. There was no pretension in

of *Mémoires sur l'Egypte publiés dans les années VII, VIII, et IX pendant les campagnes* (4 vols., Paris, 1799–1800).

[41] Though the publication of such letters can be observed throughout much of the nineteenth century, their popularity reflected current interests and concerns, and it is not surprising that there was a resurgence of such publications in the wake of the Franco-Prussian War (when the failure of Napoleon III to resort to some form of *levée en masse* was much criticised and unflattering comparisons made between the armies that had defended the Revolution and those that surrendered so rapidly at Sédan), in response to the resurgence of republican sentiment in the 1880s and 1890s, and especially in the years leading up to 1914.

their writing, no literary craft. They wrote simply, often falteringly, in the only writing style they knew. For this was still a semi-literate generation that went to war, men who had little reason to write letters in the course of their everyday lives, who travelled little and could communicate what they had to say by word of mouth. In the army, however, these assumptions were turned upside down as they crossed continents, had undreamt-of adventures, and grew accustomed to hearing a multitude of languages and dialects as they travelled around. French soldiers – artisans and journeymen, shopkeepers and peasant boys in their civilian existence – suddenly found themselves released from the constraints of village life, yet curiously alone in an alien environment, from which they felt impelled to write, to communicate with their villages, their culture, the world they had left behind. Writing was for many of them a source of solace, a way of keeping in touch with some far-off reality that was home. It broke the boredom of military life, the drab uniformity of camps and bivouacs, the tiring, tedious drudgery of the road. As in other modern armies, the prospect of a letter from home, from a loved one back in France, raised spirits and contributed to morale. It convinced many soldiers that there was benefit to be derived from literacy, and many were the infantrymen in the Revolutionary and Napoleonic armies who cursed their inability to read or who entrusted their thoughts to a third party – often a friend, a corporal or sergeant in their regiment, who would write on their behalf as an act of friendship or in return for food or drink. It was a reason, too, for officers to encourage their troops to take up writing, seeing the exchange of letters as a source of relief and reassurance, a barrier against homesickness and depression, the universally feared *nostalgie* that broke men's spirits and destroyed their health.[42] Men sweated over these letters, struggling to find the right words, to devise a polite form of address, or to give adequate expression to their emotions; that, too, gave their simple texts an added poignancy for those who came after.

So what might the nineteenth-century reader find in soldiers' correspondence that he would not expect to find in more reflective writings like memoirs? He would not turn to them for outpourings of patriotism and revolutionary commitment, except for those letters, semi-public in character, which the most committed Jacobins among them wrote to their clubs, sections or municipal councils in 1793 and the Year II – the letters that had been read out by the mayor or president to an admiring audience, winning the praise and gratitude of their fellow citizens

[42] Marcel Reinhard, 'Nostalgie et service militaire pendant la Révolution', *Annales historiques de la Révolution Française* 30 (1958), pp. 1–15.

at a moment when the *patrie* was indeed *en danger*. But these were not in any sense typical of soldiers' writings, written to reassure mothers and fathers at home, to learn of the most recent happenings in the village, the quality of the harvest, or their younger brothers' fortunes when facing the draft. The content of their correspondence was largely dictated by the conditions under which they wrote and the expectations of the readers at the other end. For whereas a man might write to his club or popular society praising republican virtue and deriding the treachery of priests and counter-revolutionaries – indeed, there were moments during the Terror when it was almost obligatory that he should write in these terms – this was not the stuff of family conversation, and declarations of political faith surfaced only occasionally in letters home. For the reader, this made them all the more exceptional and worthy of comment: that in the midst of so much routine exercise, so many deaths and injuries, so much suffering, ordinary Frenchmen had still felt the need to repeat their faith in the ideals for which they were fighting. It provided reassurance that they were still citizen-soldiers, committed to the cause of the Revolution and to the defence of their new-won liberty.

But if this was a welcome message to the patriots and republicans of later generations, their importance does not really lie in their politics.[43] Rather, they were treasured as evidence of what life was like in the armies, the experience of ordinary men caught up in events that had marked the history of a continent. Letters might hint at bravery or cowardice; they sometimes broached the question of fear, gave graphic descriptions of a cannonade or artillery barrage, or described the wounds suffered by their comrades-in-arms. But in the main they dealt with aspects of army life that were far more prosaic – those questions that were uppermost in the young soldiers' minds because their comfort and their very survival depended on them. For every mention of the national cause or statement of republican beliefs there must have been a score that talked of the poor quality of their rations, their unfamiliarity with local food, the shortage of boots and uniforms, or the strangeness of the landscape through which they passed. Their thoughts were on their immediate environment, the next day's march, the dangers of hospitalisation, the quality of the food in the houses where they were billeted. They wrote as human beings, as sons and brothers, more confused and vulnerable than they were heroic.

[43] For a full discussion of the content of soldiers' letters home from the revolutionary armies, see Alan Forrest, *The Soldiers of the French Revolution* (Durham, N.C., 1990), pp. 155–79.

In their correspondence the young soldiers complained that they had no money, that their pay was late, that their *assignats* were refused by local farmers and businesses or that they had, through no fault of their own, run up debts to their friends and officers, debts which they were honour-bound to repay. Indeed, many of their letters struggled to rise above the level of simple requests for money, for a loan or the present of a few francs to pay off their creditors or buy the most basic creature comforts that could help to make life bearable. Again and again we find sons pleading with their mothers not to abandon them to the state of penury to which army life had condemned them, so as to allow them to enjoy a drink with their comrades, or to help compensate them for their sufferings and their sacrifice. They treasured the human warmth provided by the comradeship of other soldiers, and expressed their fears and their grief when they became separated from close friends, or when they were wounded or died in battle. They marvelled at the great cities they passed though on their march – from Paris and Brussels to Berlin, Milan or Warsaw; others owed to the army their first view of France overseas, of Saint-Domingue and the other French islands in the Caribbean. And they admitted to feelings of homesickness, often spurred by the sight of the harvest being brought in, of vines ripening in the sun or of the priest outside a village church on a Sunday morning. Their descendants, eager to learn more about members of their own family, and future generations of Frenchmen, captivated by the ideals of the Revolution or by the story of a whole society at war, read these letters avidly in their quest for the moments of courage and grandeur that brought their ancestors back to life or confirmed their own romantic vision of the nation-in-arms. They clamoured for the publication of personal correspondence and revelled in the banal – but personal and human – detail they provided about the day-to-day experience of war.

It was through their writings that the soldiers of the Revolution first entered the imagination of nineteenth-century France, the voices of a lost generation providing inspiration for those who would follow. Their voices would be taken up by others, imitated, romanticised and inserted into the literary canon of the nineteenth century. But that insertion would take time. In the years immediately following the Restoration of the Bourbons, it was the more immediate legend of the Napoleonic army that left the more indelible mark, even on the Left: the men who had fought under the Emperor were more numerous and more clearly etched in popular memory. They were closer in time, fathers and elder brothers, hundreds of thousands of whom had returned to civil society and were familiar figures to a new generation of adolescents. Their letters and memoirs conjured up images of glory and national pride, and they enjoyed an instant vogue in the battered, humiliated France of the Bourbons. It was the Napoleonic legions, too, which – much more than the columns of the Year II – became the favoured theme of popular prints and *images d'Epinal*, figuring on the many lithographs and engravings sold in print shops, reproduced in books or peddled at the fairs and markets of *la France profonde*, where they were bought by the families of a new generation of soldiers fighting in Europe or in Africa.[44] In the immediate aftermath of Waterloo it would be they – the soldiers of the *Grande Armée*, citizen-soldiers, too, conscripted and judged fit for service ('bons pour le service'), who became the new paradigm for the nation-in-arms to which the opposition appealed. Those of the Year II would have to await their moment. For some that moment would come with the Second Empire, when republican writers like Victor Hugo and Jules Michelet lavished praise on the troops raised by the *levée en masse* as they poured scorn on Napoleon III's attempts to provide for national defence. For the population at large it would take the military disaster of the Franco-Prussian War, combined with the fall of the Empire and the proclamation of a new republic, for the legend of the soldier of the Year II to assume its place in France's national pantheon. The explanation is, of course, political. Before 1871, in John Horne's words, 'military mythology was much more important to the regime than to the Republican opposition'.[45]

[44] René Perrout, *Trésors des images d'Épinal* (Paris, 1985), pp. 161–2.

[45] John Horne, 'From *levée en masse* to total war: France and the revolutionary legacy, 1870–1945', in Robert Aldrich and Martyn Lyons (eds.), *The Sphinx in the Tuileries, and Other Essays in Modern French History* (Sydney, 1999), p. 322.

5 The hollow years

The role of nostalgia was crucial in keeping memories of the *levée en masse* alive in the years that followed Waterloo. References to the army of the Year II conjured up images of violence, political terror and regicide in royalist minds, as well as associations with the Napoleonic regime, and these, of course, were anathema to the new political rulers of France. They were anathema, too, to the Restoration Church, which, following Joseph de Maistre, denounced the Revolution as a form of divine punishment for the sins of the nation and urged that France could only avoid further punishment by 'wiping out the crime that made it necessary, or by prayer'.[1] With the blessing of the government, it sought to eradicate the ideological legacy of the Jacobins through an intensive campaign of missions to those regions of the country which the Catholic hierarchy, many newly returned from emigration, deemed to be especially decadent and in need of spiritual redemption. In particular there was concern that in areas that had been systematically dechristianised during the Revolution, church attendance was resumed more quickly than the practice of the sacraments.[2] Memories of the Year II outraged opinion in those deeply divided regions of the country – like the west or the Rhône valley – where memories of terror and massacre were still vivid and where a resurgence of White Terror always threatened. The threat of renewed violence had diplomatic resonances, too, as it risked upsetting the Allied powers with whom France had been forced to negotiate at Vienna. Much of Talleyrand's skill as a diplomat was based, after all, on his espousal of the principles of legitimacy and the presentation of France as a responsible member of the international community. Talleyrand might have worked for both the Revolution and the monarchy, but he never doubted that interest of state must prevail, or that it was his duty to make the restored monarchy acceptable both to French

[1] Robert Gildea, *The Past in French History* (New Haven, 1994), p. 227.

[2] Gérard Cholvy and Yves-Marie Hilaire, *Histoire religieuse de la France contemporaine* (2 vols., Toulouse 1985), vol. I, 1800–80, p. 23.

domestic opinion and to the crowned heads of Europe.[3] Napoleon's call to partisans in 1814 to fight the invading Prussian forces had already reminded the allies of France's recent revolutionary past, since they constituted a democratic and undisciplined force incapable of abiding by the accepted rules of war. It was a spectre which the Bourbons, anxious for the opportunity to arbitrate once again in European affairs, had every interest in burying.

Their concern to play down the tradition of spontaneous revolutionary violence was only increased by the fact of occupation after the fall of Napoleon, when for three years, from 1815 to 1818, two-thirds of the departments of France were occupied by Allied troops, troops from all over Europe, delighted to mark their symbolic and material victory over the Empire. Prussians and Austrians, British and Spaniards, Russians and Swedes were all on French soil, their mission to impose on the population the totality of their victory and of France's defeat. They were billeted on French homes, requisitioned French food, ate and drank lavishly in French inns with scant regard for the feelings of the vanquished. Appearance was part of the purpose of the occupation, to drill into the minds of the French people that their war effort had failed, that their adversaries were triumphant, and that they must accept to pay the cost of rash wars entered into recklessly and driven by ideology or national pride. The other part was repressive, reflecting the determination of the Allies to impose their dominion, rooting out where necessary those aspects of France's revolutionary and imperial past which, they believed, threatened the peace of the continent. The response on both sides was fairly measured. There were thefts, assaults and rapes, as would be expected when a tired occupying force tried to impose its authority on civilians. But these were limited in number, just as the cases of assault, robbery and murder committed by the French population on their occupiers were relatively infrequent. Local communities were exhausted by the long years of war and had little interest in stirring up animosity or seeking retaliation. The government had no wish to extend the period of occupation; administrators urged obedience to the law; local notables feared renewed disorder; and amongst the population at large there reigned a spirit of weariness and resignation. There was only very limited local rioting and no sign of a general insurrection. Circumstances simply did not demand a new *levée en masse* and it found no legitimacy in the public.[4]

[3] Philip G. Dwyer, *Charles-Maurice de Talleyrand, 1754–1838. A Bibliography* (Westport, Conn., 1996), pp. 13–14.

[4] Jacques Hantraye, *Les Cosaques aux Champs-Élysées. L'occupation de la France après la chute de Napoléon* (Paris, 2005), p. 274.

Political suspicion continued to be directed against soldiers who had served the Revolution and Empire and, even after the bulk of Napoleonic officers had been retired or put on *demi-solde*, the army was still seen by the authorities as a possible hotbed of conspiracy. It continued to be perceived as a mixture of interests, some loyal to the Bourbons, others lured by nostalgia for the Emperor or inspired by the reflexes of their predecessors of the Year II. It was widely supposed that both serving troops and former soldiers, often adjusting with great difficulty to the demands of civilian life, might be tempted to reject legitimacy in favour of a romantic vision of the republic or of imperial glory. This was, after all, a period characterised by secret societies and underground political movements, whether the *Carbonari* on the republican Left or the *Chevaliers de la Foi* on the Catholic Right. The *Carbonari*, or *Charbonnerie Française*, seemed to pose a particular threat, as it united a series of secretive republican splinter groups to make common cause against the Bourbons, formed alliances with liberal movements abroad, especially in Italy, and brought together, after the Emperor's death, men nostalgic for the Empire and committed republicans, their republicanism now integrating something of the Napoleonic myth.[5] Indeed, for many of the middle-class students and the young romantics attracted to *charbonnerie*, the attraction of Napoleon's name was as strong as the memory of republican constitutionalism, and in the symbolism of insurrection the Bonapartist violet mingled effortlessly with the *bonnets rouges* of neo-Jacobinism.[6] After 1830 some prominent members of the movement went so far as to admit that in the aftermath of defeat in 1814 they been dazzled by the popular image of Napoleon and seduced by his military success to the point where they had difficulty in distinguishing between the Republic and the Empire. Both appealed to men nostalgic for military glory, especially to the more disaffected of the *demi-soldes*;[7] and both seemed steeped in the spirit of the sovereign people.[8] The consequence for the 1820s was, in Alan Spitzer's felicitous expression, 'not only a tactical alliance but an ideological amalgam whose contradictions were not yet apparent'.[9] They would become so in the Revolution of 1830, but by then the nightmare of a secret, insurrectionary society

[5] Jean-Pierre Chaline, *La Restauration* (Paris, 1998), p. 46.

[6] Robert Alexander, *Re-writing the French Revolutionary Tradition* (Cambridge, 2003), pp. 175–7.

[7] P. Savigear, 'Carbonarism and the French Army, 1815–24', *History* 54 (1969), pp. 200–2.

[8] Ulysse Trélat, 'La charbonnerie', in *Paris révolutionnaire*, vol. II (Paris, 1833).

[9] Alan Spitzer, *Old Hatreds and Young Hopes. The French Carbonari against the Bourbon Restoration* (Cambridge, Mass., 1971), p. 278.

backed by hundreds of thousands of army veterans had taken root in the royalist imagination.

The Restoration monarchy was obsessed by the threat of military plots, most frequently involving young officers in active service who were lured by the temptations of liberalism or by the pseudo-masonic rites of *charbonnerie*. Events suggested that they were right to harbour suspicions. Following the assassination of the Duc de Berry in 1820, state paranoia attained new levels of intensity, and 1821 and 1822 were years of heavy undercover policing in military towns. A succession of plots and conspiracies were uncovered, leading to arrests, show trials and feverish press coverage. In 1822 alone, the police unveiled a series of anti-government plots organised by suspected units of the *charbonnerie*. In the first of two conspiracies at Saumur, the military academy was supposed to have been infiltrated by conspirators calling themselves the 'chevaliers de la liberté', though little could be proved and, when the trial was over, only one man was executed, a *maréchal des logis* by name of Sirejean. In another town with a strong military tradition, Belfort, both soldiers and civilians were implicated in a plot and a failed insurrection, whose exposure led to the arrest of an army captain in the Midi as a fellow conspirator. Captain Vallé was the very stereotype of the liberal romantic produced by the ideals of the Revolution and Empire – he was a member of the *charbonnerie*, had helped the nationalist insurrection in Greece and had made indiscreet boasts about freeing France from monarchy – crimes that led him, alone of the many conspirators, to the steps of the guillotine. General Berton, leader of the second Saumur plot, was another to be denounced and tried. He had led the national guardsmen of Thouars to raise the *tricolor* and ring the tocsin, after which he had openly denounced the monarchy. Evidence was again given of their membership of a secret society, which sufficed to condemn Berton and two of his fellow conspirators to summary execution. Most notorious of all among the neo-republican trials of 1822, however, and a case that became a favoured subject for popular chapbooks and cheap woodcuts, was that of the four sergeants of La Rochelle – young men whose boasting in bars and barracks from the Montagne Sainte-Geneviève in Paris, by way of Orleans and Poitiers, to their final posting in La Rochelle, led to their arrest for political conspiracy and membership of an illegal organisation. They were members of a unit of *Carbonari* organised by Sergeant Bories, who talked openly of his plans and of the sympathy he felt for the plotters at Saumur, leading to the arrest of the four sergeants. Offered their lives in exchange for the names of their superiors in the order, they refused to cooperate and were sent to the guillotine, four humble cogs in a much more sinister machine. The story, as it entranced the nation, emphasised their honesty, their simplicity, their loyalty and lack of guile, the tale of four brave and handsome young soldiers, attracted by republican ideals, then inveigled into conspiracy by dark and mysterious forces, only to die before their time. In the opinion of many readers and of the onlookers at their execution, they were not the dangerous criminals denounced by the state, but young men committed to a republican tradition for which they were prepared to die. They were obvious recruits to the new, romantic republicanism of the 1820s.[10]

But if it was clear that the Restoration was not going to trust soldiers it had inherited, men who had sworn loyalty to a ruler now denounced as a usurper, the government still faced the overriding question of how to provide for national defence. How best could they serve the needs of the restored monarchy and construct an army that would be well fitted to a peacetime role – riot control and the maintenance of public order – and to the smaller, geographically limited wars of the first half of the nineteenth century? The character of such wars would soon become apparent, with French operations in Spain (1823–4), Greece (1827–9) and Belgium (1831–2), European campaigns that would be complemented by early colonial engagement, most notably in Algeria from the late 1820s. These wars are best regarded as limited missions, rather like peacekeeping campaigns in recent times, since they deliberately avoided head-on conflict with other great powers. As such, in the generals' view, they were best fought by small, mobile and tightly organised columns that would give maximum manoeuvrability and have the benefit of precise and repeated drilling.[11] They rejected any return to the huge size of the Napoleonic armies, which were now thought of as unmanoeuvrable on the battlefield and unfeedable off it, conjuring up the huge supply problems that had contributed so much to Napoleon's undoing. It was a strategic choice, and one that implied the rejection, for the next generation at least, of the revolutionary idea of the *levée en masse*. In this respect the military were at one with the political leaders of the Restoration, who, once they had disbanded Napoleon's huge conscript armies, had no wish to put their trust in political ideals that had been invented by the French Revolution.

Among the conservatives who formed the new majority, fear of the legacy of the revolutionary and Napoleonic army was accompanied by

[10] André Zeller, *Soldats perdus. Des armées de Napoléon aux garnisons de Louis XVIII* (Paris, 1977), pp. 319–41.

[11] Paddy Griffith, *Military Thought in the French Army, 1815–51* (Manchester, 1989), pp. 8–9.

something more brutal, a disdain for the common soldier, a rejection of his person and a degree of antipathy for the values and lifestyle which he represented. Armies were, of course, necessary to state security and the safety of persons and property; the mood was not one of anti-militarism, even if many did want to see the exceptional role of military values in the Napoleonic state reduced to more normal proportions. Rather it was the rejection of the idealisation during the previous quarter-century of the soldier as an apostle of liberty, the soldier preaching the benefits of republicanism, or secularism, or equality before the law to the subjects of kings and emperors. And with it went the end of the idealisation of the soldier himself, in the way that republicans and Bonapartists had repeatedly done, the myth that the soldier of the Year II was himself driven by ideals, that he was different from the troops who since time immemorial had plundered, looted and bullied their way across the continent. For many royalists, the adulation that had been poured on the revolutionary and Napoleonic infantry was itself an offence to their sensibilities and they reverted to eighteenth-century type, seeing the soldiery as violent, uncultured, prone to criminal behaviour, lecherous and brutal, in short as men whom it was probably safer and more pleasant to avoid.[12] After 1815 the image of the infantryman, which the Revolution had devoted so much effort to burnishing, was once again allowed to be dragged through the mud of public condescension. It was, perhaps, an appropriate mood for a society with a mission to demilitarise the state, to reduce France's armed forces from the highest levels of manpower that Europe had known and replace them by a small, well-drilled and thoroughly professional standing army.

The task of creating this new army – as well as of disbanding the remains of the imperial army – fell to the Restoration authorities. Early signals were not promising, with the constitution outlawing any return to conscription and manpower dwindling. Under the ministry of Marshal Henri de Clarke between 1815 and 1817 the army was allowed to run down to only 117,000 troops, a figure insufficient even to provide minimal defence for France's frontiers; the failure to attract new recruits meant that in 1817 the army was forced to use 18,000 national guardsmen to fill gaps in their ranks and mount guard in the fortresses around France's borders.[13] To resolve the crisis the King was persuaded to restore to the War Ministry the man he had briefly turned to after the Restoration, Marshal Gouvion Saint-Cyr, who had made his reputation

[12] Raoul Girardet, *La société militaire de 1815 à nos jours* (Paris, 1998), pp. 14–15.
[13] William Serman and Jean-Paul Bertaud, *Nouvelle histoire militaire de la France, 1789–1919* (Paris, 1998), p. 207.

as a brilliant tactical commander and defensive strategist and as one of Napoleon's more idiosyncratic marshals, headstrong, individualistic and disliked by the King for his outright hostility to the expansion of the Royal Guard or the conferment of privilege upon it.[14] But Gouvion Saint-Cyr got his way, expressing his view that the peacetime strength of the army should be capped at 240,000 men – as much a question of budgetary constraints as of manpower targets – and introducing a new recruitment law that would meet this target. It was this measure, finally passed in 1818 after a week of debate in the Chamber, which more than any other defined the character of the army for the next half-century. The debate was vigorous, the proponents of professionalism and a noble officer corps arguing fiercely against the supporters of republicanism and meritocracy. As one historian perceptively noted, the debate about conscription was not limited to questions of military efficacy. It brought to the surface many of the lingering divisions of the previous half-century, providing 'a sort of laboratory of political ideologies at the dawn of modernity'.[15]

Aware of the level of public hostility to any suggestion of conscription, Gouvion insisted that the army should be manned by volunteers wherever possible – volunteers for six years in the infantry, eight in the cavalry and artillery. But he knew that, to get manpower to the required level, an element of compulsion was necessary, and wrote in a 'selective service' clause whereby all the males domiciled in an area were asked to register with a local board, which would then use a ballot or lottery to determine who would be called upon to serve. The aim of this clause was to raise around 40,000 troops each year, though, given the state's anxiety not to create unnecessary political opposition, the law left many possible loopholes. Those who drew a low number could hire a substitute to serve in their stead; they could claim an exemption; and even then, those condemned to serve might not be called upon to leave their homes. This was not full-blown conscription, and was marked by little of the spontaneity of the people-in-arms of revolutionary legend; it also had little appeal to the emotions at a time when Prussians were still stirred by memories of the *Ehrhebung* and the sacrifice of romantic patriots like Theodor Körner.[16] But Gouvion Saint-Cyr had not set out to betray every tenet of his revolutionary inheritance. The principle had

[14] David Chandler, 'Gouvion Saint-Cyr', in *Dictionary of the Napoleonic Wars* (New York, 1993), pp. 391–2.

[15] Thomas Hippler, 'Conscription in the French Restoration: the 1818 debate on military service', *War in History* 13 (2006), p. 297.

[16] Daniel Moran, 'Arms and the concert: the nation in arms and the dilemmas of German liberalism', in Daniel Moran and Arthur Waldron (eds.), *The People in Arms*.

been accepted that the army had the right to call upon its citizens, and that there should be a visible equality before the recruiting sergeant. In the words of Royer-Collard, what was essential here was the equality of all: 'The Charter declares all Frenchmen equal before the law; by virtue of the Charter, then, it is fate, the minister of equality, who will preside over the process of recruitment.'[17] To that extent, at least, the principle of the soldier as a citizen – the *soldat-citoyen* if not the *citoyen-soldat* – had been preserved in law.[18] In almost every other respect, the spirit of the *levée en masse* had been put firmly to one side in favour of training and drill. The Restoration had set the military agenda for the greater part of the nineteenth century by putting their trust in a small, largely professional army.

There were, it must be emphasised, good military arguments in defence of this position, most notably the fact that, even under the Revolution and Empire, large armies of citizen-soldiers or conscripts had proved ill-trained, difficult to supply adequately in the field and prone to unnecessarily high casualties. There were many, even among Napoleon's officer corps, who would plead the case for smaller, better-trained units, or who pointed out that the Emperor's greatest exploits had been achieved in relatively small-scale operations like Marengo, Ulm, Jena and Austerlitz.[19] The kinds of warfare which threatened in the nineteenth century emphasised the primacy of the infantry and underlined the case for small, highly-drilled units that could respond quickly in an emergency. In Spain, Greece and Belgium they were engaged in specific, limited manoeuvres that had no use for massed armies; and the same lesson would be learned from France's many colonial campaigns across the nineteenth century, beginning in Algeria in 1830. Here the initial French response – to send in a large mass of troops poorly prepared for the conditions they met – was rewarded with horrific levels of fever and death among the soldiers. It was quickly accepted that to fight in the desert, or the Caribbean, or in other parts of the Empire, the advantage lay in deploying small, tough columns that could be manoeuvred with relative ease, bound together by a sense of duty, by military spirit and by experience and familiarity.[20] Colonial wars, increasingly fought by French officers leading native

Military Myth and National Mobilization since the French Revolution (Cambridge, 2003), pp. 56–7.

[17] Annie Crépin, *Défendre la France: Les Français, la guerre et le service militaire, de la Guerre de Sept Ans à Verdun* (Rennes, 2005), p. 182.

[18] Gary P. Cox, *The Halt in the Mud: French Strategic Planning from Waterloo to Sedan* (Boulder, Colo., 1994), pp. 41–4.

[19] Griffith, *Military Thought*, p. 8. [20] *Ibid.*, p. 9.

soldiers, had little use for conscription, or for the spontaneity of the traditional revolutionary *levée en masse*. Hence for many French observers, the reforms initiated in 1818 responded perfectly to the country's defence needs. What they also did, however, was to cut the size of the army to the bone and virtually ignore the need for a viable reserve, something that could prove terribly costly in moments of national emergency. This omission placed the French in a diametrically different situation from the Prussians, who continued into peacetime the principle of universal conscription that had been adopted in the War of Liberation against Napoleon. The Law concerning Compulsory Military Service of September 1814 laid down that all Prussian men aged between seventeen and forty were obliged to serve in the militia, which was defined as an independent military organisation alongside the standing army.[21]

What the French had was another institution created by the Revolution, the National Guard, though a guard that was already, long before 1815, stripped of most of the powerful political symbolism of the revolutionary years. The National Guard had been created as a revolutionary institution, a force that had its origins in the Great Fear and the right of local communities to oversee their own defence, and which increasingly devoted itself to the ceremonial and policing work needed to protect the institutions of the republic. In the early 1790s, dressed in their patriotic uniforms or marching behind their sectional banners, electing their officers and proclaiming revolutionary principles, national guardsmen had encapsulated the optimism of the young Revolution and had enjoyed a high degree of popular support. But public respect soon plummeted. Under the Directory much of the initial spontaneity disappeared, until by 1799 it was a tired and ageing institution, little more than a means of recruiting auxiliaries to the army and the *gendarmerie*.[22] Their status only worsened under the Empire, since Napoleon had little time for the notion of a patriotic force of order and preferred his soldiers to be at his command, until the guards were little more than reserve infantry battalions, to be used in battle should circumstances require. Thus by 1810 four battalions of the National Guard had been incorporated into the *Garde Impériale*, while for civil defence and police duties Napoleon favoured the *gendarmerie*, whose

[21] Karen Hagemann, 'German heroes: the cult of death for the fatherland in nineteenth-century Germany', in Stefan Dudink, Karen Hagemenn and John Tosh (eds.), *Masculinities in Politics and War: Gendering Modern History* (Manchester, 2004), p. 119.

[22] Georges Carrot, 'Une institution de la nation: la Garde Nationale, 1789–1871' (thèse de doctorat de 3e cycle, Université de Nice, 1979), p. 107.

numbers he expanded by over 50 per cent, from 10,000 to 15,600.[23] The public image of the Guard had been obscured, and its popularity with the French people suffered in consequence. Indeed, as Louis Girard perceptively remarked, the periods when the Guard enjoyed high levels of popular support were more and more restricted to those when France was at war or when French territory was threatened with invasion.[24] It was at such moments that the Guard ceased to be a purely sedentary force, an institution perceived as being of and for the propertied classes, and became an active part of the nation's defence, mingling with the troops of the line to make common cause against the enemy or to push the invading force beyond France's frontiers.[25] Then – most notably in the crisis years of 1814 and 1870 – the men of the National Guard once again became soldiers, soldiers who had risen from the midst of the people to defend their fellow citizens.

But for most of the nineteenth century, and most particularly during the Bourbon Restoration, their image was very different. After the Hundred Days, when the King harboured such distrust for the regular army, he had to turn to the Paris National Guard, which had turned a deaf ear to Napoleon's call to insurrection, in an effort to consolidate his throne. In the months that followed, indeed, the Guard would constitute the only force in the country capable of defending the monarchy and the country.[26] This would mark its image throughout the decades of the Restoration and the July Monarchy – an image of respectable conservatism, men of property defending property rights against popular anger, men of order defending monarchy against insurgency and the threat of anarchy, and providing a useful counter-weight to the notorious fickleness of the military. Gone was any association, other than in popular memory, between the Guard and the forces of popular revolution, any equation between its new role and the streets of revolutionary Paris. Its essential values were no longer political, but social, as Brun de Villeret was quick to recognise. 'The shining element among the national guards', he wrote, 'the men of substance who can contribute their own money and who today are the very soul of the Guard, will continue to assure the peacefulness of our cities and provide relief to the monarchy'.[27] The Guard was, in effect, given a simple policing role, that of maintaining public order and controlling the rowdier elements of Paris society. It was a role that implied neither the spontaneity nor

[23] Carrot, 'Institution de la nation', p. 123.

[24] Louis Girard, *La garde nationale, 1814–71* (Paris, 1964), p. 8.

[25] Archives Nationales (A.N.), F9 357, Levée en masse de 1814, decree of 6 January 1814.

[26] Cox, *Halt in the Mud*, p. 23.

[27] Quoted in Girard, *Garde nationale*, pp. 99–100.

the patriotism that had characterised the guard during the early revolution, none of the qualities associated with the *levée en masse*. Indeed, it was increasingly contaminated by its political associations, at least in the eyes of the Left. From defending the *patrie en danger*, it was now condemned to officiate at a seemingly endless stream of royalist ceremonies which were greeted by the mass of the population with cold indifference – like the anniversary of the death of Louis XVI, a religious office for Marie-Antoinette, the birthday of the Duchess of Angoulême, or the mass of the Holy Spirit.[28] The 1830 revolution changed little, the new government using the Guard only as a colourful force for public parades, leading to widespread alienation among the guardsmen themselves.[29] Service had been relegated to a matter of routine, while membership in the guard – and especially a place in its officer ranks – was now a reward for social distinction, a sign of wealth and status in Paris society. All trace of the revolutionary Guard, any echo of the nation-in-arms, was scrupulously excluded.

Both the National Guard and the army, military strategists insisted, had to be protected against contamination from the more revolutionary elements in the civilian population. It is this that explains the repeated insistence in the 1820s on the need for the French infantryman to be well trained and of sound judgement, a skilled skirmisher who could apply his intelligence to combat roles. He was not, in other words, like his predecessor of the eighteenth century, a common soldier recruited at random from among the prisons and hospitals of rural France. He was an elite soldier, morally as well as technically, to be housed in barracks rather than billeted on the citizenry, and required by his position in the army to hold himself apart from the civilian population. In contrast to the soldier of the Year II, he was to be buffered against popular turbulence; indeed, his usefulness was largely judged by his ability to deal with civil disorders and crowd control at home in France. In 1827 the army was ordered to destroy the barricades thrown up by food rioters in Paris. In 1830 it faced a full-scale revolution in the streets of the capital, and Marshal Marmont responded by leading his army against the barricades in an operation that left 200 soldiers and 1,800 insurgents dead in the fighting. To make matters worse, the army was shown to be powerless to stop the force of popular insurrection, while large numbers of soldiers deserted and joined the insurgents. In Paris

[28] *Ibid.*, p. 112.

[29] Annie Crépin, 'La Garde Nationale, les gauches, et l'idéal de la nation armée sous la monarchie de Juillet', in Serge Bianchi and Roger Dupuy (eds.), *La Garde nationale entre nation et peuple en armes. Mythes et réalités, 1789–1871* (Rennes, 2006), pp. 455–6.

the revolutionaries prevailed in spite of, not because of, the army.[30] And along with the violence shown by the military in quelling the silk-workers' risings in Lyon in 1831 and 1834 – in 1831 the military lost 11 per cent of the 3,500 men deployed, killed or wounded[31] – it succeeded only in creating an image of the military on the left of the political spectrum as a force of popular repression. The July Days in particular ensured that the army was treated with great distrust by republicans and socialists. From being the cherished agent of revolution and the defender of the sovereign people, the army had turned into a force for repression, the defender of government interest and private property.[32]

The army of the Year II, in other words, had passed into legend, the legend of the other, popular army to which the people had turned in times of turmoil to protect their liberties. It was quite distinct from people's current experience of the military, whether under the Restoration or the July Monarchy: in that sense 1830 was seen to have made scant difference. Rather it was inextricably linked in the popular mind with conscription, civic equality and the right and duty of all to rise in defence of the people, in short with a project that was necessarily revolutionary and played on the idealism and patriotism of the people. The new regime had little reason to revive it, and even less reason to impose universal conscription on an unwilling population. Instead, the new war minister, Soult, sought in 1832 to strengthen the army created by Gouvion Saint-Cyr by extending the period of service for those who drew a low number to seven years, of which two should be devoted to service in the reserve. In this way, Soult believed, the real weakness revealed by the revolution of 1830 – the failure of the French army to create a trained and efficient reserve – could be addressed without moving away from the principle of an army of well-trained long-service soldiers, and without risking the instability of a return to broad conscription. Half the contingent would be allowed to stay at home, but in times of war it would no longer be necessary to pass special laws to bring them back to the colours. And the relatively lengthy period which each soldier had to spend in the army meant that he could undergo thorough drill and weapons training, and be psychologically prepared for war, without the government having to take the political risk of arming

30 Griffith, *Military Thought*, pp. 43–4.

31 For an account of the 1831 uprising and its repression, see Robert J. Bezucha, *The Lyon Uprising of 1834. Social and Political Conflict in the Early July Monarchy* (Cambridge, Mass., 1974), pp. 48–72.

32 Cox, *Halt in the Mud*, p. 97.

the popular classes.[33] France had taken a further step away from the ideal of the *levée en masse*, placing her trust, both politically and militarily, in professionalism and training, the virtues of a small, structured and long-serving army over the revolutionary siren-calls of equality and citizen-soldiers.

For the officers placed on *demi-solde* after the Restoration, the July Monarchy offered no return to active service; only a tiny proportion of those who had served in Napoleon's armies found their way back into uniform.[34] Yet in more symbolic ways the accession of Louis-Philippe did bring France closer to its revolutionary and Napoleonic roots, as the new constitutional monarchy sought to dissociate itself from the immediate past and appeal directly to the traditions of the Revolution and Empire. The men who had served their country during the long years of war now found their service honoured and their sacrifice recognised; they were no longer treated as embarrassing pariahs of a legitimist state. And yet, in the rush to gain credit through association, it was again the soldiers of the Empire, rather than of the Revolution, who found themselves honoured. Orleanists who lacked any powerful tradition of their own were keen to identify with those who had served the Emperor, not only because they increasingly identified with the liberal values of the revolutionary tradition but, more importantly, because they were seen as the principal opponents of the Bourbon Restoration. The government was well aware that there was a huge reservoir of public sympathy which it could exploit. The Emperor, for many, was not just the man who had brought France military success and glory, or who had given Europe the benefits of law and a constitution. There was something Christ-like in the way he was talked about and portrayed; and 1840 was his Second Coming, hailed in the images of Pellerin and the popular songs of Béranger. Béranger, in particular, directed many of his words towards the shades of the Emperor, encouraging nostalgia for past glories at a time when French arms had stood for deeper, more permanent values. Napoleon, he insisted, had led the army he had inherited from the French Revolution, 'the army of the revolution that was the enemy of the feudal regimes of Europe that had come together to crush the achievement of revolutionary France'.[35] A golden age was being unveiled to a new generation of admirers, and the soldiers who had

[33] Annie Crépin, *La conscription en débat, ou le triple apprentissage de la nation, de la citoyenneté, de la République, 1798–1889* (Arras, 1998), p. 84.

[34] Stéphane Calvet, 'Les officiers de l'armée impériale et le pouvoir royal: tensions et conflits en Charente, 1814–32', in Natalie Petiteau (ed.), *Conflits d'Empire: Les Cahiers du GERHICO 9* (Poitiers, 2006), p. 126.

[35] Pierre Brochon, *La chanson sociale de Béranger à Brassens* (Paris, 1961), p. 25.

fought with him found their own past also was rehabilitated. The July Revolution, in Sudhir Hazareesingh's words, was not so much a return to 1789 as a specifically nineteenth-century conflict, what he sees as 'the final act of the persistent confrontation that had pitted Napoleonic and Bourbon factions in France against each other throughout the Restoration years'.[36]

What the July Monarchy did not change, however, was the strategic approach to the army, which retained its commitment to a small, largely professional force and had not made significant changes to its strategic plans since 1818. When revolution came in 1848, therefore, the government was forced to respond with an under-strength and badly underfunded army whose budget had been seriously reduced and whose morale was undermined. The soldiers were being deployed against armed crowds of their own citizens who initially took the authorities by surprise, and whose violence and resort to street-fighting behind hastily constructed barricades tied down large numbers of troops while making outright victory almost impossible. To increase their problems, since February there had been a widespread attitude of mistrust towards the army, shared not just by the radicals in the streets but also by many in the provisional government itself. So when Cavaignac was recalled, he was given the task of rebuilding the trust that had been lost between the army and the civil authorities; his mission quite specifically stated that he should be a republican general, 'the republican leader of our rehabilitated army, the man who could safeguard public order'.[37] His primary responsibility was to build up troop numbers in Paris, and he insisted that this should be achieved with troops of the line, the battle-hardened veterans of campaigns in North Africa. They did what they could, resorting to plans that had been made as far back as 1830 in anticipation of another revolution, and concentrating their forces around Paris so that they would be able to intervene wherever necessary, especially in the eastern suburbs of the city. The various sectors of the city were to be contained and cordoned off so that the rebels could not make common cause, and key revolutionary quarters like the Faubourg Saint-Antoine were particularly targeted.[38] Meanwhile, the popular image of French troops resorting to savage acts of repression created bitter antagonism between soldiers and rioters as the insurrection spread from Paris to the major provincial cities, and from there

[36] Sudhir Hazareesingh, *The Legend of Napoleon* (London, 2004), p. 150.

[37] A. Doumenc, 'L'armée et les journées de juin', in *Actes du Congrès historique du Centenaire de la Révolution de 1848* (Paris, 1948), p. 255.

[38] Roger Price (ed.), *1848 in France* (London, 1975), p. 54.

to large swathes of the countryside. In Lyon, where General Gemeau called on two divisions of the Army of the Alps to prevent the insurrection in the silk-workers' suburb of the Croix-Rousse from spreading across the city, there was no attempt to be conciliatory: four and a half battalions of infantry and eight cannon were deployed in a two-pronged operation against the workers that inflicted terrible casualties and left a burning hatred of the military.[39] By the end of 1848 a total of more than 48,000 troops – including some 5,300 cavalry – had been deployed in the countryside to deal with over 250 incidents of rural unrest. Less than three years later they were expected to support the overthrow of the republic in favour of the Second Empire. In other words, the work of the army was no longer specifically republican; it had been transformed into a force whose function was to maintain public order, if necessarily repressing the people mercilessly in pursuit of its mission.[40]

There remained, of course, the National Guard, which, as we have seen, had strayed mightily during the first half of the nineteenth century from its revolutionary role of the 1790s but which was still linked in the public imagination with republican values. How far could this identity be maintained against a backcloth of popular revolution, when guns and weapons were being handed out to the citizenry at large (between 24 February and 20 June around 450,000 rifles were handed out, in the belief that in a republic, every citizen should also be a soldier, or at least a national guardsman)?[41] The question was all the more compelling in that the public still tended to confuse two distinct images of the National Guard, that of the partisans who rose spontaneously to defend the motherland in crises like 1792 and 1814, and that, rather less revolutionary, of the bourgeois militiamen of the post-1815 world, a sedentary force which – if it had any role at all – was there to defend property and the social order. Their image was steadfastly conservative: if they were associated with disorder, it could only be with its repression, and in many provincial towns and cities they did not even have any obvious purpose, since after the mid-1830s they had practically stopped all pretence of training or exercising and many of them had not even bothered to elect their officers.[42] Only sporadically did radicals recall an earlier tradition of revolutionary spontaneity, or imply that the nineteenth-century *garde* should revert to its revolutionary origins. In 1831, for instance, the prospectus for a patriotic paper that was about

[39] Mary Lynn Stewart-McDougall, *The Artisan Republic. Revolution, Reaction and Resistance in Lyon, 1848–51* (Kingston, Ontario, 1984), p. 131.

[40] Griffith, *Military Thought*, p. 44.

[41] Girard, *Garde nationale*, p. 292.

[42] Georges Carrot, *La Garde Nationale, 1789–1871.* Une force publique ambiguë (Paris, 2001), p. 267.

to be launched in Bordeaux, *Le Garde National de la Gironde*, addressed the new generation of guardsmen in terms that were heavily tinged with nostalgia for a past age and which suggested that they see themselves as part of a revolutionary continuum, as the sons and grandsons of the men who had marched to the rescue of the Great Revolution. But even here the essence of their duty, however enthusiastically and spontaneously it was carried out, was defined as the defence of order, albeit of a revolutionary and republican order. The paper's editor appealed openly to the young men's sense of history. 'You did in 1830', it argued, 'what your fathers had done in '89: in these two moments two generations paid their debt in equal measure to the *patrie*'.[43] And the features that linked these two moments were, of course, republicanism and the violence of revolution.

That the *garde* remained a symbol of the republic was not in doubt: indeed, the moral influence which they retained in Paris in 1848 was largely due to their refusal to betray the *tricolor* and their singing of the Marseillaise, gestures which identified them with the republic in the eyes of republican Paris. The fact that, in contrast to 1830, the people were organised and armed, and the regime based on manhood suffrage, made it important that Paris made this identification, that the National Guard was shown to be truly popular, an ally of the Parisian population. In the banquets and festivities that took place throughout the spring and summer of 1848, steeped in republican gestures of unity with the people and reciprocal fraternity with the army, that identification was repeatedly rammed home to the population. In local ceremonies, in particular, the Guard paraded among maypoles and liberty trees and sang the praises of a Marianne who was at once militant, republican and democratic. For a brief moment, it seemed, it had returned to its revolutionary persona, incorporating some of the tropes and symbolism of the old *fêtes révolutionnaires*.[44] But if it was relatively easy to associate the Guard with the revolution – a largely symbolic association – it was more difficult to transform the institution from what it had been – a force paid by and answerable to the monarchy – into one that was truly popular and prepared to side with the insurgents against the regime. To achieve this, the republican authorities expanded the numbers in the guard, organised elections for officers and threw guard membership open to all without regard to social background.[45] In the process

[43] *Le Garde National de la Gironde*, prospectus, le 7 août 1831.

[44] Rémi Dalisson, *Les trois couleurs, Marianne et l'Empereur: Fêtes libérales et politiques symboliques en France, 1815–1870* (Paris, 2004), p. 158.

[45] Girard, *Garde nationale*, p. 293.

they once again politicised at least a part of the Guard, with the consequence that the more radical among them refused to countenance the election of Louis-Napoleon as president, preferring to make common cause with the insurgents against the agents of the state.

But the Paris Guard was not destined to become an effective revolutionary force.[46] It was composed of too many conflicting factions, among them the former elite units which remained faithful to the idea of social order, and which feared that they were being sacrificed in the cause of the democratic republic. And if it gained a fleeting legitimacy from the populace in the days following the February days, that legitimacy was soon lost.[47] There followed open demonstrations by the guardsmen on the Place de Grève, and a deeply humiliating moment when the radical clubs, rather than look to the Guard for support, sent their members into the streets to block the guardsmen's route. The result was predictable. Fearing a plot by the clubs, the government called on the guard for protection against the radicals of the Paris streets – a gesture which once again put the National Guard on the side of political conservatism. Their brief cameo appearance as a radical force was over, as they were increasingly used by a conservative republic for policing turbulent areas of the city and suppressing insurrection. When on 2 December Napoleon staged his coup d'état, even that degree of influence would be removed. The *garde*, aware, no doubt, of the strength of Napoleon's forces, made no effort to defend the republic and its institutions and stood by as the popular districts of Paris were crushed and silenced by the regular army. Its prestige as an instrument of popular revolution lay in tatters, though it seemed since 1848 to have done just enough to lay claim to its republican credentials. Louis-Napoleon had no use for such an institution, and under the Second Empire the National Guard would be disbanded, then reluctantly restored to perform rather anodyne ceremonial duties. From being a vital part of the republic's nation-in-arms, it had by 1852 sunk to the position of a 'decorative sinecure'.[48]

Napoleon III had little interest in the National Guard or in the civic values it stood for in republican eyes. His conception of the army was more imperial than revolutionary, as was shown in his frequent references back to the imperial *Grande Armée*, his frequently stated desire

[46] The essential ambiguity in the role of the National Guard is discussed in a number of the essays in Serge Bianchi and Roger Dupuy (eds.), *La Garde nationale entre nation et peuple en armes. Mythes et réalités, 1789–1871* (Rennes, 2006).

[47] Louis Hincker, 'Officiers porte-parole des barricades: Paris, 1848', in Bianchi and Dupuy (eds), *La Garde nationale entre nation et peuple en armes*, p. 488.

[48] Louis Girard, *La Deuxième République, 1848–51* (Paris, 1968), pp. 291–3.

to reward those men who had followed his great-uncle, and the lavish celebrations that surrounded the award of the *médaille de Sainte-Hélène* to veterans of the First Empire – some 400,000 of them – in 1857.[49] As he dreamt of recreating the pomp and military glory of his ancestor, the new emperor wanted an army on whose loyalty he could depend, one that would defend the imperial throne against attack, whether from outside France or from within. He need hardly have worried, since from the moment when he was elected president of the Second Republic in 1849, it was apparent that the army was at his back. The Second Republic had done nothing to undermine that monarchical model of an army in which a small proportion of the population was condemned to perform seven years' service, while the vast majority escaped scot-free.[50] Napoleon shared the preference for a small, highly trained army of the kind that Gouvion Saint-Cyr had created in 1818 and which would remain untainted by the revolutionary connotations of the *levée en masse*. Economics may have dictated this, too, since the French preference for a relatively small force, dispersed around the country in regimental garrisons, was seen as a cheaper solution in peacetime than the recruitment of massed armies or the construction of large permanent camps. Besides, until 1848 nothing had occurred to suggest that this strategy was ill conceived, since in colonial operations, in particular, the army had demonstrated high levels of training and effectiveness. Only then, when France was swept by a brief war scare, did levels of manpower and the dispersal of the army across far-flung garrison towns present a problem for the state. Low manning levels remained a serious issue throughout Napoleon's reign, and the issue was made more sensitive by the Emperor's expansionist foreign policy. In 1851, for example, the army could assemble only some 230,000 troops, and of these a substantial number – around 50,000 – were already committed to colonial duties in Africa.[51]

If the call for large-scale conscription and appeal to the ideal of the citizen-soldier were confined to radicals and neo-Jacobins on the republican Left, the practical problem remained unanswered. A solution had to be found for what was increasingly recognised as a manpower crisis in the French army. Fighting colonial campaigns in Africa and keeping the peace in the streets of Paris or Lyon were very different in scale to the full-blown European warfare which Napoleon's aggressive foreign

[49] Sudhir Hazareesingh, *The Saint-Napoleon. Celebrations of Sovereignty in Nineteenth-century France* (Cambridge, Mass., 2004), pp. 82–5.
[50] Crépin, *La conscription en débat*, p. 96.
[51] Cox, *Halt in the Mud*, pp. 162–3.

policy always risked, and which finally came – despite his desperate attempts to secure a diplomatic solution to what he dismissed as 'the foolish affair of the Holy Places' – in 1854 in the Crimea, and later in the decade in Italy.[52] In these campaigns even the Emperor admitted that the performance of the army was only mediocre, though he at no time envisaged the levels of military disaster that would follow during the next decade. But this realisation, and the heavy losses that were sustained – 100,000 men in the Crimean War alone – did nothing to convert him to more generalised conscription, a solution that continued to be seen as redolent of the French Revolution. Instead he sought to improve the army's effectiveness by other means – by introducing new rifles, improving medical provision and offering bounties to those professional soldiers who agreed to extend their periods of service. The most significant reform in these years was the law of 26 April 1855 which aimed to increase the number of soldiers available to the army – something which, it was agreed after the Crimean experience, was urgently needed – without offending public opinion or placing an intolerable financial strain on the state. Conscripting large numbers of young men was deemed to cause anguish to countless families and to pose a threat to agriculture and the economy, while at the same time imposing huge numbers of reluctant soldiers on French regiments. So no attempt was made to increase levels of conscription, to reduce the period of service demanded, or to allow the sons of the rich to buy their way out. Instead, the new law transformed the traditional *remplacement,* whereby anyone drawing a low number in the ballot could buy the services of someone else to serve for him, with the rather different idea of *exonération*, or personal exemption. Both the army and the state's coffers, it was suggested, would benefit, since exemption would be bought by paying a tax which would then be used by the army to re-engage non-commissioned officers and private soldiers who had already acquired experience of soldiering. The cost of the tax would be fixed each year: originally pitched at 2,800 francs in 1856, it would oscillate between 1,800 francs in 1858 and 3,000 francs in 1867.[53] In this way manpower needs could be addressed without resort to compulsion, and the commanders could take comfort in the fact that the men they received into the regiments had greater experience and professional skill. But the new law did not solve France's recruitment problems at a stroke. The number of engagements and re-engagements seldom met the requirements of the military; and in every year except

[52] James F. McMillan, *Napoleon III* (London, 1991), p. 76.
[53] Serman and Bertaud, *Nouvelle histoire*, p. 310.

1860, 1861 and 1862 it was lower than the number of exemptions purchased, leaving the army to make up numbers by buying replacements in the traditional way. There were other problems, too, for recruitment. Conditions of service were regarded as too primitive, and barracks too overcrowded and insanitary, while pay lagged behind what was offered in civilian life. The French army had to accept a painful truth: that the Prussian and German states, using a system more akin to the former French system of conscription, could put several hundred thousand more men on the battlefield than could France.[54] By 1866 – the year of the Austro-Prussian War – even Napoleon himself was driven to accept that some form of obligatory military service was necessary if France were to have the troop strength necessary to take on the other great powers of Europe.[55]

Though the Emperor might be convinced of the need for a mass army of the people, implementing it would have meant winning over the Imperial establishment of ministers, deputies and army generals, most of whom were deeply conservative and distrustful of any reform which they associated with the Jacobin republic. Napoleon, by comparison, came across as radical in his pursuit of change, setting up a parliamentary commission to formulate reform and publicising his own ideas both in the pages of the *Moniteur* and in a minute to the Conseil d'Etat, in which he advocated the resumption of full-blown conscription. He favoured the call-up of everyone who was liable for service, though for a shorter period – the length of service was to be reduced to six years with a part of that time spent in the reserve – and urged that the number exempted be limited to the number of men who had been engaged the previous year.[56] The Emperor, in other words, was convinced of the need for France once more to have an *armée de masse*, as it had had in the Year II or under the First Empire. He made no secret, in the aftermath of Sadowa, of the size of the threat facing France, the threat of Prussia's army of 730,000 men.[57] But to get any kind of military reform through the Assembly and past the critical eye of the high command, his Minister of War, Marshal Niel, had no choice but to be conciliatory and to seek a compromise with the conservatives. He met strong opposition to compulsory service from the bourgeoisie and from agricultural regions like the west and Burgundy. In the Chamber the Party of Order took sides with conservatives in the army, arguing that

[54] Cox, *Halt in the Mud*, p. 166. [55] Serman and Bertaud, *Nouvelle histoire*, p. 313.
[56] *Ibid.*, p. 314.
[57] Crépin, *Défendre la France*, p. 276.

the long-service soldiers of France, even if their number were cut to 300,000, had nothing to fear – and little to learn – from the military models adopted by Prussia or Switzerland. And even those generals who admired the Prussians, like Trochu, saw little in the Prussian system that could be easily transferred to France, and so they limited themselves to advocating minor changes. Niel had no option but to side with these conservative voices in preparing a more moderate army bill which kept the annual ballot, but maintained the principle of long service for relatively few men rather than a short period of military training for the mass of the population. The length of service was extended from seven years to nine, with five in active service and a further four in the reserve. Exemption was abandoned and *remplacement* restored, so that once again the well-to-do could buy their sons out of soldiering. And – the major innovation in the law – a *garde nationale mobile* was established to incorporate all those judged fit for service who by one means or another escaped recruitment to the army proper (whether through drawing a high number in the ballot, or by being exempted, bought out or replaced). It was a modest enough reform, too modest in the view of many to answer the needs of the military, since it left the Emperor, in moments of emergency, with only the regular army of around 400,000 men on whom to call.[58] But it had, perhaps, symbolic significance, since it was the first time since 1818 that the French government had openly discussed the possibility of a return to conscription, and that arguments about civic obligation and equality had been made in the context of national defence.

That they were not made with greater urgency is a reflection of the ambition and the perceived success – especially, perhaps, in Africa and France's overseas colonies – of the army of the Second Empire. Army morale and the standing of the officer class were high, and there was less impetus to question the roots of the institution than there had been in the dog-days of the Restoration, when the fortunes of the military had hit their nadir. But that is not to ignore the anxieties about the state of the military which were expressed in certain quarters, the criticism that tactics were largely unchanged since the eighteenth century, or the suspicion that an army increasingly cut off from its civilian roots was open to abuse and moral decay. This view was most trenchantly expressed in 1867 by one of the army's more outspoken officers, General Trochu, soon to be pilloried by the radical Left for his role as Military Governor of Paris in 1871 and his enthusiasm for repressing the Paris

[58] Serman and Bertaud, *Nouvelle histoire*, pp. 316–17.

Commune.[59] But in his critique of military strategy during the Second Empire Trochu could himself appear as a radical critic of the establishment. In his influential study of *L'armée française en 1867*, Trochu declared himself on the side of the ordinary soldier, who, he felt, was left exposed to a raft of dangers as a result of his service.[60] The army, he believed, was responsible, and in need of reform, since it had become what he termed an 'instrument for destroying social distinction'. He went on to enumerate what he saw as the vices that emanated from army life – the forced idleness of life in barracks and army camps; the risk of moral degradation and debauchery; and the artificial division that was created between soldiers and civilians that made it so difficult for soldiers to readapt to the requirements of civilian life after their service was over.[61] In his critique there was more than a little of the republican ideal of the citizen-soldier, of the rural idyll of Chauvin, and of a timeless France of unspoilt villages, peasant farmers and *soldats-laboureurs*.[62]

Critics of France's military strategy argued that the French army had become overshadowed by that of Prussia, which was committed to a very different model of conscription and to the commemoration of the heroic sacrifice of young Prussians like Theodor Körner in the Wars of Liberation. Unlike Restoration France, Prussia did not renounce the idea of universal military service or cease to admire the ideal of the citizen-soldier as the heroic defender of family, community and nation. On the contrary, that ideal became consecrated in nineteenth-century conscription law.[63] The decrees of 1813 which had introduced conscription as a war measure were, unlike the French case, continued into peacetime by the Law concerning Compulsory Military Service, passed in September 1814. And though for much of the nineteenth century the numbers called to active service remained low, the principle that every Prussian had a military duty to serve the state was maintained. Citizenship and nationhood were more closely linked, with all those men between the ages of seventeen and forty who were subject to conscription – their numbers, admittedly, varied hugely from year

[59] James A. Leith, 'The war of images', in James A. Leith (ed.), *Images of the Commune* (Montreal, 1978), pp. 110–12; Frank Jellinek, *The Paris Commune of 1871* (London, 1937), p. 64.

[60] Trochu (général), *L'armée française en 1867* (Paris, 1867).

[61] Raoul Girardet, *La société militaire de 1815 à nos jours* (Paris, 1998), pp. 114–15.

[62] Gérard de Puymège, *Chauvin, le soldat-laboureur. Contribution à l'étude des nationalismes* (Paris, 1993), pp. 126–7.

[63] For a telling comparison between French and Prussian approaches to military service see Thomas Hippler, *Citizens, Soldiers and National Armies. Military Service in France and Germany, 1789–1830* (London, 2008), esp. pp. 163–89.

to year – obliged to offer personal service in the militia alongside the standing army. This in turn affected the image of the military and its place in German culture. Poets and novelists sang the praises of the chivalrous German boy hero, the son of good family, who volunteered to serve his country and did not baulk at the sacrifice of his own blood in the service of the fatherland. A legend of comradeship and fraternity, death and military sacrifice – a legend just as powerful among nineteenth-century German nationalists as that of the army of the Year II was for the republican half of France – had been born.[64]

For much of the century, it is true, the French leadership treated the Prussian army as a rival, but a rival they could confidently deal with in the event of war, and they comforted themselves with the belief that their forces, battle-hardened in Africa and in a succession of colonial wars, were a match for any in Europe. This was not a wholly unrealistic belief. Even within Europe they were able to win the two wars they fought during the 1850s, albeit at an exaggerated cost to human life. They therefore saw little reason to change their structures or their organisation, even though repeated experience suggested that the process of mobilisation was often painfully slow and that their supply trains were dreadfully inefficient. But their victories in the Crimea and against Austria in the 1850s caused the Prussians to reconsider their military strategy. Inspired by a new Chief of General Staff, von Moltke, who assumed his post in 1857, they took bold steps to restructure their army, revolutionising both its organisation and training. Von Moltke placed great store by the quality of his staff officers, who were chosen from among the very brightest cadets and who were given new levels of responsibility for decisions in the field. Plans were drawn up for the rapid mobilisation and deployment of the army in times of war. An Inspector-General of Communications was appointed with overall responsibility for supply. And in 1866 the potential of these reforms became apparent to the rest of Europe – and to at least some members of the French high command, among them Trochu – when Prussia trounced Austria in the Austro-Prussian War. Napoleon understood, too late perhaps, the full extent of the threat which France faced, but, as we have seen, was forced to accept a conservative compromise when Niel failed to force his more radical proposals for reform through the Chamber. Nevertheless, he had made a start to the process of reform, with the consequence that in 1870 the French had just under half a million men prepared for active service, of whom around 300,000 could be mobilised within three weeks. In addition they could call upon

[64] Hagemann, 'German heroes', pp. 118–24.

around 120,000 *gardes mobiles*. Their dilemma was that control of the North German Confederation meant that Prussia could now mobilise so many more, and do so more quickly. In 1870 Roon could put into the field an army that threatened to overwhelm the French – an army, well trained and rapidly assembled, that numbered 1,180,000 men, the result of putting their trust in a more democratic system of conscription, whereby large numbers of young Germans, sons of the bourgeoisie to the fore, were called upon to perform personal military service. Service, as redefined in the Army Law of 1868, remained for a period of three years, beginning at the age of twenty; the soldiers then served for a further four years in the reserve, before moving for two further years to the *Landwehr*. It was a model of a citizen army that came much nearer to the revolutionary idealism of 1793 than the compromise with vested interests which Niel had been forced to accept in the same year.[65]

The crucial test came, of course, in 1870 with the Franco-Prussian War, the moment which, for so many French soldiers and their officers, held out the promise of a trial of strength against their greatest continental rival and provided the opportunity for which they had been waiting to fulfil their destiny. For many it seemed a moment of release, when they could finally achieve their goal of fighting for France in a national struggle with Prussia, and make war – not peacekeeping in Spain or colonial adventures in the Maghreb, but the kind of war for which they had suffered such repetitive training, so many forced marches, so much boredom in the barrack towns of provincial France.[66] It was the moment, too, when the French military would be able to prove itself, to justify the policy that had been maintained since 1818 of putting faith in a small standing army, highly disciplined, well armed and drilled, and seething with self-belief. Confidence, of course, would prove to be tragically misplaced, as the humiliation the imperial army suffered at Sedan both administered a terrible shock to the army and destroyed the Napoleonic regime. The Emperor's indecision in the face of the enemy, the reluctance to form the divisional and corps structure before the outbreak of hostilities and the failure to grasp the potential of railways for mobilisation and supply, all contributed to the extent of the French defeat.[67] Its psychological impact cannot be overestimated. Any belief in the innate superiority of a small long-service army – the central pillar of military thought since the Restoration – was brutally shattered.

[65] Michael Howard, *The Franco-Prussian War. The German Invasion of France, 1870–71* (London, 1961), pp. 18–39.

[66] Girardet, *La société militaire*, p. 116. [67] Cox, *Halt in the Mud*, p. 183.

Sedan not only ensured the return of republican institutions; it also guaranteed a resurgence of republican sentiment and renewed demands for an army of citizens, for a return to the *levée en masse*. During the July Monarchy and the Second Empire, when republican ideas had been silenced and republican sympathisers forced into clandestine activity, the dream of a citizen army had proved stubbornly persistent on the political Left. In particular, romantic writers had helped ensure that the idea remained alive in popular memory throughout the hollow years of the nineteenth century. Victor Hugo's poem, *Châtiments*, published in 1853, famously contrasted the heroic soldier of the Year II, driven by his patriotism and his love of liberty, with the repressed troops of Louis-Napoleon, bereft of ideals or any concern for the people of France, who staged the *coup d'état* that would destroy the republic.[68] And Jules Michelet, in *Légende d'or*, expressed the gratitude felt by a nineteenth-century republican for the soldiers of the Revolution. He emphasised the total equation between the army and the people, and underlined the youth, the idealism and the heroism of that people. The army of the 1790s, he insists, was 'nothing other than France itself, fighting and dying to defend its laws'. It was an army united by bonds of friendship and fraternity, words which he consciously borrowed from the language of the First Republic. The soldiers, for their part, were the men of the federation, who had made common cause in the summer of 1790 'to unite and love one another in a shared *patrie*'. It is a memorable image. 'The federations of 1790', he writes, 'were the battalions of 92. Friends with friends, neighbours with neighbours, they set out hand in hand, fulfilling a commitment they had made two years earlier on the altar of the nation'. For Michelet, that was what distinguished the army of the French Revolution from the successive French armies of the nineteenth century: it was built on passion and hope, dedicated to the cause of the nation and to 'an immense crusade of fraternity'.[69] After defeat in 1870 it would again prove to be an intoxicating dream.

[68] John Horne, 'Defining the enemy. War, law and the levée en masse from 1870 to 1945', in Moran and Waldron, *The People in Arms*, p. 103n.

[69] Jules Michelet, 'Nos armées républicaines', in Paul Viallaneix (ed), *Oeuvres complètes de Michelet* (21 vols., Paris, 1980), vol. XVI, pp. 29–31.

6 The Franco-Prussian War

The Franco-Prussian War would be a turning point in nineteenth-century French military thinking, one that gave new impetus to those who saw in France's revolutionary past an answer to the problems of the present. In part, of course, this stemmed from the sheer scale of the defeat suffered by Napoleon III's armies, and by the humiliating speed of their collapse. The armies of the Second Empire were constructed on three principles which France had consistently applied since the Restoration and the recruitment law of Gouvion Saint-Cyr: the soldiers were long-service recruits, they were selected by ballot, and those who could afford to buy themselves out were authorised by law to do so.[1] The nation was shocked by the enormity of the defeat in 1870, inflicted not by a massive coalition of foreign powers of the kind France had faced in the past, but by a single state with a population scarcely larger than France's own. But it was not just public opinion that was shocked. So, too, was the high command, which had been so determined in its insistence that France's small, highly trained army was necessarily more effective in the field than armies based on wider recruitment where military service was a kind of rite of passage to adulthood and citizenship. They had gone into this war without trepidation, confident of the quality of their troops and training, buoyed by their successes in Africa and with a reassuring belief that their weaponry was as good as any in the world. There were reasons for this confidence. The new recruitment law of 1868 assigned men to five years' active service with a further five in the reserve, which seemed to ensure that the army would not lack in experience or professionalism (though it is important to note that the 1868 law also advocated the use in a future war of a *garde nationale mobile* and made provision for the recruitment of companies of *francs-tireurs*).[2] And they believed that they

[1] See Jean-François Chanet, *Vers l'armée nouvelle. République conservatrice et réforme militaire, 1871–1879* (Rennes, 2006), pp. 9–10.

[2] Pierre Cambon, 'Francs-tireurs et corps francs en 1870–1871: mythe et réalité' (mémoire de maîtrise, Université de Paris-I, 1976), p. 16.

were better armed than their predecessors, since the 1860s had brought new guns and more effective weaponry; in particular, the soldiers were now issued with a new breech-loading rifle with an effective range far superior to the Prussians (the *chassepot*), and with an early model of the machine-gun, the *mitrailleuse*.[3] Politically, too, all seemed set fair. Napoleon III had no sense that he was being manipulated by Bismarck into a war he would lose, and he, like his generals, headed east in July 1870 without premonition, confident of victory.

Their assurance was shattered in a few short weeks. The first encounter of the war, when the French under Bazaine took the town of Sarrebrücken, was a relatively minor engagement against markedly weaker opposition; yet it was hailed as a major victory that augured well for the campaign ahead. Everyone was in a mood to celebrate and optimism raged, both in the army and in the population at large. In the Paris press it was widely reported that Sarrebrücken had been burned to the ground and the Prussians overwhelmed; in Michael Howard's words, 'the expectations of the excited Paris public would be satisfied with nothing else'.[4] But within days these celebrations were shown to have been tragically premature, as the optimism they generated turned to bitterness and anger in the face of a series of damaging defeats from Wissembourg to Froeschwiller to Metz, each of which resulted in substantial French loss of life and the draining of any remnants of early euphoria. At Wissembourg, for instance, French losses in men dead, wounded and missing totalled around 23 per cent, while at Froeschwiller the figure rose even higher.[5] The autumn campaign culminated in the rout of the French army at Sedan and the imposition of a humiliating peace, with the army forced to capitulate to the victorious Prussians and Napoleon himself, now a broken emperor, compelled to lead his men off into captivity in Germany. The victory seemed total. The Prussians had taken 21,000 prisoners during the battle, and now what remained of the imperial army, a further 83,000 officers and men, passed into their hands.[6] The Berlin press had already been talking animatedly of the annexations that would follow, and Bismarck had made no secret of his desire to secure the western frontier of his new empire by annexing French territory. Bismarck had made this clear in a dispatch he wrote to the Prussian ambassador in London, Bernstorff, on 17 August. 'For us', he wrote, 'the only goal is the strategic security of our frontier.

[3] William Fortescue, *The Third Republic in France, 1870–1940* (London, 2000), p. 3.

[4] Michael Howard, *The Franco-Prussian War: The German Invasion of France, 1870–71* (London, 1961), p. 82.

[5] Stéphane Audoin-Rouzeau, *1870: La France dans la guerre* (Paris, 1989), p. 105.

[6] Howard, *The Franco-Prussian War*, p. 222.

Until such time as this is achieved through the cession of Alsace and Lorraine, we are resolved to pursue the war'.[7] For the French, too, the cost of peace was clear – the loss of large areas of French territory, payment of a large indemnity and acceptance of an army of occupation. These terms were made known to the French, and they were an important factor in strengthening their resolve to fight on.

Sedan proved a terrible psychological blow for the French military, a humiliating defeat that resulted from poor tactics and leadership as much as from the intrinsic failings of the army itself. The commander-in-chief, Bazaine, had fought a poor war, partly because of the instructions he received from Napoleon, but largely through his native caution and failure to press home his advantage when opportunities arose. In the bitter recrimination that followed, he was lampooned for incompetence, most notably when he failed to break out from Metz when he had the chance to do so, and accused of treachery in his diplomatic dealings with the Prussians. These were damaging charges, and his belief that he could win better terms by mediation with the Prussians was little more than self-deception. The Prussians made few concessions. They did not grant the defeated French army the customary honours of war, and the 83,000 French prisoners were herded off to Germany in demeaning circumstances, unkempt, unfed and with only the remnants of military discipline. Nor did the Prussians hold back from seizing their arms and equipment; Bazaine, it seemed, had failed to send out the order that flags and weapons must be destroyed.[8] In a highly critical article published in the *Revue des Deux Mondes* in 1871, Alfred Mézières noted that, when he took leave of his men, Bazaine 'imprudently' recalled the past achievements of great Napoleonic marshals like Masséna, Kléber and Gouvion Saint-Cyr. The inappropriateness of the parallel was obvious to all. 'Before they would negotiate', claimed Bazaine boldly, 'the soldiers of the Republic and Empire exhausted every form of resistance, threw themselves into combat and soaked up enemy assaults; they were never seen to capitulate on French territory, agree to hand over their weapons, or cause a French stronghold to be lost'.[9] He could scarcely make the same claim for his own army. His words were mocked by a Paris crowd baying for him to be put on trial, convinced that the army had been betrayed by their commander and that Bazaine was guilty of both cowardice and treason, charges that

[7] Quoted in François Roth, *La guerre de 1870* (Paris, 1990), p. 175.

[8] For an extremely hostile account, see Alfred Duquet, *Les derniers jours de l'Armée du Rhin* (Paris, 1888).

[9] Alfred Mézières, *Récits de l'invasion. Alsace et Lorraine* (Paris, 1913), p. 262.

were subsequently examined by a *conseil de guerre* at Versailles in 1873. Bazaine himself would later claim that his actions during the siege of Metz were dictated by his concern for his men, by the lack of food and fodder and their vulnerability to fevers and malnutrition; and his criticisms were reserved for those whose advance planning of the war had been so hasty and ill-conceived.[10] But the court did not see things that way, and he was found guilty on four charges, including those of laying down his arms in mid-campaign and surrendering the citadel of Metz to the enemy. He was sentenced to death and, though he was later reprieved, the stigma of failure lived on.[11] His generalship was widely condemned as a source of national shame, and the battles fought in August and early September 1870 did nothing to recall the heroism of Valmy or Jemmapes. The revolutionary tradition, many felt, had been allowed to die.

But if the generals were viewed as weak and self-seeking, and Napoleon's own position as the ultimate commander in the field as untenable, little of the criticism fell on the men in the regiments, the ordinary soldiers who had fought in the imperial cause. The Army of the Rhine, for instance, was an army of peasants, a young army drawn largely from rural areas, and its bravery would continue to evoke praise even after the fall of the imperial regime. Indeed, during the Third Republic the heroism of these young soldiers 'would assume the dimensions of a myth', albeit a myth with a strong basis in reality.[12] Republicans could reassure themselves that it was not the army of France that had been defeated so comprehensively, but the imperial army, an army loyal to, and recruited in accordance with the desires of, the imperial regime. In the same way, when Napoleon surrendered his sword to the Prussian victor at Sedan, his action was represented as an act of personal submission, not as the surrender of France. This was a distinction of huge significance, since it implied that the French people had not been defeated, and that the new government of the French people, in whatever form it emerged from the political vacuum created by the Emperor's departure, had an obligation to fight on. This message was most strongly upheld on the left, among those republicans who

[10] Achille Bazaine, *L'armée du Rhin, depuis le 12 août jusqu'au 29 octobre 1870* (Paris, 1872), pp. 206–8.

[11] The evidence presented at Bazaine's trial before a *conseil de guerre* was published in full by the *Moniteur universel* in Paris in 1873. He was found guilty and sentenced to death, stripped of the Legion of Honour and the military medal that had been awarded to him, and suffered *dégradation militaire*. See *Procès Bazaine (capitulation de Metz). Seul compte rendu sténographique in extenso des séances du 1er Conseil de Guerre de la 1ère Division Militaire* (Paris, 1873), p. 799.

[12] Audoin-Rouzeau, *1870*, p. 101.

had kept faith with the tradition of the Revolution, and especially in the capital. There had been, ever since 1792, a clear association between the republic and war, and on repeated occasions during the nineteenth century Paris had seen bellicose crowds demanding mobilisation for war or demanding popular sovereignty. They had made their mark in 1814, in the 1830s, in 1840, in 1848 and, most recently, in 1859 and 1863.[13] Once again, following news of Sedan, the more radical Parisian republicans faced the prospect of an expanded people's war with undisguised relish and optimism.

For Sedan did not just destroy Napoleon's army; it ended the Empire and provided republicans with the opportunity to seize control of the state. Imperial agents and administrators, with no government to report to, resigned or melted away, leaving local republican leaders in effective control. As news of the defeat reached the major provincial cities – Lyon, Bordeaux, Marseille – republicans simply took over office. In Paris there was a peaceful, bloodless revolution, with the deputies to the Napoleonic *corps législatif* declaring the demise of the Empire, which allowed Paris's republican deputies to proclaim the republic to an enthusiastic crowd from the balcony of the Hôtel de Ville and to reform themselves as a Provisional Government of National Defence.[14] In effect they had been legitimised by a popular revolution in Paris, with a mission to steer a defeated nation in war. This became ever more urgent as, in the days following Sedan, the character of that war changed. The French were no longer fighting on the frontier, but in the interior, with the main theatres of operations centred around Paris and along the Loire. The German high command was now installed in Versailles, not Berlin, and the next phase of the war would be fought in the heart of the French provinces. The government was geared for that war, and the new republic was visibly, like the republic of 1792, *en danger*. Indeed, the question was no longer whether France should fight on, but how she could most effectively harness the resources and energies of the people in the cause of national defence.

Republicans might have been harshly critical of Napoleon's war leadership and the levels of military preparedness under the Second Empire, but they did not question the need to finish the war, to salvage French honour and territory from the abyss of 1870. The republican tradition was still staunchly patriotic; it continued to equate the republic with the defence of the French people and to look back to the First Republic, and to the government of the Year II, for its symbolism and for much of its inspiration. And, like its revolutionary predecessor,

[13] Robert Tombs, *The Paris Commune, 1871* (London, 1999), p. 42. [14] *Ibid.*, p. 43.

the Third Republic came into existence through war, as an emergency government to stave off military disaster, a government founded on the ashes of French defeat. The republic was proclaimed on 4 September from the balcony of the Hôtel de Ville in Paris, in an address read out by Parisian radicals and counter-signed by the prefect of police of the Seine. Theirs was an act of revolution which, as they never tired of repeating, was not a usurpation of power but rather the filling of a void, a power vacuum that threatened the country with anarchy.[15] The address explicitly called on the citizenry to rally to the cause of the *patrie*, quite unashamedly using the language of 1793 and conjuring up memories of the nation-in-arms. It talked of resuming, after eighteen years, 'the traditions that were interrupted on 18 Brumaire and 2 December', the days when the first two republics had been overthrown.[16] It addressed a generation of French republicans who instinctively looked back to the 1790s and appealed to a Jacobin heritage to which they still believed they belonged. What they overlooked was the extent of the change in political culture which distinguished the France of 1870 from that of 1793. It was not possible in 1870 to recreate the 'unity and indivisibility' of the French Revolutionary years, and the new republic would be characterised by bitter factionalism. In particular, it failed to win over the majority of provincial Frenchmen to the patriotic cause or to persuade them of the need for sacrifice; at the same time Paris itself refused to be swayed by a moderate government and preferred to suffer the miseries of a long and harsh Prussian siege.[17] Parisian radicals tended to blame provincial France for a lack of patriotism, and to assume that this had its roots in self-interest. But for much of France the war seemed distant; it was fought somewhere else, far from where they lived and, increasingly, around Paris. With no French army opposing them, the Prussians advanced rapidly on the capital, reaching the suburbs on 19 September and immediately laying siege to the city.[18]

There was nothing ambiguous about the language of the appeal to arms, no suggestion of weakness or of a willingness to compromise with the military traditions that had prevailed since the Restoration monarchy. Those proclaiming the republic used a discourse that was uncompromisingly republican and which, in the tradition of Valmy, united army

[15] Eugène Pelletan, *Le 4 septembre devant l'enquête* (Paris, 1874), p. 59.

[16] A.D. Seine, Atlas 508, document 43, Declaration of the Republic, 4 September 1870.

[17] James R. Lehning, *To Be a Citizen. The Political Culture of the Early Third Republic* (Ithaca, N.Y., 2001), p. 9.

[18] Charles Freycinet, *La guerre en province pendant le siège de Paris, 1870–71* (Paris, 1871), p. 6.

and people in a common cause. It also, quite deliberately, drew parallels with the revolutionary era, parallels which a mid-nineteenth-century audience could not fail to recognise. 'The revolution which has been brought about', they insisted, 'has stayed entirely peaceful; it has understood that French blood should not be spilt other than on the field of battle. Its aim, as it was in 1792, is the expulsion of foreigners from French soil'.[19] On the following day the new mayor of Paris, Louis Arago, addressed his fellow citizens in similarly resounding tones, again reminding them of the triumph of their revolutionary forebears. 'Just as our fathers did in 1792, so I call on you today: Citizens, the fatherland is in danger!' He did not hesitate to remind them that the greatest signs of patriotism had always come from the city of Paris – 'in 1792, in 1830, in 1848' – nor that he himself spoke as 'an old soldier of the republic'.[20] Paris and the republic were as one, and it was for them, as citizens, to be vigilant and mindful of their great history. The same message was put forcibly to the people of France in an address of 5 September signed by Arago and a dozen other republicans, now appealing to the entire country for support. 'Frenchmen', they thundered,

> the people have gone beyond the wishes of the Chamber, which has allowed itself to hesitate. To save the *patrie en danger* they asked for the republic. They placed their deputies not in power but in peril. The Republic was victorious in 1792. The Republic has once more been proclaimed. The Revolution is made in the name of the law, of public safety. Citizens, watch over the polity that is confided in you: tomorrow, with the army, you will avenge the *patrie*.[21]

Once again, as in the 1790s, France was threatened from outside its frontiers, even if on this occasion it faced a single enemy, Prussia, rather than a Europe-wide coalition. Once again, a republican administration was calling on the French people to join a national crusade against the invader in order to save the nation and the republic.[22]

It had, as in 1792, little choice, since the imperial army had not simply failed on the battlefield, but had been decimated, its remnants melting away into prisoner-of-war camps in Prussia. If the new government were to fight on, then it had to find a new army, and find it rapidly, even before elections could be held. The urgency, the shock at the speed of

[19] A.D. Seine, Atlas 508, document 43, Declaration of the Republic, 4 September 1870.

[20] A.D. Seine, Atlas 508, document 44, *affiche* signed by the mayor of Paris, Etienne Arago, 4 September 1870.

[21] A.D. Seine, Atlas 508, document 45, *affiche* signed by Arago and a dozen other leaders (including Gambetta, Crémieux, Jules Simon and Jules Ferry), 5 September 1870.

[22] Philippe Darriulat, *Les Patriotes. La gauche républicaine et la Nation, 1830–70* (Paris, 2001), p. 272.

the Prussian advance, the humiliation of capitulation, the slow realisation that there was no longer a frontier to defend to the east and that what was left of the existing troops had been ordered to fall back to defend Paris, these all added to the sense of national emergency. In September 1870 there was a political as well as a military void that had to be filled, and without the luxury of time in which to plan. The provisional government reassured the population as well as it could, telling them of the bravery of their troops in the east, and of the rapid troop movements that would ensure the defence of Paris. In the capital, in advance of elections, a provisional municipal commission was set up to run the city until such time as a regularly elected body emerged. As early as 6 September the first decrees were being issued, and with them the first exaltations to patriotism and sacrifice. In the seventeenth *arrondissement*, François Favre, signing himself the provisional mayor of the quarter, made it clear that the authorities would count upon the patriotism of the population, but also – and this risked being more divisive – on their 'devotion to republican institutions'. And once again he spelt out what this implied. 'As you all know', he wrote, 'the word Republic signifies public order and respect for property; and when the enemy violates the sacred soil of France, it particularly means that all the citizens should be ready to accept any sacrifice, up to and including death'.[23] He warned that the commission would do everything in its power to defend the republic, and that, in this same spirit, it would repress acts of disorder and public resistance.

Within days the provisional government had put in place a series of republican measures which it saw as necessary to national defence, measures which often had their roots in the wars of the 1790s. In December the various *mairies* of the capital organised elections in the National Guard, elections to choose their officers, NCOs, sergeants and corporals, and they called on all members of the Guard to take part in the ballot. The guardsmen were reminded that they were free to select as officers whomsoever they wished: they were under no obligation, for instance, to choose men who had military experience or who had already fought in military campaigns.[24] Two days later, a poster addressed to the women of the fifth *arrondissement* reminded them that in a free society they, too, had an important role to play in war. So it had been, of course, in 1793 with the *levée en masse*, though interestingly

[23] A.D. Seine, Atlas 508, document 58, *affiche* addressed by François Favre to the *habitants du dix-septième arrondissement*, 6 September 1870.

[24] A.D. Seine, Atlas 508, document 78, *Avis de la Mairie du 5e arrondissement*, 10 September 1870.

it is with another republic, the United States, that the poster invited comparison, at the time of the Civil War. Here, too, the soldiers were civilians thrown into uniform by the outbreak of war; and here, as in revolutionary France, they had performed prodigious acts of courage and sacrifice. But it was the role of the women of America that attracted special attention: 'American women, taking initiatives in the serious and rational way we associate with free peoples, spontaneously organised – quite apart from aid societies – a complete ambulance service; and never has an army medical service found more intelligent or more devoted helpers.' They, too, were republicans, and in making their contribution to the war effort they were showing their republican credentials; and they could usefully act as an example to the women of Paris in France's current plight.[25]

All, it seemed, had a part to play, women and children as well as the male and able-bodied. The call was for volunteers, for a truly national effort to save France and French honour. And what did France mean to the radical generation of 1870? From the start the government emphasised the yawning moral chasm that separated a kingdom or empire like Prussia from a republic like France. In a call to arms to the inhabitants of the sixth *arrondissement*, the mayor, Hérisson, explicitly linked the impending battle to the rights of citizenship and membership of the French people. As citizens, as Frenchmen, they must enter 'that patriotic communion which will cause us to march as one against the enemy'. Patriotism in a republic, he reminded them, was a very special sentiment. It was not just a matter of defending their lives, their families or their property – the appeal that was routinely made to every citizen-army – but rather it had to do with the nature of France, 'that France which had been so great, so generous of spirit before the Empire', a France which represented 'civilisation itself, liberty, progress and the future of the world', values that now found themselves under attack from 'the bloody and barbarous invasion by German princes'. That, he concluded with a characteristic reference back to the 1790s, was why the French people would rise against the enemy, and would recreate 'the fiery passion of patriotism which, in 1792 and 1793, allowed our fathers to save the human race through the defence of our country'.[26]

Behind the rhetoric and the egalitarian ideals, the new republic had to have solid policies for war, and had to institute measures of policing

[25] A.D Seine, Atlas 509, document 93, *Aux Femmes du 5e arrondissement*, 12 September 1870.

[26] A.D. Seine, Atlas 509, document 113, *Le maire du 6e arrondissement, Hérisson, aux habitants*, 16 September 1870.

and repression to ensure that they were enforced. Mass recruitment, as the experiments of the French Revolution had demonstrated, was never going to be popular with everyone; there would be avoidance, attempts by individuals to buy themselves out or to bribe the recruitment officer to grant dispensations, cases of draft-dodging and desertion by those too frightened, exhausted or self-interested to carry on. The republic had to be severe if it was to be successful, and – as, once again, during the Revolution – savage penalties were prescribed for those who tried to shirk their civic responsibilities. In a series of decrees in the weeks following 4 September the new Minister of the Interior, Léon Gambetta, ordered the arrest of any soldiers found on their own in Paris, of possible deserters and of those suspected of spreading panic in the ranks. The death penalty was prescribed for those who deserted in the face of the enemy and a court martial set up in Paris. Once again everything was to be sacrificed to the cause of the nation. Individual freedoms could not take precedence over public safety, as the government did everything possible to throw large numbers of men against the rear of the Prussian army. All available forms of military force were to be used – whether regulars, volunteers or national guardsmen – and they were to be deployed as circumstances dictated. In the words of the decree of 24 September, they could be used 'either as guerrillas or as regular troops', an open acknowledgment by the government that they were prepared to use irregular forces where these offered a strategic advantage, and to appeal to the spontaneous anger of the population in the defence of the nation.[27]

In his appeal to the people Gambetta did not hesitate to summon up memories of France's republican heritage. On 21 September, the anniversary of the foundation of the First Republic, he issued a proclamation to the French people that reminded them what they owed to the Revolution and what they could learn from the patriotism of the first republicans. 'Citizens', he declared, 'today is 21 September. Sixty-eight years ago on this day our fathers founded the Republic and took an oath, faced with a foreign invader who defiled the sacred soil of the fatherland, that they would live in freedom or die in combat'. The Government of National Defence could not allow this glorious anniversary to pass, not just as a moment to savour, but so that it might serve as 'a great example' to the current generation of republicans. Gambetta noted that the revolutionaries had kept faith and had gone on to a memorable victory, with the consequence that 'the Republic of 1792 has remained in men's memories as 'the symbol of heroism and national greatness'. He expressed the hope that 'the powerful breath that stirred

[27] A.D. Seine, Atlas 509, document 152, decree of 24 September 1870.

those who went before us will pass into our souls', so that France might once more, as in 1792, be victorious.[28]

The Franco-Prussian War had been transformed into a people's war, fought by the Prussians against the people of France; it was therefore logical that the people were now called upon to rise against the aggressor. Although more moderate republicans, alert to the threat of social revolution, were reluctant to arm the working people of Paris, they were rapidly overtaken by the national emergency and the sudden centrality of Paris to the war effort. On 6 September the size of the Paris National Guard was increased by 90,000 men as the decision was taken to arm the populace, whatever the social risks this involved. The response was massive, as patriotism and social pressure combined to drive the young and able-bodied to enrol at the emergency recruitment stations set up in the streets and squares of the capital. From 12 September they had the additional stimulus of a daily indemnity to reward them for their service, a sum which would become vital to their families' survival during the 132 days of the siege. Parisians flocked to volunteer, in numbers that greatly exceeded the government's own targets, so that by the end of September 1794 new battalions had been formed. The National Guard now formed an army of 340,000 men, equipped with some 280,000 rifles and a small number of artillery pieces paid for by public subscription. Companies were locally recruited, neighbours from tightly-knit quarters of the city, sometimes from just a few adjoining streets. Many, especially those from the radical working districts of the north and east, were intensely politicised, breathing the fierce radicalism of Belleville, Ménilmontant or Montmartre.[29] Individual battalions took pride in their specifically Parisian inheritance, and gloried in their identification with the *sans-culottes* of the Year II; others, from the more bourgeois districts of the west of the city, were equally committed to the protection of property and to a more moderate definition of the republic. Such distinctions were in the nature of a people's army drawn from a burgeoning and increasingly disparate city, a city which had experienced massive immigration, especially to the east, and the expulsion of ordinary men and women from the city centre as a result of the ambitious urban renewal projects of Baron Haussman.[30] Battalions and companies became associated with a particular politics, some fighting for their ideology as much as for the nation as a whole.

[28] Reproduced in André Rossel, *1870. La première grande guerre par l'affiche et l'image* (Paris, 1970).

[29] Tombs, *The Paris Commune*, p. 46.

[30] Jeanne Gaillard, *Paris, la ville 1852–1870: L'urbanisation parisienne à l'heure d'Haussman* (Paris, 1977), pp. 204–8.

In Lyon, the effect was even more sectarian, with different units of the National Guard inheriting conflicting political ideologies from their revolutionary past – the egalitarian Jacobinism of Chalier, the moderate republicanism of the federalist municipality, even a residue of Catholic royalism. These tensions would be played out in the politics of the guard units.[31]

But in popular areas of Paris there was no such ambivalence. Here the call for volunteers to enrol in the Guard evoked pride in the city's republican past and was unambiguous in summoning up the spirit of 1792. A good example is the call for volunteers for the Guard of the fifth *arrondissement* on 26 October, by which time the siege of the city had begun to cause real suffering among the inhabitants. The mayor, Bentillon, warned of the increasing danger which Parisians faced and talked of Prussian confidence that they would starve the city to surrender. He called on his fellow citizens to form what he called 'an army of deliverance' to rescue Paris from encirclement, and he repeatedly referred to their ancestors, the 95,000 volunteers from the city who had marched resolutely against the invader in 1792, 'cutting them to pieces' at Valmy and Jemappes. 'Let us imitate them', he cried, and prove that the people of Paris have not degenerated since the time of Valmy. In a surge of oratory he appealed to the young men to join up en masse: 'In the name of national honour, in the name of your wives, your mothers, your children, in the name of your old folk, in the name of this great city which fought in 89, 92, 1830, 1848 and 1870, stand up and march against the enemy!'[32] A number of common themes are repeated here – the comparison of past and present, with the revolutionaries of 1792 held up as paragons for a new generation to emulate; the time-honoured appeal to masculinity in wartime, the young men the protectors of the old and weak, of women and children; and the identification with '89' and '92', which, unlike more recent historical precedents, are cited in a familiar, shortened form without fear that the reference would be missed or misconstrued. It was understood that the National Guard had been reborn in its revolutionary form, as an army of citizen-soldiers committed to the defence of the republic against its enemies.

This was less a deliberate measure of policy than a response to defeat in the field and, with it, a realisation that the existing National Guard – the guard that had been recruited following the law of 1868 – lacked

[31] Bruno Benoît, 'Garde nationale et tensions sociales à Lyon, 1789–1871', in Serge Bianchi and Roger Dupuy (eds.), *La Garde nationale entre nation et peuple en armes. Mythes et réalités, 1789–1871* (Rennes, 2006), pp. 449–50.

[32] A.D. Seine, Atlas 512, document 322, *Enrôlements pour les bataillons de volontaires de la Garde Nationale, 5e arrondissement*, 26 October 1870.

sufficient idealism and patriotism. Napoleon III had shown little faith in the institution of the Guard, always seeing it as potentially revolutionary and going so far as to dissolve it completely in 1852. And what had re-emerged after 1868 was often a socially conservative body, whose officers were representative of the property-owning classes of society. This was the force that would be formed into companies for active service in 1870, and the composition of local units suggests that they were far from the revolutionary avant-garde of mythology. The case of Nantes provides an interesting insight into the kind of men who became officers and non-commissioned officers in the volunteer companies of the National Guard that were raised for war service. They were not drawn from the working classes or those who had manual jobs, but almost entirely from the merchant community of a large port city. Their captain was an inspector of gambling and gaming; the lieutenant and second lieutenant a sailor and a commercial agent in a trading company; the sergeant-major a lawyer; and the sergeants an entrepreneur, a banker, a driver with the highways department, and two clerks in trading houses. They were, in other words, solidly representative of respectable, commercial circles, the majority unmarried (only two of nineteen in this sample had wives or families), and generally aged twenty-five or over. They had volunteered for guard service, had a taste for adventure, and claimed to have been inspired by their patriotism to offer themselves in the defence of the nation.[33] That was, however, the extent of their debt to the National Guard of 1792, and they had little reason, as professional men and sons of bourgeois families, to associate themselves with the tradition of revolutionary Paris. The Guard of 1870 was seldom a force for social revolution, despite the propagandist efforts of some republicans to make it so.

In republican memory, on the other hand, the National Guard was an essential element in the nation-in-arms, its contribution marked as much by its spontaneity as by its equality of sacrifice. And in the second, republican phase of the war, when the defence of the country could easily be confused with that of Paris, that identity was more firmly based in fact. In Paris and its suburbs, in particular, guardsmen fought tirelessly to defend their townships, their streets and homes, and to protect the capital against the enemy. But there was another source of confusion, with the *franc-tireur*, the irregular partisan who, in 1870 as in 1814, rose to defend his immediate community when it came under attack, and who came to represent those quintessentially French military qualities

[33] A.D. Loire-Inférieure, 2R 140, register of the officers of the Compagnie des volontaires de la Garde Nationale de Nantes, 1870.

of energy and selflessness. The *franc-tireur* was not a member of any official force: he was, at least in principle, an irregular fighter, a partisan in the tradition of the Spanish guerrillas of the Peninsular War, who took up arms spontaneously, as a citizen and a Frenchman, to fight off the hated *Uhlans* and defend his town or village. He was often the product of one of the many shooting clubs that had sprung up in the 1860s, and had to provide his own arms and equipment.[34] His valour was all the greater in that he enjoyed none of the privileges accorded to soldiers in wartime: the Prussians regarded irregular troops as brigands and common criminals, and they were liable to summary execution as criminals if they fell into enemy hands. But, especially in the early stages of the war, not all the *francs-tireurs* conformed to this image. Their recruitment was authorised by law, first in 1868 – when the same law that created the *Garde Mobile* allowed for the recruitment of companies of 'Francs-Tireurs Volontaires', to be employed 'for the defence of their region and to ensure the security of their homes' – and later, in some desperation, during the summer of 1870 as the news from the front grew worse. Some were even incorporated into regular companies, with batteries of artillery in support. Guardsmen and *francs-tireurs* fought alongside one another in the same battles, until by July 1870 they were being talked of as a valuable resource for the nation, and not just as defenders of their local communities. On 12 August, indeed, as France struggled to build up numbers in the army, prefects in a number of regions were asked to encourage, quite indiscriminately, 'the formation of units of volunteers, *gardes mobiles* and *francs-tireurs*'.[35]

It was the defeat at Sedan and the creation of the republic that changed the role and image of the *franc-tireur*, transforming him into an archetypal republican military hero, risking all to save his country. In response to Sedan, men flocked to enlist, so that for the first time the partisans could be equated with the people in arms, enthusiastic and dedicated to the cause of France. Their image was a heroic and exemplary one, that of the ordinary citizen who turned into a resistance fighter and so exposed himself to the most barbarous reprisals in the cause of the people. The actions of the *francs-tireurs* attracted admiration from the French as much as they attracted the opprobrium of the Germans. In prints and lithographs they were usually depicted, brimming with self-belief, rising spontaneously from the midst of the people in the best traditions of the Year II and recalling the acts of self-sacrifice of the

[34] Cambon, 'Francs-tireurs et corps francs', p. 12.
[35] Robert Molis, *Les Francs-tireurs et les Garibaldi: soldats de la République, 1870–1871, en Bourgogne* (Paris, 1995), p. 13.

partisans of 1814. Some formed themselves into *corps francs* to engage in military operations against the Prussians, while others indulged in disorganised guerrilla activity, taking pot-shots at German soldiers from hiding places behind hedges, often armed with no more than old hunting rifles. All were volunteers, local men who had responded to the call of the *patrie en danger*, amateurs in a republic increasingly suspicious of professional armies. They volunteered in thousands, in Paris especially where over 20,000 men came forward, but there were solid responses, too, in many parts of the provinces – 1,132 in the Ardennes, for instance, 1,165 in the Gironde, 1,250 in the Indre-et-Loire, 1,823 in the Bouches-du-Rhône, 2,807 in the Seine-inférieure, 3,325 in the Nord.[36] Units proliferated throughout the country, encouraged by the new republican government to think of themselves as the saviours of the polity. Gambetta's appeal in *Le Siècle* of 25 September expressed this eloquently, in a tone and a tradition that they understood. The *patrie*, he declared, was again *en danger*. It was a moment when every Frenchman had a part to play, and he called on his fellow countrymen to take up whatever weapons they had to hand, 'scythes, axes, sticks, come in vast numbers, and torment the enemy army. Stop its convoys, cut its lines of communications, and destroy its provisions'. Soldiers and partisans, he implied, should make common cause, since they were equally essential in the defence of the republic.[37]

This was the image of the Franco-Prussian War which republicans treasured, an image that linked the patriot of 1870 to his revolutionary ancestor and revived memories of the people in arms. It was also an image of tragedy, of sacrifice by the French people, and of the martyrdom of the republic. Nothing could mask the fact that France was badly defeated, though explanations were quickly offered. If the early weeks of the war were inglorious, that could be explained by the political context of the 'emperor's war', a war fought without enthusiasm for a cause in which few believed. If the French lost, it was not because of the fighting qualities of their soldiers, but because of poor leadership, inadequate mobilisation plans, a lack of trained reserves and the absence of an effective general staff.[38] Instead, the myth grew of a glorious 'people's war', called for by the new republic, that involved high casualties among the volunteers and inordinate suffering by the civilian population. The

36 Exact figures are disputed, and these should be taken as indicative only. Cambon, 'Francs-tireurs et corps francs', p. 74.

37 *Ibid.*, p. 68.

38 Terry W. Strieter, 'The impact of the Franco-Prussian War on veterans. The company-level career patterns of the French army, 1870–1895', *War and Society* 7 (1989), p. 25.

levels of popular resistance and the exemplary courage shown by both soldiers and civilians allowed France to claim a moral victory amidst the defeat inflicted by Bismarck. That they were defeated was never challenged: as at Waterloo, there developed a culture of defeat that was also a culture of sacrifice, a celebration of France's ability to survive lost battles and summon up its moral strength in a glorious act of patriotic resistance.[39] What historians have challenged is the validity of the myth itself, the belief that a large segment of the population rushed to make sacrifices in the name of the republic, or that the advancing Prussians inflicted huge damage on the civilian population. This, it has recently been suggested, was an invention, a convenient alibi for failure, since in many parts of the country the call for a partisan insurrection was met with embarrassing indifference, especially among the peasantry, while agriculture was largely left undisturbed by the Prussian invasion, even in many departments that lay directly in the invader's path.[40] The *francs-tireurs* who fought, and fought courageously, in the *corps francs* were as likely to have come from Rio, Buenos Aires or Montivideo as from the departments of rural France; Garibaldi supplied his revolutionary force from Italy; and in the *Armée des Vosges* there were Poles, Greeks, Spaniards and even some Egyptians, as well as a sprinkling of French volunteers.[41] As for France itself, it was not the nation as a whole that responded to the challenge of a people's war. The provincial cities – Lyon, Bordeaux, Rouen and the rest – provided their share of soldiers. But, to a quite disproportionate degree, it was a single city, Paris, besieged, isolated from the national government and increasingly a prey to radical and insurrectionary ideas, which responded to the call for volunteers and made the language of the people's war its own.

The long siege of the capital, dragging through the winter months, would lead to revolution and civil war and ended any pretence of republican unity. The insurrection of 18 March divided the new republic against itself, with conservatives denouncing radicals, and provincial France blaming Paris for the failure of the armistice and for the continued presence of German troops on French soil. And the Commune ended in bloodshed, arson and the savagery of a bitter civil war. For the

[39] The theme of sacrifice is developed in Jean-Marc Largeaud, 'Waterloo dans la mémoire des Français, 1815–1914' (thèse de doctorat, Université de Lyon-II, 2000). See Robert Tombs, 'Making memories of war: images of heroism and turpitude, 1870–1871', in *French History in the Antipodes. Proceedings of the Twelfth George Rudé Seminar on French History and Civilisation* (Wellington, New Zealand, 2001), p. 64.

[40] Sanford Kanter, 'Exposing the myth of the Franco-Prussian War', *War and Society* 4 (1986), pp. 20–1.

[41] Molis, *Les Francs-tireurs et les Garibaldi*, pp. 28–36.

government at Versailles the radicals of the Commune were rebels to be hunted down and punished, rebels who were responsible for the torching of the finest buildings in the city, the heinous murder of priests in the Rue Haxo and a paroxysm of violence in the streets of the capital. No compromise could be considered; the battle between the republic and the Commune was fought to the death, the republic levying terrible reprisals on those who had taken part. Yet it is impossible to dissociate the violence of the Commune from its revolutionary rhetoric and its insistence on arming its citizens, which rapidly led to disorder and to a loss of political control. Whereas in September 1870 the defence of the city was left largely to the National Guard, who had a commitment to maintaining public order, that discipline evaporated under the Paris Commune. After March 1871 control increasingly passed to informal units or *corps francs*, some of whom were former guardsmen, others citizens who had found weapons by the simple expedient of disarming soldiers of the national army as they fled the city. The result was a proliferation of units and commandos, of revolutionaries committed to defying the national government or harbouring a romanticised idea of the revolutionary traditions of the city. The *corps francs* were formed in response to the siege, spontaneous creations with colourful names often redolent of 1793, the *Enfants du Père-Duchesne*, the *Tirailleurs de la Marseillaise*, or the *Légion des Enfants Perdus*. In all, there were twenty-eight *corps francs*, with around 11,000 men. They attracted men with a romantic sense of adventure, among them some who had deserted from the regular army or moved across from the National Guard. Many were committed to the republican cause or were romantic revolutionaries who volunteered because they believed in the republican and socialist ideas which the Communards preached. But their lack of discipline and a marked taste for violence meant that they helped to increase levels of disorder in Paris and added to the sense of anarchy in the city.[42]

The Communard leaders took every opportunity to link their cause with that of the French Revolution, and parallels with the army of the Year II were ubiquitous. The Paris National Guard shared this vision, and by the spring of 1871 they were calling on the people to rise, spontaneously, in defence of their fellow citizens and against the forces of invasion and occupation. This in turn called for a 'patriotic fever' that reflected the commitment of the people themselves; it could not be achieved by the deliberations of bureaucratic commissions. 'In the same way', explained the central committee of the Guard in an appeal to

[42] Georges-Ferdinand Gautier, *Les Francs-tireurs de la Commune* (Paris, 1971), pp. 4–17.

Parisians on 4 March, ‘the patriotic fever which in a single night raised and armed the entire National Guard did not result from the influence of a provisional commission appointed to create legal statutes; it was the real expression of an emotion felt by the population’.[43] Spontaneity and enthusiasm had become the most treasured of qualities, the spark that could turn the anger and suffering of Parisians into revolutionary commitment. The government, of course, regarded this as a dangerously Parisian vision, one they denounced as subversion, and in a virulent campaign of counter-propaganda Thiers appealed to self-interest and to the desire for public order. He urged the majority to make their views known, and sought to defend France against what he saw as an irresponsible and insurrectionary movement that was unelected and had little support in the wider community. To this end he called on the National Guard to defend the republic against the Communards, men who were ‘almost all unknown to the population’, who pillaged and murdered in the name of their ‘communist doctrines’.[44] The difference between them lay, of course, in their opposing definitions of the republic and of the revolutionary tradition on which it was built. For the Commune the Versailles government and its army did not constitute a truly republican government; it was better understood as a government of the bourgeoisie. They believed that the true republic could not exist without the support of an army of the people, a revolutionary army answerable to the population. Hence they called for the dissolution of the permanent army on which the government relied, and the right of the National Guard to assure the defence of Paris – a National Guard which had the right to elect its own leaders and would be reorganised so as to guarantee the rights of the people,[45] a National Guard that could pull France back from the abyss ‘as our fathers did in ‘93’.[46]

Their language only confirmed this. The military arm of the new republic had to behave in the manner of the soldiers of the First Republic, whereas the troops of the Versailles government ‘placed themselves beyond the laws of war and of humanity’, which in turn left the Commune with no option but to resort to reprisals. The struggle, to their eyes, was little different from the wars of the 1790s that pitted

[43] A.D. Seine, Atlas 527, document 1, *Appel du Comité Central de la Garde Nationale*, 4 March 1871.

[44] A.D. Seine, Atlas 527, document 4, *Adresse aux Gardes Nationaux de Paris*, 18 March 1871.

[45] A.D. Seine, Atlas 527, document 37, *La Fédération Républicaine de la Garde Nationale aux citoyens de Paris*, 24 March 1871.

[46] A.D. Seine, Atlas 527, document 55ter, *affiche of the Démocrates socialistes du 17e arrondissemont*, March 1871.

republicans against royalists, the revolution against its enemies. The threat to the sovereignty of the people had not changed. In the words of an address by the Commune to the people of Paris on 5 April, this was still a war between revolution and counter-revolution, exactly as it had been in 1793.

> Each day the bandits of Versailles murder or shoot our prisoners, and there is not an hour that passes that does not bring news of one of these massacres. The guilty men, as well you know, are the policemen and *sergents de ville* of the Empire, the royalists of Charette and Cathelineau, who march against Paris to cries of 'Long live the King', with the white flag of the Bourbons at their head.[47]

The language of royalism and the easy references back to civil war in the Vendée are eloquent here, the struggle between good and evil where the soldiers of the good were necessarily recruited in the tradition of the Year II. The people, the Communards insisted, had the right to defend themselves from oppression, against an enemy that was now routinely condemned in the language of the first revolution. The government forces were no longer acknowledged to be in any sense republican. They were regularly vilified as 'royalists', '*chouans*' or 'Vendeans' – direct references to the enemies of the republican armies in the previous civil war – while the government that claimed to speak for the republic was dismissed as 'the clerico-royalist forces of reaction in Versailles'. In the rather Manichean way of all civil wars, that of 1871 equated the republican cause with the moral character of its armed force.[48]

Art and caricature played a leading role in the service of the Commune, and they employed a wide range of revolutionary symbolism, some of it dating back to the 1790s, though supplemented by more recent additions to republican iconography. Significantly, the temptation was still strong to justify Paris's military effort in traditional terms that recalled the sacrifices of the Jacobin republic. Paris itself was represented as a militant female figure in the mould of a radical Marianne, leading the people of the city towards the Promised Land and driving back the Versailles leaders, often depicted as diminutive pygmies or with men of the regular army at their back. In several cartoons the Commune is presented as the latest of a long series of Parisian revolutions, dating back to 1830 and suggestive of a revolutionary spirit in the city which successive moderate and socially conservative governments had failed to quench.

[47] A.D. Seine, Atlas 527, document 103, address of the Commune to its citizens, 5 April 1871.

[48] A.D. Seine, Atlas 527, document 137, *affiche* of the deputies of the fourth arrondissement, n.d.

A poster printed in praise of the National Guard was illustrated by a whole panoply of revolutionary symbols linking the present revolution with the Paris of 1792, symbols which James Leith pithily synthesises as 'the liberty bonnet, the pike as weapon of the common people, the cannon standing for popular force, and the fasces representing republican unity'.[49] Such caricatures could not fail to make a deep impression. They were reproduced in the pages of left-wing and radical newspapers, printed as wall bills and posters, displayed in shop windows and, as single printed sheets, included in the stock of pedlars and street vendors. Unsurprisingly, they unleashed a barrage of counter-images from the government, as Versailles took up the cartoonists' challenge, manipulating images of anarchy and destruction to blacken the reputation of the Commune.[50] The French Revolutionary tradition was transformed into a wanton rage of destruction and arson, the view on the Right being as apocalyptic in this matter as that on the Left.[51] Notably, many of the conservatives who were driven to intolerant invective by the violence of the *francs-tireurs* and the destruction of the *pétroleuses* focussed their anger on that which they saw as most monstrous and unnatural, the presence on the barricades and in soldiers' uniforms of women of the popular classes. Caricaturists like Charles Bertall emphasised the prominent part played by women in the Commune's lines, their hair and dress deliberately made to appear harsh and masculine, stressing a barbaric, unnatural appearance which came close to disguising their sex in a disturbing image of the world turned upside down.[52] What for one side constituted the revolutionary valour of the people only confirmed for their opponents their brutishness and lust for violence.

The venom with which the Commune was greeted by moderate republicans guaranteed that, when the insurrection was quelled, the vengeance and retribution that followed would be exemplary in its scale. The radical leaders of Paris, some Jacobins in the tradition of 1793, others socialists and anarchists born of nineteenth-century class struggles, were rounded up and summarily executed during the *Semaine sanglante* that followed its final defeat, those who had borne arms for the Commune being mown down in their thousands as provincial France

[49] James A. Leith, 'The war of images surrounding the commune', in James A. Leith (ed.), *Images of the Commune/Images de la Commune* (Montreal, 1978), p. 116.

[50] David A. Shafer, *The Paris Commune. French Politics, Culture and Society at the Crossroads of the Revolutionary Tradition and Revolutionary Socialism* (London, 2005), p. 87.

[51] J.M. Roberts, *The Paris Commune from the Right* (London, 1973), p. 32.

[52] Gay L. Gullickson, *Unruly Women of Paris. Images of the Commune* (Ithaca, N.Y., 1996), p. 195.

exacted terrible revenge on the people of the capital. Paris, so long looked up to by writers and artists as a city whose master narrative was revolution, was now reviled as a treacherous city that undermined order and placed national security at risk in the pursuit of its sectarian goals.[53] In the process the National Guard, too, fell from favour, along with the Commune's vision of a spontaneous army of the people, that revolutionary ideal of the people in arms that had been revived, if only briefly, in the desperate weeks of the siege. Like the Allies in 1814 and the Prussians in 1870, republican France insisted that its army must remain the monopoly of the state, and it showed little sympathy for partisans and irregulars, little tolerance of the revolutionary ideal of an army drawn from and answerable to the common people of the capital. That the new republic would have to reform the military was not in doubt: the scale of the military disaster in 1870 had exposed the weaknesses of the military philosophy that had been dominant since the reforms of Gouvion Saint-Cyr. But for the moment, at least, radical critics of that philosophy had also been silenced. The revolutionary ideal, which had been reborn in the context of the Prussian invasion, had failed to provide the unity that France craved, instead turning Parisians against provincials, fathers against sons, Frenchmen against Frenchmen in the bitterness of a civil war. There could therefore be no simple return to the army of the Year II. Instead the conservative republicans of the 1870s, in an attempt to come to terms with the double disaster of 1870–1, sought to reconstitute the national army by a series of partial reforms which would, in the words of Fustel de Coulanges, create the 'necessary link' between the country's military and its political institutions. Without that link, he warned, neither the army nor the state could function adequately, and the inevitable result would be what Thiers and the government feared most, another revolution: 'If the army is not fashioned in the image of the State, then after a short time it will mould the State to its own image.'[54]

[53] Priscilla Parkhurst Ferguson, *Paris as Revolution. Writing the Nineteenth-century City* (Berkeley, Calif., 1994), pp. 197–200.

[54] Fustel de Coulanges, 'Les institutions militaires de la République romaine', *Revue des deux mondes*, 15 November 1870, p. 314, quoted in Jean-François Chanet, *Vers l'armée nouvelle*, p. 11.

7 The army of the Third Republic

After 1870 the military debate remained closely aligned to the character of the state and reflected the sharp divisions within the French political class. France was now finally a republic, a regime whose identity would evolve until, within a decade, it was defined not only by constitutional rules and a juridical system, but, in Maurice Agulhon's words, by 'a complex set of values' that were subject to 'opposing interpretations and rival passions'.[1] At the heart of these lay a republican ideal of citizenship, a male, secular citizenship rooted in universal suffrage and in revolutionary concepts of liberty and equality before the law. But it was an ideal that could not be achieved overnight. From its faltering beginnings in national defeat in September 1870, the Third Republic was a desperately insecure regime, fighting off the ambitions of both monarchists and Bonapartists as it groped to create new institutions and establish its legitimate authority. It was a task made all the harder by the recent bloodletting of the Commune, which led to widespread fear of disorder and antagonisms between Paris and the French provinces.[2] Politics became polarised between the Right and Left, until in 1873 France came close to seeing the restoration of the monarchy, as an alliance of monarchists and conservative republicans seized the initiative and elected Marshal Patrice MacMahon, the military commander who had suppressed the Communards, to the presidency. It would be 1875 before the Third Republic had a constitution, or a series of constitutional laws, and they would be of a rather timorous, conservative character, far removed from the rhetoric of the more radical republicans like Gambetta or Clemenceau. Legislative authority was divided between the president and two chambers, the National Assembly and the Senate, instead of being concentrated in the legislature as the Left demanded. Senators had to be forty years of age, and three-quarters of

[1] Maurice Agulhon, *The French Republic, 1879–1992* (Oxford, 1993), p. 1.
[2] James R. Lehning, *To Be a Citizen. The Political Culture of the Early French Republic* (Ithaca, N.Y., 2001), pp. 1–13.

them were to be elected by French departments and colonies. Mayors were appointed rather than elected. In the minds of the founding fathers of the Third Republic, social order was paramount.[3]

The political landscape of 1870 would be rapidly transformed during a decade of manoeuvring by the various factions within the republican elite. Alert to the threat of reaction, they sought to isolate the monarchists and protect France from the threat of a Bourbon restoration. A new consensus had to be found, recent hatreds laid to rest and the supporters of the Commune reintegrated into the ranks of a republican Left who combined ideas of social justice with a rabid anti-clericalism born of the tradition of the 1789 revolution. In the immediate aftermath of the Commune, that Left had been held in check, and its ideals restricted to the sphere of political rhetoric by an administration committed to the restoration of moral order. By 1876, however, the ultraconservative regime had given way to the so-called 'Opportunists', republicans like Gambetta, Grévy and Ferry who would provide the bedrock of French republican politics in the years ahead. Their first aim was to reunite public opinion behind the republic. To this end they appropriated the person of Adolphe Thiers, the arch-conservative of 1871, now resurrected as the very embodiment of responsible republicanism.[4] His death in 1877, and the state funeral that followed, allowed for a public celebration of his life, 'a public ceremony performing republican political culture on the streets of Paris'.[5] The police and the press alike noted the mood of calm and reverence in the streets of the capital, and Paris began once again to be considered as part of the political nation, its republican character defined not by violence and brutality, as it had been in 1871, but by political participation and a respect for the institutions of the state. Radical politicians were no longer cowed into silence by fear of being identified with mob violence and were able to espouse with undisguised enthusiasm policies that had their roots in the revolutionary politics of the 1790s. From 1879, with the return of the Waddington administration, the radical republic had come of age. With its emphasis on anti-clericalism and secularisation it embraced revolutionary values of liberty and equality and openly identified with its Jacobin heritage.

François Furet goes so far as to end his history of 'revolutionary France' in the late 1870s, when the radical republicans established a

[3] William Fortescue, *The Third Republic in France, 1870–1940. Conflicts and Continuities* (London, 2000), pp. 28–9.

[4] Bertrand Taithe, *Citizenship and Wars. France in Turmoil, 1870–71* (London, 2001), p. 169.

[5] Lehning, *To Be a Citizen*, p. 64.

new era of political stability and asserted once more the supremacy of the law over individual rights, what he terms 'the reunion of the republican country and its tradition'.[6] This was achieved symbolically in 1880 by the designation of 14 July, a day forever associated in the public mind with the assault on the Bastille, as France's national festival, the day which above all others stood for the values of the new republic.[7] The national anthem would be the Marseillaise, the battle-song of the First Republic which commemorated the bravery of the soldiers of the Year II, and which – or so republican mythology has it – had been penned in a spurt of patriotism by the young officer Rouget de Lisle in response to a challenge from Mayor Dietrich, in April 1792 in Strasbourg.[8] It was an uplifting story, which evoked concepts of fraternity and was the subject of a famous painting by Pils that proved one of the most popular and enduring images for the new generation of republicans. The Marseillaise had not lost its radical associations: it had been sung by republicans and radical workers' associations in 1848 and had helped unite the opponents of the Second Empire during the 1850s. And it was adopted as the new French anthem in 1880, at that moment when the men proscribed after the Commune were allowed by a general amnesty to return from exile. The whole of republican Paris could again unite and rejoice in the words of the former battle-song of 1794.[9] But there was, for Furet, a third element of republican symbolism that was every bit as important as the choice of anthem or of the day for a national festival. In 1875 the new constitutional law had laid down that 'Versailles is the seat of government and the seat of parliament'. Yet four years later the two chambers left Versailles for Paris. It was a symbolically powerful moment, since they were following the same road as that taken by Louis XVI and his family in 1789. On that occasion the King had been forced to leave the safety of Versailles and place himself in the custody of the Paris crowd. But 'when the deputies and senators followed the same route, ninety years afterwards, it was as representatives of the people, reconciling the nation with its capital. The French Revolution was coming into port'.[10]

With them the new generation of radical deputies brought clear views about the proper character and composition of a republican army, ideas which derived from their republican reading of French history,

[6] François Furet, *Revolutionary France, 1770–1880* (Oxford, 1993), p. 537.
[7] Christian Amalvi, 'Le 14-juillet. Du dies irae à jour de fête', in Pierre Nora (ed.), *Les lieux de mémoire. 1 – La République* (Paris, 1984), pp. 421–72.
[8] Hervé Luxardo, *Histoire de la Marseillaise* (Paris, 1989), esp. pp. 91–6.
[9] Frédéric Robert, *La Marseillaise* (Paris, 1989), p. 93.
[10] Furet, *Revolutionary France*, p. 537.

the romantic view of a citizen army which they had ingested from the writings of Victor Hugo and Edgar Quinet, Alfred de Vigny and especially Michelet.[11] But until the radical victories of the end of the decade, there had been no such consensus, as the political leadership lived in fear of popular revolution. They were faced with the contradictory lessons of the Franco-Prussian War and the Paris Commune, the one pointing to the need for broad, national recruitment, the other warning against the revolutionary tradition of a people's army as it had manifested itself on the barricades of the capital. They were cautious men, fearful for public order, but aware, too, of just how strongly popular opinion had opposed the reintroduction of conscription when the idea was floated in the 1860s after the shock administered by the Prussian victory at Sadowa. Of course opposition had fallen away in 1870, when the frontiers of France were exposed and the country invaded. Emergencies justified emergency measures. But the evidence so carefully collected by the prefects after 1866 and during discussion of the Loi Niel showed that the French remained hostile to military conscription in peacetime, or for use in overseas adventures like Napoleon III's incursion into Mexico. Prefect after prefect reported that the wealthier sections of society – the *classes aisées* – continued to oppose any measure that would force their sons to serve in person, believing that their interests and those of the army would both be best served by retaining *remplacement* in some form. Some, like the *procureur impérial* in Nancy, even made the case for privileged treatment in terms of France's sacred duty to equality, arguing that 'a farmhand, a day labourer or countrydweller has more to gain than to lose by spending six years in the regiment'. On the other hand, there was little benefit for the young man who 'through the chance of birth or the often excessive sacrifices made by his family could have devoted himself to serious study', and who, almost by definition, saw his whole future shattered by army service.[12] Officials pointed to the high levels of resentment caused by the threat of compulsory service in rural areas, where farm labour was at a premium and the fields risked being left untilled. The arguments used, indeed, are strikingly similar to those that greeted the first conscriptions of the Napoleonic Wars, with peasant France to the fore in protecting its sons from the recruiting-sergeant.[13]

[11] See Christian Croisille and Jean Ehrard (eds.), *La légende de la Révolution. Actes du colloque international de Clermont-Ferrand, juin 1986* (Clermont-Ferrand, 1988).

[12] Letter to the Garde des Sceaux, 14 January 1867, quoted in Annie Crépin, *Défendre la France. Les Français, la guerre et le service militaire, de la Guerre de Sept Ans à Verdun* (Rennes, 2005), p. 297.

[13] Alan Forrest, *Conscripts and Deserters. The Army and French Society during the Revolution and Empire* (New York, 1989), pp. 110–11.

The *procureur* at Caen went so far as to emphasise the link between the current threat of military service and the memory of Napoleonic conscription among the rural communities he administered. Local people, he reported, and especially rural communities, 'imagined that we were going to renew the *levée en masse* of the First Empire and herd them off again to the end of the world'.[14] There was a crying need, in his opinion, for greater public awareness, for more education and understanding of their civil obligations. It was a lesson that the radical politicians of the Third Republic would take to heart.

But in the immediate aftermath of the Commune, the political argument for conscription had been won. The new republic, while it distrusted Paris and rejected the sort of revolutionary spontaneity that had pushed the country to the brink of civil war, was committed to some form of conscript army. The conscription laws that had been rejected in 1867 had been adopted as a military necessity in 1871, and they were widely accredited with restoring something of France's battered pride after the humiliation of the Prussian invasion. If France had lost, indeed, it was because the Empire had been so reluctant to accept an all-encompassing system of military service, in marked contrast to the Prussians, whose national army elicited grudging admiration from among the French high command. If the Prussians were able to put more men in the field than the French, and if their soldiers conducted themselves so effectively, it was because they imposed a three-year period of military service on the young, creating a truly national army of the sort of which the French revolutionaries had dreamed. In 1871, as in 1813, many saw in Prussia, not in the various French army reforms since Waterloo, the model for a modern nation-in-arms. And, it was argued, the introduction of universal personal service would bring important civil benefits to match the improvements to the military. Against the backcloth of popular violence and amid memories of Paris in flames, the draft was also seen as a salutary form of social discipline for France's youth. It was in these terms that the conservative Marquis de Chasseloup-Laubat recommended a conscription law to the National Assembly in 1872: 'When all classes of society are mingled together in a body of men, especially in an army where discipline reigns, it is the noble sentiments that emerge triumphant, the good examples that are followed, and the whole moral level that is raised.'[15] For liberals

[14] Letter to the Garde des Sceaux, 11 October 1866, quoted in Crépin, *Défendre la France*, p. 293.

[15] J. Monteilhet, *Les institutions militaires de la France, 1814–1932. De la paix armée à la paix désarmée* (Paris, 1926), p. 136.

and conservatives the mingling of the social classes would have another advantage. They saw it as a useful form of social cement, a means of reducing popular violence and social anger, and hence of restricting the appeal of working-class politics and socialism. The army, in other words, could be turned into an instrument of social reconciliation and help to create a nation that was finally at peace with itself.[16]

The most significant change in public opinion in 1870 was undoubtedly in the conservative camp, among men who in the past had argued fiercely for the virtues of a professional army and who instinctively distrusted the notion of an 'army of the people'. Conservatives looked to the army to impose strict discipline on the young, and through discipline to induce a sense of patriotism and duty. Chasseloup-Laubat did not renounce his conservative social values, or the interests of the rural *hobereaux* among whom he counted himself. When he introduced his bill to the Assembly he pointed to the social benefits that could be derived if a whole generation of young Frenchmen were made to serve in the military. He reminded his listeners that the army had twice saved France from social upheaval, in 1848 and in 1871, and suggested that it would now save a new generation from the dangers of moral corruption: 'So let all our children go there, so that compulsory service may become the *grande école* of generations to come!' He believed, as did many of his conservative colleagues on the benches of the Chambre des Députés, that corruption was especially rampant in countries with democratic regimes, where the poor and ill-educated always posed a threat of violence. 'The more a society is based on democratic principles', he proclaimed, 'the more it needs that obedience to a higher authority which is military discipline, the submission to the law which is civil discipline, and – let us dare to say it openly – severity towards anyone who breaks the rules which society itself has imposed'. Only in that way, he concluded, could order and liberty be assured for the population at large.[17]

Throughout the debates that preceded the new recruitment law ran a dual strand of argument. The law must produce an efficient and well-trained army, and it must also suit the needs of a French society which, the politicians insisted, was more anarchic in spirit, less naturally disciplined than that of Germany. For that reason it would not be sufficient simply to imitate the Prussian recruitment of 1870 and impose a three-year term of military service on everyone. They needed a model to suit the French temperament, not the German. But there was no

[16] Michel Auvray, *L'âge des casernes. Histoire et mythes du service militaire* (Paris, 1998), p. 195.

[17] Raoul Girardet, *La société militaire de 1815 à nos jours* (Paris, 1998), pp. 122–3.

easy solution, no text that would satisfy all interests. It was pointed out that neither the *armée de métier* nor the citizen-soldiers who had served in the Franco-Prussian war had fared very well against the Prussians. Many in the military argued that effective army training took longer than three years, and that by imposing a relatively short term of universal military service they would produce a large, straggling and undertrained force that would be incapable of defending France's frontiers when war was resumed – as everyone assumed it would be – against the new German *Reich*. Besides, there were important budgetary considerations at a time when the relatively modest level of German armaments could not justify the maintenance of a large French standing army in peacetime. The government believed that a force of around 450,000 men would suffice for the needs of defence, of which 120,000 would be career soldiers who could provide qualities of professionalism and tactical awareness.[18] But they knew that money could not be the only consideration. In particular, they could not ignore the republican tradition of equality, or the argument that universal military service was a key adjunct of citizenship.

The generals remained unconvinced. If applied literally, universal conscription would result in a large, young and unwilling army of short-term soldiers, poorly trained and posing huge problems of barracks accommodation. For many parents, moreover, the image of the French army in peacetime was still the classic image of the 1850s and 1860s, of young men corrupted by the temptations of the tavern and the brothel, who risked losing the habit of work and with it any ambition for social advancement. It was further damaged by its identification in the minds of many Frenchmen as an army of the poor, an army in which, right through to the Crimean War, the system of *remplacement* had effectively preserved the sons of the rich from the need to serve in person. With the onset of that war replacements were so coveted that their costs had spiralled, with the result that many of those called up in 1854 and 1855 had been obliged to renounce any dream of finding someone to serve in their stead.[19] There was a booming trade in replacement insurance for those unlucky enough to draw a low number in the ballot, a further index of the desperation of better-off families to extract their sons from soldiering.[20] As a result, the Law of 1872 was scarcely the product of

[18] Richard D. Challener, *The French Theory of the Nation in Arms, 1866–1939* (New York, 1955), p. 38.

[19] Bernard Schnapper, *Le remplacement militaire en France. Quelques aspects politiques, économiques et sociaux du recrutement au dix-neuvième siècle* (Paris, 1968), p. 211.

[20] M. Levi, *Consent, Dissent and Patriotism* (Cambridge, 1997), p. 89; Lars Mjøset and Stephen van Holde, 'Killing for the state, dying for the nation', in Lars Mjøset and

political idealism. It prescribed two different degrees of military service, one far more arduous and time-consuming than the other, with each individual's fate resting on the outcome of a ballot. Those who drew a *bon numéro* faced six months to a year of military training, whereas drawing a *mauvais numéro* meant a full five years in the regiment, followed by a further four in the reserve. All were then assigned for five years to the territorial army, with six more in its reserve. No-one could buy a replacement. This was a juggling exercise that allowed everyone to claim a moral victory: it provided the army with the seasoned soldiers they required, answered the republican demand with at least a semblance of universality, and limited the total size of the army. It also demanded a degree of personal service from everyone, including those sons of the bourgeoisie who were widely supposed to have escaped scot-free in the past.[21] But the more radical republicans saw it as a shabby compromise that created two distinct classes of service and left the army desperately short of officers and *sous-officiers*. By 1881, following the disappointments suffered by the French in Tunisia, Léon Gambetta himself was won over by calls for a new law that demanded a minimum of three years' military service for all.[22]

For the radicals, who after 1880 enjoyed an increasingly powerful parliamentary position, the main flaw in the 1872 law was the continued inequality between those who were drafted into the army for long-term service and the majority who escaped with a year or less. In some cases it was much less: 30 per cent of the annual contingent was completely exempted, while a further 20 per cent served for only a year. The burden of army service was still falling on only half the cohort.[23] They argued that this was an affront to the sacred principle of equality, a denial of the ideal of the nation-in-arms, in short, a betrayal of the heritage of the Year II. It did little, they insisted, to resolve the issue of national morale or to educate the next generation of Frenchmen in their patriotic duty, the civic role which they saw as essential to the regeneration of the country after 1871. Charles de Freycinet was not alone in declaring that the French had a passion for equality, a passion born of republican principles; or in concluding that 'the day when the conception of a national army, or the nation in arms, was born,

Stephen van Holde (eds.), *The Comparative Study of Conscription in the Armed Forces (Comparative Social Research,* vol. XX, 2002), p. 43.

21 Auvray, *L'âge des casernes*, pp. 107–8.

22 Jean-Claude Jauffret, *Parlement, Gouvernement, Commandement. L'armée de métier sous la Troisième République, 1871–1914* (2 vols., Vincennes, 1987), vol. I, p. 359.

23 Challener, *French Theory*, p. 60.

the idea of absolute equality imposed itself as a natural consequence'.[24] Egalitarianism thus became the subject of impassioned debate, with increasing pressure to legislate an equal period of service for all – an argument that dominated in the lower house, but which met with resistance from the army high command and with repeated rejection by the Senate, which continually intervened to protect those in cultural and educational careers from the need to serve in person. The liberal professions, argued the senators, required long years of preparation and study, and they applied the same argument to schoolteachers and to the *bêtes noires* of the radicals, the clergy. It was only in 1889, following years of political speeches and newspaper editorialising on the issues of equal obligation and the benefits and disadvantages of a mass army, that the 1872 law was reformed and the obligation to serve in person shared more widely. The 1889 law was still something of a compromise, in that not all had to make an equal contribution. But neither was anyone completely exempted from service. Around 70 per cent of young Frenchmen had to undergo a full term of service, now pegged at three years instead of five; the other 30 per cent, including many in the professions, had to spend a year in the military, so that all young males had acquired some military training in the event of another war. In this way, the politicians argued, the country had learned from the mistakes of the Second Empire; and the nation was prepared, once again, to take up arms to defend French soil.[25]

It is instructive how far the debates leading up to the law of 1889 were predicated on the principles of the French Revolution, and the discussions littered with references to Valmy and the sacred ideals of equality and citizenship. The parliamentary debates of the 1880s constantly returned to the question of equal obligation, which would in turn mould individual Frenchmen into a single, cohesive nation. Sharing the same conditions and the same sacrifices with others would, it was believed, create national identity and root out class antagonisms and resentments. Paul Bert, in a speech to the Chamber in 1884, put this case uncompromisingly when he argued that 'there is only one way by which you can create a true unity of spirit in this country, and that is a uniform period of service and absolutely equal conditions for everyone'.[26] It was an increasingly prevalent view in the Radical party, where many saw the 1889 law, like its predecessor, as an unsatisfactory compromise that

[24] Freycinet, *Souvenirs, 1878–93* (Paris, 1914), quoted in Challener, *French Theory*, p. 58.
[25] Challener, *French Theory*, pp. 59–60.
[26] Speech of 29 May 1884, quoted in Crépin, *Défendre la France*, p. 342.

continued to draw arbitrary distinctions between citizen and citizen, and to leave young Frenchmen at the mercy of the *tirage au sort*.

Throughout the nineteenth century the moment of the *tirage* had weighed heavily on every town and village in France, the moment that would determine whether a young man could continue his civil existence and devote himself to his career and his family, or whether he had to leave the community behind and spend long years in the military. For many republicans it was the epitome of inequality and unfairness, something that jarred with the egalitarian principles at the heart of the republican tradition. Among those who faced the next *tirage*, the looming threat of military service was also a shared bond, a common identity as a *classe*, which provided a natural friendship group, a category of belonging identified by their youth, their gender and the shared circumstance imposed by the law. On the eve of the ballot they were given the freedom of their communities, celebrating together their virility, their lifelong friendships and the threshold of their adult lives. It was a moment when they were expected to dress up, to drink copiously and to celebrate their youth, and the public space – the streets, the market square, the bars – was theirs for two or three noisy, bibulous days of celebration. A high level of licence was afforded to the *conscrits*: the boys of the *classe* would shout and sing, sound horns, get wildly drunk, and take part in the dances and banquets that marked the *fête*, and in the evening there was considerable sexual licence, too. Older men, those of previous *classes*, had their place in the ceremonies, as did the families of the young. As for the conscripts themselves, it was a ceremony to mark their transition into manhood, a rite of passage marking their departure from the protection of their families to play their own part in the nation and the wider community. During the Third Republic it became the principal rite of passage between first communion and marriage.[27] Printed tickets bearing the number drawn by each man were produced and distributed, and the conscripts traditionally stuck them on their hats to boast of their new status. That is how they would be remembered in nineteenth-century songs and lithographs, while their village balls and popular festivities were widely celebrated on cheap etchings and woodcuts.[28]

Of course, these popular celebrations were not just statements about friendship and adolescence; the young men who drew low numbers, those deemed 'bons pour le service', were also conscious of their

[27] Michel Bozon, 'Conscrits et fêtes de conscrits à Villefranche-sur-Saône', *Ethnologie française*, nouvelle série 9, numéro 1 (1979), pp. 29–46.

[28] Henri George, *Conscription, tirage au sort et imagerie populaire* (Paris, 1981), pp. 7–11.

vulnerability, and no doubt apprehensive about the challenges that lay ahead. The ritual itself was curiously ambiguous, what Michel Bozon defines as 'a strange mixture of maturity and immaturity, of imagination and conformity, aggressive virility and sentimentality'.[29] And of course the celebrations were soon ended, and with them the moment arrived when the new conscripts had to leave their family and village behind and head off for life in the regiment. They were often accompanied by parents and siblings to the village boundary or the outskirts of the town, but then they were on their own, their minds concentrated on the unfamiliar lifestyle that lay ahead, and which they knew only through rumour and the stories brought home by those who had gone before. Life in the barracks would mean more than the new challenges of bearing arms and undergoing training exercises. It involved accepting new constraints and military discipline, looking after personal effects, washing and cleaning – in short, a degree of independence and autonomy that came as a shock to most young men of their age. It involved acclimatising to a new sociability, a certain gregariousness that many peasant boys found dauntingly unfamiliar; gone forever, it seemed, was the opportunity for silence or solitude. The moment of departure for the army was often one of muted conversation as the reality dawned that their lives would never be the same again.[30]

Some among them faced the reality of war, for even in years of peace between European nations, France's armies were engaged in colonial adventures and in policing insurgency in her African possessions. For raw recruits this could be a most daunting assignment, with the perils of heat and disease adding to the military dangers that they faced. It was a test of physical endurance as much as of courage or tactical skill, and was one of the principal reasons why so many army officers, even in the republic, were reluctant to endorse the revolutionary view of the nation-in-arms or advocate a short period of military service for all. In Africa, they pointed out, this was not a practical option, since it took months to train the new recruits, plus the long periods required to ship them to and from the colonies. Colonial service filled the fever wards and took a heavy toll in young lives. The result was a new form of inequality which the polemical Urbain Gohier denounced as a glaring injustice. With the 1889 law the period of service in the colonies was fixed at two years; hence it was from among the men called upon to serve for three years that France filled her colonial units, while the more privileged, who

[29] Michel Bozon, *Les conscrits* (Paris, 1981), p. 10.

[30] Odile Roynette, '*Bons pour le service*'. *L'expérience de la caserne en France à la fin du dix-neuvième siècle* (Paris, 2000), p. 214.

served for only one year, were effectively exempted. 'As a result, the inequality in their period of service is aggravated by a terrible inequality in the level of risk to which they are exposed'.[31] The extent of that 'terrible inequality' became clear during the colonial campaigns of the 1890s, when thousands of young Frenchmen died in the colonies, the majority from diseases like typhoid and dysentery. In Indochina between 1884 and 1896 the official death toll was 12,555 in a force of fewer than 20,000 soldiers and seamen. Public outrage greeted the news of French losses in Madagascar in 1895, where malaria cut down the young conscripts in their thousands, assisted by poor healthcare in the regiments and an almost total lack of immunisation. Of 15,000 soldiers sent on the expedition, 8,000 were conscripts, drawn from garrisons across France. The expedition was a disaster in human terms, resulting in the deaths of nearly 6,000 soldiers, of whom only twenty-three were killed in battle. The rest were the victims of disease, of the army's inadequate medical provisions and of its failure to take steps to acclimatise its men to what awaited them in Africa.[32]

Increasingly, too, the young soldiers came to accept the likelihood that they would be called on to serve in a new war in Europe, the war of revenge against Germany to liberate the 'lost provinces' of Alsace and Lorraine to which the political leadership made repeated reference before the turn of the century. As they marched forth from their villages, the new conscripts sang of war and revenge as much as of comradeship; they looked to a future of victory and bloodshed. On leaving Villefranche-sur-Saône, for example, the local conscripts' 'Chanson de la Classe 1900' promised action and revenge. The song talked of the 'blessed day that brings revenge', when, they promised, 'we will pick up our weapons and fight for our country, for the country we love'.[33] As the new century approached, they were no longer playing at war; they were actively training for a conflict in which they might be asked to lay down their lives, and which, as the Franco-Prussian War had demonstrated, would be conducted against well-armed and well-trained troops. It was a context in which the issue of equality rapidly assumed renewed importance.

Historians disagree about how immediate the threat of war really was during much of the Third Republic, and in particular during the 1890s when relations between the republic and its army were often

[31] Urbain Gohier, *Le service d'un an* (Paris, 1899), p. 21.

[32] Auvray, *L'âge des casernes*, pp. 126–7.

[33] 'Chanson-marche offerte à l'occasion de la Fête du tirage au sort des conscrits de la classe 1900', in *Salut la classe! Exposition de l'Ecomusée Nord Dauphiné* (catalogue, Villefontaine, 1986), p. 24.

tense, and when the language of *revanche* was heard far less often than in the immediate aftermath of 1870. Alsace and Lorraine seemed to have slipped from the political agenda, as a series of colonial rivalries with Britain, and most notably the confrontation at Fashoda in 1898, served to divert public attention from the renewal of a continental war with Germany.[34] This was not, however, the thinking of the military themselves, since the army's raison d'être was closely linked to the belief that war with Germany would soon be resumed. Military planning concentrated heavily on the defence of France's new eastern frontier, and between 1887 and 1892 alone five new plans were drafted on the shape of the war to come, while the signature of a defence treaty with Russia in 1894 opened the way to a more offensive foreign policy.[35] Was there, however, the political will to match the resolve of the general staff? And did the distrust of the politicians not undermine the army's strategic goals? The campaign by General Boulanger during the 1880s had underlined the danger inherent in a politicised military, reviving the fears of a military putsch that had convinced the politicians of the First Republic of the need for a citizen-army in the first place. His ability to appeal both to disgruntled Bonapartists and to disempowered royalists showed how much of a threat the Right, in the person of a charismatic army officer, could still pose to the republic and its institutions.[36] One effect, inevitably, was to increase republican suspicions of the officer corps, suspicions which republicans felt were justified by the evidence of political plotting and of a damning cover-up within the army as the Dreyfus Affair unfolded. In its attempt to defend its reputation at the expense of Dreyfus' liberty, in its willingness to launch attacks on the republic's Jewish supporters – most notably Joseph Reinach – as in its choice of political allies in the bitter public recrimination that followed, the army high command opened itself to charges of political machination against the same republic that it was paid to serve. It also showed how isolated it had become from French society, with its own values, its own system of justice and a wide net of patronage.[37] The fact that the Catholic hierarchy leapt to the army's defence only strengthened the conspiracy theories and hastened the army's political isolation.[38]

[34] Eugen Weber, *France, fin de siècle* (Cambridge, Mass., 1986), p. 195.

[35] Guy Chapman, *The Dreyfus Trials* (London, 1972), p. 4.

[36] William D. Irvine, *The Boulanger Affair Reconsidered. Royalism, Boulangism, and the Origins of the Radical Right in France* (Oxford, 1989), p. 20.

[37] Robert Gildea, *The Past in French History* (New Haven, Conn., 1994), p. 142.

[38] See Pierre Birnbaum, *Les fous de la République. Histoire politique des Juifs d'Etat de Gambetta à Vichy* (Paris, 1992), pp. 204–5.

The implication of some of France's best-known generals in political scandal did much to destroy what was left of the army's prestige among republicans, and contributed to the growth of anti-militarist sentiment on the Left, a development which could not but further weaken the bonds between the republic and its military. Anti-militarism among republicans had a number of roots and sources of inspiration. They condemned the army's role in the colonies, where they saw it as an instrument of repression used for political goals against indigenous populations. They questioned its use to maintain public order in France itself – a traditional role for the military, but one which, with the advent of the industrial age, had come increasingly to be identified with strike-breaking and the repression of workers' movements. And they disputed the role of the general staff in war, when the territory of France was exposed and its people endangered.[39] Increasingly, socialists took up the cause of anti-militarism, arguing that the army represented not the nation or the people of France, but rather the interests of the ruling class, and especially of the factory owners and capitalism. They believed that capitalists made wars to expand their business interests, killing workers to increase their already bloated profits. This argument grew more vociferous after the massacre of ten textile workers by troops at Fourmies in the Nord, killed while demonstrating for better working conditions, and other massacres followed, especially in coal-mining towns. Working-class anger was increasingly directed at the army, and its paymaster, the republic. In his *Cathéchisme du soldat*, in 1894, Maurice Charnay gave memorable expression to this new militancy among socialists. Militarism he condemned as an 'instrument of servitude' to keep the working classes in order; barracks were likened to prisons for workers in uniform; and wars were denounced as 'meaningless orgies of killing and destruction' fought in the dual interests of capitalism and government.[40] Charnay expressed himself more uncompromisingly than most, but he was not alone in adopting an anti-militarist position or in denouncing the military goals of the republic. An increasing number of socialists took up one of two positions – either that wars should be fought democratically by the nation-in-arms, or that war must be rejected in all circumstances as meaningless butchery. *La Voix du Peuple*, the official mouthpiece of the socialist union, the CGT, gained particular notoriety for its fierce anti-militarism in the early years of the twentieth century, presenting the

[39] Gildea, *The Past in French History*, pp. 140–1.

[40] Paul B. Miller, *From Revolutionaries to Citizens. Anti-militarism in France, 1870–1914* (Durham, N.C., 2002), p. 27.

conseil de révision as a meat market where the naked bodies of conscripts were cursorily inspected before being stamped on the shoulder with the words, 'fit to kill', like cattle about to be driven to the slaughterhouse.[41] Jaurès was far from the only socialist to have become a convinced pacifist in the years before the Great War.

If the spread of pacifist sympathies dimmed enthusiasm on the Left for the idea of the nation-in-arms, there were counter-currents at play in the 1890s and the first years of the twentieth century which helped restore faith in the old revolutionary mantra. The political distrust which the generals brought down on themselves brought professional soldiering into disrepute, with the consequence that many on the Left demanded that France turn once more to an army of citizens, on the model of those mythical heroes of the Republic, the victors of Valmy. They were helped, of course, by a generation that had served in 1870 and had seen the motherland once again in danger, and by a republic that increasingly looked back to the French Revolution for its inspiration. Nationalism and the Revolution were more and more linked in the public imagination, especially after the institution of Bastille Day as France's national festival in 1880.[42] The choice of the *Quatorze juillet* may seem doubly significant, since it both identified the new republic with its revolutionary inheritance – a vague inheritance, as much the bourgeois revolution of 1789 as the republic militant of 1793 – and chose a moment within the Revolution when the actor was the people themselves, a symbol of popular sovereignty, a moment that was democratic and distinct from the part of any single leader or statesman.[43] And it was not only men of the Left who were glad to embrace this revolutionary inheritance. Authoritarian republicans and nationalists also looked to the Revolution as a great vector of national energy, and they gave particular emphasis to the role of the revolutionary armies as they spread the doctrine of liberty across Europe. From Maurice Barrès to Paul Déroulède, nationalist republicans praised the energy of the Great Revolution, looking back with pride to the achievements of the soldiers of the Year II who not only defended France's frontiers but led a successful imperial crusade across the European continent.[44] Even Boulanger himself declared his loyalty to both the army and the republic, two institutions which, he declared, were not irreconcilable. He

[41] *Ibid.*, pp. 78–9.
[42] Jean-Pierre Bois, *Histoire des 14 juillet, 1789–1919* (Rennes, 1991), pp. 148–51.
[43] Amalvi, 'Le 14 juillet', p. 426.
[44] Christian Amalvi, 'Nationalist responses to the Revolution', in Robert Tombs (ed.), *Nationhood and Nationalism in France: from Boulangism to the Great War, 1889–1918* (London, 1991), p. 39.

reminded Frenchmen that, as Minister of War in 1886, he had helped to form republican opinion; and if now he was returning to the army, it was as a 'simple soldier', called to the colours by the seriousness of the military threat that France faced. It was, he insisted, his way of proving 'that in all circumstances I know how to be loyal to my duty both as a soldier and as a republican'.[45]

The French were further reminded of their debt to their revolutionary past by the celebrations organised to mark the centenary of the Revolution in 1889 and during the years that followed. In Paris the inhabitants were treated to a succession of festivities and commemorations, from the festival to mark the opening of the Estates-General at Versailles on 5 May through to the closure of the Universal Exhibition on the Champ de Mars on 6 November.[46] For many, the essence of 1889 lay in the Exhibition and the Eiffel Tower, as much a celebration of modernity and the age of steel and electricity as it was a reminder of the sacrifice of their ancestors.[47] But here and throughout France the celebrations that were organised by mayors and municipalities placed the accent on the most memorable moments of the Revolution, its great men, its soldiers and its triumphs, while the militants of the Ligue de l'Enseignement ensured that it retained a pedagogic role in alerting the young to the rights and obligations of citizenship.[48] In Paris statues were erected to Danton and, more symbolically, to the Triumph of the Republic, while several of the Revolution's greatest soldiers – Carnot, Marceau and La Tour d'Auvergne – were granted the honours of the Pantheon. And while Pascal Ory is undoubtedly right to point to the importance of local initiatives in acts of collective memory, with societies, associations and municipalities to the fore, there was no doubting their direction or their import.[49] The Centennial was an act of republican piety, presenting the Revolution in its most progressive light and emphasising the sacrifice of those who had helped Frenchmen to enjoy the political and civil rights of citizenship.[50] It also provided a fitting

[45] Georges Boulanger, *La Lettre Patriotique du Général Boulanger: sa déclaration républicaine* (Paris, 1887).

[46] For a discussion of the different aspects of these celebrations, see the brochure produced by La Documentation Française, *Le Centenaire de la Révolution, 1889* (Paris, 1989).

[47] The divisions produced by the planning of the centennial are discussed in Brenda Nelms, *The Third Republic and the Centennial of 1789* (New York, 1987).

[48] Pascal Ory, 'Le centenaire de la Révolution Française. La preuve par 89', in Pierre Nora (ed.), *Les lieux de mémoire. 1 – La République* (Paris, 1984), p. 531.

[49] See, for instance, detail of the Centenary as it was celebrated in the Dauphiné in Philippe Nieto, *Le centenaire de la Révolution dauphinoise. Vizille, un mythe républicain* (Grenoble, 1988), *passim*.

[50] Pascal Ory, *Une nation pour mémoire. 1889, 1939, 1989, trois jubilés révolutionnaires* (Paris, 1992), pp. 146–7.

tribute to its military traditions and a reminder of the debt that all Frenchmen owed to the soldiers of the Year II.

Celebrations of the centenary of the Revolution were a skilful mixture of public entertainment and military pomp, as befitted public festivals in the last years of the nineteenth century. The government and local councils were eager to encourage an enthusiastic attendance, peppering the celebrations with banquets and fireworks, dances and *bals publics*. The fireworks were a matter of pride and artistry, with professional companies of artificers and 'entreprises de fêtes publiques' hired to guarantee displays that would amaze and entertain the audience. Just as with the *fête nationale* on 14 July, soldiers marched and paraded, and the celebrations were interspersed with the spectacle of military bands and the blaring of martial music. In Nantes in 1892, for instance, the proceedings opened with a twenty-one gun salute on the eve of the *fête*, followed by a torchlight procession by the army; on the fourteenth itself there were two further salvos of gunfire, a military procession and a review of the troops, before the rest of the day was given over to a patriotic play, a *kermesse*, balls and carnival, ending with the launch of a hot-air balloon and fireworks over the harbour.[51] So with the *fête* to mark the centenary of the Republic two months later, when again the Nantais were treated to a round of military salvos, popular festivities on the major squares, an exhibition of gymnastics and free theatrical presentation, boat races on the Loire, a free orchestral concert, games and the illumination of public buildings.[52] On neither occasion were the proceedings directly propagandist, though their political purpose was not in doubt, the presence of the troops serving as a reminder of the solemnity and patriotic ardour of the occasion. They were there to provide colour and a symbol of national unity.

Some, however, could not bring themselves to unite under the banner of a republican tricolor. Devout Catholics were outraged to find that they were expected to celebrate a republic which conjured up images of padlocked churches and guillotined priests. If in 1889 the Archbishop of Paris was prepared to come to Versailles for the ceremony to mark the centenary of the Estates-General, in 1892 – the centenary of the republic – he was understandably more circumspect. Many Catholics regarded this phase of the Revolution with abhorrence, preferring to offer expiatory masses each 21 January for the soul of Louis XVI, a king who, they believed, had been murdered – some would say martyred – by the republican state. This time the Archbishop politely declined,

[51] A.M. Nantes, I-1 23, programme of the *fête nationale* of 14 July 1792.
[52] A.M. Nantes, I-1 23, programme of the *fête nationale* of 22 September 1892.

reminding the minister that, although the Church felt no hostility towards the institutions of the republic, the seizure of the historic Eglise Sainte-Geneviève by the state to create the Pantheon had made too recent and too painful an impression on the clergy, and he took the opportunity to remind republicans, with the slightest hint of a threat, that 'the best guarantee of stability for the republican government lies in respect for the Christian traditions of France'.[53] The Catholic press was rather less diplomatic. In the *Revue des conférences populaires*, for instance, Gailhard-Bancel was scathing in his attack on the politicians of 1789, the men who, in his view, had corrupted the wishes expressed by the French people. 'There are', he insisted, 'two eighty-nines: the 89 of the people and the 89 of the disloyal deputies; the 89 that leapt out of the heart and soul of France, and the 89 that resulted from the errors, the cowardice, and the treason of an assembly that had usurped power'. And, the article concluded, since 'the one is the contradiction of the other' it was unthinkable that Frenchmen should be asked to confuse them or to celebrate their centenary without drawing a clear distinction between them.[54]

In the west, where any mention of the Revolution still evoked memories of burned-out churches and of atrocities committed by republican soldiers, the language of the Centennial did little to popularise military service. This did not mean that Catholic boys made reluctant soldiers; it merely made the point that the cause they served was that of France rather than the Republic. Throughout Brittany and western France, retreats were held for conscripts before they left for the army and after their service was complete, gatherings which served to unite them in a Christian as well as a national cause. At Machecoul in 1896, for instance, 150 young men responded to their bishop's call to spend four days of retreat from civil society, four days of 'paternal guidance' from their priests, four days when conscripts and those the Church described as 'hommes libérés', men freed from military service, could share each other's company and enjoy the support of their local community. It was, reported the local pastoral news-sheet, 'a moving occasion', and especially the religious service that brought the retreat to a close. 'Most of the priests from neighbouring parishes were in attendance. The general sense of communion, the renewal of baptismal vows, and the consecration to Notre Dame des Armées, read in unison by all the soldiers, left many of those present in tears.'[55] The accounts of these

[53] A.N., F19 5582, letter from the Archbishop of Paris to the Minister for Religious Affairs, 21 September 1892.

[54] A.N., F19 5611, *Revue des conférences populaires*, 6e année, 3e numéro, janvier 1889.

[55] Raymond Poincaré, *La Semaine religieuse du diocèse de Nantes* 32 (1896), p. 1086.

retreats left by conscripts who participated in them – or such of them as were printed in the Catholic press – suggest a mood of fellowship and subdued joy, at least in peacetime. There is nothing of the morosity that had marked the religious rituals of the Bretons in the Napoleonic Wars, when villagers had led their sons to the village boundary, saying prayers, reciting the *de Profundis*, bidding them an 'eternal farewell'.[56] This generation of young men, it would seem, enjoyed their retreat – the prayers, the renewal of their vows, the pilgrimage together to a local shrine; but also the sense of comradeship, the communal dinners and the exhortation to courage. They took their vows in the presence of the Holy Sacrament, a new unity was forged among them, the language of the priest mingling with that of their future general in battle. 'Be strong in war! It is Our Lord who asks for our love and our fidelity! Better death than dishonour! Catholic and Breton forever![57]

For the majority of Frenchmen, however, commemoration of the Revolution was also a reminder of past military triumphs by the French people, which underlined the extent of their debt to their citizen-soldiers as they fought and conquered in the name of liberty. And if the army tended to sacrifice public sympathy at this time – both through the threat of military rule represented by Boulanger and the unscrupulous politics of its generals at the time of the Dreyfus Affair – there was general recognition that France needed a strong army for the trials that lay ahead. The language of *revanche* did not, it is true, figure largely with the political leadership of the 1890s, for whom the imminence of war had receded and the wounds of 1870 were at least partly healed. In the election campaign of 1893, most notably, there was little place for nationalist rhetoric of this kind, and increasingly it seemed to be accepted that Alsace-Lorraine was being absorbed into a greater Germany, its citizens apparently resigned to their new identity. There were, of course, exceptions, most particularly in the far-right rhetoric of Paul Déroulède and the *Ligue des Patriotes*, though even they had faded from the front of the political stage since the heady days of the 1880s, only to be rescued by the public storm over Dreyfus.[58] But the desire for revenge and images of a victorious army still figured in the pages of the polemical press and in popular visual culture. This imagery, as Richard Thomson has demonstrated, did much to rehabilitate the army in the eyes of the citizenry. In particular it displayed the

[56] Jean Waquet, 'La société civile devant l'insoumission et la désertion à l'époque de la conscription militaire', *Bibliothèque de l'Ecole des Chartes* 126 (1968), p. 191.

[57] Poincaré, *La Semaine religieuse*, p. 1089.

[58] Peter M. Rutkoff, *Revanche and Revision. The Ligue des Patriotes and the Origins of the Radical Right in France, 1882–1900* (Athens, Ohio, 1981), p. 84.

soldier as the community knew him, as a citizen as much as a hero, an ordinary peasant or tradesman who found himself temporarily under arms. This was a reassuring image, and one that presented a socially inclusive image of the army as a reflection of society at large.[59] It was a reminder of the extent to which the army after 1889 had again been transformed into the *nation armée*, the people organised in their collective defence.

While the compromise reached in 1889 satisfied the more conservative among the republicans, radicals were increasingly disillusioned by a system which, to their way of thinking, still fell short of the republican ideal. During the 1890s there were repeated demands for more liberal recruitment laws that would end the distinction between *bons* and *mauvais numéros* and the iniquity of the ballot. By 1899 as many as 200 deputies had already come out in favour of a further democratisation of recruitment and a flat term of two years' service for all, without distinction.[60] The arguments on both sides were strikingly familiar, the latest stage in a seemingly eternal battle between those who believed that an effective army must at all costs be professional, well trained and thoroughly disciplined, and those, mainly on the Left, who harked after the tradition of the citizen-soldier which had served the people so well during the French Revolution. Advocates of the two opposing standpoints were as far apart at the dawn of the twentieth century as they had been for most of the nineteenth; all that had changed, it seemed, was the power of the republicans and the balance of parliamentary advantage. Speaking in the Senate in 1902, de Lamarzelle made an eloquent plea for 'military spirit' to be maintained and nurtured in the army, for without it, he believed, France's military capacity would be fatally undermined. 'You want soldiers devoid of military spirit', he accused the republicans opposite, 'and officers without military spirit. In your report you say that officers, like soldiers, should be citizens to be mobilised . . . You seem to believe that the disappearance of military spirit is a consequence of the evolution of the army'. This, he insisted, was a complete misunderstanding of how armies operate, and it would result in a force unable to function well in the heat of battle. To him, 'military spirit' was an essential ingredient in any army, and it could not be created by conscription. He went on to explain just what he meant. 'Military spirit means an absolute and unreasoning submission to orders while in army service. It is not only material discipline but moral discipline, the abdication of the individual will in the face of a

[59] Richard Thomson, *The Troubled Republic. Visual Culture and Social Debate in France, 1889–1900* (New Haven, Conn., 2004), pp. 172–3.

[60] Challener, *French Theory*, p. 60.

superior, any superior.'[61] In reply, radical deputies asserted that military service was the first duty of citizenship, just as the vote was its first right. Soldiers must be citizens, and that implied a new sort of discipline, a different kind of army. The socialist Gérault-Richard put this starkly in a speech to the Chamber during the debate on a new army law in 1905, which finally introduced universal two-year conscription and abandoned any distinction between long- term and short-term service. 'It will be necessary', he said, 'to introduce civilian habits into the barracks. Two-year conscripts cannot be treated like mercenaries. Repressive discipline must be replaced by a moral discipline in which mutual confidence, a spirit of solidarity and a consciousness of civic duty replace fear and severity in the minds of citizens who are armed in defence of their liberty'.[62]

In this republican project, consistent with the radical vision of Jules Ferry and his republic of schoolteachers, two-year military service was not only a civic obligation, but a method of education.[63] The two years were to be an apprenticeship for the struggles ahead, the regiment assuming the role of *l'armée-école* and instilling civic values as much as training in the manipulation of weapons. This was a specifically republican vision of the army, an army of national defence to which the Third Republic remained firmly committed in spite of the pacifist instincts of so many of its founding fathers.[64] With the approach of war in 1914 their belief became even more determined, and with it commitment to the principle of universal conscription. Two years' service might be the ideal, but in an emergency even radicals and socialists were prepared to extend that period, provided that it was clearly understood that it should be imposed on all alike. In contrast to Britain, where neither parliament nor public opinion was prepared to impose compulsory service in 1914, there was seeming agreement in France that the state should resort to some form of conscription to find the manpower required for the defence of its territory.[65] Even the pacifist Jean Jaurès accepted that, for as long as France had to have an army, it should be based

[61] Speech of de Lamarzelle to the Senate, 19 June 1902, quoted in Crépin, *Défendre la France*, p. 369.

[62] Speech of Gérault-Richard to the Chambre des Députés, 16 March 1905, quoted in Crépin, *Défendre la France*, p. 370.

[63] See, especially, the polemical work of Albert Thibaudet, *La république des professeurs* (Paris, 1927), a work where the image of the regiment of 1914 looms almost as large as that of the school classroom.

[64] Philip Nord, *The Republican Moment. Struggles for Democracy in Nineteenth-century France* (Cambridge, Mass., 1995), pp. 247–8.

[65] Alan Forrest, 'Conscription as ideology: revolutionary France and the nation in arms', in Mjøset and van Holde (eds.), *Comparative Study of Conscription* vol XX, pp. 109–10.

on conscription, since 'it would be a crime against France and against the army itself to separate the army from the nation'.[66] Public debate focussed elsewhere – on demographic decline and fears that France had been weakened by years of low birth-rate and faced depopulation in the face of a resurgent Germany; or on the actual size of the country's manpower needs against a country that could now draw on the added population of Alsace and Lorraine. Louis Barthou's government responded in 1913 not by questioning the adequacy of conscription but by increasing the basic period of service for all from two years to three. National unity was not put at risk. As Charles de Gaulle noted with undisguised approval, there was 'not a single group to protest against the mobilisation; not a single strike to interfere with it'.[67] The French nation was once again in arms, united in the face of danger, and acceptant of a long-assimilated tradition of service and citizenship.

[66] Jean Jaurès, *L'armée nouvelle* (Paris, 1910), p. 44.
[67] Alexander Werth, *De Gaulle* (London, 1965), p. 71.

8 Educating the army

For the radicals of the Third Republic the task of creating a republican army was one of some complexity that could not be limited to imposing conscription on a reluctant nation and legislating for equality of sacrifice, important as these were. The failures of the French army in 1870 had been there for all to see, and they were failures of tactics and military preparation, as well, the republicans insisted, as failures of leadership by the officer class of the Second Empire. They sought to explain these failures by pointing to the lack of morale in the military, and the lack of any sense of public service among the officers. In particular, they felt that the social background of many army officers and the military preparation provided for them at academies like Saint-Cyr made them aloof and aristocratic, remote from their men and out of sympathy with the ideals of the republic. For though entry to the leading military academies had increasingly become a matter of public examination and open competition, the sons of nobles still enjoyed privileged access to some areas of the officer corps, most visibly in the cavalry, and there were those, principally among the royalists, who continued to believe that the best officers came from military families and therefore sought to favour the transmission of military vocations from one generation to the next.[1] But they were fighting for a lost cause: the reforms of the Second Republic were not reversed by Napoleon III, so that by 1870 the principal danger for the republic came from the presence of Bonapartist officers in the high command rather than royalist ones. Gambetta, as a staunch republican, was deeply aware of the chasm in outlook between the political and military leadership, which, he believed, both weakened the regime and led to widespread mutual distrust. He accepted that, once in power, the republicans would have to undertake a major reform

[1] William Serman, 'Le corps des officiers français sous la Deuxième République et le Second Empire', 3 vols., thèse de doctorat, Université de Paris-IV, 1976 (Lille, 1978), p. 348.

of the officer corps if they were to assume control of the major services of the state.[2]

Throughout the nineteenth century the army – and with it the officer class – had allowed itself to become associated with the politics of the Right, a political stance that made it very difficult to reconcile with a republic whose roots were so patently with the Revolution. The Second Republic, like the First, had shown its mistrust of its military commanders by insisting that officers take a new oath of loyalty to the state, repeating the article of faith of the revolutionaries that the army was expected to obey the government of the day, passively and without question. It was not expected to have a political voice of its own, and where soldiers did hold political opinions, their duty was to remain silent. Any suggestion of political opposition, any trace of criticism of the government or of *cris seditieux*, could lead to prosecution and an appearance before a *conseil de guerre*. In moments of political tension, all governments, republican as well as Bonapartist, had imposed this rule, and, as William Serman has shown, had rigorously punished political opponents in the military. Key years for such prosecutions were those between 1848 and 1852 – there were seventy-five prosecutions in 1850, sixty-eight in 1851 and a further sixty-six in 1852 – and again in 1870 on the outbreak of the Franco-Prussian War.[3] The regular changes of regime in the nineteenth century, combined with the natural tendency of the military to defend the social order, meant that governments treated army officers as little more than military functionaries whose focus of loyalty must be to the civil authority. It was not always a lesson that the military were prepared to accept. Some high-ranking officers responded angrily to the treatment they received, claiming that republican demands demeaned their professionalism and amounted to the destruction of all independent military authority. General Picard, for instance, observed that the spirit of democracy was itself harmful to military morale, while for General Du Barail the republic was 'the negation of the army, since liberty, equality and fraternity spell indiscipline, a failure to obey, and the negation of principles of hierarchy', without which, he argued, no successful army could function.[4] Such views were, of course, extreme, since the army also contained sizable quotas of officers and *sous-officiers* who shared the republic's ideals. But it is easy to see why Gambetta was alarmed: he had to be sure that the army would obey the new republican order, and its obedience could not be taken for granted.

[2] François Bédarida, 'L'armée et la République', *Revue historique* 88 (1964), p. 135.
[3] Serman, 'Le corps des officiers', p. 1147. [4] *Ibid.*, p. 1140.

Gambetta came to be seen as a spokesman for republicans within the army, who shared their fears with him as well as their plans to revolutionise the military. Their advice was invaluable, especially in the 1870s, when the radical republicans were just coming to power and had to acclimatise to the nature of the institutions they inherited. They looked to the republic for support in their struggle and for protection from their more reactionary commanders, and in return they provided Gambetta with information about the state of the military and the degree of anti-republican prejudice in high places. With this information Gambetta compiled his own inquiry – or *enquête* – during the mid-1870s which revealed the extent of the hostility towards the republic that permeated the officer corps. He used a network of informants inside the military, informants whom he could trust in a military machine he could not: they included *sous-officiers* willing to inform on their superiors, known republican sympathisers in a strongly Catholic institution, and, in all probability, networks of freemasons whose identities would be easier to conceal. Their evidence provided the political leadership with all the ammunition they required to justify political intervention, for it showed how slight was republican sympathy in the higher echelons of the army. Among *généraux de division* 88 per cent were classed as anti-republican in outlook (a mixture of royalists, Bonapartists and reactionary conservatives); among brigade commanders the figure fell to 61 per cent.[5] The evidence suggested conclusively not only that the army was led by men whose political sympathies lay with the enemies of the regime; but that, with its love of order and hierarchy and traditional vision of military discipline, it risked being a force for conservatism and social authority.

The inherent dangers were obvious, evoking fears of military coups and political ambitions, of a new Cromwell or Bonaparte, and fears for the very survival of the republic itself. These fears would become even more vivid during the 1880s with the emergence of General Boulanger as the political champion of a populist, anti-democratic Right; and again in the 1890s during the Dreyfus Affair. In both affairs, the army high command confirmed the worst republican image of the military as elitist, xenophobic, ultra-catholic and anti-republican, choosing their political allies among the most right-wing groups and naturally attracted to the language of patriotism and strong government. By the time of the 1898 election, the army had become a political pawn, as royalists and other enemies of the democratic republic campaigned on the issue of *revanche*, making impassioned pleas to the electorate to vote generous

[5] Bédarida, 'L'armée et la République', pp. 142–3.

military credits and thus save the army from its political detractors. The Duc de Broglie, for instance, a new convert to the cause of Alsace and Lorraine, was unashamed in his wooing of support among the military top brass; his appeal for solidarity with the army was aimed as much at them as it was at the electorate. 'For our army, for our navy', he intoned, 'I have voted all the credits asked for, since nothing must be refused when it concerns the power and security of the country'. And he went on, with a barbed reference to the Dreyfusards, to defend the army's position in the 1890s: 'With you I have suffered, with you I have protested when the army, which is the incarnation of the honour of France, was insulted and dragged through the mud by the leaders of the hateful campaign for the rehabilitation of a traitor.'[6] For republicans army officers were not just political opponents; they had become a threat to the fabric of the regime, and to the core values of liberty and equality which they held to so devoutly.

It was not enough, therefore, to reform military service through conscription, important as that was, since the conscript had no power or authority in the army, and he was placed at the beck and call of officers who despised and rejected the republic he was called upon to serve. The citizen-soldier could ensure that the ranks of the army were not distanced from society, in this way keeping some vestige of the myth of Valmy alive at a time when France was not threatened, and when the role of the military was increasingly being played out in colonial wars in North and West Africa. Meanwhile, at home, the reputation of the army was put at risk in many of the new industrial areas because it was increasingly being deployed to break strikes and curb the militancy of French workers' movements.[7] It was not a task that conscripts relished – in one of the most notorious incidents, in the northern textile town of Fourmies in 1891, nine demonstrators were killed by troops – but at least, even here, the soldier could reason that he was serving the republic, carrying out the orders of the elected government. He could do nothing, however, to counter the orders of his officers, or to prevent them from pursuing their own deeply conservative and anti-democratic agenda. That would call for government intervention of a very different kind, aimed at reforming the spirit and morale of the army by exercise, training and education, issues dear to the hearts of republican politicians of the generation of Jules Ferry.

[6] Herbert Tint, *The Decline of French Patriotism, 1870–1940* (London, 1964), p. 107.

[7] Odile Roynette, 'L'armée dans la bataille sociale: maintien de l'ordre et grèves ouvrières dans le Nord de la France, 1871–1906', *Mouvement Social* 179 (1997), p. 41.

Central to this discussion was the issue of military preparation, or how best to train France's armies for the next war with Germany, the war which the political leadership all believed would have to be fought. The issue was debated in a wide range of tracts and pamphlets, in speeches at Saint-Cyr and other military academies, as well as in the press, and it continued to fascinate political opinion throughout the quarter-century leading up to the outbreak of war in 1914. Interestingly, the debate focussed as much on the social and moral role of the army, and especially of officers, as it did on more material questions of manpower and weaponry. With the introduction of two years' compulsory service, their role suddenly became more important, as the educators of an entire generation, who could mould and develop the martial qualities of the young as had never been possible in the past. It was, in the words of an anonymous article in the *Revue des Deux Mondes* in 1891, a precious opportunity, with universal service 'a marvellous agent of social action'.[8] Suddenly, 20,000 army officers had the chance to influence the youth of France, and to countermand what many saw as the damaging tradition of the school system, which encouraged book learning and the development of the mind, but to the detriment of physical prowess and activity. For too long, in this writer's view, the French had shown an exaggerated respect for intellectual achievement and had deprecated, even despised, what the officer corps represented. Here was the opportunity to restore some pride and prestige to military values and to implant in the next generation something that had for too long been lost – the 'rational balance between the development of the body and that of the mind' which had been so praised by the authors of antiquity and for which the nation now had such an evident need.[9]

Like much of the republican literature of the period, the starting point was that there was something gravely wrong with French morale, and hence with the values inculcated into the country's young men. They were too passive, too unmoved by the exhilaration of sport and physical activity. They did not have an adequate understanding of the nation, of patriotism, or of the honour of France. And given that this generation would face war to defend its territory and its coastline, the priorities of education must necessarily change to accommodate this need. In *Le Livre de Tous. Le soldat français, aujourd'hui et demain*, written in 1893, the imminence of war takes first priority, the pamphlet arguing that because of her extensive frontiers and lack of natural defences, France, of all European nations, was most exposed to future

[8] Anon., 'Du rôle social de l'officier', *Revue des Deux Mondes* 194 (1891), p. 445.
[9] *Ibid.*, p. 446.

attack. Hence the country must be prepared, which means that the young must be educated for war, educated to understand military honour and to respect the patriotic mission of the soldier. The notion of duty takes precedence: every young man had a duty to serve France, a duty to honour his regiment, a duty to his family as much as to his country, since when he is serving in the army 'the good son is the man who observes his family's traditions and who keeps up his relations with his parents'.[10] The parents have duties, too, of course, since they must support their son, encourage his patriotic devotion and persuade him of the importance and honour of his mission. Now that soldiering is the vocation of all rather than a selected few, there is new reason for the people of France to respect and honour the profession of arms and to offer themselves selflessly for the service of the nation. 'In every respect the profession of arms is noble', the pamphlet concludes, 'because for all it is composed of sacrifices and it is rewarded, above all, by public esteem and glory'.[11]

Republican writers repeatedly contrasted the army which had served Napoleon III with the army which the republic was trying to create through the courses it organised in schools and in the *écoles militaires*. The transition could not be achieved overnight: after 1870 the tradition of the officers at Sédan had not been broken, while the men of the Second Empire were usually maintained at the head of the military. Indeed, as Emile Terquem noted with regret, since the training of future army officers was the preserve of serving officers, there was every reason to suppose that little would change, with the *écoles* continuing to produce new cohorts of young officers in the image of the old. This, he believed, explained the political profile of the army as an institution, and its behaviour at the time of Dreyfus, since 'the clerical-conservative coterie' had proved impossible to dislodge, its interests carefully cultivated by the clergy and the military. How could the ideal of a citizen-army be encouraged in such circumstances? Terquem was scathing about clerical self-interest in the educative process; but, like other critics of the officer corps, he was equally dismissive of the efforts made by the secular teachers in the *lycées*, who had been largely responsible for the lack of interest among the young in things active and military. Schools had passed over in silence the whole area of nationalism and the national interest as though no such thing existed; while the university had to bear a special responsibility for 'creating generations

[10] J.S.G., *Le Livre de tous. Le soldat français, aujourd'hui, demain* (Paris, 1893), p. 10.
[11] *Ibid.*, pp. 6–7.

of bourgeois who are sceptical, indifferent, in short bad citizens'.[12] Only since the Dreyfus Affair, he believed, has the army recognised the scale of the problem of disaffection, and, through General André in particular, sought to reduce its sense of autonomy from the political world. By the beginning of the twentieth century, the army was integrating civic and moral education into its curriculum, and bringing in lecturers from outside to provide its officer cadets with an element of republican pedagogy. André went so far as to get the philosopher and former socialist deputy, Eugène Fournière, to give Polytechnicians a course in labour legislation, a dramatic change in emphasis and one that seems all the more timely in view of the army's increased role in policing social movements at home.[13]

Curiously, it might seem, Catholic writers had very similar ideas about the moral failings of the population and their lack of patriotic commitment, though, of course, they did not ascribe these to the malign influence of the clergy. But they agreed with their secular counterparts in questioning the abstract quality of much of French education, and the loss of manliness and virility which, they supposed, naturally followed. Vuillermet, whose text on education as 'moral preparation' went through many editions in the years immediately preceding 1914, denounced the cult of the abstract as offering a diversion from the moral purpose of education, and emphasised that education meant leadership, offering answers to doubt, and forming character; education, he stressed, was different from instruction, and it was instruction that schoolmasters were content to provide to the young.[14] Boys had to be encouraged to develop qualities of *volonté* that would make them willing to take initiative, to serve others, and to avoid the pitfalls of moral laxity and depravity. Catholic writers were prone to contrast generations, and to blame the lack of patriotism in the 1890s on the baneful pessimism of their elders, of that 'lost generation' born after 1871.[15] Teachers and parents, they argued, had been particularly prone to despair and to the temptations of 'nihilism, anarchism, and destructiveness', which in turn had led to materialism and individualism amongst the young. What was now needed was a new self-confidence, and the recognition by young Frenchmen that the nation, not the individual, is

[12] Emile Terquem, *Comment on fait une armée réactionnaire: comment on fait une armée républicaine* (Paris, 1906), p. 4.
[13] *Ibid.*, p. 6.
[14] F.-A. Vuillermet, *Soyez des hommes. A la conquête de la virilité* (Paris, 1909), pp. 17–18.
[15] Agathon, *Le goût de l'action – la foi patriotique – une renaissance catholique – le réalisme politique* (Paris, 1913), p. 6.

the principal organism of human society, that humanity is composed of nations just as it is of families.[16] To achieve this, boys must be shown the benefits of an active lifestyle and encouraged to take initiative; only in this way could they avoid the pitfalls of passivity, which led to a selfish commitment to pleasure, characterised by alcohol abuse and urban degeneracy.[17]

Like secular educationalists, the Catholic authors emphasised again and again the need for teachers to recognise the qualities of the army and to communicate to their pupils some understanding of its role in the service of the *patrie*. Schooling, declared one Jesuit priest addressing a prize-giving ceremony in 1898 – and the address was immediately printed and distributed – must have a clearly focussed patriotic mission and take pride in the country's glorious and chivalric past. It is a deeply conservative view of the purpose of education, and one that draws heavily on the ideas of Maurice Barrès. In the classroom, he insisted, 'we teach them patriotism. The army, we tell them, is the living image of our fatherland. Young men, we must respect it, we must love it'. But the teacher's role goes further: 'The army, we tell them, is the visible force of the fatherland. Young men, it is our duty to prepare valiant recruits to join it.' He is not just instructing his class; he is helping to 'forge in them the men of the future'.[18] This he presents as a lesson in morality and in citizenship, since military spirit is a form of discipline that is useful to society, and which is closely attuned to the 'strong, male education of the will' which France so badly needs. And if this moral attainment is gained at the expense of more traditional book learning, is this, he asks, such a bad thing? 'Our century believes in the cult – I was about to say the superstition – of science; to satisfy its limitless demands, we have overloaded the curriculum, multiplied the number of teachers, and transformed sixteen-year-old brains into living encyclopaedias.' He urges that schools should concern themselves more with things that matter.[19]

If Catholic authors berated schools for their failure to teach moral values, a more fundamental responsibility lay with the universities, and especially the Sorbonne. Here was the cradle of that effete intellectualism which they detested, and which had seeped from the university into the classrooms of provincial France, the root of the intellectual

[16] Henri Didon, *L'esprit militaire dans une nation* (Paris, 1898), p. 5.

[17] Vuillermet, *Soyez des hommes*, p. 240.

[18] Le R.P. Caruel, *L'éducation nationale et l'armée. Discours prononcé à la distribution des prix de l'Ecole libre Saint-Joseph de Reims* (Reims, 1898), p. 4.

[19] *Ibid.*, p. 12.

distortion of which they complained. It was only too easy to pass from criticisms of this intellectual tradition to an open anti-intellectualism, and some tracts did not hold back from venting their spleen on all forms of abstraction, indeed on the entire university system. Looking back to the 1890s, Agathon regretted the climate of the age, when there had been such a passion among the young for abstract ideas and when 'the philosopher, the scholar were then the masters of our lives'.[20] Scathingly, he drew attention to the conceit of the intellectuals of that time, their disdain for the provinces, and their arrogant self-sufficiency in the ivory towers of the Sorbonne, the same ivory towers where they had taken shelter when Germany seized Alsace and Lorraine. Abstraction was everything: 'Such was the astonishing *logomachie* that they taught in the Sorbonne, scarcely ten years ago: they would maintain the fatherland on condition that it served a humanitarian ideal, and, in the final analysis, they sacrificed it to that ideal!'[21] Nationalists denounced this as insupportable arrogance; and they agreed instinctively with an article in the *Journal des Débats* of 1898 which rejected pure intellectualism and saw the advantage to the nation which the Sorbonne could bring in terms of the message it could teach to the young. Otherwise, 'if the University of France was nothing more than a seminary of mandarins, ideologues and intellectuals, a factory producing bachelors, graduates, even *agrégés*, nourished with subversive ideas, then we should close its doors tomorrow'.[22]

For many nationalists of the period, the new emphasis on activity, on force, even on violence, was itself invigorating. As Henri Didon explained, the use of force, whether in defence of France against attack or in the many colonial adventures of the nineteenth century, was morally as well as militarily justified. Like many of his peers, Didon was an uncompromising apologist for empire. French colonialism was a moral crusade to bring civilisation and the Catholic faith to the unenlightened; it was a civilising force, allowing truth to be told and justice to reign. The idea that this could be achieved without force, or that it should be left to France's European rivals, he dismisses as 'sentimentalism' of a sort that might 'appeal to poets', but which must be 'banned from the hearts of leaders'.[23] Understanding the moral value of physical force was, like an appreciation of the value of the military, part of the battle that must be fought against pacifism and intellectualism. Didon sees no contradiction between the use of force and the republic, any more than between the spirit of the military and democracy. He admits

[20] Agathon, *Le goût de l'action*, p. 43. [21] *Ibid.*, p. 28.
[22] *Journal des Débats*, 7 February 1898. [23] Didon, *L'esprit militaire*, p. 17.

to liking force which he represents as the 'guardian of law', and urges that teachers have a duty to explain the value of force as an aspect of a successful nation. As he explained to a school prize-giving in Paris in 1898, he thought it a 'sacred duty of his function as an educator' to encourage in the minds of the boys he taught both the cult of the army and the cult of what he called 'sacred force'. By this, he adds, he means that degree of force which the law permits and which in turn leads men to respect and obey the law, and hence to a strengthening of the country's institutions.[24]

It is noticeable how this campaign for more emphasis on activity, for a moral education that would train the young in patriotism and educate army officers in civic values, was concentrated in the last decade of the 1890s, and especially the immediate aftermath of the Dreyfus Affair. By the early twentieth century the campaign became less strident, and the pamphlets changed in tone, praising the increasing patriotism of the young and congratulating schools and military academies on reforms to their curricula.

The mood of the country had changed, it seemed, as war hysteria began to grow, there were increasing calls for rearmament, and the nationalists' propaganda campaign made the new generation of adolescents and young men much more aware of their patriotic duty. More and more young men were enjoying sport and other outdoor activities, with football and rugby clubs, cycling clubs and *sociétés de gymnastique et de tir* sprouting on all sides, encouraging the young to exercise their bodies and to escape from their own company into that of like-minded companions. And the army itself was taking its civic duty very much more seriously, educating its officers in social values and in military history as well as in the more practical aspects of leadership and the science of war. By the early years of the twentieth century republican writers were commenting on the degree of change, and believing that the secret lay in civic education and the spread of republican values inside the army. There was, Emile Terquem acknowledged in 1906, a new mood of solidarity in the military, which had its roots in 'the common origins of the soldiers and their leaders, and especially the community of sentiments that unite them'. These stemmed from their shared republican values: 'an enthusiasm for new ideas, hatred of privileges and of the rich and powerful, compassion for the common man, love of one's country and of its independence'. United by these values,

[24] *Ibid.*, p. 27.

he believed, 'soldiers and officers are convinced that they hold the key to regenerating the world'.[25]

The growth of sporting societies and especially of clubs devoted to gymnastics, exercise and military training was especially noteworthy from the mid-1880s, providing young men with the opportunity to handle weapons, hone their bodies, and acquire the sort of physical fitness which the army would require. The movement had grown rapidly: the first properly constituted gymnastic organisation, the Union des Sociétés Françaises de Gymnastique, was formed by a handful of clubs in 1873, yet by the eve of the First World War it had grown to be a national body with 350,000 members and a periodical, *Le Gymnaste*, that was distributed throughout France.[26] In addition there were around 1,600 Catholic sports clubs and 2,000 military preparation societies.[27] These societies became part of the social fabric of cities and small towns across France, their *fêtes* and festivities taking their place in the calendar of village celebrations and popular culture.[28] They were actively encouraged by the Ministry of War, which looked to them to prepare the people for army service, especially those able-bodied males in their late teens and twenties who formed a natural reserve should an emergency arise. They would not be disappointed as the gymnastic movement spread across the country. Many of the clubs were given deliberately martial names like *L'Estafette* or *L'Avant-garde*,[29] and almost all made specific reference in their statutes to military preparation. Indeed, the Union itself, in its original constitution, made it clear that its primary goal was to 'increase the defensive strength of the country by promoting the development of its physical and moral strength through the rational application of gymnastics, shooting and swimming'.[30] They were more concerned with training and muscular development than with team sports, revelling in the new popularity that gymnastics enjoyed and in what they saw

25 Terquem, *Comment on fait une armée réactionnaire: comment on fait une armée républicaine*, p. 27.

26 *Le Gymnaste. Moniteur officiel de l'Union des Sociétés de Gymnastique de France*, founded in 1873.

27 Richard Holt, *Sport and Society in Modern France* (London, 1981), p. 40.

28 P. Arnaud and J. Camy (eds.), *La naissance du mouvement sportif associatif en France. Sociabilités et formes de pratiques sportives* (Lyon, 1986), pp. 223–39.

29 Georges Vigarello, 'Le gymnaste et la nation armée', in Alain Corbin, Jean-Jacques Courtine and Georges Vigarello (eds.), *Histoire du corps* (3 vols., Paris, 2005), vol. II, p. 366.

30 Joseph Sansboeuf, 'Les sociétés de gymnastique en France', in Philippe Tissié (ed.), *L'éducation physique* (Paris, 1901), p. 64.

as its particularly French character, which was 'considered too bold by some, and dangerous by others'.[31]

But the republic also counselled a degree of prudence. It did not want to put weapons in the hands of its opponents – prefects always seemed to enquire more thoroughly into the purposes of Catholic than of secular gun clubs, for instance – or to encourage the formation of paramilitary units. Clubs were invited to register with the Ministry of War, successful registration bringing with it a privileged status and significant benefits – a free allocation of rifles, distribution of ammunition and the right to enter prestigious *concours* and *prix du tir*. Foreigners were not allowed to register, and those administering clubs were subjected to routine police vetting to establish their republican credentials.[32] But once this investigative process was complete, the republic was very supportive, seeing the clubs as an important nursery for future soldiers. Those who ran the societies agreed that this was their principal purpose, and they did not hesitate to link gymnastics and body-building with military service in the future. Thus the president of one regional association, in Normandy, wrote in 1895, in the *Bulletin* of one of the clubs in his region, comparing their work with that of the ancient Greeks. 'May I go back to the Ancients', he asked rhetorically, 'to remind your readers of those annual battles between the youths of Greece, when the population of an entire town would turn out to sing the praises of a young fellow-citizen who had won against their fearsome and well-coached rivals from other towns? Must I remind you that the heroes of these competitions, as the most treasured prize, won the right to march first to the next war?'[33] War and fitness, it would seem, were complementary parts of the same challenge.

Societies applied for affiliation, inviting the prefecture to carry out certain basic checks on the organisers and the declared purpose of their work. In 1909, for instance, when a long-established Bordeaux club asked to be affiliated, the prefect duly confirmed that it looked both thoroughly respectable and sincere in its profession of republicanism. The *Ligue girondine de préparation militaire et d'enseignement physique*, he reported, had been set up in 1889, was active, and its members answered to the administrative and military authorities; indeed, the courses it offered were 'professed by officers and special army instructors, supported by officers from the reserve'. They had no reason to deny affiliation; this was exactly the sort of cooperation with the

31 *Le Gymnaste*, 19, issue 26 (26 December 1891), pp. 437–8.

32 A.D. Gironde, 1R 103, *Instruction ministérielle sur le fonctionnement des sociétés de tir et de gymnastique*, 1885.

33 A.M. Elbeuf, 57Z 1, *Bulletin de l'Alsacienne-Lorraine d'Elbeuf*, 2 (January–March 1895), p. 1.

military authorities which the republic had hoped to develop.[34] There were already several gymnastic clubs and shooting clubs in the city, all deemed to be worthy of support, with each appealing to a slightly different clientele. For instance, the *Patriotes Bordelais*, also founded back in the 1880s, was a 'republican society for gymnastics, shooting and military instruction'. The aims of the society are clearly set out in its prospectus: to 'develop the strength and the suppleness of the body, maintain good health by varied exercises – gymnastics, military instruction, shooting, and the preparation of young men for service in the army'. The second aim appeals especially to the patriotic republican ethic of the time – 'to study and defend the moral interests of the young people who take the society's courses, and to initiate them into the rules of discipline'. There is no limit to the number of members who can be admitted; women can join as well as men; and, it is quite expressly stated, 'all discussion of politics and religion in the meetings of the society is forbidden'.[35]

Gymnastic and sporting clubs seeking affiliation in Bordeaux generally took care to emphasise their military links, or to insist that their main purpose was to provide some military formation. That, after all, was what the government wanted, and most of those running sports clubs seem to have concurred. A shooting club known as *L'Avant-Garde*, founded in 1888 and recruiting mainly from the world of artisans and shopkeepers, was duly approved by the prefect, subject only to the requirement that the organisers should obtain parental consent for their young members' involvement. Their principal aim was defined as the provision of military instruction for young men from Bordeaux and the suburban town of Bègles: the president was the mayor of Bègles, the mayor of Bordeaux had offered his support, and the organisers were all deemed to be business people in good financial standing. The society's statutes, after defining the physical activities they would support, made clear their seriousness about military preparation. They sought, they said, 'to prepare, with a view to military service, a contingent of men who would be agile, robust, with a thorough grounding in shooting and in handling firearms, subjected to discipline and inspired by noble and patriotic sentiments'.[36] Members were mostly men in their twenties, usually their mid- to late twenties, unmarried or without children. A significant number of them were bachelors who still lived at home

[34] A.D. Gironde, 1R 103, letter from the Minister of War to the Prefect of the Gironde, 5 March 1909.

[35] A.D. Gironde, 1R 109, prospectus of the *Patriotes Bordelais*, 1885.

[36] A.D. Gironde, 1R 104, statutes of the *Société de gymnastique et de tir* '*L'Avant-Garde*', submitted 4 March 1889.

with their parents. In other words, they came from exactly that constituency to which the army would hope to turn for recruits.[37] Young men were indeed being prepared for military service, as they were in France's neighbours, where sporting clubs experienced an equally impressive explosion in membership: by 1896 there were some 120 societies in Belgium, 12 in Holland, 50 in Sweden and 448 in Switzerland. The republic could feel very satisfied with what it had achieved, even if these numbers were dwarfed by those of Germany, which already had over 5,000 gymnastic and shooting clubs.[38] There was some way to make up.

The republic was often aided in its task by local industrialists who shared the enthusiasm for gymnastics and military training and saw it as their patriotic duty to get the young men of their community prepared for a new war with Germany. An excellent example is that of Jules Blin, owner of a textile firm in Elbeuf, near Rouen, and one of the biggest employers in the region. He founded a highly successful gymnastic society, with the patriotic name of *L'Alsacienne-Lorraine d'Elbeuf*, in 1890, and within a few years it had branches in the nearby towns of Orival and Saint-Aubin as well as its main premises in Elbeuf itself. Its aim, like that of all such societies, was as much the moral education of the young as their physical development; like muscular Christianity in England, it sought 'to strengthen the body and tone the muscles', and 'to inspire the soul through vigorous moral discipline'.[39] As a factory-owner, Blin clearly had an interest in the moral regeneration of the young, not least of his own workforce, but his passion did not end there. He took a personal interest in the work of the club, financed it, served as its president, and published a volume of *Portraits de gymnastes* to help publicise the place of gymnastics in the community.[40] Its bulletin, like many of its kind, carried patriotic poems, articles about the history and tradition of the French army, and reminders of the sad fate of Alsace and Lorraine; it also had a regular feature listing those of its members who were serving in the army, and took up the call for their experience as gymnasts to be rewarded with rapid promotion to the rank of corporal or sergeant.[41]

[37] A.D. Gironde, 1R 104, membership list for *L'Avant-Garde*.
[38] A M. Elbeuf, 57Z 1, *Bulletin de l'Alsacienne-Lorraine d'Elbeuf*, 6 (January–March 1896), p. 1.
[39] A.M. Elbeuf, 3Z 1052, *Bulletin de l'Alsacienne-Lorraine d'Elbeuf*, 1 (January 1895), p. 1.
[40] Jules Blin, *Portraits de gymnastes* (Elbeuf, 1897).
[41] A.M. Elbeuf, 57Z 1, *Bulletin de l'Alsacienne-Lorraine d'Elbeuf*, 14 (January 1899), p. 7.

The other overriding interest of the War Ministry in these years was the level of education and training made available to officers, and a concern that this preparation should produce officers who were good republicans as well as good strategists. Before the shock administered by the defeat of 1870, there is little to suggest that the training of future officers had been much thought about. There had been an attempt, instituted by Gouvion Saint-Cyr after the Restoration, to make future officers follow a *cours d'application*, but it was not till the early years of the Third Republic that serious consideration was given to the overall shape of officer training. In 1876 the Minister of War, General de Cissey, took the first step towards formalising the education of officers by instituting special military programmes (*cours militaires spéciaux*), which in 1878 were rationalised into an Ecole Militaire Supérieure. With the structures in place, legislation followed to ensure that all officers were made to undergo appropriate training – a significant innovation in an army where, many felt, etiquette had too often been allowed to take the place of knowledge or experience. The curriculum that was developed placed due emphasis on tactics and the deployment of arms, but it was also careful to teach military history and to make a real attempt to integrate the various disciplines into a single, coherent education. In the view of Maillard, who taught the course on infantry tactics, it was important that the course should be broadening, and that history was given a central place in the programme. Its purpose, he said, was 'to explain the character of war, to show what it was possible to achieve, and to offer some understanding of the influence of external circumstances'.[42] Officers were to be taught about the profession of soldiering as well as the evolving character of military science; and history served both. Military science, it was believed, had its roots in the history of past battles, in a study of the decisions and the qualities of great generals, in reflection on the reasons for past failures. Of the second-year course in military history at Saint-Cyr, for instance, the end-of-year report for 1909 commented that the main purpose had been to acquaint pupils with the transformation of military tactics across different historical periods. They had visited the battlefields of Beaumont and Sedan, to which five lectures had been devoted, in order to bring to life the realities of the Franco-Prussian War and to learn from the reverses that had been suffered.[43] It was through studying

[42] Yoann Brault, Frédéric Jiméno and Daniel Rabreau (eds.), *L'Ecole Militaire, et l'axe Breteuil-Trocadéro* (Paris, 2002), p. 190.

[43] A.G. Vincennes, Xo 16, Ecole Spéciale Militaire de Saint-Cyr, end-of-year report, 1909, pp. 12–13.

history in this way, it was believed, that young officers could be initiated into their craft, and introduced to what Napoleon had called 'the higher aspects of war'.[44]

The purpose of including history in the curriculum was not only to help explain the complexities of warfare; it also was deemed to have a moral value that went beyond technical instruction. The high point for the study of history at the Ecole was, perhaps significantly, in the five years after the Dreyfus Affair broke, when Colonel Foch held the Chair in History, Strategy and General Tactics. Foch believed in the inherent value of history to the soldier, since 'the best method of ensuring the development of his spirit and character is to make history the foundation of his learning'. He argued that by studying great generals of the past the young officers would be encouraged to reflect before taking action themselves. He also drummed home another lesson dear to republicans, showing how across time small professional armies had given way to mass conscript armies, to 'nations in arms' on the republican model. With citizenship came an age of citizen armies, which fought differently from smaller *armées de métier*, and whose potential had to be appreciated before it could be exploited. Foch taught that they were well tuned to the needs of attack, and emphasised the value of offensive and counter-offensive tactics.[45]

To teach military history, guest lecturers could be brought in from the outside, and *conférences* at Saint-Cyr, then as now, were often given by the leading academics of the day, chosen by the ministry for their historical scholarship, but also for their republican credentials. In 1898 at Saint-Cyr, for instance, a course on military history was offered, introduced by Ernest Lavisse and incorporating lectures from specialist historians from the Sorbonne. Lavisse was, as always, unrepentant in his partisan approach, and he made no secret either of his republicanism or of his longstanding affection for the army. His subject, he explained, was not just military history, but the current state of French arms and the military duty that fell on every young Frenchman in the last decade of the nineteenth century. It is in this vein that he proposed to teach the course, discussing the relationship at various historical moments between military institutions and the political and social customs of their day, and offering answers to a number of questions, all with clear contemporary resonance. 'How was the army recruited?

[44] A.G. Vincennes, 1N 16, Centre des Hautes Etudes Militaires, Cours. 'Notes sur les modifications qui pourraient être apportées au programme', décembre 1913.

[45] Brault *et al.*, *L'Ecole Militaire*, p. 190.

Was one a soldier by obligation or by profession? On what principle was discipline structured? How did the officer and the soldier feel about military duty and military honour?' The course, in other words, was not just about battles and historical events. It discussed what Lavisse termed 'a philosophy of soldiering through the ages'.[46]

The specialist lecturer on the French Revolutionary armies at Saint-Cyr in 1898 was Albert Sorel, who exuded a passion for his subject that stemmed from his personal beliefs. Sorel did not try to discuss tactics or movements on the battlefield; rather, his concern was with the morale and spirit of these armies, produced from within the people of France and filled with an enthusiasm and idealism that was 'the very soul of France'. He waxed lyrical about the *volonté* of the young soldiers – especially the volunteers of 1791 and 1792 whom he dubbed 'the pure military generation of the Republic' – and inspired his audience with descriptions of their patriotism and sacrifice. The France they defended was more than the France of the Revolution, for it encapsulated the country's history, the nation's past: 'It is the Gaul of Vercengetorix, the France of the Crusades, the France of Joan of Arc. The voices that they heard were the same voices that called to Joan; they came from above – from the skies of France – as they have done throughout our history.'[47] This was not history; it was pure republican rhetoric. He offered an idealisation of the French soldier which stood, he openly admitted, in stark contrast to the darker aspects of the Terror, as he quoted the words of those young Frenchmen of the 1790s who had so unflinchingly demonstrated their courage and their love for France. Some went on to enjoy exemplary careers under the Empire, like Davout, who, in September 1792, could write that 'We received their bullets with cries of "Long live the Nation! Long live liberty and equality!".'[48] Of course, this is not innocent historical anecdote. Sorel's theme is the importance of patriotism, of sharing the spirit and the soul of the army of revolutionary France. He concluded his lecture by directing his audience to the challenge of the present and urged them to conjure up once more 'the great epoch of the Republic, to relive its soul in your soul and recreate it in our times'.[49] Behind the thin veil of a historical lecture, Sorel was talking to the officer cadets about their values and the careers that lay ahead of them. By preaching the virtues

[46] Ernest Lavisse, *L'armée à travers les âges: conférences faites en 1898 à l'Ecole Militaire de Saint-Cyr* (Paris, 1899), p. 4.

[47] Albert Sorel, *cours* on the French revolutionary armies, in Lavisse, *L'armée à travers les âges*, p. 192.

[48] *Ibid.*, p. 200. [49] *Ibid.*, p. 200.

of the men of the First Republic, his real aim was to rally this new generation to the Third.

The systematic teaching of military history was only part of the new pedagogy which André and others introduced to French military academies in the last years of the nineteenth century. Courses were also given in civic morality, with the aim of bringing the army and the republic together and of destroying the sense of military autonomy that had characterised officers in the past. A new generation of instructors were employed to deliver these courses, men of fixedly republican views like George Duruy at the Polytechnique, Colonel Ebener at Saint-Cyr, Commandant Sarrail at Saint-Maixent and Colonel Valabrègue at Versailles.[50] Their classes would form a crucial part of the new republican project, since they brought a new and specifically republican ethic to the training of officers in the different arms which, it was hoped, would help to break down decades of tradition and introspection in the academies. As Ebener expressed it in one of his lessons at Saint-Cyr in 1901, 'it is my hope that I will inject into the spirit and heart of these gentlemen the fruitful notion that, alongside their professional obligations, they also have duties to fulfil towards the Nation'.[51]

Behind this concern for the nation, there lay, of course, a familiar demographic argument that had its roots in a sense of weakness. At a moment when Germany had a clear advantage in terms of her birth rate and the size of her population – and when the loss of Alsace and Lorraine was keenly felt, strengthening Germany's military potential just as it weakened that of the French – it was incumbent on France to maximise such advantages as she still possessed. For the republicans these advantages were real, and they lay in the moral sphere; here, they believed, the French enjoyed a substantial advantage that would bring benefits on the battlefield. It was no accident, for instance, that George Duruy, one of the champions of the new republican pedagogy, chose to write under the pseudonym 'Lieutenant Marceau', so playing on the memory of one of the Revolution's military heroes. As he explained to his readers, the *nom de plume* was carefully selected to evoke the memory of the revolutionary wars, since the ideas he expressed in his study had all been 'inspired by the patriotic, humane and generous sentiments that characterised the hero of Altenkirchen, a model for

[50] Terquem, *Comment on fait une armée réactionnaire: comment on fait une armée républicaine*, p. 5.

[51] Charles Ebener, *Conférences sur le rôle social de l'officier: faites en 1901 aux élèves de l'Ecole Spéciale Militaire* (Paris, 1901), p. 5.

the modern French officer and soldier alike'.[52] In the German army, he explained,

> there is no moral union between the different elements of which it is composed. A sense of caste, at once narrow, aloof and harsh, reigns in the officer corps, which in other respects is so courageous. The NCOs are infected with the worst Prussian traditions of militarism, and the acts of odious brutality which they carry out on their men occur so frequently as to prove that, even if the Sergeant King has long been dead, his spirit and his methods live on in the army on which he has left his mark forever.[53]

The French, he went on, had different strengths, and since they could no longer hope to recruit more soldiers than the Germans, they had to play to these strengths to have any chance of victory. They had to create tight bonds between officers and men, to persuade the soldiers, as they had done in the Revolution, that they were all citizens fighting for the common good. Then, and only then, once the officers and men had become friends in peacetime, would it be possible to ask the soldiers to rise to the challenge of war, to ask them amidst the perils of battle for 'miracles of devotion', confident that the men would not let them down.[54]

In their teaching they all drew strength from France's history and military tradition, and while they praised the spirit of the republic and the principle of universal service and saw this as the platform on which the future national army would be built, they did not dismiss the legacy of the past. The eighteenth-century officer, as Ebener reminded them, had possessed superb military qualities. He might have suffered from shortcomings in his treatment of the men under him; he might have been too prone to adopt a caste mentality, but 'by temperament and by family tradition he was a warrior through and through, and that from his earliest years'.[55] Courage and devotion were qualities which he had learned in his boyhood, following in the footsteps of such heroes of the royal army as Bayard and Boufflers. He understood discipline, shared a tradition of honour, and readily accepted that he must sacrifice himself for the greater cause of his king. These were qualities, even republicans believed, that must be carefully preserved and nurtured, though they argued that the spirit of caste and belief in hereditary superiority should be replaced by that new, republican virtue, a spirit of solidarity.[56] The revolutionary armies were praised less for their military value – there was general acceptance that on the

[52] George Duruy (ed.), *L'officier éducateur national* (Bordeaux, 1905), p. xviii.
[53] *Ibid.*, p. viii. [54] *Ibid.*, p. ix.
[55] Ebener, *Conférences sur le rôle social de l'officier*, p. 16. [56] *Ibid.*, p. 8.

battlefield the exploits of Napoleon had quickly made them obsolete – than for their moral properties, properties which the new republican pedagogy valued especially highly. In his widely-read text *L'officier dans la Nation*, published in 1903, Coste argued that they were much more than national armies; they were the entire nation in arms, and 'rank was given to the most valiant, the highest ranks distributed on the basis of merit and service'. This was the principle, he declared, that should survive into the new century, for 'their example proves to us that it is not in an army of professionals, however well it is recruited, that we should in future search for the secret of victory, but in the nation itself, rising as a man, weapons at the ready, to defend its interests, its independence, or, that which is inseparable from it, its happiness'. For, he concluded in a crescendo of patriotism, 'no instruction, no military education in the world can supplant love of one's country'.[57] With war again threatening, Coste preached to the officer cadets that France was once again in the era of the French Revolution. Traditional military honour was dead; what counted now was the honour of serving one's country.[58]

The new doctrine was at pains to emphasise that there was no tension between military values and those of society at large, just as there was no contradiction between military service and democracy. As a result of the evolution of the French army and the principle of universal service, army and nation were one, and army officers shared with schoolteachers the 'honourable role' of educating the nation's young.[59] There should, Duruy argued, be greater cooperation between schools and the army, from the *lycées* right down to the level of the *instituteurs*, whose words to the children in their care might germinate and produce 'the splendour of rich harvests in the future'.[60] It was a dream worthy of the generation of Jules Ferry, that generation of radical republicans who cherished schooling above all else and looked to the country's teachers to produce both citizens and republicans. The role of the army, of the officers whom Duruy addressed, was the natural continuation into adult life of the civic education which youngsters were to be given in school. They were to have a triple purpose in the cultivation of the young men ranged before them. First, they had to turn them into soldiers, convincing them of the necessity of the service they were called upon to undertake. Second, they had to raise their morale, by impressing on them that they were not to think of themselves as individuals but

[57] Commandant E. Coste, *L'officier dans la Nation* (Paris, 1903), p. 9.
[58] *Ibid.*, p. 11. [59] Ebener, *Conférences*, p. 73.
[60] Duruy, *L'officier éducateur national*, p. xvii.

as members of society, of a nation which valued justice and fraternity. And, third but most important, they had to give the young soldiers a sense of what it meant to be citizens, to make them aware of their rights and obligations. Military education, they believed, was also an education in citizenship that would in turn make them better, more passionate and more devoted soldiers.[61]

[61] *Ibid.*, pp. 8–28.

9 Educating the republic

To make citizen-soldiers, republicans believed that they first had to make citizens, which they would achieve by a concentrated programme of education starting from the very young years at school. Education in citizenship must be for all, and not just for the young men admitted to Saint-Cyr or France's other military academies, if they were to create a society inspired by the ideals of liberty and equality, where every citizen was conscious of his civic duty and of the sacrifice he might be called upon to make for the fatherland. The message which the political leaders of the Third Republic sought to convey – especially after the arrival in power of the radicals with the presidency of Jules Grévy in 1879 – was a simple one. The new republic, like the First Republic of 1792, was one and indivisible, its ideals inseparable from its revolutionary origins.[1] This heritage was celebrated through a variety of strategies and media: the erection of statues in public squares; the resort to republican symbols on coins and banknotes; the imposition of busts of Marianne in every prefecture and every *mairie* in the land; the choice in 1880 of 14 July as France's national day, evoking quite explicitly the link between social progress and revolutionary violence; and the grandiose celebration in 1889 of the Centenary of the Great Revolution itself.[2] These years also saw the debating chambers and function suites of town halls across France transformed by paintings, sculptures and ceremonial ceilings that celebrated the great moments of the Revolution and represented the political virtues of the republic in a triumphal display of symbolic decors.[3]

[1] I gave an earlier version of part of this chapter, entitled 'La représentation de la guerre et des armées dans les manuels scolaires', to a conference on 'Tra insegnamento e ricerca: a storia della Rivoluzione francese', held at the Università di Napoli Federico II, in Naples, in October 2003. I wish to express my thanks to Anna-Maria Rao for inviting me to speak on that occasion and for providing a forum to discuss some of the views that follow.

[2] Maurice Agulhon, *Marianne au pouvoir. L'imagerie et la symbolique républicaines de 1880 à 1914* (Paris, 1989), pp. 113–26.

[3] *Le Triomphe des mairies. Grands décors républicains à Paris, 1870–1914* (Catalogue d'exposition, Musée du Petit Palais, Paris, 1986).

In the battle between Left and Right the key issue was increasingly this: how should one position oneself in relation to the political and social heritage of 1789?[4] Every image that was used was a poignant reminder of the debt of gratitude owed by present-day Frenchmen to their revolutionary ancestors. They had sacrificed themselves so that their descendants might be free; and among their sacrifices none was greater or more heroic than that of the soldiers who had fought and died for freedom. They had an honoured place in the new republican pantheon.

The preferred image of the revolutionary soldier during the Third Republic was a highly romantic one that encapsulated the full pathos of his sacrifice and played on the emotions of the onlooker. It was reproduced in pamphlets and school textbooks, but was most memorably described by Jules Michelet in historical writings that depicted the army as enthusiastic and idealistic, comprising a generation of young men bound together by their shared ideals of patriotism and fraternity. In *Les soldats de la Révolution*, published in 1898 at a time when many felt that France was once again under threat from across the Rhine, Michelet recalled his childhood memories of war, his admiration for the troops who went off to fight for Napoleon, and his belief that all were individuals who deserved to be honoured. 'I was a child in 1810', he wrote, 'when on the Emperor's birthday the drapes were pulled aside that hid the monument on the Place Vendôme and the column was unveiled. I watched in admiration like everyone else. Only, I should like to have known the names of the men depicted in bronze on the bas-reliefs. All those, I asked, who are shown climbing up the column, what were their names?'[5] The picture that Michelet paints is of an army that was born of 1789 itself, of the National Guard, the Bastille and the first federations; it is an army taking part in 'an immense crusade of fraternity', when 'the federations of 90 were the battalions of 92', and when 'friends left with friends, neighbours with neighbours, they left hand in hand, honouring the vows they had made two years earlier on the altar of the Nation'.[6] Such was Michelet's reputation on the Left and so powerful his prose that this image went on to inspire a generation of Frenchmen, none less than the schoolteachers brought by Jules Ferry into every town and village in the land. His lyricism, it seemed, knew no bounds as he made war itself an act of purity and idealism: 'Such touching origins! Such admirable armies formed by fraternity

4 Christian Amalvi, *La République en scène. Les décors des mairies parisiennes, 1873–1914* (Paris, 2006), p. 11.

5 Jules Michelet, *Les soldats de la Révolution* (Paris, 1898), p. 23.

6 *Ibid.*, p. 31.

itself! Sublime wars, wars that were created by love! For what was it that France was asking for? Liberated herself, she wanted to free all the nations of Europe; she had no expectation of gain, only a desire to save the world.' In this period, in Michelet's view, France fully merited a description coined in another age and a different context. France, he declared, had finally become in these revolutionary years the 'soldier of God'.[7]

What gave the soldier his special status in Michelet's eyes was the fact that he was the product of the people, a man of arms who had risen from the population to defend the lives, homes and territory of the French people themselves. For Michelet this was not a matter of philosophical abstraction, but a powerful and frequently repeated rhetorical device. The people for him had an almost mystical status, linked to the land of France and to centuries of past history. It was united in its love of liberty, and united by the revolutionary tradition in whose name Michelet wrote with such compelling eloquence. Above all, it was a term implying integration and social inclusiveness, in contrast to the newer nineteenth-century discourses of class. He repeatedly used the word to refer to the peasantry, to the poor, to those who had been denied rights by previous regimes but who were now engulfed in the fraternity of the French republic. They were now integrated into French society, into the *patrie*, and integrated by the culture that was the Revolution. All three terms were crucial here – *peuple*, *révolution*, *patrie* – to what one recent critic has called Michelet's 'strategy of persuasion', a strategy that gave a distinctly ideological tone to the idea of the Nation.[8] It was a strategy that found avid listeners among the political class of the Third Republic, who warmed to his lyrical style as much as to his fervent patriotism. Jules Simon had been one of his students; Georges Clemenceau had been raised on Michelet; while Jean Jaurès spoke of him as one of the political writers who had most inspired him in his youth.[9]

Michelet's histories led a generation of writers and historians to think of the French Revolution in positive, romantic terms, as the embodiment of the French nation and its people. He had a particular influence over those who were introduced to the French Revolution in the schools of the Second Empire, at a time when the Empire was eager to identify

[7] *Ibid.*, p. 34.

[8] Chaâbane Harbaoui, 'Le statut rhétorique du "peuple" et de la "Révolution" dans Michelet', in Christian Croisille and Jean Ehrard (eds.), *La légende de la Révolution* (Clermont-Ferrand, 1988), pp. 380–1.

[9] Gordon Wright, editor's introduction to Jules Michelet, *History of the French Revolution* (Chicago, 1967), p. xiv.

with the Revolution's achievements and present itself as its heir.[10] For while Michelet might admit the more brutal excesses of the Revolution, he was always careful not to condemn them, in striking contrast to the more conservative historians like Hippolyte Taine who were so influential in the early years of the Third Republic.[11] This approach won him immediate popularity with a younger generation, men who came to maturity in the 1870s and 1880s and would identify with the patriotism and anti-clerical outlook of the radical republic. Prominent among them was Alphonse Aulard, who in 1870, while still a student at the Ecole Normale Supérieure in Paris, had enlisted in the army with several of his friends to help repulse the Prussian invasion. This experience served to strengthen Aulard's republican convictions, helped to forge his identification with the Revolution and its prosecution of national interests. He believed staunchly in the values of the republic and shared in its traditions, and he equated the defence of the First Republic with the defence of the Third.[12]

This implied that the revolutionary army should again be elevated to its true position in French society and honoured for its pivotal role in saving the First Republic. In the years of conservative ascendancy after 1871 the volunteers of 1792 had received scant attention. It was not that they were actually criticised, for their stock remained high in the wake of the Franco-Prussian War; but their role was deliberately played down, their contribution passed over in silence, in a historiography that was intensely hostile to the politics of the Revolution and sought to equate the army with the nation, but not with the regime.[13] This rather conspiratorial silence was dramatically reversed with the coming to power of the radicals after 1879, when the public mood that produced cheering crowds on 14 July and gloried in the republican tradition also sought to revive the place of the French Revolution in the history of the nation. The Revolution must again take its place among the great moments of world history, an event which the people of France understood and in which they took pride. For this reason, as one aspect of the centenary celebrations in 1889, the government decided to found a Chair in the history of the Revolution at the Sorbonne, a

[10] Jacques Godechot, *Un jury pour la Révolution* (Paris, 1974), p. 231.

[11] Norman Hampson, 'The French Revolution and its historians', in Geoffrey Best (ed.), *The Permanent Revolution* (London, 1989), p. 225.

[12] James Friguglietti, 'Alphonse Aulard and the republicanization of the Revolution', in Michel Vovelle (ed.), *L'image de la Révolution Française* (4 vols., Paris, 1989), vol. II, p. 1092.

[13] Annie Crépin, 'L'image de l'armée dans l'historiographie du dix-neuvième siècle', in Michel Vovelle (ed.), *L'image de la Révolution Française*, vol. II, p. 1103.

measure which, they believed, would restore it to its rightful place in the historical firmament. The first holder of this Chair was none other than Alphonse Aulard, chosen for his scholarship and erudition, of course, but also for his staunch republican beliefs, as someone who saw teaching the French Revolution as an important part of the wider process of instilling the values of modern citizenship. Aulard was a devout believer, his political cause being the sort of anti-clerical republicanism best illustrated by the Radical Socialist Party.[14] He could be relied upon to stay loyal to the essential precepts of republicanism. Above all, he adhered to a longstanding Jacobin tradition which linked patriotism to the French Revolution and did not conceive of the army as being a force for maintaining the status quo.[15]

But to the wider French public it was Jean Jaurès who in the years before the First World War most cogently preached the cause of a people's army, as clearly aligned to the nation in spirit and ideology as it was by the nature of its recruitment. This was a major reason why he looked back to the Revolution with affection, and saw in the composition of the revolutionary armies, in the enthusiasm of the *masse*, the only means of defending the nation's frontiers should they again come under attack. He had, as a pacifist, no truck with wars of expansion or empire of the kind France had repeatedly launched during the nineteenth century. The only reason for a people to make war, as Jaurès interpreted it, was in a just cause, when its territory was invaded and its homes and livelihoods put in danger. And even then the people must have right on their side. That, for Jaurès, was what had most clearly characterised the Revolutionary wars: 'It is the fact that the high moral conscience of the armies remained intact, or was perceived as being intact, that gave them their superb faith in success; it was the certainty of being right that produced the certainty of victory.'[16] It was this, he believed, that allowed the generals to impose strict discipline on the armies, discipline that was fair and consented to by all, a discipline, moreover, that was clearly republican and which derived from the ideology of the regime. For, he argued, 'it was not by isolating from the Revolution the armies that were fighting for the Revolution that the Committee of Public Safety maintained and re-imposed order; it was, on the contrary, by assuring communication between the army and revolutionary thought'.[17] It was this that had sustained the morale of the troops and had, in Jaures's view, contributed so markedly to victory.

[14] Alfred Cobban, *Aspects of the French Revolution* (New York, 1968), p. 49.
[15] Crépin, 'L'image de l'armée dans l'historiographie du dix-neuvième siècle', p. 1103.
[16] Jean Jaurès, *L'armée nouvelle* (Paris, 1910), p. 217. [17] *Ibid.*, p. 218.

While writers like Michelet and Jaurès developed their concepts of a republican army for a largely adult readership, the principal target for the politicians of the Third Republic was always the young. In the wake of the humiliation of 1870, they sought to inculcate in future generations a love of France and a sense of republican duty that would prepare them for the war to come, and to inculcate in the young those values which their elders identified as necessary to national salvation, courage and obedience.[18] The new republic took the view that the military defeat which France's armies had suffered was as much that of the French schoolteacher at the hands of his Prussian counterpart as of the French soldier on the field of battle, and that this alone made it essential to institute a system of free and universal primary education where the young could be shaped and their republicanism formed at a tender age. In this pedagogy the republic was France, and the people and the nation – as for Michelet – were fused into a single entity, one and indivisible as in the earlier republic in the Year II. But it showed much greater awareness of provincial difference, recognition of the patriotism of men like Maurras and Barrès but also a nod in the direction of the lost provinces of Alsace and Lorraine. It emphasised the variety and the richness of France, and acknowledged the complementary character of its provinces. It gloried unashamedly in the *petites patries* of which France was composed, their complexity and difference as well as the common history that united them. It even encouraged the literary regionalism of the age, expressing that consciousness of local difference that animated a generation of provincial writers who popularised their local customs and local traditions in novels, plays and ethnographic writings.[19] For many Frenchmen – and not only men of the Right – found the central tenets of the republic too abstract, too centralist, too rooted in enlightened humanism. They pressed for changes to the centralised state, and argued, with the regionalist movement of Jean Charles-Brun, that a truly democratic republic must be grounded in the ideas and interests of families, communes and provinces. It should be united but it should also be heterogeneous.[20]

This passion for the heterogeneity of French culture and French landscape soon found its way into the school curriculum, where it was presented as one of the glories of the very special country to which

[18] André-Roger Voisin, *L'école des poilus. L'enseignement de la guerre dans les écoles primaires de 1870 à 1914* (Paris, 2007), p. 9.

[19] Anne-Marie Thiesse, *Écrire la France. Le mouvement littéraire régionaliste de langue française entre la Belle Époque et la Libération* (Paris, 1991), pp. 183–203.

[20] Julian Wright, *The Regionalist Movement in France, 1890–1914. Jean Charles-Brun and French Political Thought* (Oxford, 2003), p. 98.

French schoolchildren had the enviable good fortune to belong. It was a land like no other, a land whose virtues and beauty evoked patriotism in all who lived there. Schoolteachers were urged to adapt the national curriculum to local circumstance – the local economy, local history, local folklore – for if the school was a powerful symbol of the nation in every village in France, it was also an institution that brought republican values into the heart of the community and which, like the railway, should be encouraged to adapt to local demands and conditions.[21] In the textbooks used in primary schools, especially, France was always presented as a country with special privileges – it was 'blessed', as the authors liked to say – with a rich landscape and a sophisticated culture, a landscape as varied and timeless as the provinces of France themselves.[22] Exile, enforced absence from the *patrie*, was, in consequence a sad and solitary experience, something that diminished a man and destroyed his morale.[23] Hence the Frenchman could love his country and appreciate the values of the republic without uprooting himself from the traditions of his locality. Many textbook writers followed Maurice Barrès' lead in urging that he should remain attached to his *petit pays*, where the soil of ages ran through his fingers and where successive generations of his family had farmed the land. And though nationalists were wont to link this romantic attachment to tradition and locality to right-wing politics, and even (in Maurras's case) to monarchism, many republicans shared their concern for keeping contact with one's roots. The nation was first understood at home, and only by appreciating the defining qualities of the Brie, the Pays Basque, or Poitou, could a Frenchman come truly to love France.[24]

Underlying this new concern for France's geographical and cultural diversity lay the desire to inculcate patriotism, to create the sense of being French and members of a shared community. For republicans one of the most natural appeals was to their own republican past, to the sense that the French people were united by a shared republican history. For this reason they made repeated appeals to their ancestors of the 1790s, their 'fathers' in the France of the Revolution. Among them were, of course, the *philosophes* of the eighteenth century and the great

[21] Jean-François Chanet, *L'école républicaine et les petites patries* (Paris, 1996), pp. 45–57.

[22] The timelessness and the eternal reassurance to be derived from the landscape are themes taken up and expanded by François Walter, *Les figures paysagères de la nation. Territoire et paysage en Europe, 16e au 20e siècle* (Paris, 2004).

[23] Jacques Ozouf and Mona Ozouf, 'Le thème du patriotisme dans les manuels primaires', *Mouvement social* 49 (1964), p. 6.

[24] See Maurice Barrès, *Les Déracinés* (Paris, 1897).

orators of the Convention, as were the many men of letters, scientists, artists, musicians and soldiers who were held to have contributed to the greatness of the French republic. This lesson was repeated on all sides and through a variety of media – at school, most obviously, but also in the pages of newspapers and magazines, in popular lithographs, cartoons and the statuary of the Third Republic. It was a period when there was a new vogue for erecting statues in city streets, and most notably in Paris. The choice of figures to celebrate was quite catholic, with scientists, educationalists, actors and philosophers all to the fore; indeed, the republic seemed to prefer these as being less divisive, less open to criticism.[25] Nonetheless, the years after 1871 saw monuments erected to Etienne Marcel, the medieval peasant leader, and to a number of France's more recent revolutionary heroes, to leading eighteenth-century philosophers (Voltaire, Diderot, Beaumarchais and Rousseau), and to the republic itself. Images of soldiers were less commonplace, largely because relations between the Third Republic and its army remained strained and because politicians feared that adulation of the military might unleash a new upsurge of popular Bonapartism. A statue was raised to Danton on the Place de l'Odéon in 1891, presenting him as the 'soul of national defence', while the early death of Gambetta provided an excuse for a new explosion of patriotism and republican statuary. In the ensuing competition, the winning design specifically linked the new republic to the old, the sacrifice of Gambetta to that of the Revolution. In the statue, which was unveiled in 1888 in front of the Louvre, Gambetta is shown against the backcloth of the *Marseillaise* of François Rude, an image that necessarily recalled the volunteers of the French revolutionary armies. Behind the main figures of Force and Truth, two boys shake hands, making common cause in the name of the Republic. The boys represent Labour (shown holding a hammer) and National Defence (with a sword), and they are united when the *patrie* calls. Onlookers are reminded that, now as in 1792, the republic can look to its young, to its citizen-soldiers, in its hour of need.[26]

The unity of soldier and civilian, labour and nation, became the single most important message that the republic sought to transmit to its people, and it became one of the principal hallmarks of the French education system. Since this was a republic that believed deeply in the value of education, it entrusted to its army of schoolteachers the important task of preparing the next generation for citizenship. Of course, this was

[25] June Hargrove, *Les statues de Paris: la représentation des Grands Hommes dans les rues et sur les places de Paris* (Paris, 1989), p. 375.

[26] *Ibid.*, p. 109.

not unique to France, or to the Third Republic, though the intensity of the ideological battle between Church and state for control over the minds of the young made educational policy in France seem more ideologically directed than in most other European countries. Modernity, as the political scientist Ernest Gellner has made clear, almost necessarily favours education, since education defines the quality of the contribution which each individual can make to society as a whole; this makes it, in his view, the most precious investment that a society can make to guarantee its future, to protect its culture, and to guarantee citizenship itself.[27] In a society marked by new levels of social mobility, one of the most productive elements in this investment was the school textbook (*manuel scolaire*), especially in rural areas where books were scarce and where few homes could boast reading matter beyond a few sacred texts. Here the school textbook could introduce the habit of reading not just to the pupils themselves, but also to their brothers and sisters, their parents and the community. Indeed, one of the principal collections published by the Maison Hachette – a major publisher of classroom primers – was entitled the 'Library for Schools and Families'. In his preface to one of the volumes Henri Vast noted that 'children will take pleasure in this little book ... young people and their parents will find profit in it ... and so it will be welcome in schools of all kinds, in secondary education, and in public libraries'.[28] Compared to most adult literature, schoolbooks were undoubtedly influential. They enjoyed very large print runs, were often reprinted many times and, of course, had that rarest of privileges in the world of publishing, a guaranteed distribution. It followed from this that the image and representation of events which they conveyed gained access to innumerable young readers and enjoyed that rather special authority which came with the imprimatur of the educational authorities.

Some books were, of course, more successful and more prized than others, and some authors listened to with greater reverence. In school classrooms across the country and in thousands of French homes the richness of France's heritage was taught through the medium of a patriotic tale written in the years following the Franco-Prussian War, *Le tour de la France par deux enfants*, published in 1877 by Augustine Fouillée, though under the much more famous pen-name of 'G. Bruno'. In its pages French children were awakened to the wonderland of forests

[27] Ernest Gellner, *Nations and Nationalism* (London, 1983), p. 36.

[28] Christian Amalvi, 'Les représentations du passé national dans la littérature de vulgarisation catholique et laïque', in Stéphane Michaud, Jean-Yves Mollier and Nicole Savy (eds.), *Usages de l'image au dix-neuvième siècle* (Paris, 1992), p. 63.

and meadows, streams and mountains, rivers and aqueducts that were France, in the company of two orphaned brothers, André and Julien Volden, who in 1871 left their home in Phalsbourg in occupied Lorraine, crossed secretly on to French soil, and went in search of the uncle they hoped would look after them. Its impact was immense, especially after 1882 when the new state primary schools of Jules Ferry tried to turn it into a sort of republican catechism. Its message was vigorously and at times sentimentally patriotic, as when the two boys look down on a little stream in the Vosges and they picture its course, joining the Meurthe, then the Moselle, and on to their German-occupied homeland. The younger boy turns sad and melancholic as he recalls that 'the Meurthe and the Moselle are rivers of Lorraine' and that 'the Moselle passes through Alsace-Lorraine where we were born, where we shall never return, and where our father has stayed for ever'.[29] *Le tour de la France* is in its literary form partly a novel, but its main function is topographical and educational, to convey to the young something of the geography and history of each region of France through a series of short vignettes reminiscent of an encyclopaedia or gazetteer.[30] The conversation between the two boys is always a source of information and insight, the message made more graphic by the inclusion of nineteen maps and '212 illustrations instructive for teaching things'.[31] Buoyed by its rapid adoption in primary schools, it became one of the country's all-time bestsellers, selling three million copies in its first ten years in print and six million by the turn of the century, thus justifying the sobriquet given to it by Jacques and Mona Ozouf, of 'the little red book of the Republic'.[32] This was most especially true of later editions, which saw confessional references expunged, with the book's message mirroring more closely the 'independent morality' of the anti-clerical *Ligue de l'enseignement*.[33]

The diversity of France and the variety of its landscape are recurrent themes in the reading prescribed for the young, a richness that

[29] G. Bruno, *Le tour de la France par deux enfants: devoir et patrie* (Cours moyen conforme aux programmes du 27 juillet 1882, 283rd edition, Paris, 1898), p. 36.

[30] John Strachan, 'Romance, religion and the Republic: Bruno's *Le Tour de la France par deux enfants*', *French History* 18 (2004), p. 99.

[31] Ségolène Le Men, 'La pédagogie par l'image dans un manuel de la Troisième République: *le Tour de la France par deux enfants*', in Michaud *et al.*, *Usages de l'image au dix-neuvième siècle*, p. 122.

[32] Jacques Ozouf and Mona Ozouf, '*Le tour de la France par deux enfants*. Le petit livre rouge de la République', in Pierre Nora (ed.), *Les lieux de mémoire: 1 – La République* (Paris, 1984), p. 291.

[33] Katherine Auspitz, *The Radical Bourgeoisie. The Ligue de l'Enseignement and the origins of the Third Republic, 1866–1885* (Cambridge, 1982), p. 162.

was often contrasted with Germany whose main characteristics were ethnic or racial unity.[34] To this was added something of France's history and shared experience, a history which enabled republican teachers to identify the French nation with high moral values and enlightened ideas. Indeed, of all the subjects on the school curriculum it was history that offered the radical republic the greatest opportunity to present its humanist and secular vision, just as it was the French revolutionary period that provided the preferred battlefield in the educational war against reaction and the Catholic Church. This privileged position resulted in the creation of two rival pedagogies during the years up to the First World War – that of the republican, anti-clerical textbooks which identified with everything the Revolution had achieved and insisted, like the political leadership, that the Revolution should be regarded as a single block, as an indivisible morality; and that of the rival confessional textbooks which denounced the atheistic philosophy of the revolutionaries and drew attention to the excesses of the Terror. Both presented the history of France as a Manichean struggle between the forces of Good and Evil, and both saw history lessons as the place where these forces could most appropriately be explained. Neither believed that there was any room for compromise, and their respective representations of the French Revolution did much to embitter feelings between them. For Catholics religion was and should remain a matter for all Frenchmen, and hence for the French state, whereas the radicals saw it as an entirely private affair that should have no place in either the public sphere or the school curriculum.[35] The level of bitterness is well reflected in a speech by the radical deputy Gerard-Varet in the Chamber of Deputies in 1910, when he derided the Catholic school texts for their cynical dismissal of the Revolution and their refusal to see any good in it. They continually emphasise the faults of the revolutionaries, he claimed, and 'do not have a word to say that might describe what was great and noble in the revolution, or its prodigious fertility'. On the contrary, he added, citing the manual of Abbé Gagnol which he took as typical of many, they exaggerate the effect of the Terror (which 'struck down lives in their millions') and hurl abuse at the work of deputies on mission ('When the proconsuls had eaten and drunk well, they went, as an aid to their digestion, to see fall beneath the guillotine the head of an unfortunate servant-girl who had heard mass from a non-juring priest').[36] Each side

[34] Ozouf and Ozouf, 'Le thème du patriotisme dans les manuels primaires', p. 7.

[35] Gérard Cholvy and Yves-Marie Hilaire, *Histoire religieuse de la France contemporaine* (2 vols., Toulouse, 1985–86), vol. II (1880–1930), pp. 171–2.

[36] Christian Amalvi, *Les héros de l'histoire de France. Recherche iconographique sur le panthéon scolaire de la Troisième République* (Paris, 1979), p. 288.

saw the other's views as an intolerable moral outrage which increased their own determination to control the historical record that was offered to the young.

Both sides also sought to present a heroic narrative of French history, the heroes who had helped create their France and defend their values. All textbooks, whether of a republican or a confessional persuasion, indulged in a cult of heroes that could give some structure to the history of the nation. Some of these predated the Revolution, medieval heroes like Vercengetorix or Charlemagne, who could be linked to the expansion and greatness of France, and these were largely uncontroversial, the shared heroes of two competing nations. Most notably there was the military figure of Joan of Arc, heroic, nationalistic and (to the Church) defined by her piety and Catholic faith. In the words of one leading text, addressing its primary-age readers, 'you will love Joan with all your heart, my child, as the martyr of the motherland and the patron saint of France'.[37] What is most significant here is that the text in question was strongly republican, sharing, it seems, the enthusiasm of Catholic authors for the piety of a medieval national heroine. But once the book moved on from the medieval to the modern period, it became far more partisan in its choice of heroes.[38] It presented the history of France as a story of progress, happiness, courage and civilisation, and – like most books aimed at impressionable young boys – it placed a disproportionate emphasis on military figures. For instance, it lingered lovingly on the person of Lazare Hoche, the son of a humble groom in the royal stables at Versailles and the sort of person with whom the audience could easily identify. No fewer than three pictures are devoted to Hoche. In the first he is a small boy in the kitchen of the family home, facing punishment from his father for forgetting to prepare the stew for supper. In the second he is a sergeant in the *Gardes françaises*, working in the gardens to earn extra money to buy books and further his studies. And in the third – by implication as a consequence of these studies – he is the saviour of France, a general of the Republic at the tender age of twenty-five, and chasing the invader out of Alsace.[39]

Modern heroes, as related to schoolchildren, were almost always partisan figures – the heroes of the republic, and hence of laicity, or of the Church and the Catholic faith, men who had risked death for the cause of God or of the French republic. The one side had Le Peletier or Marat, the other Louis XVI or the Vendean Cathelineau. Or they

[37] Ozouf and Ozouf, 'Le thème du patriotisme dans les manuels primaires', p. 9.
[38] A. Aymard, *Histoire de France en images – cours Gauthier-Deschamps* (Paris, 1933).
[39] Aymard, *Cours Gauthier-Deschamps*, pp. 48–9.

were national heroes, like Joan of Arc, who could bring a vital symbolic unity to a fractured society. Or else they symbolised the values of the nation in times of great danger: one such was the young revolutionary army officer, Rouget de Lisle, the composer of the Marseillaise whose singing before the mayor of Strasbourg decorated so many school texts of the Third Republic.[40] The textbooks always emphasised the same qualities: generosity of spirit, self-sacrifice, faith (in lay textbooks religious faith was transformed into patriotism or love of France), and dignity or stoicism when faced by an unjust death. For these texts did not depend solely on the power of words; they also included large numbers of images to impress their readers, especially powerful when they illustrated a military feat or exemplified the glory of French arms. France witnessed during this period a technical revolution in the printing industry, allowing writers to incorporate for the first time illustrations drawn from high-quality lithographs rather than from the vivid images of Jean-Claude Pellerin and his fellow imagists in Epinal.[41] School texts were transformed, becoming a more direct and more powerful medium, and primary schools were treated to what Christian Amalvi calls 'a veritable theatre of memory' in which was re-enacted 'a heroic ballet both well staged and highly effective, a sort of totemic dance in honour of the great forebears of the national clan'.[42]

Of course, the most imposing regime since the Revolution to republican eyes was the Third Republic itself, which had built on the humanistic achievement of its ancestor and had, like the First Republic, championed religious tolerance at every opportunity, to Protestants and Jews, Jansenists and Freethinkers; the only religious group who were missing, it seemed, were the Catholics themselves.[43] The Republic was praised for its loyalty to the ideals of the Revolution, but also for something that was decidedly more military – its capacity to prepare the French people psychologically for the war to come.[44] For in this new civic republicanism there was a strong element of national pride, the pride of a strong nation able to succeed where the Second Empire had failed, by delivering an adventurous and successful foreign policy. That in turn meant that the role of the army and the importance of military expenditure had to be recognised by the Republic, even if its political

[40] Michel Vovelle, 'La Marseillaise. La guerre ou la paix', in Pierre Nora (ed.), *Les lieux de mémoire: 1 – La République* (Paris, 1984), pp. 89–90.

[41] See Nicole Garnier, *Catalogue de l'imagerie populaire française. 2- Images d'Epinal gravées sur bois* (Paris, 1996).

[42] Amalvi, *Les héros de l'histoire de France*, p. 78.

[43] Ozouf and Ozouf, 'Le thème du patriotisme dans les manuels primaires', p. 10.

[44] Alice Gérard, *La Révolution française, mythes et interprétations* (Paris, 1970), *passim*.

leaders still eyed the military high command with ill-disguised distrust. In the process, building up France's military strength came to be a significant priority for republicans, as significant, in its way, as the reform of the educational system which Ferry, Combes and others treasured so highly. In the words of one primary-school history textbook, written by Devinat for use by nine- and ten-year-olds, the case for the military was baldly stated. 'Today', the book rejoiced, 'the French army is formidable'. To make the point more forcibly, he went on to boast that 'if it marched past four abreast, without stopping day or night, it would take more than half a month before the last man had passed'.[45] The point was well made; it was an image to dazzle its schoolboy audience.

Already, in the years that followed the Franco-Prussian War, France's political leaders were planning a war of revenge, and the moral battle for the minds of the nation had begun. Schools were bombarded, especially during the 1880s and 1890s, with an avalanche of titles about civic duty which sought to offer an education in citizenship, a citizenship in which military service played a significant part. In the process the army of the republic was increasingly lauded, while in history lessons the generals of the French Revolution were introduced into the revolutionary pantheon. It was a theme that could unite everyone regardless of political preference. Even the Catholic Right could join in the celebration of national victories. This is shown in the textbook of the ultra-royalist René-Jean Durdent in 1815, deliberately entitled *Memorable Periods and Events in the History of France from the Beginnings of the Monarchy to the Arrival of Louis XVIII in his Capital.* During the revolutionary years, Durdent claimed, it was in the armies that 'French honour took refuge', adding for good measure that 'it is right that we should lavish praise of those brave men, so many thousands of whom died in the belief that they were defending their country's cause'. Even Carnot, a member of the Jacobin Committee of Public Safety, escaped censure because of the quality of his military leadership, while the victories at Fleurus and Jemappes were hailed as 'the prelude to the greatest feats of arms which History has ever related'.[46] The Revolution might represent a grim and dark period in the minds of the French Right, but the army could count as a salutary exception. 'Only the glory of the armies, the sacrifice of countless numbers of republican soldiers and the valour of raw and youthful generals illuminate a period that was

[45] Ozouf and Ozouf, 'Le thème du patriotisme dans les manuels primaires', pp. 12–13n.

[46] Paul Gerbod, 'La Révolution enseignée à la jeunesse française dans la première moitié du dix-neuvième siècle', *Revue historique* (1988), pp. 438–9.

at once painful and odious.'[47] Even for much of the twentieth century, when the textbooks that were used in Catholic schools remained highly critical of the Revolution and its ideology, it is noticeable how positive images of the period relied on the army and military glory. Of twenty-four pro-revolutionary pictures identified in textbooks in use in 1959 – compared to thirty-one that were critical or overtly hostile – it is images of the war that dominate: republican soldiers, the enrolment of volunteers, Valmy and Rouget de Lisle together account for seventeen of the twenty-four illustrations.[48] And it is valour and patriotism, not vestiges of revolutionary idealism, that elicit admiration.

The sheer negativity of many of the Catholic textbooks was roundly denounced by the republican majority and led to numbers of them being banned in 1901.[49] A good instance is the *Histoire de France* of Abbé Vandepitte, which epitomised for many on the Left the outrageous lack of patriotism and civic commitment of those teaching in the *écoles libres*.[50] The reasons are not hard to find. The book, aimed at primary-school children, laid out four main periods of the French Revolution: those of the Constituent Assembly, 'or the period of destruction'; the Legislative Assembly, 'or the period of persecution'; the Convention, 'or the period of terror and bloodshed'; and the Directory, which it condemned as 'the period of anarchy'.[51] In short, there was nothing in the Revolution from which to take pride, and little that could be discussed without outright condemnation. When the text turned to the wars of the Convention, it immediately plunged into the question of civil war, emphasising the popular character of the revolt in the West and the piety of the Vendean forces. 'The death of Louis XVI', Vandepitte declared, 'had the effect of mobilising the Vendée for God and the King', with the consequence that today 'France refers with pride to the heroes who fell in the struggle, a struggle that was primarily about religion'.[52] If that was not bad enough, the more rabid Catholic textbooks poured scorn on the revolutionary volunteers. They could accept the quality of some of the Revolution's generals, and they might go so far as to praise the wisdom of Carnot's measures for national defence. But those who volunteered to fight for the Revolution they often dismissed as rabble. In

[47] *Ibid.*, p. 446.

[48] Jacqueline Freyssinet-Dominjon, *Les manuels d'histoire de l'école libre, 1882–1959* (Paris, 1969), p. 189.

[49] Among the more intransigent were Melin, *Petite histoire de France* (Paris, 1885), Girard, *Année préparatoire d'histoire de France* (Paris, 1886), and Abbé Gagnol, *Histoire de France* (Paris, 1901); also the work of Abbé Vandepitte cited below.

[50] Abbé Vandepitte, *Histoire de France, à l'usage des maisons chrétiennes d'éducation* (Lille, 1895).

[51] *Ibid.*, p. 397. [52] *Ibid.*, p. 435.

the opinion of Vandepitte, 'those miserable recruits from Parisian riots had neither value nor discipline; they took fright when the Austrians advanced and lost Neerwinden for Dumouriez'. Only later, when the armies had been trained to behave more like professional soldiers, did clerical manuals begin to ascribe some military worth to them and to their commanders.[53]

If Catholic authors treated the revolutionary armies with less hostility than the politicians, even admitting that they fought bravely in defence of French soil,[54] they still hesitated to create the impression that the Revolution had any real merit. They thought, in the tradition of Monseigneur Dupanloup (then Bishop of Orleans) and others, that there was a real danger in leaving the education of the young to a generation of teachers who did not believe in God, and they used the history of the Revolution to rectify imbalance and prejudice. It was not that the schools of Jules Ferry omitted all reference to religion; far from that. But they did not understand or feel for it as only a believer could. 'They turn Christianity', wrote Dupanloup, 'the divine work which has regenerated mankind and changed the face of the world, into something that is no doubt beautiful and admirable, but it is human, purely human in inspiration, and as a result, in spite of the ostentatious and hypocritical praise they heap upon it, it is vain and perishable like everything that is made on earth'.[55] Between this and the dominant view of the Third Republic there could be little common ground.

For republicans school textbooks had a strong civic purpose. They had to be patriotic in sentiment and were expected to hold true to the revolutionary faith. They were preparations in citizenship and moral conduct as well as primers in French history, and France's heroes were presented as exemplary lives, to be admired and imitated. For this purpose it was important to be able to present France as a united country, open to enlightened ideas and working for the benefit of mankind. The unity of a society of citizens allowed France to overcome more shallow sectional divisions, of religion or wealth or social class. French patriotism was about taking pride in these values and exporting them across the globe; it could be presented as a virtuous form of nationalism that contrasted with the ignoble and imperialistic chauvinism of others. French wars had been fought out of an innate sense of justice; they were

[53] *Ibid.*, pp. 437–8.

[54] Vincent Cavalier, 'La représentation de la Révolution française à travers les manuels scolaires de 1870 à 1914' (mémoire de maîtrise, Université de Provence Aix-Marseille I, 1996), p. 79.

[55] Félix-Antoine-Philibert Dupanloup, *Conseils aux jeunes gens sur l'étude de l'histoire* (Paris, 1872), p. 26.

unavoidable, indeed necessary, and the republic existed to bring peace and to establish the basis on which a lasting peace could be guaranteed. Texts portrayed war, generically, as something odious and ignoble, leading to death and physical destruction; so the republican soldier was presented, not as aggressive and warlike, but rather as the defender of his community and the hero of a just cause.[56] This was the message that was conveyed in the depiction of exemplary soldiers, mild-mannered, courteous and heroic, ready to sacrifice their lives for a greater good. General Marceau, for instance, was an emblematic figure for many republicans, a young officer who led an exemplary life, won rapid promotion – he was a general at twenty-three – before dying in battle at the age of twenty-seven, loyal to the end to the republic he loved.[57] And it was accentuated – for schoolboys, especially – by elevating tales of revolutionary youngsters like Bara and Viala, who died heroically at a tragically young age to destroy treason and save the republic. They had been hailed as heroes in 1793; now, ninety years and two republics later, they were once again presented to a new generation as exemplars to be admired and followed. This was especially true in primary schools, where images were starker and textbooks routinely devoted a page or two to them as models of 'heroic childhood'.[58] Often the message was clearly spelt out. In 1882, for instance, Charavay asked, rhetorically, whether telling children about the 'sublime' actions of Bara and Viala was not 'a means of developing selflessness in the hearts of the young and inspiring them to seek to emulate their fine example'.[59] The writers of texts for the *cours moyen*, and the schoolteachers who read them out in front of their classes, were in little doubt about their civic value.

This civic message was omnipresent during the radical years of the Third Republic, especially in the 1880s when anti-Prussian feelings ran high, and in the early years of the twentieth century when the whole country was uncomfortably aware of the approach of another war. It was not confined to history lessons, but insinuated itself into every aspect of the syllabus – into drawing and music classes, geography, lessons in composition and essay-writing, and into the regular

[56] Ozouf and Ozouf, 'Le thème du patriotisme dans les manuels primaires', p. 20.

[57] Michel Vovelle, 'Fortunes et infortunes de Marceau', in François Gendron, *Le général Marceau, figure emblématique du héros révolutionnaire*, catalogue d'exposition, Musée des Beaux-Arts de Chartres (Chartres, 1996), p. 17.

[58] François Wartelle, 'Le thème de l'enfance héroïque dans les manuels scolaires de la Troisième République', in *Joseph Bara, 1779–1793: pour le deuxième centenaire de sa naissance,* published by the Ville de Palaiseau and the Société des Etudes Robespierristes (Paris, 1981), p. 83.

[59] E. Charavay, *Viala, Bara, Sthrau, les enfants de la République* (Paris, 1882), quoted in Wartelle, 'Le thème de l'enfance héroïque', p. 98.

dictations through which generations of schoolchildren were taught to spell, to write grammatically, and to listen to the spoken sounds of their native tongue.[60] Nine- to eleven-year-olds were also given classes in 'civic instruction', a subject introduced into the primary-school curriculum by the law of 28 March 1882, with the explicit aim of ensuring that children grew up to 'know and love France'. The character of this France was clearly explained. It was a France of cities and departments, of schools and tribunals that guaranteed the spread of order and civilisation. But it was also a France imbued with patriotism and military valour, a country that was proud of its past and of the republic that sustained it. Increasingly, indeed, patriotism became equated with military and soldierly values. In Louis Mainard's *Livre d'or de la Patrie*, for instance, a book often offered as a school prize to outstanding pupils, the reader was regaled with great exploits from France's past, from the epic stand of Roland at Ronceveau to, once again, the patriotic devotion of the volunteers of 1792. 'Roland', it was explained, 'was the hero of the chivalric past', in the same way as 'the volunteers of the Revolution represent the chivalry of the modern world'.[61] Textbooks in daily use put the case even more straightforwardly. Civic instruction was included in the curriculum to make every child aware of the privileges he enjoyed, but also, more importantly, of the obligations that followed from them. Lessons emphasised the cohesion of the country and its people, and they insisted on a number of core duties that were incumbent on all: the obligation to do military service; the respect due to the flag; the duty to love France and what it stood for; and the meaning of patriotic festivals like 14 July. This was not empty rhetoric. As the threat of war grew, teachers made every effort to explain to their pupils that they might, in turn, be called upon to fight and, if necessary, to die for the nation they loved.[62]

History and civic instruction, in the eyes of both schoolteachers and politicians, went hand-in-hand, and the need to perform military service was emphasised over and over again in the textbooks of the period. We find it in a whole range of schoolbooks, not least in the writings of Ernest Lavisse, whose teaching position in the Sorbonne and influence with the Ministry of Education, presence on educational commissions and in the publishing houses of Paris, made him a national figure in the educational world, and – in the words of Pierre Nora – a

[60] For a range of texts illustrating the theme of patriotism and military preparation, see Voisin, *L'école des poilus, passim*.

[61] Louis Mainard, *Le livre d'or de la Patrie* (Paris, 1885), p. vii.

[62] Voisin, *L'école des poilus*, pp. 45–63.

sort of '*instituteur national*'.[63] Lavisse was ubiquitous, his encyclopaedia a republican icon and his many schoolbooks and works of historical synthesis the subject of innumerable editions and reprints. He heaped praise on the values of the republic, contrasting republican liberty and monarchical tyranny; and he did not forget the value of military service or the need to remind his readers of their patriotic duty. It is to be found, of course, in his history, in the exemplary lives he evokes. But he also made more direct appeals to his readers. In the last paragraph of his history of France for the *cours moyen*, published in 1912, Lavisse turned to the present, and to the war that was to come. 'War', he said, 'is not probable, but it is possible'. He declared that, in the event of such a war, they all have a duty to perform. 'In defending France, we are behaving like good sons. We are fulfilling a duty to our fathers, who have taken such pains over the centuries to create our country. In defending France, we are working for all the men of all the countries in the world, for France, since the Revolution, had spread throughout the world ideas of justice and humanity.' He concluded with an undisguised cry of patriotism: 'France', he said, 'is the most just, the most free and the most humane of fatherlands'. And for that reason if for no other, France must be defended.[64]

It is this belief in the essential humanity of France that, for Lavisse and so many of his generation, tied the legacy of the revolutionary armies to the needs of the present. In his view the history of the First Republic and the exploits of its soldiers provided an unrivalled source of civic pride and of instruction in civic duty, and he never tired of praising the devotion and patriotism of the revolutionary volunteers who had given so much for the republican cause. He was similarly concerned to laud the sacrifice of those he saw as their direct descendants, the young men who had answered the call of the Third Republic in the dark days of the Franco-Prussian War. The only difference between the two wars, one that was brought out in many of the texts, was that in 1792 men were fighting for liberty and for the cause of the Revolution, whereas by 1870 the defence of the republic implied a struggle to save France from foreign invasion and aggression.[65] It was, he believed, vital that France

[63] Pierre Nora, 'Lavisse, instituteur national', in Pierre Nora (ed.), *Les lieux de mémoire: 1 – La République* (Paris, 1984), pp. 247–8.

[64] Ernest Lavisse, 'Le devoir patriotique', quoted in Nora, 'Lavisse, instituteur national', p. 284; for a fuller text see Ernest Lavisse, *Histoire de France: cours moyen* (Paris, 1912), p. 246.

[65] Danielle Perrot, 'La thématique politique des manuels d'histoire du cours élementaire de l'enseignement public' (mémoire pour le diplôme d'études supérieures de science politique, Université de Rennes, 1973), p. 84.

should be protected and defended by its own people, and to this end he did not hesitate to preach at his readers. It was his mission to offer a new form of legitimacy to the cause of French patriotism. Patriotic duty, in his view, was 'the corollary of republican liberty', with the history of France best seen as 'a repertory of examples for the manual in civic instruction'.[66]

This theme was taken up even more directly by his younger brother, Emile, a cavalry officer and, like Lavisse himself, a committed republican. In a work published in 1888 and subtitled 'The history of a French soldier', Emile related the sufferings of the men of the 1870 war through the person of his hero, Bautry, a young volunteer who had abandoned his studies to defend France against the Prussians. Bautry was held up as a paragon to the young: he had been a devoted scholar and had, of course, been preparing to be a warrior in the Third Republic's other great war, as an *instituteur* in the school classroom.[67] Lavisse did nothing to hide his intentions here; he went out of his way to mould the ideas of the young, and made clear that 'history here is what it was for many republicans, a form of civic education'. By teaching pupils about the miseries which France's soldiers had endured and reminding them on every page of the cost of the German invasion, he aimed to inculcate a spirit of patriotism and love for their country. 'By explaining the noble mission of the army, proving its usefulness and its necessity, and recounting instances of discipline and devotion given by its officers and soldiers', he added, 'I wanted to teach the children to love their country and to prepare them to fulfil a sacred duty, their military service'. In the atmosphere of these years, with international tension mounting and the French press ever-more strident in its demands for a war of revenge, this was not a purely academic stance. And lest there be any doubt as to his ultimate goal, he concluded with the wish 'that in every school in France the teacher should repeat to each and every one of his pupils the words which I have inscribed in large letters on the title page of this modest book'. Those words were unambiguous: *Tu seras soldat*. It was a call to arms, a call to a new generation to defend the republic as their ancestors had done before them, and a bald statement that this generation would be called upon to make that sacrifice.[68]

[66] Nora, 'Lavisse, instituteur national', p. 276.

[67] Mona Ozouf, *L'école de la France. Essais sur la Révolution, l'utopie et l'enseignement* (Paris, 1984), pp. 231–49.

[68] Emile Lavisse, *'Tu seras soldat'. Histoire d'un soldat français: récits et leçons patriotiques d'instruction et d'éducation militaires* (Paris, 1888), p. 2.

10 The First World War

Preparing France psychologically for war had posed a huge challenge for the authorities, but fighting that war would provide an even sterner test of the bold words and egalitarian resolutions of the pre-war years. The French government did not, of course, hesitate when war was declared; it did not challenge established ideas of duty or the need for universal conscription. Nor did the young men who were called up flinch from their duty, and the myth grew, as powerful in its way as the myth of the *levée en masse* itself, that they had come forward willingly, sharing a common enthusiasm for their country's defence that recalled the valour of their forebears in the revolutionary armies at Valmy and Jemappes. It was even claimed that they rushed headlong to the front, chatting, laughing, some cheering, all intent on gaining belated revenge for the French defeat in 1871 and the loss of Alsace and Lorraine. The truth, of course, was less heroic. There were isolated instances of joy and exhilaration expressed in public, largely in Paris; and certain newspapers made it their business to repeat such stories as they desperately tried to stir up patriotism among their readers. But these were rare aberrations in a country where the general mood was much more sombre. The great mass of French people did not whoop with joy or long for a war of revenge, and the dominant mood in the country was one of resignation and acceptance, often mingled with anguish and scarcely concealed fear.[1]

Yet the manner of raising an army in wartime was not an issue for debate in France – unlike in Britain, where it took two years of trench war and unsustainably high losses before the government was forced to accept that it was no longer possible to rely on volunteers. Conscription to British ears still conjured up ideas of foreignness, of Continental rather than British traditions, whereas in France it was already firmly

[1] André Latreille, '1914: Réflexions sur un anniversaire', quoted in Jean-Jacques Becker, 'La fleur au fusil: retour sur un mythe', in Christophe Prochasson and Anne Rasmussen (eds.), *Vrai et faux dans la Grande Guerre* (Paris, 2004), p. 154.

encased in republican culture. In wartime, in times of crisis for the nation, it was taken for granted that national defence should be assured by the young men of France, without distinction of class or creed; that was the tradition they understood, and which they had inherited from the Revolution. In 1914 it was evident that the *patrie* was once again *en danger*, and republicans knew that there was but one way in which to respond, the way in which their entire history and culture pulled them. The political parties rallied to the cause of winning the war, preaching an *Union Sacrée* and urging their constituents to unite in the cause of the nation and forget traditional social and sectional divisions, political differences and trade-union demands. All had sacrifices to make, and the fact that military service was so widely accepted, and so seemingly palatable to the public, can only be explained by the open appeal that was made to egalitarian sentiment and republican tradition.[2]

Under the recruitment law of 1913, the first to be conscripted for active service were those aged between twenty and twenty-two. They were the unlucky generation, whose period of active service had been controversially raised from two years to three, followed by long years in the reserve, while older men who had already completed their period in uniform found themselves recalled to the colours. As the early euphoria died and the realities of trench warfare came to be understood by the civilian population, it is interesting that it was the supposed inequalities that caused by far the greatest disquiet, what critics saw as a fundamental breach of republican principle. In a pamphlet published at the end of the war – the censorship laws ensured that little was written at the time – the Socialist Party reserved its greatest scorn for the *Loi de Trois Ans*, which had created, they believed, significant inequities in the levels of sacrifice it demanded. There were both economic and military arguments against the law, the authors agreed, but most importantly, there were political reasons to oppose it, because, in their view, 'it runs counter to the entire democratic and republican tradition of France which has worked tirelessly, by every possible means, to reduce the time during which soldiers would be shut away in barracks and thus eliminate the praetorian spirit of the army and help to fuse the army and the nation more closely together'.[3]

Back in 1914, too, organised labour had been rather less united behind the war effort than subsequent propaganda was wont to suggest. Many trade unions and socialist groups had followed Jean Jaurès in

[2] John Horne, '"L'Impôt de sang". Republican rhetoric and industrial warfare in France, 1914–18', *Social History* 14 (1989), pp. 201–2.

[3] Parti Socialiste, *La Loi de Trois Ans et la guerre* (Limoges, 1918), p. 7.

his support for pacifism, and persisted in seeing the bourgeoisie rather than the Germans as the real enemy of the French workers. The manner of Jaurès's death, his murder outside the offices of *L'Humanité*, served only to focus attention on his pacifism and attract further sympathisers on the Left. Anarchist groups had been among the first to adopt pacifist slogans and denounce the war; more important, however, was the response of the socialist trade union, the CGT, as its views risked carrying the support of millions of workers. Hence the speech made by Léon Jouhaux at Jaurès's funeral, in which he spoke both for himself and his organisation, was widely seen as a key moment in winning over the Left for the cause of war. Jaurès, said Jouhaux, had looked to the future and had preached peace and internationalism even when others had not followed him. He was courageous, and he had been right. And it was not his fault if that peace had been betrayed, if France and all of Europe had been plunged into war. Now that France was at war, Jouhaux felt able to break with Jaurès's legacy and urge French workers to forget their class interests, at least for the duration of the conflict: it was, he said, a means to a greater end of which they must not lose sight. They did not want, he said, to lose the very liberties for which they had fought so passionately in the past. And though they had been duly horrified by Jaurès's assassination, they could not simply abandon their motherland at a moment when once again, as so often in the past, it was in danger. Besides, he said, seizing at a familiar trope, 'This working class, which has always been nourished on the traditions of the Revolution, on memories of the soldiers of the Year II taking liberty to the ends of the world, must remember that it is not hatred of a people that drives it to take up arms, but of despots and bad governments'. He went on to urge his audience to take up arms in their turn: 'We shall be the soldiers of liberty to bring a regime of liberty to the oppressed, to create harmony among the peoples of Europe by establishing a free agreement between nations, by the alliance between peoples.' With this mission he believed that they could not only succeed, but could take over where the men of the First Republic had left off. Now that the nation was once again the Republic, he believed that they were fully justified in taking up arms in its defence.[4]

For socialists persuaded that wars were waged by capitalist imperialists to further their economic interests, accepting that they had a duty to rally to the national cause in 1914 was not easy. They needed persuasion, and among the most persuasive arguments were those that

[4] Annie Kriegel and Jean-Jacques Becker (eds), *1914. La guerre et le mouvement ouvrier français* (Paris, 1964), pp. 142–3.

characterised this new war as a war for liberty, a war that united the whole people in a crusade against tyranny. Parallels with the army of the Year II came easily to them, as they sought justification in the exploits of their forefathers for what many still saw as a betrayal of their pacifist principles. They looked back to previous wars, to 1870 and the Wars of Napoleon, but it was to the French Revolution that socialist journalists and intellectuals most naturally turned. The common thread, of course, was liberty: the Great War could be presented in the same tenor as the Revolutionary Wars because, unlike colonial or imperialist warfare, it was fought to liberate the people from despotism. It was not just the *patrie* that was in danger, noted Gustave Hervé, it was 'the *patrie* of the Revolution', which socialists could be proud to defend.[5] For Vincent Auriol, the future president of the Fourth Republic writing in *Midi Socialiste*, 'the soldiers of the Republic are the sons of the soldiers of the Revolution', both entrusted by the people of France to resist oppression and fight for their liberties.[6] Interestingly, some radical papers resorted to the same images and a virtually identical language, their readers' identification with eighteenth-century Jacobinism seemingly intact. On 2 August 1914 the newspaper *Le Radical* reminded its readers that the words 'republican' and 'patriot' were synonymous and praised the ardour of the French soldiers now leaving for the front, which matched that of their 'glorious ancestors' of 1789.[7]

The government, of course, could not have wished for more, since some of its major propaganda offensives were aimed at precisely that section of the working class most open to the siren voices of pacifism. Tales of German atrocities and the cruelties of occupation were one part of this process; so, too, were French images of their own troops as the heroic sons of France, steeped in their country's military virtues and history, the innocent victims of a savage martyrdom.[8] They are pictured being led by Joan of Arc against the invading army, just as they are shown being counselled by Napoleon's *grognards* or by the soldiers of the Year II. From each there was a vital lesson to be learned, a lesson that was as much about morale and hope as it was about the science of war.[9] French wartime propaganda was deliberately shaped

[5] Jean-Jacques Becker, 'Le souvenir de la Révolution pendant la guerre de 1914', in Christian Croisille and Jean Ehrard (eds.), *La Légende de la Révolution: Actes du colloque international de Clermont-Ferrand*, juin 1986 (Clermont-Ferrand, 1988), p. 606.

[6] *Ibid.*, p. 607. [7] *Ibid.*, p. 608.

[8] John Horne and Alan Kramer, *German Atrocities, 1914. A History of Denial* (New Haven, 2001), pp. 302–3.

[9] Laurent Gervereau and Christophe Prochasson (eds.), *Images de 1917* (Paris, 1987), p. 120.

to strengthen national pride and reinforce mental resolve, which made images binding the republican present to the revolutionary past particularly evocative, recalling not only the sacrifice of the men of the Year II but also the cause for which they were willing to die. It was not just a question of informing or misinforming, of spreading news and information which the government thought useful for the war effort. It was about drawing on well-rehearsed images, the pictures that young Frenchmen had pored over in the pages of their school textbooks, and about updating them for the current crisis. It was also about sensitising the population, a process which Georges Demartial termed the 'mobilisation of consciences'.[10] With mass citizen-armies again defending French frontiers against invasion from the east, it was only logical that the French Revolution should once more have become a model to be followed, and that the parallels between the fallen soldiers of the 1790s and France's new generation of *poilus* should have been so sharply drawn in the images and the language that were invoked.[11]

The language of 1914 was still the traditional language of republican patriotism, the language of the *manuels scolaires* of the 1880s and the *sociétés de tir* of the 1890s, a rhetoric steeped in republican imagery and often seasoned with revolutionary fervour. The consistency of the references, the frequent repetition of key words, and the familiar symbolism of particular events, all contributed to the impression that this was a very republican call to arms. It was, it was inferred, a short step from civic education to the defence of France in war, as the nation's citizen-soldiers would once again rush to their posts. A good instance of this is the patriotic periodical *Le Soldat de Demain et l'Elève Soldat Réunis*, published in the years up to the Great War and described as the 'official bulletin of the Union of Societies for Military Preparation in France'.[12] In tone and content it was typical of the defensive, rather pessimistic patriotism of the age, warning its readers of the dangers that lay ahead, lamenting France's historically low birth rate and the consequent shortfall in boys of military age, and urging rigorous military training for all in preparation for war.[13] In many respects, it was

[10] Georges Demartial, *La guerre de 1914. La mobilisation des consciences* (Paris, 1927). See also John Horne, '"Propagande" et "vérité" dans la Grande Guerre', in Christophe Prochasson and Anne Rasmussen (eds.), *Vrai et faux dans la Grande Guerre* (Paris, 2004), pp. 76–95.

[11] George L. Mosse, *Fallen Soldiers: Reshaping the Memory of the World Wars* (New York, 1990), pp. 35–6.

[12] *Le Soldat de Demain et l'Elève Soldat Réunis. Bulletin Officiel de l'Union des Sociétés de Préparation Militaire de France.*

[13] *Le Soldat de Demain*, 18 January 1912, editorial by Adolphe Chéron on 'La préparation militaire dans les villages'.

the sort of publication that appealed to the nationalist Right as well as to the republic's schoolteachers and youth leaders. But it was staunchly republican, even citing its date of publication in terms of the revolutionary calendar of the 1790s, in the form '1 January 1912 (nivôse an 120)'. Many of the local organisers were indeed schoolteachers who saw their role as extending beyond the classroom to preparing the youth of France for war. The pages of *Le Soldat de Demain* praised their work in their local communities, in establishing societies in such communes as Archiac and Etaules, Jonzac and La Jarne Champagne (four of a dozen *sociétés de tir* affiliated to the Union in the single department of Charente-inférieure).[14] It also gave full vent to their particular view of the nation and its army. The paper reported, for instance, a patriotic speech by one Veunac, the director of *L'Avant-garde lindoise*, its affiliated shooting-club in the village of Lalinde in the Dordogne. Veunac is a primary-school teacher, and he claims that the school is and should continue to be 'the first rung in military education' and a means to help stop the 'degeneration of our race'. In the best tradition of the *instituteurs* of Jules Ferry, he places his work in preparing the next generation of soldiers squarely in the tradition of Valmy. His speech at a local prize-giving ceremony in Lalinde is quoted, approvingly, word for word:

> And the grandsons of these heroes of 92, of these volunteers shod in clogs who astonished the world with the victories they won singing the *Marseillaise*, who had only one love, the *Patrie*, and only one goal, to defend it, immediately came forward and grouped themselves around us, and have come to us each Sunday to learn to love their country better, to serve and defend it better.[15]

The words came straight from the pages of Lavisse, from lessons learned on the benches at primary school, and their familiarity and their appeal to republican idealism only gave them added potency.

When the government invoked memories of the Revolution, it had to proceed with greater caution. The *Union Sacrée* was supposed to unite the French people, not to revive memories of the ideological schisms that had split public opinion in the previous thirty years, causing such bitter animosity during the Dreyfus Affair and the subsequent separation of church and state. For many on the Right, especially amongst devout Catholics, any attempt to place the preparation for war in the context of the French Revolution was likely to be seriously counter-productive. For this reason the words used by Raymond Poincaré to announce the

[14] *Le Soldat de Demain*, 18 January 1912, p. 54.
[15] *Le Soldat de Demain*, 20 January 1912, p. 75.

state of war were carefully weighed. He noted the patience the French people had shown, the unity demonstrated by all in the face of provocation, and the sympathy that he had received from every corner of the 'civilised world'. For France, he declared in a phrase that invoked memories of 1789, 'represents today, once again before the world, liberty, justice and reason'. In this highly moral cause, France could rely on her army, and would be 'heroically defended by all her sons, whose sacred union before the enemy nothing can destroy, and who have assembled today in a spirit of fraternity, united by a common indignation at the actions of the enemy and in a shared spirit of patriotism'.[16] The reference to justice and to the country's past, the insistence that France would be defended by 'all her sons', these were suggestive of the army of the Year II, but Poincaré was careful not to make the identification too partisan. In 1915, after a year of war and a level of suffering that was just beginning to sink in, his message to the nation was necessarily inclusive. The army, he reminded them, is the people; 'the beauty of the people is luminously reflected in its army', for the most modest soldier understands the role he has been given, the sacred role that falls to him as a Frenchman. 'The army, which the nation has formed from its own substance, immediately understood the grandeur of its role. It knows that it is fighting for the security of our race, our traditions and our liberties. It knows that the future of our civilisation and the fate of humanity depend on the victory of France and its allies.' Nor is the sacrifice limited to the fighting men of France. In a passage reminiscent of the *levée en masse*, Poincaré emphasised that the war effort must be the affair of all. 'Each day, in the smallest communes, the spontaneous involvement of old men, women and children ensures that everyday life continues, prepares the sowing season, cultivates the land, brings in the harvest, and, through the organisation of work, helps to keep the soul of the people patient and strong.'[17]

As the war years passed, it is noticeable how rare were official references to the soldiers as the heirs of the Revolution, and how the praise lavished on the army tended to be self-contained, acknowledging their losses, their valour, the qualities of patience and steadfastness which they had shown in carrying out their duties. It is not difficult to see why. Experience of the Great War was like no other, either in the scale of losses or the seeming senselessness of the slaughter, as armies remained

[16] Raymond Poincaré, *Au service de la France: Neuf années de souvenirs, vol. 4, L'Union sacrée, 1914* (Paris, 1929), p. 546.

[17] Raymond Poincaré, *Message à la France*, 5 August 1915 (*affiche*, Historial de la Grande Guerre, Péronne, 15696).

immobile for weeks on end and men died in their thousands defending rat-infested trenches in the mud of Picardy. In technological terms, too, it was a new kind of warfare which depersonalised the fighting and made comparisons with previous wars clumsy and inept. It was not long before the image the young soldiers took with them to the front – an image which, like soldiers before them, they had gleaned from stories of past wars, from the armies of Napoleon, the Crimea or 1870 – was cast aside, and war was experienced in new and devastating terms. They were not the men of the Year II, and they knew it; faced with the daily reality of the slaughter, the Revolutionary idea of taking war to tyrants and peace to the peoples of Europe lost much of its resonance. References to Valmy were increasingly restricted to particular political families, principally those of the radicals and socialists, while others, on the Right or the Catholic centre, preferred to ignore it altogether. For the Church, especially, any equation with a revolution that had shut churches and guillotined priests seemed repellent. Catholics continued to believe that the war had been inspired not by historical precedent but by God; as Albert de Mun phrased it, 'any resurgence of warrior spirit in a nation is accompanied by a renaissance in religious life'.[18]

In the event, even the most republican of celebrations, Bastille Day, was muted during the war years. News from the front was too serious, too disturbing, to permit of extravagant display, and the government recognised that the public mood called for the exercise of economy and an air of dignified sobriety. In 1915, the memory of the Revolution was evoked when 14 July was chosen as the day when the composer of the Marseillaise, Rouget de Lisle, was buried with national honours in Paris. Originally it had been proposed to transfer his ashes to the Pantheon, but the decision had been taken at the very last minute, without the special legislation required for *panthéonisation*; so they used the Invalides instead. The ceremony was simple and rather moving, as the coffin was borne from the Arc de Triomphe down the Champs-Elysées on a military waggon of the First Republic. There were few men of military age along the route, and the crowd who turned up were largely the old, army veterans, nurses and children.[19] Most importantly, the second burial of the author of the Marseillaise was not conducted in a spirit of ideological triumph, but rather as a conscious celebration of national unity. The outbreak of war had made the national song popular again, on the streets and in cafes, without regard to the politics of Left and Right. It

[18] Becker, 'Le souvenir de la Révolution pendant la guerre de 1914', pp. 608–9.

[19] Raymond Poincaré, *Au service de la France: Neuf années de souvenirs*, vol. 6, *Les Tranchées, 1916* (Paris, 1930), account of the ceremony of 14 July 1915.

conjured up images of patriotic heroism and national resistance to the invader, not the partisan politics of the Jacobin republic. And the focus on the young musician, the transfer of his body through the streets of Paris to a hero's burial, was part of accepted public ritual for the citizens of Third Republic France. The destination, the Invalides, was the recognised resting place for military heroes and served to raise the patriotic tone of the ceremony.[20]

In the following year Raymond Poincaré spoke of his government's approach to the national festival when it was being celebrated against the backdrop of war. On the one hand they were marking the liberties of the French people. 'The government of the Republic', he told his listeners, thought that 'on the day when France celebrated the origin of its political liberties', they should not cease to do so because of war; they would continue to respect a tradition 'which gives concrete form to our national consciousness and to the unity of our native land'. But he also wished to mark the sacrifice of the troops. 'Nothing', said the President, 'could better respond to the feelings of the country than a simple act of homage, made with due piety and in the bald setting of a military ceremony, to the soldiers who have died at the hands of the enemy and to the families who grieve for these brave men with such noble resignation'. His language still betrayed traces of Lavisse as he paid tribute to the men who, 'when they heard the call of the *patrie en danger*, rose up, gathered their weapons and rushed to the frontiers'; they came from all walks of life, and from all corners of France; 'they have shed their blood for a sublime cause, the salvation of the fatherland and the future of humanity'.[21] But he stopped short of making direct comparisons with the men of the Year II, or of reminding his listeners that they were citizens. 1915 was the bloodiest year of the war for the French army. Citizen-soldiers just might be tempted to lay claim to their rights of citizenship and mutiny, as would happen in 1917 when the soldiers' consent to the war finally snapped.[22]

But where ministers saw dangers in exaggerating the parallels between the wars of the French Revolution and the war which France was now fighting, more radical deputies were quite prepared to stir the embers of Jacobin egalitarianism, especially over military service. Throughout

[20] Avner Ben-Amos, 'The Marseillaise as myth and metaphor', in Valerie Holman and Debra Kelly (eds.), *France at War in the Twentieth Century. Propaganda, Myth and Metaphor* (Oxford, 2000), p. 44.

[21] Raymond Poincaré, *Discours prononcé le 14 juillet 1916 par Raymond Poincaré, Président de la République, à l'occasion de la remise des diplômes d'honneur aux familles des morts pour la patrie* (*affiche*, Historial de la Grande Guerre, Péronne, 24859).

[22] Leonard V. Smith, *Between Mutiny and Obedience* (Princeton, 1994), esp. pp. 186–7.

the war the issue of equality of sacrifice continued to be raised, especially when thousands of younger conscripts were withdrawn from the front line to man munitions factories. They were visibly not at war, and that at a time when the government was seeking ever more desperate measures to fill the regiments, even proposing the call-up of eighteen-year-olds two years early.[23] For many people, including the parents of serving soldiers, the presence in their communities of able-bodied men of military age was the cause of deep resentment and indignation, and the workers were widely denounced as *embusqués*, shirkers who were favoured by the authorities. For the men in the trenches, too, the inherent injustice of the situation was what caused the greatest outrage. The *journaux du front* returned repeatedly, almost obsessively, to the inequalities of treatment that persisted in the army itself, where the privileges accorded to administrators, clerks, truck drivers and even artillery gunners were contrasted with the lot of those condemned to fight in the front line. Here, too, there was a constant suspicion of favouritism, and it was assumed that those favoured with the safer jobs had benefited from personal influence and protection – the *piston* that was the source of endless jibes during the war years. The period from 1914 to 1916 represented the high point of *embuscomanie*: in 1915, indeed, a whole issue of the satirical weekly, the *Canard Enchaîné*, was devoted to the *embusqués* and the affront they posed to France's republican traditions.[24]

The issue also caused outrage among left-wing deputies, who twice tried to overturn the wishes of the government and force the *embusqués* back into uniform. The details of these proposals, introduced by back-bench deputies and hotly opposed by both the army and the administration, need not concern us, since on neither occasion did the measure passed lead to the return of workers from the war industries to the front. What is of interest here is rather the language used by supporters of these bills, who did not hide their belief that the inequities that were being tolerated in the name of efficiency were an affront to the ideals of the French Revolution. During the debate on Dalbiez's bill of April 1915, for instance, the Republican-Socialist deputy Durafour urged that more was at stake than finding workers for iron foundries. Soldiers' morale was also at risk. 'Let us give our soldiers the impression', he cried, 'that they are governed with method and equity, that they are still

[23] This discussion of the parliamentary debates on the Dalbiez and Mourier laws is based on John Horne's article, "L'Impôt de sang". Republican rhetoric and industrial warfare in France, 1914–18', in *Social History* 14 (1989), pp. 201–23. The translations are John Horne's.

[24] Charles Ridel, *Les embusqués* (Paris, 2007), p. 47.

fighting for the country of the French Revolution, and that the chain of tradition has not been broken'.[25] In 1917, with the manpower crisis even more urgent, those who opposed the government again demanded total equality before the recruiting officer. Again the bill – presented by Mourier, a Radical from the Gard – responded to the threat to call up young men two years early by turning on the *embusqués* sheltering in factories and in government offices. Mourier wanted a simple, Jacobin solution to the problem, proposing that everyone who was mobilised, aged between nineteen and thirty-four, should be sent to a fighting unit. The soldiers in the trenches, he argued, demanded that justice should be seen to be done, just as the young men of the first requisition had demanded in 1793 that no one should be allowed to use favours or connections to avoid the danger of the front. Mourier did not hesitate to associate his bill with that of the Jacobin Convention; indeed, the parallels were all too clear. The *embusqués* were a revival of the *muscadins* under the Directory, the privileged, protected *jeunesse dorée* of the twentieth century; and 'at 123 years' distance the same protests are rumbling and rising from the depths of the muddy trenches; we hear echoes of the same indignation from the four corners of France. It is our task to allay this anger by following the example of the Committee of Public Safety, and at last learning to recall everyone "rigorously to their post"'.[26]

To the voices of newspaper editorials and deputies in the Assembly were added those of France's intellectual elite, ready as always to throw themselves into the task of analysing contemporary politics and to offer themselves as the conscience of the nation. Intellectuals wrote manifestos extolling ideas of nationhood, citizenship and civilization and – particularly in this post-Dreyfus generation – focussing particularly on the nation and the values that it stood for. In 1914 and throughout the war years, writers, poets and philosophers expressed their views on the morality of the conflict that raged before them and on the need to defend civilization against its enemies, a civilization which they equated with France against enemies identified all too easily with Huns and barbarians come from the East. For writers who were still smarting from the defeat they had suffered in the Dreyfus years, the advent of war could even seem like a sought-after opportunity for a new generation of Frenchmen to gain their revenge. For if among the intellectual generation of the Great War there were men who followed Jaurès into a pacifist stance or who, like Henri Barbusse, wrote of the horrors of life in the trenches, they were more than matched by the fervent

[25] Horne, 'L'Impôt de sang', p. 205. [26] *Ibid.*, p. 211.

nationalists who saw war as a cleansing, edifying experience, one that would bring out the best in the nation's youth, would rekindle its energy and national spirit, and would finally purge France of its decadence. Writers like Ernest Psichari and Henri Massis heaped praise on the 'simple, chaste' lifestyle of the warrior, and painted the war, just as the revolutionaries had done a century earlier, as a conflict dedicated to liberation and to the freeing of enslaved peoples.[27] As the months passed and the toll of war deaths grew – among them the very students they would have taught in the last years before war broke out – more and more writers felt the call of patriotism, demonising Germany on the one hand, and on the other lionising the virtues of the republican nation. They attacked even those aspects of German culture for which they felt a sneaking respect – German poetry, music, science and medicine. These they now felt it necessary to belittle, as they contrasted German functionalism with French spontaneity and artistic genius. Germany had *Kultur*, it was implied, France *civilisation*. There was a striking difference between them: indeed, for many French intellectuals, that difference was so fundamental that it came to represent the future of civilisation itself.[28]

Most of these writings were aimed at an educated civilian audience, though some, like Barbusse's *Le Feu*, reached out more widely to become bestsellers during the war years, read by soldiers in the trenches as well as by a civilian readership. But what did the soldiers themselves think? Did they, too, draw parallels between the cause in which they were fighting and that of the revolutionary years, or compare themselves with the citizen-soldiers of the 1790s? The letters they wrote home to their parents offer some clues, though, given the highly personal nature of the correspondence and the difficult circumstances in which letters were written, relatively few offer detailed political testaments or declarations of faith. Like soldiers writing home from any war – and it is as true of Napoleon's *grognards* as it is of American servicemen in Vietnam – they felt constrained by filial affection, by a desire not to shock their loved ones or reveal the true degree of their unhappiness.[29] The soldiers in the Great War had the additional problem that they knew that their letters were subject to censorship, and that loose words could lead to interrogation and punishment. By late 1916 that censorship was tightened as

[27] Christophe Prochasson and Anne Rasmussen (eds.), *Au nom de la Patrie. Les intellectuels et la Première Guerre Mondiale, 1910–1919* (Paris, 1996), p. 129.

[28] *Ibid.*, pp. 203–9.

[29] Samuel Hynes, *The Soldiers' Tale. Bearing Witness to Modern War* (London, 1997), pp. 1–30; Alan Forrest, *Napoleon's Men. The Soldiers of the Revolution and Empire* (London, 2002), pp. 21–52.

the *Contrôle Postal* sought to prevent ideas it considered seditious from destroying morale on the home front; and the soldiers responded by taking greater care, expressing themselves less freely and discouraging their parents from pressing them with too many questions.[30] Some admitted that they had taken a conscious decision to tone down their letters so as not to frighten or disappoint, to say as little as possible about the conditions they were experiencing so as not to hurt or worry those at home.[31] On the other hand, when they are compared with the citizen-soldiers of the Year II, they had the inestimable advantage of a much higher level of literacy. This did not just mean that a higher proportion of them wrote home. Men filled every spare hour with writing; many wrote daily letters; some were so passionate about communicating with their families that they wrote several times each day, telling them how they were feeling, asking after the health of relatives, or seeking reassurance about the state of the harvest.[32] Greater literacy gave them greater facility in writing, and the confidence to express feelings more subtly, more accurately, with nuances of emphasis and irony that had rarely been available to earlier generations. Their letters were more varied, less formulaic than those of the soldiers who preceded them. But we must not exaggerate their fluency. Most letters were still very short, and soldiers, like other men of their generation, experienced great difficulty in sharing their emotions or admitting to fear. A letter was also a celebration that one was still alive.[33]

In these circumstances it is unrealistic to expect to read in soldiers' letters any profound statements of ideology or political faith. They were written on the spur of the moment, and most of them concentrate on the essentials of life and the simple pleasures of home. Soldiers from peasant stock might comment on the state of the harvest in the regions they passed through, or they might note differences in the seasons or in farming techniques; but their letters were more concerned with food, and their greatest joy was reserved for food parcels they received from home.[34] Besides, by 1915 they knew very clearly the nature of the war they were being sent to fight, and they hated it. Few still shared the illusion that it would be soon be over, and there are many more references to war-weariness, their desire to get home, their longing for peace, than

[30] Anick Cochet, 'L'opinion et le moral des soldats en 1916, d'après les archives du Contrôle Postal' (thèse de doctorat, Université de Paris-X, 1986), p. 15.

[31] *Ibid.*, pp. 46–7.

[32] Gérard Bacconnier, André Minet and Louis Soler, *La plume au fusil. Les poilus du Midi à travers leur correspondance* (Toulouse, 1985), p. 19.

[33] *Ibid.*, p. 21.

[34] Paul Raybaut, *Correspondance de guerre d'un rural, 1914–17* (Paris, 1974), p. 26.

there are to heroism or their thirst for victory. Like the men who fought for the Revolution and Empire, they constantly refer to their duty, to the sufferings they must endure, the obedience they owe to their officers, the sacrifice they owe to their country. These are the recurrent themes of soldiers' writing, themes which are repeated hundreds of times over. Indeed, what is most striking is how little the language had changed since the Napoleonic Wars, and how widely these mantras were shared, for the letters they received from their mothers and sisters were often written in a similar style, urging them to make precisely these sacrifices because their country demanded it.[35] It is evidence, if evidence were needed, of the power of popular patriotism in a war that was perceived as being that of the entire nation. The young men of 1914 had assimilated the language of the newspapers, and, above all, they had learned, in the army as in the school classroom, the republican gospel according to Ernest Lavisse.[36]

Direct references to the Revolutionary Wars are less frequent. If there is a political message to be found, it is the sense that they are fighting for the republic, for humanistic values and the security of France, which predominates in the soldiers' writings. They lay claim to defending ideas of Liberty and Justice, values which they specifically associate with French traditions and which some relate to the French Revolution. But analogies with the citizen-soldiers of the Year II are few and far between. Letters, diaries, even the *carnets de route* in which they record their thoughts about the war as well as the immediate events that surround them, are firmly rooted in the present, the terrible bleakness of the front, the loss of sensibility that comes with months and years in the army.[37] There was too much happening around them to allow the luxury of historical reverie, not least the death of friends and comrades. 'A week ago we had dinner together in a sunlit barn at Magnicourt', wrote Paul Tuffrau in 1915, 'We had a lot of shared memories. Yet his death did not come as a terrible blow. You become hard, indifferent, rather passive, resigned to anything'.[38] Besides, the Great War itself threw up its own icons, its geography of national symbolism: there seemed little reason to look further back when the present war

[35] Cochet, 'L'opinion et le moral des soldats', pp. 492–4.

[36] Pierre Nora, 'Lavisse, instituteur national', in Pierre Nora (ed.), *Les Lieux de mémoire, vol. 1 – La République* (Paris, 1984), p. 282.

[37] See, for instance, excerpts from wartime diaries in the North in Annette Becker (ed.), *Journaux de combattants et civils de la France du Nord dans la Grande Guerre* (Lille, 1998).

[38] Paul Tuffrau, *1914–1918: Quatre années sur le front. Carnets d'un combattant* (Paris, 1998), p. 86.

had given France symbols of courage and sacrifice like Verdun (which was honoured by the republic as a site of memory during the War itself, and was visited by the President on no fewer than six occasions in 1916 alone).[39] When soldiers do draw comparisons with the past and with the military exploits of the Revolutionary and Napoleonic Wars, they are as likely to paint themselves as being the descendants of Napoleon's *grognards*, about whom they knew far more. The *poilu*, wrote one soldier, shared the 'gaiety' of the *grognard*, an attitude to life that set him apart and made him his worthy successor.[40] There was a certain poignancy in the comparison, since, like Napoleon's Grande Armée, they were setting out on a grandiose adventure from which, for many, there would be no return.

The same sense of patriotism is to be found in the pages of the *journaux de tranchées*, the cheaply produced papers which were written and produced, often on crude printing presses, by serving soldiers, and which were circulated among the men of particular regiments or in defined areas of the trenches. They were much enjoyed by the troops, who turned to them for jokes and irreverent comment that would be censored in more official publications.[41] They contained little hard news; that was not their purpose. Their readers knew enough about the realities of war and the terror of the trenches, and the trench newspapers had no reason to conceal what was a daily reality. Rather, they indulged in a mocking, satirical humour which, their editors believed, the troops needed if their morale was to be sustained in the face of terrible physical hardship, and if the destructive impact of depression – the feared *cafard* – was to be held at bay.[42] They satirised the national press which the troops so violently disliked, since they felt aggrieved that journalists ignored their sufferings and used them as pawns for government propaganda.[43] And they rejoiced in their amateur character, and the fact that they were written by ordinary men, not staffed by the great and the good. 'This paper does not have a single academician among its editors', mocked one, 'but simple civilians – they used the rather pejorative army term for civilians, *pékins* – from every region and

[39] Antoine Prost, 'Verdun: the life of a site of memory', in *Republican Identities in War and Peace* (Oxford, 2002), p. 50.

[40] Becker, 'Le souvenir de la Révolution pendant la guerre de 1914', p. 613.

[41] Stéphane Audoin-Rouzeau, 'Les soldats français pendant la guerre de 1914–18 d'après les journaux de tranchées. Une étude des mentalités' (thèse de doctorat, Université de Clermont-Ferrand, 1984). For a revised version of this thesis, see *14–18: Les combattants des tranchées* (Paris, 1986).

[42] Pierre Albin (ed.), *Tous les journaux du Front* (Paris, 1916), p. 10.

[43] Guillaume Leveque, 'L'image des héros dans la presse photographique française de la Première Guerre Mondiale' (mémoire de DEA, Université de Paris-I, 1989), p. 40.

every social class, civilians who have been transformed by four months' campaigning into brave *poilus*'.[44] But what bravery they had shown! What soldiers they had proved to be! The papers do not conceal their pride in their achievements, in their suffering and their ability to hold firm. Throughout the war they remained stoutly patriotic, even when, after the terrible losses of 1917, traces of despair set in. They continue to fight, they make clear, because they have no choice but to do so: 'We fight', declared *Le Tord-boyau* in August 1917, 'because we cannot do otherwise'.[45] They cannot believe that they could lose, because they believe that right is on their side, and that right must ultimately prevail. And so they fight on, and even in victory continue to express a curiously generous form of patriotism. Urging the *poilus* to treat the defeated Germans without hatred or malice, *La Mitraille* in January 1919 associates such generosity with the identity they have fought to preserve. 'What makes France truly immortal, wrote the paper, 'is that she has always known how to show itself generous and fraternal towards everyone, even a defeated enemy'.[46]

They also tended, far more than the official press, to link the war to the tradition of the French Revolution, and to identify the soldiers of the Year II with the men in the trenches. One paper, *Télémail*, went so far as to claim that '1915 is to the twentieth century what the Year II was to the eighteenth'.[47] Another, *L'Écho des Marmites*, a trench newspaper produced by the soldiers of the 309th infantry regiment, to whom it was distributed freely, announced in its first number that 'without any pretension, it hopes to be welcomed by all our comrades with the same cordiality that it tries to bring to its columns'. It then turned its mocking eye on those official republican historians and journalists who pontificated on their place in history, and in a special supplement it offered its own analysis of 'the soldier of 1914'.[48] The article does much to encapsulate the mischievous spirit of the trench press, while also adding the soldiers' own slant on a well-known trope of republican journalism. It is a powerful piece of journalism and for that reason it seems worth examining in some detail.

The article, the paper proudly announced, was the work not of an Academician but of a soldier, second class, who wrote under the name of 'Ajax'. It took the form of a chapter, written in advance, from a school history of France for secondary pupils that would be published in 1952.

[44] *L'Écho des Marmites*, editorial to the first issue, 7 December 1914.
[45] Audoin-Rouzeau, *14–18: Les combattants des tranchées*, p. 209. [46] *Ibid.*, p. 199.
[47] Becker, 'Le souvenir de la Révolution pendant la guerre de 1914', p. 613.
[48] *L'Écho des Marmites*, 7 December 1914.

It was, in other words, a Lavisse for future generations, a Lavisse whose portentous style and republican patriotism were mercilessly lampooned. The text included the obligatory quotations from the nationalist writers of the pre-war era, Barrès and Péguy, Maurras and Bergson; it cited the traditional comparisons with the soldiers who had preceded them, and claimed that they were driven by an idealism that singles them out from others.

> The little soldier of 1914 understood that life is only worth as much as the ideal that guides it, that war can be ennobled by its purpose, and that the word *patrie* has a deep and lasting meaning. That was his strength. Napoleon's Grande Armée had worshipped one man. But the armies of the Republic fought for an ideal, like their ancestors during the Crusades, or the volunteers of 1792. That is why they brought to this war virtues that the soldiers of the Grande Armée had not known.

These virtues, 'Ajax' explains, were peculiar to the Great War, and were a response to the circumstances of the Western Front. They helped to maintain morale, good humour and discipline in a different kind of warfare, where men did not see the enemy, where the cavalry did not ride out and the infantry rarely moved, where soldiers were destroyed by shells fired from ten or fifteen kilometres, killed by bombs dropped from planes above the clouds, or blown up when they stepped on landmines. Fighting in this war clearly took a special sort of valour, one that a Lavisse of the future would surely write up for the edification of future generations of schoolboys. Not without a certain bitterness, yet with an impressive sense of humour and mockery, 'Ajax' could imagine himself and his comrades reinvented as republican military icons for French nationalists later in the century.[49]

It took some imagining, given the conditions in the trenches and the lack of any obvious parallel between their war and the heroic tales they had heard of the armies of the Revolution. The daily experience of the *poilu* had little about it that was romantic or glorious; the drudgery, the mud, the daily exposure to shells and the sight and smell of death offered little to fire their imaginations with memories of previous wars when the conditions of fighting had been so very different. The threat of death and mutilation might seem inescapable, at least after the first months when some still dared to believe in a short war and a rapid return to civilian life.[50] Men encountered death on a daily basis, in hospitals, in the trenches, even by the side of the road; they cared for

[49] 'Le Soldat de 1914', supplement to *L'Écho des Marmites*, issue 1.

[50] Thierry Hardier and Jean-François Jagielski, *Combattre et mourir pendant la Grande Guerre, 1914–25* (Paris, 2004), p. 126.

dying comrades, wrote letters to the loved ones they left behind, acted as stretcher-bearers for the wounded and scoured the battlefield to identify corpses and bury the dead.[51] In such circumstances it was not easy to convince soldiers that they were fighting in the glorious tradition of 1792, and it is perhaps to their credit that their commanders rarely tried. Rather, they turned their minds to more immediate problems, seeking answers to the waves of demoralisation and depression that afflicted the troops. By 1915 the young men who only a year before were being portrayed as strong and heroic in recruitment literature and political speeches appeared haunted by uncertainty. In the eyes of the military authorities they had ceased to be the regenerated race of the immediate pre-war years. Instead, they seemed traumatised by their experience, their thoughts turned to the comforts of home, or to sexual gratification and the pleasures of the flesh.[52] Wartime exaltation to the troops was more concerned with the moral dangers of prostitution and venereal disease than with memories of Valmy.[53]

In the propaganda of the First World War, indeed, it is notable that the images of revolutionary heroism are much more common in posters and billboards aimed at the civilian population than they are in those directed at the troops. Wartime *affiches*, both those calling for recruits and a spirit of patriotic sacrifice in the first months of the war and those from the later years of fighting which sought to conjure up war loans from the people of France, had every interest in suggesting the strength of the link between the Great War and French wars of the past. This was especially true of her republican past, whose wars were fought in the name of the people; and the call of '*la patrie en danger*' immediately conjured up associations with the 1790s. Marianne is omnipresent in war propaganda, whether as the protector of her people, as the symbol of a violated republic, or as the avenger of the war crimes of the German enemy. On a variety of war posters she is depicted wearing a Phrygian cap, holding the French flag or strangling the German eagle.[54] It is rare, though, to show her in the thick of the fighting; she is not a warrior figure like Joan of Arc, but a feminine icon, frail, vulnerable and sharing the suffering of her people; most commonly she

[51] *Ibid.*, pp. 178–99.
[52] Jean-Yves La Naour, *Misères et tourments de la chair durant la Grande Guerre. Les moeurs sexuelles des Français, 1914–18* (Paris, 2002), p. 18.
[53] François Rouquet, Fabrice Virgili and Danièle Voldman (eds.), *Amours, guerres et sexualité, 1914–45* (Paris, 2007), pp. 88–91.
[54] See, for instance, the lavishly illustrated catalogue of the Collection Lafond (series 169 Fi) in the Archives of the Seine-Maritime, *Affiches et documents iconographiques, guerre de 1914–1918* (Rouen, 1997), pp. 69–73.

stands side by side with French troops in the trenches or appears as gentle and compassionate, offering sympathy to the wounded or the grieving. In Sabattier's etching of 1919, after peace is finally theirs, Marianne is shown thanking the troops by kissing a French soldier on the cheek.[55] In this art form the republic may be militant and defiant, but it is most conspicuous in being a victim, wronged and violated by its enemies.[56] Only as the moment of peace approaches does Marianne forsake this role to become once again France's leader in war, the leader of the nation guiding French soldiers to victory and pointing to the Promised Land.[57]

Most often the French soldier of these posters is recognisably modern, a son of the twentieth century fighting in the uniform of the *poilu*, the figure with whom men's families at home could most readily identify. But he retained many of the attributes of the revolutionary soldier, those traits that for generations had been, in Peter Paret's words, 'part of the French self-image: individualism, quickness, enthusiasm, *esprit*'.[58] Sometimes the artist appealed more directly to history, to moments in France's military past. In a poster for the Crédit Lyonnais in 1918, for example, the artist Jules-Abel Faivre emphasised the vulnerability of the army by depicting a French soldier fighting, single-handed and naked, with only his sword to defend him against the claws of the German eagle as he ripped the French flag from its beak.[59] In this instance the image was not specific to a particular moment of the past; instead, it recalled figures from classical mythology and the tropes of eighteenth-century history painting. But the very fact of fighting unclothed, without shield or armour, meant that it emphasised every sinew of the soldier's body as he fought for his country, and underlined the extent to which that body was exposed to wounds and mutilation in the nation's service. On other occasions artists appealed more specifically to the citizen-soldier and to the republican tradition of the *levée en masse*, depicting recognisably revolutionary troops in action. Heroic soldiers from the Year II were evoked as exemplars to those who now served

[55] Hoover Institution Archives, Stanford University (HI), FR 180, dessin de L. Sabbatier, 1919.

[56] Maurice Agulhon, 'Marianne en 14–18', in Jean-Jacques Becker, Jay M. Winter, Gerd Krumeich, Annette Becker and Stéphane Audoin-Rouzeau (eds.), *Guerres et cultures, 1914–1918* (Paris, 1994), pp. 379–81.

[57] HI, FR 328, 'La victoire en chantant', dessin de Maurice Neumont, November 1918.

[58] Peter Paret, Beth Irwin Lewis and Paul Paret, *Persuasive Images: Posters of War and Revolution* (Princeton, N.J., 1992), p. 40.

[59] Alain Weill, 'L'affiche de guerre', in Véronique Harel (ed.), *Les affiches de la Grande Guerre* (Péronne, 1998), p. 12.

in their stead. *L'Hommage aux anciens*, a much-reproduced engraving executed by Alphonse Lalauze in 1915, showed the ghost army of the First Republic saluting France's new heroes as they were led wounded from battle, with, symbolically, the windmill of Valmy as a backcloth.[60] Other posters, especially those issued by the banks as they competed to raise war loans and sell bonds to fund reconstruction, played variations on the same theme. Georges Seignac, for the Banque Privée, drew a peasant woman carrying wheat in her apron as she worked on the farm, wearing a revolutionary liberty cap on her head.[61] The need to put farms back to work lay at the heart of the government's appeal in 1918. The Société Générale's campaign again mingled soldiers and civilians in the cause of the *patrie*: the bank's poster showed a woman and a young child harvesting their crops, the sky filled with the image of soldiers at war. It was a potent reminder of the message at the core of the *levée en masse*, that everyone, male and female, soldier and civilian, had a duty to perform in the service of the nation.[62]

It also drew attention to another favoured theme of wartime propaganda – the timeless quality of France and the strength and constancy of her people, an agricultural nation linked inseparably to the soil and to history. Circumstances might change and there might be short-term crises, but France was eternal. This theme was evoked in many etchings and posters calling on the new generation to match the sacrifices of generations past. Fraipont, for instance, depicted a tall column from which a procession of soldiers marched down from the sky, representing the major periods of French history from the earliest times to 1914. 'France', or so the caption ran, 'is eternal, and nothing of what is France should perish!'[63] The same message was hammered home in Alsace, where Lucien Jonas drew a moving scene in a military cemetery that again linked present sufferings to France's past. As an ethereal host parades across the sky, the ghosts of former soldiers from the Great War kneel by their graves and look on. By the nearest grave a woman stands, dressed in French national costume with a young child in each hand; the caption reminds us that under the Revolution and Empire 72 generals from Alsace and Lorraine had served France, while in this war 171 generals and more than 20,000 soldiers from

[60] This image was drawn to my attention in a paper by John Horne on 'Myths and symbols of the *levée en masse* – image and text', presented at the Seminar on Force in History at the Institute for Advanced Study at Princeton in 1999.

[61] HI, FR 707, 'Emprunt national 6%', drawing by G. Seignac, 1918.

[62] HI, FR 671, 'Pour nous rendre entière la douce terre de France', Emprunt national, 1918.

[63] HI, FR 385, 'France toujours! France quand même!', etching by Gustave Fraipont.

the two provinces were fighting in the French army.[64] Perhaps the most famous image of military tradition, however, and one reproduced many times between 1914 and 1918, is François Rude's panel on the Arc de Triomphe, *La Marseillaise*. Serge Goursat's poster for the Banque Nationale de Crédit in 1916 takes Rude's sculpture as its central motif, showing past generations of soldiers streaming through the Arc in a seamless flow, each new generation called forward by the revolutionary volunteers in whose footsteps they marched. The message was in no way ambiguous. It preached a republican sermon, that the ideal of the citizen-soldier was still alive, and that it extended not only to all classes and conditions of men, but also across time, bridging the chasm between past generations and the young men who filled the regiments in the trenches. The spirit of the revolutionary armies lived on in the breasts of the *poilus* of the Great War, who were fighting for their country and its ideals with the same selfless passion that their ancestors had shown back in 1792.[65]

This was the imagery that appealed most strongly to civilian France, and which helped persuade those on the home front to give more, or subscribe more, or tolerate greater sacrifice. The experience of the armies might have changed radically since the time of the Revolutionary and Napoleonic Wars, just as the methods of fighting had changed, but the thread of continuity between Valmy and Verdun continued to exercise huge emotive appeal. In towns and villages across the country, more even than in the armies, the myth continued to resonate. But it no longer divided the nation: the cult of the dead was not restricted to republicans or radicals. There was also an *Union Sacrée* in death, and the sheer scale of that death, and the trauma it caused in so many French families, ensured that it would not be shattered in the moment of victory. The country wanted to remember, to commemorate and to grieve, and Frenchmen were in no doubt about what and whom they were commemorating. Memorials were seldom built for generals or in celebration of victories on the battlefield, as had occurred after previous wars. Nor was there any popular pressure to celebrate civilian losses, the annihilation, in extreme cases, of whole towns and villages, obliterated from the map in the *zone rouge* of the Aisne or the Somme.[66]

[64] HI, FR 460, 'Debout! Nos morts pour la patrie', etching by Lucien Jonas.

[65] HI, FR 428, 'Pour le triomphe, souscrivez à l'emprunt national', design by Sem (Serge Goursat), 1916; for comment see Daniel Moran and Arthur Waldron (eds.), *The People in Arms. Military Myth and National Mobilization since the French Revolution* (Cambridge, 2003), p. 35.

[66] A moving instance is the town of Albert and its surrounding countryside, devastated by fighting in the Somme. See Matthew Tomlinson, 'Rebuilding

The focus of remembrance, in France as in all the other war-shattered countries of Western Europe, was on the ordinary soldier, the lost generation of 1914. They saw no reason to commemorate the living when so many real heroes lay dead on the battlefield.[67]

The *poilus* were not the first French soldiers to be given their memorial in the midst of their community, though the level of commemoration and public mourning was unprecedented. Indeed, the scale of the losses was so great, and the clamour for monuments so unremitting, that every village in France seemed to demand its share of commemoration, its own plaque in the church or monument across from the *mairie*, and the landscape of the 1920s and 1930s became dotted with parochial *lieux de mémoire*, precious to local communities and a poignant symbol of the democratization of warfare in the modern era. They were a symbol, too, of a more general democracy, of the value of the common man in society, which had first appeared in the years that followed the Franco-Prussian War, when both French and Germans began to build memorials to their war dead.[68] Often the names of particular regiments or units were cited as the memory of whole communities turned to the young men they had lost. A good example is the monument erected in 1893 in the commune of Le Pallet, near Nantes, in memory of the men of the *ambulance* of Le Pallet who had died in the war: the monument was paid for by public subscription and placed in the village cemetery on land donated by the town council for the purpose. Its appearance was markedly modern, taking the form of 'a truncated four-sided pyramid crowned by a funeral urn, protected by four granite boundary stones joined together by iron chains'.[69] It was simple, direct, uncluttered by statuary and devoid of political symbolism, a poignant memorial that foreshadowed the thousands erected all over France in the aftermath of the Great War.

1871 had been, of course, a moment of defeat when there was little reason for expressions of triumph, whereas 1918 marked a victory, albeit a very costly one. Yet it is notable how few of the monuments erected by local initiative after 1920 were tempted to wallow in images of victory, far less to place the men who had died in the trenches in a

Albert: reconstruction and remembrance on the Western Front, 1914–1932' (PhD thesis, University of York, 2005).

67 Annette Becker, 'From war to war. A few myths, 1914–1942', in Valerie Holman and Debra Kelly (eds.), *France at War in the Twentieth Century. Propaganda, Myth and Metaphor* (Oxford, 2000), p. 20.

68 Annette Becker, 'Monuments aux morts après la Guerre de Sécession et la Guerre de 1870–1871', *Guerres mondiales et conflits contemporains* 167 (1992), pp. 25–7.

69 A.D. Loire-inférieure, 2R 377, report on the monument at Le Pallet, 1893.

long and glorious military tradition.[70] Sculptures, where there were sculptures, were generally ordered from local artists, allowing for a degree of regional variation in the themes and tone of presentation: in the deeply Catholic west, for instance, there is a marked Christian presence, with crosses and crucifixes sculpted on many of the memorials. And some communes did stress the glorious deaths of their soldiers, showing them nestling in the arms of a winged Victory. But most often what was depicted was the fragility of the soldier's life, and the sadness and emptiness that his death left behind: for every Marianne and every patriotic cockerel there were sculptures showing the soldier suffering and dying, the grief and mourning of mothers and sweethearts, or the children, now orphaned, playing at his feet. There is also a realism about many of these images that contrasts with the more abstract or allegorical forms of previous generations. The images are about individual men and families more than they are about nation and patriotism, the language of remembrance emphasising the loss of their 'children', their fellow villagers who had not been allowed to grow to manhood.[71] In a small number of communes the hatred of war ran so deep, indeed, that the monument they chose was dedicated to peace, and avoided any direct reference to the cause in which their soldiers had died.[72]

France's political infighting was, of course, far from over. Disputes between Left and Right, as well as between factions within the Left, would re-ignite during the inter-war years, while local communities would remain marked by religious difference, by their Catholic, Protestant or anti-clerical pasts. But in this moment of remembrance and communal grief these divisions were largely forgotten. There was a scramble to honour the dead, whether in churches, in town halls, or on village greens. Minds were concentrated on the immediate past, on the extent of death and destruction, and on the intensity of personal loss, and here republican propaganda had little place. The patriotic rhetoric of the war years gave way to a new rhetoric of peace and reconciliation as the country turned to the problems of reconstructing the national community. France, and with France the republic, was eager to turn

[70] An excellent survey of the designs of the war memorials erected in the aftermath of the First World War, with lavish illustrations, is the catalogue issued by the Secrétariat d'Etat aux Anciens Combattants et Victimes de Guerre, *Monuments de mémoire. Monuments aux morts de la Grande Guerre,* eds. Philippe Rive, Annette Becker, Olivier Pelletier, Dominique Renoux and Christophe Thomas (Paris, 1991).

[71] Yves Hélias, 'Les monuments aux morts: essai de sémiologie du politique' (mémoire dactylographié, Université de Rennes, 1977), pp. 32–3.

[72] Monique Luirard, *La France et ses morts. Les monuments commémoratifs dans la Loire* (Saint-Etienne, 1977), p. 31.

a new page. There were new challenges to address, new divisions, new foreign threats, in a Europe increasingly divided between the ideological forces of communism and fascism. The army of the Year II and the legend of the *levée en masse* appeared destined, after over 120 years, to pass into history as the nation turned to the new challenges of the twentieth century.

11 Last stirrings

If the myth of the soldier-citizen was struck an immense blow by the sheer scale of the human destruction that resulted from the Great War, remnants of it survived into the post-war world to re-emerge in moments of national crisis. But these were usually desperate, transient phases when France faced the threat of invasion or the republic itself was under threat. In years of peace, or while the French government was screwing up its courage to cope with Hitler or respond to the civil war in Spain, there was little reference to republican tradition, no appeal to the citizen-soldier of republican legend. Conscription had been turned into a chore, a source of fear and resentment; it seemed inconceivable that young men would again march joyfully off to war as they had done in 1914. For the post-war generation the reality of modern warfare was too well known, the evidence of its destructiveness there to be studied on the street corners of every city, on the plinths of the now-ubiquitous war memorials, and in the sanatoria of the 1920s. Besides, the character of warfare had changed too drastically, far more even than during the colonial wars of the 1870 and 1880s which had already driven a wedge between past and present. It had become a prey to mechanisation – the phrase used by the Marquis de Vogüé in 1889 when commenting on the manner in which the army was presented at the exhibition to mark the centenary of the Revolution – and the central role of flesh and sinew had given way to a brave new world of *matériel*, of hardware and technology. On the faces of visitors from the countryside Vogüé read the same expression, the same helplessness that he had seen in the machine gallery, a 'stupor brought about by the dominance of diabolical forces'.[1] Soldiers' lives changed in consequence, their motivation, training and morale, as what Michael Neiberg has termed 'the age of men' was transformed into 'the age of

[1] Marie-Eugène-Melchior de Vogüé, *Remarques sur l'Exposition du Centenaire* (Paris, 1889), pp. 196–7.

machines'.[2] There was so little common ground with the soldiers of the French Revolutionary wars, so little in the impersonal killing and mechanised warfare of the twentieth century that could compare with the bright uniforms and personal engagement which, for many, still encapsulated war in the revolutionary and Napoleonic years. Warfare had become industrialised, artillery and aircraft fire remote and depersonalised, the role and skill of the individual soldier reduced to an irrelevant sideshow. Too often he was seen – and came to see himself – as little more than cannon fodder for the enemy artillery. If there was an element of glamour and personal valour in twentieth-century wars, it was restricted to the few, representatives of a new elite who could, in the manner of fighter-pilots, still pit their skill and military prowess against the enemy in one-to-one combat. War had, it seemed, passed on, abandoning the citizen-soldier in its wake.

The Great War marked a watershed, and it left a very uncertain legacy. Some on the Left were so sickened by the scale of death and human destruction that they followed the pacifist strategy of Jean Jaurès and Gustave Hervé, rejecting war, and in particular all forms of expansionist and imperial warfare. Others remained faithful to the anti-militarist line of pre-war socialist policy-makers, continuing to distrust professional armies and to put their trust in the democratic ideal of the nation-in-arms. In the 1920s the socialists had no choice but to evolve a new defence policy, especially in the colonial field where the threat of foreign war was most immediate. They consistently opted for caution, and spoke out against several colonial expeditions, to the Levant in 1925 and 1927 and to Morocco in 1925 and 1926.[3] But in the European sphere there was less clarity. They still clung to the ideal of the 'nation armée', but in the era of the League of Nations they believed that the concept was in need of some reworking, some reinterpretation, and that they should turn to the international community for arbitration which would obviate the need for war. Their belief that their nation was essentially just – and that France could therefore accept the outcome of international arbitration with confidence and equanimity – helped cement this view, so that the socialists increasingly looked to the nation-in-arms as a means of avoiding war and countering the belligerency they associated with professional armies. This also dovetailed neatly with their class ideology of supplying 'not a *sou*, not a single man for the military

[2] Michael S. Neiberg, *Soldiers' Lives Through History: The Nineteenth Century* (Westport, Conn., 2006), p. 95.

[3] Patrice Buffotot, *Le socialisme français et la guerre. Du soldat-citoyen à l'armée professionnelle, 1871–1998* (Brussels, 1998), p. 92.

machine of the bourgeoisie'.[4] Instead, they advocated reorganising the military for national defence. France should have an army sufficient to deter attack while still reassuring others that it was not threatening enough to become an instrument of aggression. So what did this mean in practice? For most it meant turning once again to a citizen army, an army that would be composed principally of reservists. The socialists argued that it was no longer necessary to prove the efficacy of such a force, as Jaurès had tried to do before 1914, since the experience of the French armies in the Great War had demonstrated it. So encouraged, Paul-Boncour reaffirmed the plan that had earlier been proposed by Jaurès – based on large-scale training for the army, to be followed by a term of military service for all, and by periods in the reserve.[5] Dogma and practicality seemed happily in tune, since for many socialists, putting their faith in a citizen army not only provided a moral defence for their country, but also minimised the chances of future involvement in an aggressive war.

But unanimity on the Left on the subject of defence is easy to exaggerate, and if there was a general acceptance that France should turn to a citizen army if war should break out, that cannot conceal the wide divergence of views on rearmament during the 1920s and 1930s. The French Communist Party illustrates this dilemma nicely. On the one hand, it could glory in the 'revolutionary democratic tradition' of warfare, seeing the *tricolor* as a representation of France's commitment to the nation-in-arms and remaining faithful to the Party's much-vaunted role as the 'new Jacobins' of the twentieth century.[6] But it also took its instructions on European defence issues from the Soviet Union and the Comintern, and its response was somewhat confused as to the overlapping issues of patriotism, defence policy and anti-militarism. For if the PCF remained loyal to the republican ideal of the citizen-soldier and saw it as an important part of its ideology in wartime, it was not immune to the effects of pre-war factional struggles between those who had advocated rearmament and conscription, and those who had toyed with pacifism. These included many on the Left – including *guesdistes*, *allemanistes* and *vaillantistes* – who had opposed the institution of a standing army on the grounds that it would produce some form of conscription. These divisions had been temporarily concealed by the needs of the Great War; but they resurfaced in the post-war years, putting anti-militarism once more on the agenda of at least part of the Left

[4] *Ibid.*, p. 107. [5] *Ibid.*, p. 102.

[6] Daniel Brower, *The New Jacobins. The French Communist Party and the Popular Front* (Ithaca, N.Y., 1968), pp. 197–9.

and threatening to efface the traditional commitment of radicals to the nation-in-arms.[7] The Popular Front made use of a national rhetoric to trespass on the traditional territory of the centre-right, but it was only towards the end of the decade, when the danger posed by Hitler was clear for all to see, that the Left was able to appeal unambiguously to the national community and allow itself to use the rhetoric of national defence and commemoration.[8]

The tradition of anti-militarism was one which the authorities took seriously, since they saw it as corrosive of civic spirit and believed that it could undermine the preparedness of the people to accept sacrifice should war break out again. In wartime, of course, the expression of any form of anti-militarism was viewed as seditious and was repressed accordingly. Registers of known or suspected anti-militarists had been drawn up throughout the country on the eve of 1914, their names and addresses listed alongside those of syndicalists, revolutionary socialists and suspected spies. Some were identified as major threats to national security, and their names were included in the infamous *Carnet B*. A number of these had become known to the authorities for trade union activity, and the nature of the danger they posed was carefully noted. In the Seine-Maritime, for instance, where the register contains over seventy names, the work of each was listed in painstaking detail. They might 'frequent the leaders of the anti-militarist group', or have organised strike action, be an 'anarchist' or a 'revolutionary socialist', or have gained notoriety as a 'partisan of direct action in the event of mobilisation'. All were denoted as being anti-militarists; and several already had criminal convictions.[9] At the other end of the country, reports from Orange in 1917 suggested that pacifist groups, under the banner of the *Fédération Socialiste de Vaucluse*, had passed from door to door in many towns and villages collecting signatures and calling for the cessation of hostilities. In the eyes of the Minister of the Interior, this was dangerous behaviour, calculated to destroy civilian morale. He noted that they were corroding the tolerance of local people to the war

[7] Kevin Morgan, 'Militarism and anti-militarism: socialists, communists and conscription in France and Britain, 1900–1940', unpublished paper kindly supplied to me by the author. On the distinctions between communist politics in France and Britain, see also Morgan, 'Une toute petite différence entre *la Marseillaise* et *God Save the King*: la gauche britannique et le problème de la nation dans les années trente', in Serge Wolikow and Annie Bleton-Ruget (eds.), *Antifascisme et Nation. Les gauches européennes au temps du Front Populaire* (Dijon, 1998), pp. 203–12.

[8] Jessica Wardhaugh, 'Fighting for the unknown soldier: the contested territory of the French nation in 1934–1938', *Modern and Contemporary France* 15 (2007), p. 197.

[9] A.D. Seine-Maritime, 1M 323, 'Liste des antimilitaristes du Département de la Seine-Inférieure, révision au premier janvier 1912'.

effort by lobbying for 'a premature peace', and deplored the fact that they collected signatures from women and even children, people who did not vote and had no part in the political process. Such lobbying was, he believed, damaging to military morale and intolerable for a nation still labouring to accept the heavy costs of combat.[10]

During the interwar period the hostility of the authorities towards anti-militarism hardly abated, and the campaigns of pacifist groups like the *Combattants Pacifistes*, the *Ligue des Droits de l'Homme*, or the *Bloc des Mutilés* were subjected to rigorous police surveillance.[11] Communist meetings, too, continued to be infiltrated, even in 1936–7, when Communists were in government as part of the Popular Front, since they were widely suspected of distributing anti-militarist tracts to young soldiers and inciting conscripts and reservists to desert. There was good reason for such suspicions. Since the mid-1920s the Party had been opposed to what it saw as an 'imperialist war', fought in the interests of capital, and with the army of the Republic the unwilling instrument of that war. Young communists urged their comrades in the army to resist the call to arms, and encouraged reservists to tear up their call-up papers. They called on soldiers and workers to make common cause against the demands of the bourgeoisie, and they deplored the departure of each cohort of reservists for the army. They accosted soldiers in the street, outside their barracks, in stations and on trains, encouraging them to disobey the orders of their officers;[12] and in a tract printed and distributed by the Party in Paris, they made a special appeal to young workers who found themselves allocated to the reserve. Their message was uncompromising, and, for many, unpatriotic:

> Worker!
> Periods in the reserve prepare for an imperialist war!
> Periods in the reserve allow the army to put in place its training camps, the centres of mobilisation and new engines of war!
> Periods in the reserve help prepare you morally for the war of the bourgeoisie!
> Periods in the reserve constitute an attempt at mobilisation!
> They will be all these things if you allow it![13]

[10] A.D. Vaucluse, 1M 855, letter from the Minister of the Interior to the Prefect of Vaucluse, 5 January 1917.

[11] In the same department, see A.D. Vaucluse, 1M 846, Prefecture of the Vaucluse, reports on pacifist meetings during the 1930s.

[12] A.D. Seine-Maritime, 1M 311, letter from the Commissaire Spécial de Police de Dieppe to the Director of Sûreté Générale in Paris, 30 May 1927.

[13] A.D. Seine-Maritime, 1M 311, Anti-militarist propaganda in Rouen, 1921–1930, tract published by the Parti Communiste and Jeunesses Communistes, 'Les réservistes de la 23 partent!'.

This was a language far removed from the Left's traditional support for the nation-in-arms, a language that was intended to end popular support for the war and to destroy the identification of the people with its army.

Significantly, the PCF was now encouraging reservists to carry on their struggle in the camps as well as the factories; it urged them to join committees of activists inside the army, and to see themselves as workers before they were members of the nation, a call to political activism that alarmed the high command. As a consequence, reservists were themselves subjected to closer surveillance; their political opinions were scrutinised, as were the friends they kept and their networks of sociability. 'I should be obliged if you would let me know as a matter of extreme urgency', wrote the Prefect to his police chief in Rouen in April 1937, 'whether these reservists profess anti-militarist sentiments or have relations with revolutionary groups'.[14] Nothing, it seemed, could now be taken for granted. Throughout the 1930s the routes taken by trains carrying reservists to their training camps were a matter of intense secrecy; civilians seeking to board these trains were to be arrested; and any hint that reservists or young soldiers held anti-militarist opinions was to be investigated as a matter of urgency.[15] The bond between the people and its army had, it seemed, been severed, dissolved by the proliferation of anti-war sentiment and anti-militarist propaganda.

Even the one hundred and fiftieth anniversary of the Revolution, in 1939, did little to revive enthusiasm for the image of the citizen-soldier, for French minds were now concentrated on other revolutions, in Germany and Russia, and on the totalitarian threats which these posed for human rights and the basic principles of 1789. For many French people the very act of celebrating the Great Revolution seemed curiously irrelevant and, for some, in light of the destruction of its ideals across Europe, almost obscene. In this most ideological of decades, no gesture was innocent. On the political Right there was an almost total refusal to acknowledge that the Revolution, with its blood-letting and its sacrilegious assault on Christianity, was in any sense worthy of celebration. Even on the Left, indeed, politicians showed a degree of equivocation, an element of confusion that stemmed from that other identity of the Quatorze Juillet, as the civic festival of the now-defunct Popular Front. There was, says Pascal Ory, too much overlap between

[14] A.D. Seine-Maritime, 4M 3216, letter from the Prefect of the Seine-Inférieure, 19 April 1937.

[15] A.D. Seine-Maritime, 4M 3216, correspondence between the Commissaire Spécial de Police de Rouen and the Prefect of the Seine-Inférieure, April 1937.

the celebration of the historical Revolution and the legitimation of a republic that was now clearly dying before their eyes.[16] It seemed particularly insensitive to revive memories of war and bloodshed when the youth of France were again facing the probability of a further conflict with Germany, a circumstance which helps explain the rather low-key character of the commemorative ceremonies that were held during the summer of 1939. Nationally, the government took due note of the anniversary, assigning funds to organise a large exhibition in Paris, to establish a permanent museum in honour of the Revolution, and to hold a public celebration on 14 July, inspired by the original Fête de la Fédération. In all, the national committee spent some twenty million francs, but though there was a military presence in the festivities, the role of the revolutionary armies was given little emphasis.[17] At local level the aim was less to preach a revolutionary ideology that was recognised as being divisive, than to try to involve the whole community in a popular *fête*. The ceremony staged in Amiens, for instance, a city that had painful recent memories of war, allowed only a rather muted military involvement. The garrison was reviewed, as was traditional on such occasions, and a fanfare was struck up by the band of the local fire brigade, the *sapeurs-pompiers*. But otherwise the army was conspicuous by its absence. There were choirs and gymnastic displays, a concert in the bandstand, a procession by children from local schools, floodlights and fireworks. There was even a place for the local pigeon-fanciers, who released their pigeons at a fixed moment in front of the town hall. And a balloon was launched over the city.[18] But there was little direct celebration of the soldiers who had spread the message of Revolutionary France across Europe with rifles and bayonets; the nearest they got, two days after the *Quatorze*, was a 'grand cortège-cavalcade' through the streets of the town, organised by the tourist office, and offering a 'retrospective on the uniforms of the French army' through the ages.[19] In the summer of 1939 the country showed little of the intense patriotic fervour that had marked the eve of the First World War, and that mood was faithfully reflected in the measured tone of the celebrations.

The image of the citizen-soldier did not die, however, and it would be revived periodically, to become a standard trope of French political

[16] Pascal Ory, 'La commémoration révolutionnaire en 1939', in René Rémond and Janine Bourdin (eds.), *La France et les Français en 1938 et 1939* (Paris, 1978), p. 116.

[17] A.N., F21 4766, Commémoration de la Révolution Française, note pour M. le Directeur-général des Beaux-Arts, 8 June 1938.

[18] A.D. Somme, KZ 285, Ville d'Amiens, Fête du 150e anniversaire de la Révolution Française, programme for 14 July 1939.

[19] A.D. Somme, KZ 285, programme for 16 July 1939.

language in moments of national peril. If it played little part in the summer of 1939, it underwent a dramatic renaissance the following year, when young Frenchmen were once again urged to leave their homes and their jobs, to respond selflessly to the call of *la patrie en danger* by taking up arms and fighting as partisans. This was a traditional response that quite consciously looked back to the Revolution – and to the powerful response of the *francs-tireurs* in 1814 and 1870 – for both precedent and inspiration. It was a language that found echoes across the political spectrum, though the response was anything but uniform. This was not a return to the national mood of 1914, and any sign of exuberance, of a lust for revenge, had disappeared as the reality of the First World War inspired fear and premonition more than patriotic joy. But nor was there a total rejection of war, or an ideological embrace of pacifism; rather the mood was one of unease and anxiety, and an inability to contemplate a second hecatomb on the scale of 1914.[20] The patriotic call to arms did not go unanswered, even though the political leaders of the Third Republic showed themselves so supine in their response to Nazi demands. What was clear, though, was that the language of Valmy and the Year II had a more limited clientele, and that it appealed most strongly to the political extremes that turned a deaf ear to the siren calls of collaboration. But it was not restricted to a single faction or political cause. If young Communists rallied to it in the greatest numbers, so did Christian Democrats and followers of General de Gaulle, for whom, after the national army had surrendered and when French military power was controlled by the Pétainist regime, the main source of opposition to the German occupation necessarily came from workers and peasants, from those partisans who joined the Free French abroad or who left their homes to take up arms in the *maquis*.

In the context of the Occupation, resistance was once again represented by the opponents of Pétainism as a public duty, an act of sacrifice that was necessary so that France could again be free; and those who took to the hills, who sacrificed themselves as partisans and hostages, were hailed as heroes, as martyrs for the national cause. Their role was, as in the Revolution, a military one, albeit without the authority or the international protection that a regular military uniform conveyed. In the Vercors, the Auvergne and other mountainous regions, they contributed to the process of wearing down the Germans and driving them out of France, sapping the morale of the occupier, encircling isolated platoons and adding significantly to the atmosphere of

[20] Daniel Hucker, 'French public attitudes towards the prospect of war in 1938–1939: "pacifism" or "war anxiety"?', *French History* 21 (2007), pp. 431–2.

threat and insecurity.[21] They had much in common with the partisans of previous generations and were deeply influenced by the language of revolutionary France, by the call for liberty which was encapsulated in the Republic. For them July 14 was not only 'the national festival of France', but was also 'the world-wide festival of liberty'. This spirit was expressed with characteristic vigour in a tract entitled *Quatorze juillet 1942*, which urged the French people to remember and to celebrate the sacrifices of their ancestors. For 14 July did not represent only 'the great grief of the French people'. It was also, the pamphlet reminded its readers, 'the day when all Frenchmen should promise that they will resist the enemy who is momentarily triumphant by all the means at their disposal, so that France, the real France, can be present at the moment of victory'.[22]

After the Liberation the role of those involved in the armed struggle, whether in the ranks of the Free French or in clandestine activity in Occupied France, would be fully acknowledged by the French state, which sought to legitimate their irregular military action by identifying it with the spirit and tradition of the Revolution. It is significant that once again that identification was not limited to the Left, to the Communists and their allies who looked back to their days in the Resistance as part of the process of legitimising their politics with the electorate. It was also made by the Gaullist Right, who had their own Resistance heroes to mourn. Consider these words, by André Malraux, at the ceremony to transport the body of Jean Moulin to the Pantheon on 18–19 December 1964. 'This is the funeral march of Jean Moulin's ashes. Alongside those of Carnot and the soldiers of the Year II, those of Victor Hugo and *Les Misérables*, and those of Jean Jaurès, watched over by Justice, may they rest here with their long cortege of disfigured shadows'. Jean Moulin, tracked down and murdered by the Gestapo in Lyon, had been de Gaulle's principal ally and confidant in the dark days of the Occupation. It was a poignant moment when he and the Resistance movement he led were deliberately identified with the revolutionary armies, and with the historical tradition of the republic and its people which they incorporated.[23] It was not just the way in which the act of resistance was formulated, or the language which the *résistants* used to encourage one another, that harked back to 1793. It was also the way in which their acts of resistance were commemorated.

[21] John F. Sweets, *Choices in Vichy France. The French under Nazi Occupation* (New York, 1986), p. 200.

[22] *Quatorze juillet 1942* (Publications de la France combattante, no. 51), p. 1.

[23] Jean-Yves Boursier (ed.), *Résistants et Résistance* (Paris, 1997), p. 14.

De Gaulle was not, of course, an unqualified admirer of the Revolution, nor did he see much to emulate in the military qualities of its armies, which he was prone to dismiss as amateurish and wasteful. What he saw as most valuable in the armies of the Year II, indeed, were precisely the roots of the future professionalism of the military, personified, for him, by the contribution of Carnot, on whom he bestowed the supreme accolade of being an outstanding professional soldier and strategist. When he served as a deputy on mission to the armies, de Gaulle noted, he took the opportunity to observe the state of the troops, to assess their needs and to make an informed assessment of the quality of their leaders. He did so with all the skill and guile of a seasoned campaigner, an engineer and professional soldier of twenty years' standing. His outstanding contribution was in the area of supply, in finding sufficient men, food and munitions for the army's needs, and, most importantly of all, in fighting the fraud that was rampant among army suppliers which cost the soldiers so dearly. 'In spite of the many obstacles placed in his path, Carnot provided for a million troops on campaign, and during the winter of 1794–1795, when the armies were fully engaged, in enemy territory and far from their bases, there were fewer sick soldiers in military hospitals than there had been in the past.' That, for de Gaulle, was Carnot's most valuable contribution, and the most staggering achievement of the revolutionary armies in the field. He saw it as the most significant advance in military science of these years, more valuable than all the rhetoric and oratory of Barère and the Jacobin Club. This was the message, indeed, of his reflections on the republic and its army, published the year before the outbreak of the Second World War.[24]

But it was not the message of Jean Moulin's pantheonisation. Here, resistance activity was being compared to the generosity, selflessness and sacrifice of the *levée en masse*, the patriotic self-belief and youthful abandon of the men who responded to their nation's call to arms. This was not just a posthumous identity, supplied after the war was over to give a spurious respectability and sense of order to what the Germans and their sympathisers on the French Right had denounced as undisciplined acts of terrorism. The men of the *maquis* had themselves assumed it, consciously comparing themselves and their tactics to those who had fought at Valmy, soldiers who were young, poorly trained but glowing with self-belief, or to the partisans who had risen out of the Ardennes and the Vosges in 1814 to protect French soil against the Prussian invader. In the minds of this new generation of partisans

[24] Charles de Gaulle, *L'armée et la nation, la France et son armée* (Paris, 1938), pp. 6–7.

who left their villages, their farms and their workshops in 1940 or 1942 to take up arms with the *maquis*, it was an obvious parallel, one that had them following in the footsteps of heroes and placed them in the republican tradition of France's past. It is a point of reference which we find repeated in countless tracts and resistance newspapers, especially, though not exclusively, those written from a socialist or Communist viewpoint. They were unfailingly patriotic, reminding their young militants of their duty to France and to those who had served before them in the revolutionary cause. And there was – as there had been in the Year II – an emphasis on the need for constant vigilance, the repeated claim that the enemy is apathy and egotism as much as the foreign invader or the *milice*. They were always in danger of denunciation; for this reason, even as they repeated their mantra that the people were on their side, and the popular masses their natural supporters, they remained fearful of the local population, and were constantly on the alert for collaborators, for hoarders and egotists who might turn them in or denounce them to the authorities. They were partisans, outlaws, revolutionaries in a country that had been betrayed to their enemies, and the stakes were accordingly high.

Some of the most conscious identification with the soldiers of the Year II came from the Communist Party and its youth movement, the *Jeunesses Communistes*, whose tracts, even in rural areas, regularly appealed to the memory of Valmy, the revolutionary wars and the spontaneity of 1792. Valmy had a renewed resonance for those in the ranks of the Resistance, a reminder that victory could be won against all the odds, by an army of enthusiastic patriots against some of the best-drilled regiments that the monarchies of Europe could muster. It was a source of morale and of promise for the future, just as the image of the *levée en masse* eloquently encapsulated the unity and solidarity of ordinary people in resisting the invader. Republicans and Communists made repeated efforts to commemorate the 150th anniversary of Valmy by a mass show of strength. In the area around Angers, for instance, hatred of Pétain and Laval was linked to a resurgence of the memory of the Year II and its victorious battalions. Robert Gildea cites a tract distributed by the communist youth movement in the small town of Segré asking the youth of the area to turn up to their town hall bedecked in red, white and blue rosettes and lay wreaths at village war memorials as a sign of homage to their ancestors who had scored such a memorable victory over a previous German invader. A tract issued by another communist group, the Popular Women's Committees, appealed to French women working for the German war machine to down tools and demonstrate against the Germans. They called on them to join others of widely different backgrounds, 'housewives, wives of POWs and Catholic women', in a show of strength and defiance, 'as at Valmy the people rose up against the coalition of kings'.[25] The inspiration, it would seem, seldom varied.

In 1944, in common with many other departments, the Ardèche was the scene of commemorative processions, notably in Aubenas, Privas, Le Teil and Tournon, where thousands turned out to listen to patriotic speeches from local Resistance leaders.[26] The Communist paper, *La Voix du Peuple de l'Ardèche*, reported on the relevance of Valmy for those engaged in the current struggle against a new German invader. Those who came to the celebrations noted how perfectly the young men of the FFI paraded through their town, how impressively disciplined they were, and how committed to the liberation and renewal of France. And the comparison with the young soldiers at Valmy was not lost on onlookers. 'They were able to admire once again what our little soldiers and their young officers had learned through their patriotic faith, without any military schooling other than what they had learned from guerrilla fighting and their struggle with the Germans.' They had seen the nucleus of a new popular army for 'the France of tomorrow'. And they had drawn the obvious parallels with France in 1792, when the people of France had again risen up against oppression, and 'rushed to the frontiers to stop the army of tyrants and of émigrés from Coblenz, who at that time played the role now filled by those of whom Pétain and Laval offer the best and most sinister examples'. The same patriotic *élan* that won the day at Valmy 150 years previously, the paper concluded, could do so again; for Valmy was 'not only a military victory that overturned the prejudices of the old generals of the royal army, it was a victory that showed how a people defending its fatherland and defending its liberty is a people that is invincible'.[27]

The *fête nationale*, as we have seen, was another occasion on which to celebrate the affinity between the cause of the Revolution and that for which young Frenchmen were now laying down their lives, and again the PCF was not slow to remind people of the parallels. 'The patriots of 1942', in the words of one tract, 'see Laval and Pétain protected by German troops in the same way that the King was defended by German regiments in 1789', and the same qualities of *audace* are

[25] Robert Gildea, *Marianne in Chains. In Search of the German Occupation, 1940–1945* (London, 2002), p. 170.

[26] The examples that follow are taken from the archives of the Musée Départemental de la Résistance de l'Ardèche, in the Archives Départementales in Privas (Fonds Privés, série 70J).

[27] A.D. Ardèche, 70J 46, *La Voix du Peuple de l'Ardèche*, issue 6, 23 September 1944.

needed now as the French people displayed then. The communists call for a new *levée en masse*, involving not just the young, but the entire community, civilians as well as soldiers, united in the patriotic cause as they had been under the First Republic. All, whatever their job, whatever their political or religious beliefs, must struggle side by side in the cause of the nation.[28] The *levée en masse* was a recurrent theme in the polemical literature of the time, especially after the government tried, through STO (*Service du travail obligatoire*), to coerce all young men to leave their homes to work for war industries in Germany. This measure was bitterly resented, as it forced young workers to leave their families and friends and to uproot themselves from their communities; and for many it was the trigger to join the *maquis* and take part in the armed struggle. The communists were again to the fore in urging the young to resist what they talked of as 'deportations', pointing out that already tens of thousands of their peers had taken to the hills and the woods of the interior. Again, in resisting STO France needed a unified response, a *levée en masse* against Vichy. 'All France is mobilised to save these young men. Patriotic employers are helping their workers, civil servants are sabotaging their departments, and doctors declare the strongest of them unfit to serve. In many places gendarmes and patriotic members of the police do their duty as Frenchmen by helping the young to escape from their executioners.' As in 1793, none could escape behind titles or offices: all had a role to play.[29]

The need to preserve good relations with civilians on whom, ultimately, they depended for support meant that the young men of the FFI were made to respect strict discipline, and to avoid harassing or antagonising the local population. They could not afford to do otherwise, and had to be especially careful to avoid stealing livestock and damaging property. The documentation that was issued to them in June 1944 made this very clear. 'We are', it stated, 'the army of the French people, recruited from within the French people, and loved by the French people'. Their purpose was to chase out the invader, not to antagonise their fellow Frenchmen. Besides, the instruction continued, they were vulnerable to reprisals from the local community, since 'we have lots of enemies – not only the *boches* and the *milice*, but also a whole mob of egotists, *petits bourgeois* who could not care less about the war, black marketeers, bourgeois with vested interests, and political reactionaries

[28] A.D. Ardèche, 70J 50, tract entitled *14 juillet 1789–14 juillet 1942*, distributed in 1942.

[29] A.D. Ardèche, 70J 50, *Appel à la jeunesse française*, par Raymond Guyot, député de la Seine, distributed in 1942.

or opportunists'. They are the ones the FFI have most to fear, since they both accuse the Resistance of 'seeking to terrify local people' and condemn them for running excessive risks, risks which can bring retribution on the local population.[30] For this reason, it was the duty of every resistance fighter to establish good relations with the people among whom they operate. Those who did not risked severe punishment. One man, who pleaded guilty to stealing 30,000 francs from the owner of a shoe shop in Aubenas, and who had aggravated his crime by pretending to be an officer of the FTP, was taken before a court-martial and summarily shot. A notice announcing the sentence was printed and prominently displayed as a warning to others.[31]

As the war neared its end, the *francs-tireurs* began to savour the fruits of victory and to think more of the role they would inherit in a liberated France. In the Ardèche the newspaper printed for the FFI was, characteristically, entitled *Valmy*, a name which by this time needed no explanation. In its second issue its editorial ruminated on the kind of army France would need once the Germans had been defeated, which in their eyes meant not the restoration of the army that had brought such dishonour on itself and the country in 1940, but the creation of what it termed 'the true army of the people'. This would be very different from the army of the Third Republic, where the infantryman had been so poorly paid that he could not afford even simple pleasures like a visit to the cinema or a football match. It implied, too, the construction of barracks where the men would enjoy a basic standard of hygiene and comfort – unlike those, newly built at the Porte de Clignancourt in Paris, which had dormitories for up to sixty troops, with neither toilets nor washbasins provided in the buildings. Above all, it would necessitate a change in public attitudes towards ordinary soldiers, who, as citizens, had made sacrifices for the people and had a right to be treated decently in return. The paper wanted the new army to take forward the fraternity, the easy relationships between officers and men, which had been fostered in the Resistance, and the creation of a new, popular army that would reflect the interests of the people. It should be, it declared, an army worthy of the French people and in the tradition of the Revolution of 1789 – a 'republican and democratic army, in the sense that every man could, in principle, and providing he had the talent, rise to the highest ranks'. The author regretted that this spirit had

30 A.D. Ardèche, 70J 34, 'Documentation générale à l'usage des GM des compagnies concernant l'attitude à avoir à l'égard de la population et des autorités civiles', typed sheets, 1944.

31 A.D. Ardèche, 70J 34, Cour martiale de la Demi-brigade Joannas, jugement du 24 août 1944.

been lost during the nineteenth century, under the July Monarchy, the Second Empire and even the Third Republic. 'In spite of conscription and compulsory military service, it had maintained the spirit of a formal, professional army, and only slowly did it begin to remove a level of authoritarianism that had nothing to do with military discipline.' He finished by noting that 'the exploitation of the citizen was much greater in the barracks than it was in the factory', and that in the army it was even forbidden for French citizens to speak or to express their point of view.[32]

The Communist Party's identification with the French Revolution ran deep in their traditions, but its appeal to the memory of 1789 was also a matter of political strategy. At no time was this clearer than in the immediate post-war years, when they emphasised their links with the Revolution and with Valmy in an attempt to countermand the Gaullist emphasis on 1940 and the *appel* by de Gaulle to the French people on 18 June. But the *levée en masse* had a rather different connotation once peace was restored. The *patrie* was no longer in danger; there was no foreign invasion against which to defend the homeland. The enemy was now, as it had been for the Jacobin republic, an enemy within, and as early as 6 June 1945 the Communist paper, *L'Humanité*, appealed to the government to take the steps that would be needed to bring order to a society ravaged by division, betrayal and the effects of occupation. The party demanded the immediate arrest and punishment of those whom it identified as 'enemy agents', those who had collaborated with the occupier; and it called for a new *levée en masse* and the arming of the population 'to defend Paris and make the capital of France into an impregnable citadel'.[33] The same theme was repeated in the PCF's public ceremonies at the Liberation – both on 14 July and on 2 June, when the Party went out of its way to celebrate the one hundred and seventy-seventh birthday of the revolutionary hero and general, Lazare Hoche, in his native town of Versailles. Hoche was represented as a soldier who had risen from the ranks of the people, promoted because of the socially comprehensive society that the Revolution had created, and endowed with the courage and imagination to reshape the military into an army of the people, capable of fighting a new kind of war in the name of the whole people of France. Just as significantly, he had had to defeat treason in the Vendée, to overcome the same kinds of moral failings

[32] A.D. Ardèche, 70J 45, *Valmy: Organe des Forces Françaises de l'Intérieur de l'Ardèche*, issue 1, 21 October 1944.

[33] Gérard Namer, *Batailles pour la mémoire: la commémoration en France de 1945 à nos jours* (Paris, 1983), pp. 89–90.

as the new republic was faced with amidst the debris of Vichy.[34] Once more the people of Paris were being called upon to defend the gains of the French Revolution and of the secular republic it had brought into being. Once more they were being urged to take up arms and defend their liberties against their enemies.

There was, of course, a contrast between 1792 and 1940, for in the revolutionary wars it was the armies of the French state that had displayed the qualities of patriotism and self-sacrifice, whereas in 1940 the French army, by capitulating to the Germans, proved unequal to the task of national defence. One lesson to be drawn from the Second World War, indeed, might be that the army was no longer capable of living up to the ideals of the Year II, and that the idealism of the citizen-soldier had been betrayed by inadequacies of government and leadership. The *patrie* in 1940 had not simply been in danger. It had been invaded by Germany, and its people had suffered humiliation at the hands of a regime that imposed its own moral values on Marshal Pétain's government, arrested and imprisoned political opponents, rounded up Jews, sent its young men off to Germany to work in war industries, and introduced food rationing at a much lower nutritional level than that which was deemed sufficient for Germans. Where the spirit of the Year II did find expression was not in the military but in the civilian population. It was young civilians, especially young urban workers, who held their nerve and showed something of the alacrity and sense of patriotism that had once inspired the troops at Valmy; and it was partisans and guerrilla fighters who sacrificed themselves in the cause of the people without any mandate from the official government of the day. Their contribution was a visible and powerful reminder to the civilian population that the government had no monopoly of armed might, and that France's traditional republican values lived on elsewhere, even at the height of the German Occupation. When major cities were liberated at the end of the war, the *maquisards* often took their place in the liberating army: in the south-west, for instance, forces of Resistance fighters from the Dordogne, Lot-et-Garonne, Gers, Landes and the Pyrenean departments all joined the army that converged on Bordeaux.[35] In the post-war world that lesson would not be forgotten. Gaullists, Communists, socialists and others demanded that the sacrifices endured by the Free French and the Resistance should be honoured, and their contribution recognised as the true military voice of France. At the Liberation their leaders were decorated, their exploits extolled, and the streets of many

[34] *Ibid.*, p. 92.
[35] Pierre Bécamps, *Bordeaux sous l'Occupation* (Rennes, 1983), p. 100.

French cities renamed to commemorate their valour.[36] At the same time, the men of the official French army, those who had been overwhelmed by the invading German army, were scorned or condemned to public oblivion. It would prove difficult in the wake of their capitulation to rekindle the identification of the modern French army with ideals of patriotism and spontaneous sacrifice or to take seriously the claim that the soldiers of 1940 were the true heirs to the revolutionary tradition.

This difficulty did not ease in the post-war years, years dominated by the Cold War in Europe, and by the acquisition of nuclear warheads and deadlier conventional weaponry, which served to depersonalise war even more and to transform the role of the individual soldier. Besides, much of the fighting in which the French would be involved after 1945 was again in the colonial sphere, as the Fourth Republic fought to hold on to her remaining colonies in Africa and South-east Asia in what proved to be a losing battle against the tide of decolonisation. In Indochina and in the early conflicts in North Africa these wars were fought with professional troops, many with experience of colonial wars. But in Algeria, the longest and bitterest of these conflicts, the Fourth Republic threw in its conscripts, the young men of metropolitan France, sent across the Mediterranean to fight for a cause which few could relate to the vital interests of the nation. The first contingent left Marseille in 1955, sent by the government of Edgar Faure to reinforce a regular army that was increasingly taking on the role of policing the territory, and their fate became that of a whole generation. Between 1954 and 1962 more than 2,700,000 young Frenchmen were sent to Algeria in a war that cost some 30,000 French lives, a war in which they felt abandoned and unappreciated by a French public that had little sympathy for the *colons* and remained largely indifferent to the cause of *Algérie Française*.[37] Their bitterness only increased after 1958, when de Gaulle responded to the state of emergency in Algeria by extending the period of obligatory military service to twenty-seven months for soldiers and thirty for officers and NCOs. Many found the experience harrowing, especially after 1961, when the troops found themselves increasingly under attack not only from the Algerian nationalists of the FLN – in the eyes of many a legitimate enemy – but also from French settlers who resented de Gaulle's policy in North Africa and opposed any thought of

[36] This is illustrated in ceremonies throughout provincial France; see the various volumes in the collection edited by Henri Michel during the 1970s, *La Libération de la France* – by way of example I would cite Pierre Bécamps, *Libération de Bordeaux* (Paris, 1974), and Henri Ingrand, *Libération de l'Auvergne* (Paris, 1974).

[37] Martine Lemalet, *Lettres d'Algérie, 1954–1962. La guerre des appelés, la mémoire d'une génération* (Paris, 1992), p. 7.

an independent Algeria. The young soldiers found themselves caught in the middle of a civil war that had little to do with them, defending the economic interests of *pied-noir* landowners and business interests that many of them saw little reason to defend.[38]

They were, of course, subjected to persistent propaganda from the army itself, which recognised the degree of their alienation and understood the threat which this posed to morale. The commanders tried to explain to the young conscripts when they arrived in North Africa something of the history of the colony and the importance of maintaining a French presence there. In particular, they were issued with a fifteen-page pamphlet that sought to win them over to the cause of *Algérie Française*, informing them about the climate, the landscape and the history of the colony and making the case that Algeria could not survive without French support. Just as importantly, it pointed to the terrible economic damage which France would suffer if the army withdrew; one French worker in three, it alleged, would be reduced to unemployment and misery.[39] The pamphlet then went on to offer an explanation for the war, one which threw all responsibility on the Algerian nationalists and on those in France – the Communist Party in the main – who had offered encouragement to anti-colonial movements. There was, it was emphasised, no reason to suppose that France would lose, and nothing progressive or inevitable about Algerian nationalism. It aimed, the young soldiers were informed, only to serve the 'personal interests' of the FLN leaders and to 'assuage their desire for vengeance' by chasing out of Algeria those of a different race and religion from themselves. It followed that it was in everyone's interest, French and Muslim, for France to stay in North Africa and for the army to resist nationalist demands. Only by doing so could they prevent the crumbling of European values and the 'retreat of the civilisation which we brought'.[40] Algeria was represented as being crucial to French interests, and as French as Touraine or Picardy. When it was under attack, it was the soil of France itself that was threatened.

But the French conscripts were also exposed to counter-propaganda produced by the FLN in a campaign that was deliberately designed to undermine their self-image as a people's army. The FLN saw it as their task, especially during the first months of the war, to mobilise

[38] Martin Evans, *The Memory of Resistance. French Opposition to the Algerian War, 1954–1962* (Oxford, 1997), p. 211.

[39] *Afrique française du Nord, notice à l'usage des jeunes Français appelés à servir en Afrique du Nord*, a pamphlet of fifteen pages distributed by the government to the troops on their arrival in Algeria.

[40] Quoted in Lemalet, *Lettres d'Algérie*, p. 285.

their fellow Algerians against French imperialism, and they approached this by appealing to their sense of nationality, the fact that they were a people whose rights had been denied them by the coloniser. They made it clear that they would listen to the demands of the Algerian people, but insisted on their right to speak in its name. The FLN, declared Ramdane Abbane in June 1955 in a key tract to the population, 'affirms that the liberation of Algeria will be the work of all Algerians and not that of a mere fraction of the Algerian people, whatever its importance'.[41] The FLN claimed that their resources were limitless, both the freedom fighters who took up arms in the countryside against French police posts and local officials, and the 'urban *maquis* who are already in place and who form a second unofficial army', a terrorist army without outward emblems or uniform.[42] In other words, they made the case, both to their own people and to the French, that their power was irresistible because it rested on the will and the faith of the entire population of Algeria, that they were a true people's army in the way the French had been during the Revolution. Their cause was the cause of the people, and, like the French before them, theirs was military action in defence of freedom and self-government. In 1956 the Algerian Communist Party went further, calling for a show of solidarity between the Algerians and their natural allies, the 'working class and the common people' of mainland France. All should unite behind a common platform – 'to establish a democratic republic in Algeria, to introduce fundamental agrarian reforms that would give the land to the peasants, and to force the French government to open immediate negotiations with the representatives of the resistance movement and with the national political parties'.[43] To many of the young Frenchmen reading this, the language must have seemed hauntingly familiar, the same call to take up arms and to join a national armed insurrection that de Gaulle had issued to their fathers in 1940. Similarly, for young Algerians it was a double reminder – of the lack of gratitude shown by the French government for their sacrifice in the war against Hitler, and of the apparent double standard which the French applied when they responded to their own claims for national liberation.[44]

41 Tract by Ramdane Abbane, June 1955, quoted in Mohammed Harbi and Gilbert Meynier (eds.), *Le FLN. Documents et histoire, 1954–1962* (Paris, 2004), pp. 219–20.

42 *Le Plate-forme de la Soumman*, text of 20 August 1956, quoted in Harbi and Meynier, *Le FLN*, p. 247.

43 Text of January 1956, from *Liberté*, the official organ of the Algerian Communist Party, quoted in Harbi and Meynier, *Le FLN*, p. 225.

44 Dalila Aït-el-Djoudi, *La guerre d'Algérie vue par l'ALN, 1954–1962. L'armée française sous le regard des combattants algériens* (Paris, 2007), pp. 37–8.

It was hard for young men brought up on the history of the Second World War and taught to admire the exploits of French resistance fighters – often members of their own families – to accept the morality of the role they were expected to play in Algeria. As early as 1951 there were accusations in the Paris press that the police in North Africa were resorting to torture in order to extract confessions and information from Moslem prisoners, and parallels were being drawn with the treatment that had been meted out to Frenchmen by the Gestapo. Were the French troops not in danger, asked Henri-Irénée Marrou in *Le Monde*, of losing their souls in North Africa in exactly the way the Germans had done during the years of the Occupation? Would they be able to speak about their experiences to their children and grandchildren without themselves suffering 'the humiliation of Oradour and the Nuremberg trial'?[45] Were the values they claimed to represent, the republican ideals of the French people, not corroded by their cynical cruelty and their response to provocation in this most murderous of wars? Too often, it seemed, the soldiers were left with the responsibility for crimes of torture and brutalisation that were ordered by their officers and condoned by the French state, and this, as those intellectuals caught up in the war quickly recognised, posed problems for them as citizens. Pierre Vidal-Naquet was one of many whose exposure to the moral dilemma of torture was awakened by war service in Algeria, and he denounced it as state-authorised terrorism.[46] For those who did not share these worries or recognise the ambivalence of their actions, the Algerian Liberation Army, the ALN, was at hand to remind them of the atrocities which they were committing in the name of the French people. 'French soldier', read one tract widely distributed in 1958, 'You stigmatised the attitude of the SS in France, yet you behave exactly like them in Algeria. You shook with indignation when you heard of the crimes and atrocities that were committed at Oradour-sur-Glane, but how many Oradours are you responsible for in Algeria?' It was, they stressed, a matter of moral conscience: 'you know very well that crimes must be paid for'.[47]

There is little evidence that the French soldiers sent to Algeria took great pride in their mission, or that they used the language of their republican forefathers to describe it. Many were sent out as conscripts, as *appelés*, often against their will and in the face of opposition from

[45] Guy Pervillé, 'La génération de la Résistance face à la guerre d'Algérie', in François Marcot (ed.), *La Résistance et les Français. Lutte armée et maquis* (Paris, 1996), p. 453.

[46] See, for instance, Pierre Vidal-Naquet, *Face à la raison d'état, un historien dans la guerre d'Algérie* (Paris, 1989).

[47] Text quoted in Aït-el-Djoudi, *La guerre d'Algérie vue par l'ALN*, p. 40.

their families, to fight a war which many of them saw as pointless and irrelevant to national interest. The *patrie*, whatever Edgar Faure or Guy Mollet might say, did not appear to them to be *en danger*, and the *pieds-noirs* they were sent to defend did not always behave as their compatriots.[48] There was little in common with the war in Indochina, where the French had fought with an army of professionals, and the language used by the conscripts in North Africa repeatedly reminds us that their priorities remained elsewhere. Jean-Charles Jauffret expresses this difference quite clinically. While it is true that in battle the two armies, conscripts and professional soldiers, found bonds in *esprit de corps* and that fraternity that evolves under fire, for the men of the contingent the war raised different questions which led them to question the orders they received. They expressed doubts about the methods of psychological warfare they were expected to use, doubts, too, about the value of the counter-guerrilla methods they were ordered to adopt, and anxieties in 1961 when they were torn between the dictates of military honour and the law of the republic.[49] They increasingly rejected the policies of their political leaders, as some even came to sympathise with the Algerians in their battle for liberty. This was not the language of the Year II, of the republican nation-in-arms.

The conscripts had other grievances, too, which bore directly on their identity as citizen-soldiers, not least a realisation that they were not treated fairly or equally in this dirtiest of wars. It was bad enough in their eyes that conscripts were being used to put down a popular insurrection against colonial rule. But it was still worse for those who found themselves called back to the colours when their legal period of service was over in order to provide desperately needed experience to a young, poorly trained army in North Africa. The government claimed that these men – conscripts born between November 1932 and August 1933 – were being royally rewarded for their exceptional sacrifice, and that reasons of state made it necessary to keep them in uniform. But those unexpectedly called back from civilian life were often left bitter and angry, and a wave of protest and insubordination followed, often orchestrated by discontented *rappelés* who accused the government of a breach of faith. Disobedience took many forms. Conscripts refused to leave for their port of departure; others lay down on the tracks in marshalling yards or pulled emergency cords on troop trains. One Paris regiment, which included a high proportion of *rappelés*, gained

[48] Pierre Miquel, *La guerre d'Algérie* (Paris, 1993), pp. 173–90.

[49] Jean-Charles Jauffret, *Soldats en Algérie, 1954–1962. Expériences contrastées des hommes du contingent* (Paris, 2000), p. 10.

favourable press coverage when it directed an appeal to the people of France questioning the legitimacy of the war itself. After attending a peace mass at Saint-Severin in Paris, they wrote uncompromisingly and powerfully about the iniquities of the French presence in Algeria. 'Our conscience tells us', they proclaimed, 'that the war that we have to pursue against our Moslem brothers, many of whom died in defence of our country, is a war against all the principles of Christianity, against the principles of the French constitution, against the right of peoples to govern themselves, against all the values of which our country is justly proud'. They insisted that they were not conscientious objectors, not opposed to war when that war was necessary for national security. But they cared deeply about justice, and 'we would be ready, tomorrow, to take up arms against any army that proposed to do here in France what we are being made to do in North Africa'.[50] The government predictably took no action; but the point had been made, that they were not a professional force, and that the consent of citizen-soldiers should not be taken for granted in an unjust cause.

Algeria would prove to be a major turning point in the history of French identity, a war that brought neither glory nor public recognition to those who fought in it, which was tainted by accusations of torture, and which has proved difficult for the French republic to integrate into its national narrative. Films and novels discussed the miseries of the troops sent into the desert and lamented the misfortune of those who happened to be twenty at the moment of France's ill-judged defence of colonialism. There was a sense that this was not a proper war for conscripts, and that the cause and manner of its fighting only brought discredit on the nation-in-arms. In contrast to the celebration of those who had fought and died in the two world wars of the twentieth century, the victims of the Algerian War were remembered in silence, or condemned to public oblivion. Not before Jacques Chirac did any French president seek to rescue them from anonymity or to remind Frenchmen of the trauma that had affected the previous generation, a war that had divided them against themselves and which had ended in the bitterness of withdrawal. Chirac, to his credit, made something of a personal crusade of resurrecting the memory of those who died, by a series of commemorative gestures that began with the unveiling of a modest monument in 1996 on the Square de la Butte du Chapeau-Rouge in Paris 'to the victims of the conflicts in North Africa'.[51] He

[50] Text quoted in Jean-Pierre Vittori, *Nous, les appelés d'Algérie* (Paris, 1983), pp. 21–2.

[51] Robert Aldrich, *Vestiges of Colonial Empire in France. Monuments, Museums and Colonial Memories* (London, 2005), p. 146.

also honoured the *harkis* who had fought alongside the French and had been rejected by both French and Algerians after 1962. And finally, in 2002, and in the face of some political unease, he inaugurated a national memorial to commemorate all the servicemen who had died in Algeria, Tunisia and Morocco in France's wars of decolonisation, creating on the Quai Branly in Paris the national *lieu de mémoire* which had previously been denied them by the French state.[52] On the columns are listed the names of around 23,000 soldiers, among them 3,010 *harkis*. After being so pointedly forgotten by government, written out of history as part of a doomed and unheroic conflict for empire, the last contingent of citizen-soldiers to die in war for France finally have their memorial, and with it their place in the military tradition of the nation. It may be a small gesture, but in the context of a tradition that had lasted for nearly two centuries, it is surely a fitting one.

[52] *Ibid.*, pp. 151–2.

12 Conclusion

That France maintained the tradition of conscription until 1996 and still used a public discourse derived from the *levée en masse* is part of a wider public memory which has only recently been breached. Compared to her European neighbours, indeed, France has seemed strangely reluctant to break with her traditions, and republican politicians in particular have continued to insist, even in the twentieth century, that their legitimacy and that of the French Republic remained bound up in the values of their revolutionary past. The Revolution was to be celebrated, and its achievements – including the achievements of its army in saving the *patrie en danger* – were honoured, decade after decade, in the military processions down the Champs-Elysées every 14 July. For many the central importance of the French Revolution was self-evident; it was the event which, more than any other, had given France her distinctive character and the French people their particular form of liberty. In 1889, during the highly partisan rule of the Radicals of the Third Republic, and even, less propitiously, in 1939 as the danger of a new German invasion threatened, France celebrated the 'Great Revolution' unreservedly: it was seen as a single whole and commemorated as a key moment in the modernisation of the world. The citizen-armies that fought at Valmy and drove the Austrians out of the Netherlands were key components of this representation, and the identification of citizenship with soldiering remained largely unchallenged. And so, each time France went to war, it was an unspoken assumption that she would call upon her sons to defend her, exactly as the men of the First Republic had done in 1792 and as generations of republican pedagogy had taught that free peoples must respond in moments of national danger.

How different was the picture in 1989 when the French state planned another celebration, that of the Bicentenary of 1789! This time there would be no united view, no consensual memory across the nation, and François Mitterrand's dream of a lavish world fair to mark the event was cast aside in an atmosphere of political faction-fighting and public indifference.[1] The resultant celebrations were strangely muted, and were restricted to the celebration of a certain kind of revolution, the liberal reforms of 1789 and the civil gains promised to the French people by the Declaration of the Rights of Man. Banished were the violence and bloodshed of 1794, the bitter divisions wrought by the republic and the Terror, or the celebration of victory in war. Only in a few provinces – especially in Lyon and the Vendée – did local groups and political interests stir memories of their own experience of revolution and invoke images of violence and massacre, of an illiberal, centralist republic intolerant of opposition and incapable of accepting political pluralism. In vain did Jean-Pierre Chevènement evoke 'the old marriage that was consumated at Valmy between the Republic and its soldiers'.[2] Historians like François Furet retorted that the French people were no longer concerned by the issues that had obsessed so many of their forebears, and that the Revolution had ceased to be relevant to their lives, except, perhaps, to the degree that 1789 had guaranteed them citizenship, liberty and equality before the law. Beyond that simple, salient claim, the Revolution and its works had become an irrelevance, even an embarrassment. Colonialism, the European Union and successive waves of immigration had undermined the centrality of the revolutionary tradition and sapped the ideology of the republic. The majority of the population were, it was alleged, indifferent, if not openly hostile, to France's revolutionary achievement.[3]

This claim would seem to be borne out by opinion polls at the time of the Bicentenary, which suggested that the more liberal, enlightened figures like Sieyès and Condorcet enjoyed the favour of the public far more than did Jacobin leaders associated with persecution and Terror. Popular memory proved to be predictably uneven: the legislative achievements of the Revolution were less well-known by the general public than the granting of universal suffrage in 1848 or the educational reforms of Jules Ferry. And in the list of France's most heroic military moments, Valmy was mentioned by a very modest 2 per cent of respondents, far behind the twentieth-century achievements of the *maquisards* or the Liberation.[4] This would seem to demonstrate two parallel changes in public perception: a reduction in public sympathy for the French Revolution, which was clear in the media coverage at the time and in Furet's ability to capture the imagination of the public; and

[1] Steven L. Kaplan, *Adieu 89* (Paris, 1993), pp. 22–5. [2] *Ibid.*, p. 447.

[3] Jean-Pierre Rioux, *La France perd la mémoire. Comment un pays démissionne de son histoire* (Paris, 2006), pp. 52–64.

[4] SOFRES, *L'état de l'opinion. Clés pour 1989* (Paris, 1989), pp. 99–103.

a loosening of the bonds between France's military history, those qualities of spontaneity and *élan* that had been so central to the army's self-image, and the ideals of equality and citizenship. The citizen-soldier of the Year II no longer held the nation in thrall as he had done a hundred or even fifty years before: indeed, it is plausible that the loss of sympathy for the revolutionaries and their politics – as shown in the sympathetic treatment reserved for the Vendeans and for the defence of their 'martyred province' – had begun to affect public attitudes towards the revolutionary troops themselves. In the west they were too often portrayed massacring an innocent population driven to the ultimate sacrifice by simple values of loyalty and religious belief. Pierre Chaunu and Reynald Secher did not hesitate to use the expression 'genocide', Chaunu maintaining that 'this war was the most atrocious of the wars of religion and the first ideological genocide'.[5] It is surely significant that in the SOFRES poll almost as many people expressed their appreciation of Vendean soldiers, whom they often perceived as freedom fighters, as of the republican soldiers themselves.[6]

There is not a little irony in this, since for generations the legend that is the theme of this book, the legend of the *levée en masse*, had ensured that patriotism and military heroism were identified in the public mind with the revolutionary tradition of the citizen-soldier. Political fears on the republican Left had ensured that the state continued to call upon its citizens to perform military service as they approached manhood, and insisted that they gain an apprenticeship in arms lest France should again be attacked, whereupon they would be called upon to fight in their country's defence. Military service became a rite of passage for young Frenchmen, celebrated in towns and villages across the country on the day of the ballot when that year's *classe* would leave to join their regiment. It was a moment in their lives when they left their families and stepped into the world, and when they left childhood behind and became men. The language that was used to describe their service was one of duty and sacrifice, the words deliberately chosen to equate these duties with the treasured rights of citizenship which the state had bestowed on them. It was a reminder of a contract between the individual and society, between the citizen and the French people, a reminder that he was, as a Frenchmen, uniquely blessed with rights, and that the moment had come when he had to fulfil his obligations. It was also a call upon his qualities of martial masculinity, a discourse that

[5] Reynald Secher, *Le génocide franco-français. La Vendée-vengé* (Paris, 1986). See especially the *avant-propos* by Pierre Chaunu, pp. 21–4.

[6] Rioux, *La France perd la mémoire*, p. 59.

continued, even in peacetime, to define manhood in military terms. Under the First Republic, of course, it was the values of citizenship and republican virtue that were, at least publicly, emphasised. But during the Empire, and in the military culture of the nineteenth century, the equation was more clearly with manhood and masculinity. Under Napoleon the army did not hesitate to present its troops as the worthy defenders of a warrior nation, responding to the call of glory and honour and ready to make any sacrifice to defend the people and their emperor. They were also presented – or they presented themselves – as red-blooded males who were driven by a desire for sexual as well as military conquest. Many of the songs they sang on long marches and in the barracks of the nineteenth century explicitly linked the French soldier to an aggressive heterosexuality, and suggested that their military service only enhanced the sex appeal of young soldiers. Women would be charmed by them, and many would allow themselves to be conquered. The citizen-soldier could expect to encounter pleasures as well as dangers in the defence of the *patrie*.[7]

This book has been mainly about the implications of citizenship in a country that equated it with the values of the republic. In France, both during and after the Revolution, the conscript was made to perform military service because he was a citizen, and he owed duties that followed from his citizenship. This was an equation that was continually made, as we have seen, in politicians' speeches, in school textbooks, and in the various patriotic discourses of the nineteenth and early twentieth centuries. It was an emotive claim, and is arguably one reason why the tradition of the citizen-soldier was so enduring, and proved so difficult to excise. It is perhaps significant, too, that this is a peculiarly French formulation of the case for conscription, a case born of revolution and of the notion that war was no longer the threat of chaos – as it had been, for instance, during the Thirty Years War – but was a form of pedagogy, a means of forging sociability.[8] This was a concept that found few echoes either in Britain – which held out against the idea of a draft until 1916, claiming that a conscript army was foreign to British traditions – or in Prussia, which did adopt conscription during the Napoleonic Wars, largely in response to French victories at Jena and Auerstädt. Prussia, unlike France, had not experienced revolution, and could make no claims that its young men enjoyed the rights of citizenship, far less that

[7] Michael J. Hughes, 'Making Frenchmen into warriors. Martial masculinity in Napoleonic France', in Christopher E. Forth and Bertrand Taithe (eds.), *French Masculinities. History, Culture and Politics* (London, 2007), pp. 60–3.

[8] Alain Ehrenberg, *Le corps militaire. Politique et pédagogie en démocratie* (Paris, 1983), p. 45.

they were fighting in the name of the people. Prussia was an autocratic state whose soldiers were conscripted to serve their king. The rights of citizenship did not precede military service, but came afterwards, as a reward for their service. Nor did the Prussians make any mention of *élan* or spontaneity, preferring to place their emphasis on repeated, mechanical drill that would discipline the soldier into a machine-like obedience. Indeed, in an influential contemporary pamphlet Decken threw down a challenge to the most fundamental precepts of French warfare. Courage, he insisted, was not 'the effect of an ecstatic identification of the individual with a community, but passively cultivated through habit and obedience'.[9] Both countries perceived the move to a larger conscript army as a form of modernisation, of the increased power and outreach of the state. Each had a very different concept of citizenship, yet in both cases much of the public debate was concerned with citizenship and with the army's relationship to it. And German recruitment was in no sense undermined by the state's rejection of the revolutionary model of citizens' rights. Indeed, the principles introduced in 1806 formed the basis of a highly successful system of conscription which by 1870 had outlasted and outperformed the French tradition of the Year II.

In France conscription is also seen as part of another process of modernisation, that of the countryside, the atomised world of peasant holdings and subsistence farming which continued to characterise so much of provincial France across large swathes of the nineteenth century. Among republican politicians and their historians military service is often portrayed as one of the principal tools used by the state to create citizenship and a sense of belonging to the public sphere; it was a mechanism, in Eugen Weber's words, for turning peasants into Frenchmen. This, in Weber's view, was something that was achieved only in the last decades of the nineteenth century: he dismisses the idea that French national identity was formed in the revolutionary or Napoleonic period itself, and well into the second half of the nineteenth century he still cites evidence that rural France was resistant to the process of acculturation, whether by the army, or by emigration, or by schooling. Military service would play a key part in this process when it finally took place, but for most of the century he believes that soldiers continued to be treated as outsiders, foreigners, men who brought violence and pillage to their communities. His view has, of course, been widely contested, with some claiming that Weber selected only the remotest and most isolated regions for his study. But in these regions he

[9] Thomas Hippler, *Citizens, Soldiers and National Armies. Military Service in France and Germany, 1789–1830* (London, 2008), p. 137.

did find evidence, as late as the 1870s, of a deep antipathy to the military and a traditional desire to protect sons and brothers threatened with service. Officials reported a detestation of the recruiting officer in the Basque country in 1873; generalised indifference to the army in the Gers in 1876; and frequent cases of emigration across the Pyrenees to Spain to escape service in the Haute-Garonne in 1877. There were still villages, like one in the Allier, where 'almost all boys at birth were declared as girls'.[10] Nevertheless, the process of assimilation was proceeding apace, if, in Weber's view, very slowly, until by the first years of the twentieth century he agrees that the enforced exposure of each new generation to service in the military, and the mingling of young men from different provinces, different dialects and different social classes, created a bond of unity and a sense of identity which their parents' generation had lacked. Regiments set up their own job agencies, which meant that many peasant boys did not return to the land, but found work as building labourers, maintenance men or bus conductors in the cities. 'In sum', concludes Weber, 'the army turned out to be an agency for emigration, acculturation, and, in the final analysis, civilisation, an agency as potent in its way as the schools about which we tend to talk a great deal more'.[11] The republicans of Jules Ferry would, of course, have baulked at any such comparison. But in institutional terms Weber has a point. In the process of creating an integrated French nation, military service was a political weapon as much as it was a means of supplying the army with troops. Indeed, it is political faith rather than military utility that explains the persistence of conscription in France and the continuing resonance of the *levée en masse* long after the citizen army had outlived its tactical value in war.

[10] Eugen Weber, *Peasants into Frenchmen. The Modernisation of Rural France, 1870–1914* (London, 1977), p. 296.

[11] *Ibid.*, p. 302.

Bibliography

ARCHIVE SOURCES

ARCHIVES NATIONALES, PARIS

Algérie, 1 CM 6	Fête du 14 juillet, 1935–41
F1cIII Bouches-du-Rhône 10	Fêtes nationales, an II – 1852
F1cIII Basses-Pyrénées 5	Fêtes nationales, an IV – 1853
F1cIII Bas-Rhin 12	Fêtes nationales, an II – 1852
F1cIII Lot-et-Garonne 11	Fêtes nationales, 1792–1852
F1cIII Meurthe 11	Fêtes nationales, an II – 1852
F21 4766	Beaux-Arts. Commémoration de la Révolution Française, 1939

ARCHIVES DE LA GUERRE, VINCENNES

1 N 16	Conseil Supérieur de la Guerre, cours, 1899–1911
7N 1970	Ecole Supérieure de Guerre, cours et conférences, 1889–1914
Xo 16	Ecole Spéciale Militaire de Saint-Cyr, programmes des cours, 1905–14

ARCHIVES DÉPARTEMENTALES, ARDÈCHE

70 J 34	Francs-tireurs et partisans, Ardèche, 1942–5
70 J 45	*Valmy. Organe des Forces Françaises de l'intérieur de l'Ardèche*, 1944
70 J 50	Tracts communistes, 1940–4

ARCHIVES DÉPARTEMENTALES, CALVADOS

M 2796	Monuments aux morts de la Grande Guerre, correspondances, 1919–20

ARCHIVES DÉPARTEMENTALES, GIRONDE

1 M 721	Fête du centenaire de 1789–92
1 R 103–09	Préparation militaire – fédérations et unions de sociétés, 1883–1936

ARCHIVES DÉPARTEMENTALES, LOIRE-ATLANTIQUE

L 352 Fêtes publiques, 1790 – an IV
L 554 Commission civile et administrative: indemnités, an II- an VII
1M 674–75 Cérémonies et fêtes publiques, dossiers annuels, 1843–59
2R 377 Tombes et sépultures de la Guerre de 1870–1

ARCHIVES DÉPARTEMENTALES, NORD

M 161. 1–5 Fêtes de la République, 1871–92
M 161. 42 Monuments aux morts, inaugurations, 1904–31
M 219 Sociétés de gymnastique et de tir, 1873–1903
M 222. 1254 Sociétés militaires, Lille
M 222. 1256 Société des médaillés de Sainte-Hélène

ARCHIVES DÉPARTEMENTALES, PUY-DE-DÔME

M 122 Fêtes, an VIII – 1807
M 132 Quatorze juillet et centenaire de la République

ARCHIVES DÉPARTEMENTALES, SEINE

VK3. 87 Fêtes et commémorations, 1887–8
VK3. 90 Fêtes et commémorations, 1889
Atlas 508–12 Affiches, Guerre de 1870
Atlas 527–28 Affiches, Commune de Paris
13 Fi 4101, 4106, 4146, 4155, 4262 Affiches, Libération de Paris, 1944

ARCHIVES DÉPARTEMENTALES, SOMME

1M 772 Propagandes politiques – le Boulangisme
99 M 1–2 Mémorial aux défenseurs de la patrie, an VIII
KZ 285 150e anniversaire de la Révolution Française, 1939

ARCHIVES DÉPARTEMENTALES, VAUCLUSE

1M 846 Antimilitarisme, rapports, 1912–40
1M 855 Guerre, 1914–18 : Etat d'opinion publique
1M 856 Rapports du préfet, 1914–19
1M 876 Consulat, Empire: correspondance, fêtes et cérémonies publiques

ARCHIVES DÉPARTEMENTALES, YVELINES

4M 2/116 Anniversaire de la naissance du Général Hoche, 1882–1935

ARCHIVES MUNICIPALES, NANTES

I -1. 23 Cérémonies et fêtes publiques officielles, 1890–6

I -1. 29 Cérémonies et fêtes publiques officielles, 1790–1815
I -1. 31 Cérémonies et fêtes publiques officielles, 1790–1848

ARCHIVES DE LA PRÉFECTURE DE POLICE, PARIS

B/A 119 Fêtes pour l'ouverture de l'Exposition et du Centenaire de 1789
B/A 471 Fête du 14 juillet, 1880, 1881

BIBLIOTHÈQUE MUNICIPALE, SAINT-DENIS

Journaux de la Commune, 1870–1

PRIMARY WORKS

Agathon, *Le goût de l'action – la foi patriotique – une renaissance catholique – le réalisme politique* (Paris, 1913).

Albin, Pierre (ed.), *Tous les journaux du Front* (Paris, 1916).

Armée et Démocratie. Organe des officiers et sous-officiers républicains, later entitled *Revue militaire* (Paris, from 1906).

Aymard, A., *Histoire de France en images – cours Gauthier-Deschamps* (Paris, 1933).

Barrès, Maurice, *Les Déracinés* (Paris, 1897).

Bazaine, Achille, *L'armée du Rhin, depuis le 12 août jusqu'au 29 octobre 1870* (Paris, 1872).

Blin, Jules, *Portraits de gymnastes* (Elbeuf, 1897).

Bonnet Rouge: Quotidien républicain du soir (1915).

Bouloiseau, Marc, Lefebvre, Georges, Dautry, Jean and Soboul, Albert (eds.), *Oeuvres de Maximilien Robespierre* (10 vols., Paris, 1950–67).

Boulanger, Georges, *Lettre patriotique du Général Boulanger: sa déclaration républicaine* (Paris, 1887).

Bourdon, Léonard, *Recueil des actions héroïques et civiques des républicains français, présenté à la Convention Nationale au nom de son Comité d'Instruction Publique* (Paris, an II).

Bruno, G., *Le tour de la France par deux enfants: devoir et patrie* (Cours moyen conforme aux programmes du 27 juillet 1882, 283rd edition, Paris, 1898).

Caruel (le R. P.), *L'éducation nationale et l'armée. Discours prononcé à la distribution des prix de l'Ecole libre Saint-Joseph de Reims* (Reims, 1898).

De Gaulle, Charles, *Le fil de l'épée* (Paris, 1932).
L'armée et la nation, la France et son armée (Paris, 1938).

Didon, Henri, *L'esprit militaire dans une nation* (Paris, 1898).

Dupanloup, Félix-Antoine-Philibert, *Conseils aux jeunes gens sur l'étude de l'histoire* (Paris, 1872).

Duruy, George (ed.), *L'officier éducateur national* (Bordeaux, 1905).

Ebener, Charles, *Conférences sur le rôle social de l'officier: faites en 1901 aux élèves de l'Ecole Spéciale Militaire* (Paris, 1901).

Fédération des Bourses du Travail de France et des Colonies, *Nouveau manuel du soldat. La Patrie – l'armée – la guerre* (13e édition, Paris, 1905).

Freycinet, Charles, *La guerre en province pendant le siège de Paris, 1870–71* (Paris, 1871).
Gagnol, Abbé, *Histoire de France* (Paris, 1901).
Gambetta, Léon, *Le Général Hoche. Discours prononcé à Versailles le 24 juin 1872* (Paris, 1872).
Girard, *Année préparatoire d'histoire de France* (Paris, 1886).
Gohier, Urbain, *Le service d'un an* (Paris, 1899).
Gouvion Saint-Cyr, *Mémoires* (Paris, 1829).
Hervé, Gustave, 'La conquête de l'armée', in *La Guerre Sociale* (Paris, 1912).
J.S.G., *Le Livre de tous. Le soldat français, aujourd'hui, demain* (Paris, 1893).
Jaurès, Jean, *L'armée nouvelle* (Paris, 1910).
Lavisse, Emile, '*Tu seras soldat*'. *Histoire d'un soldat français: récits et leçons patriotiques d'instruction et d'éducation militaires* (Paris, 1888).
Lavisse, Ernest, *L'armée à travers les âges: conférences faites en 1898 à l'Ecole Militaire de Saint-Cyr* (Paris, 1899).
Histoire de France: cours moyen (Paris, 1912).
Mainard, Louis, *Le livre d'or de la Patrie* (Paris, 1885).
Markham, J. David (ed.), *Imperial Glory. The Bulletins of Napoleon's Grande Armée, 1805–14* (London, 2003).
Melin, *Petite histoire de France* (Paris, 1885).
Pelletan, Eugène, *Le 4 septembre devant l'enquête* (Paris, 1874).
Poincaré, Raymond, *Au service de la France: Neuf années de souvenirs, vol. 4, L'Union sacrée, 1914* (Paris, 1929).
Au service de la France: Neuf années de souvenirs, vol. 6, Les Tranchées, 1916 (Paris, 1930).
Quatorze juillet 1942 (Publications de la France combattante, no. 51).
La semaine religieuse du diocèse de Nantes, 32 (1986).
SOFRES, *L'état de l'opinion. Clés pour 1989* (Paris, 1989).
Le Soldat de Demain et l'Elève Soldat Réunis. Bulletin Officiel de l'Union des Sociétés de Préparation Militaire de France (1912).
Terquem, Emile, *Comment on fait une armée réactionnaire: comment on fait une armée républicaine* (Paris, 1906).
Trochu (général), *L'armée française en 1867* (Paris, 1867).
Vandepitte, Abbé, *Histoire de France, à l'usage des maisons chrétiennes d'éducation* (Lille, 1895).
Vuillermet, F.-A., *Soyez des hommes. A la conquête de la virilité* (Paris, 1909).
Wright, J. (ed.), *Copies of Original Letters from the Army of General Bonaparte in Egypt, Intercepted by the Fleet under the Command of Admiral Lord Nelson* (London, 1798).

SECONDARY WORKS

Agulhon, Maurice, *Marianne into Battle. Republican Imagery and Symbolism in France, 1789–1880* (Cambridge, 1981).
Marianne au pouvoir. L'imagerie et la symbolique républicaines de 1880 à 1914 (Paris, 1989).
The French Republic, 1879–1992 (Oxford, 1993).

'Marianne en 14–18', in Jean-Jacques Becker, Jay M. Winter, Gerd Krumeich, Annette Becker and Stéphane Audoin-Rouzeau (eds.), *Guerres et cultures, 1914–1918* (Paris, 1994).

Aït-el-Djoudi, Dalila, *La guerre d'Algérie vue par l'ALN, 1954–1962. L'armée française sous le regard des combattants algériens* (Paris, 2007).

Aldrich, Robert, *Vestiges of Colonial Empire in France. Monuments, Museums and Colonial Memories* (London, 2005).

Alexander, Robert, 'The hero as Houdini: Napoleon and nineteenth-century Bonapartism', *Modern and Contemporary France* **8** (2000).

Re-writing the French Revolutionary Tradition (Cambridge, 2003).

Amalvi, Christian, *Les héros de l'histoire de France. Recherche iconographique sur le panthéon scolaire de la Troisième République* (Paris, 1979).

'Le 14-juillet. Du dies irae à jour de fête', in Pierre Nora (ed.), *Les lieux de mémoire. 1 – La République* (Paris, 1984).

'Nationalist responses to the Revolution', in Robert Tombs (ed.), *Nationhood and Nationalism in France from Boulangism to the Great War, 1889–1918* (London, 1991).

La République en scène. Les décors des mairies parisiennes, 1873–1914 (Paris, 2006).

Arnaud, P. and Camy, J. (eds.), *La naissance du mouvement sportif associatif en France. Sociabilités et formes de pratiques sportives* (Lyon, 1986).

Audoin-Rouzeau, Stéphane, 'Les soldats français pendant la guerre de 1914–18 d'après les journaux de tranchées. Une étude des mentalités' (thèse de doctorat, Université de Clermont-Ferrand, 1984).

14–18: Les combattants des tranchées (Paris, 1986).

1870: La France dans la guerre (Paris, 1989).

Auspitz, Katherine, *The Radical Bourgeoisie. The Ligue de l'enseignement and the Origins of the Third Republic, 1866–1885* (Cambridge, 1982).

Auvray, Michel, *L'âge des casernes. Histoire et mythes du service militaire* (Paris, 1998).

Bacconnier, Gérard, Minet, André and Soler, Louis, *La plume au fusil. Les poilus du Midi à travers leur correspondance* (Toulouse, 1985).

Baecque, Antoine de, *La caricature révolutionnaire* (Paris, 1988).

Barny, Roger, 'L'image de Cromwell dans la Révolution Française', *Dix-huitième siècle* **25** (1993).

Bécamps, Pierre, *Bordeaux sous l'Occupation* (Rennes, 1983).

Libération de Bordeaux (Paris, 1974).

Becker, Annette, 'Monuments aux morts après la Guerre de Sécession et la Guerre de 1870–1871', *Guerres mondiales et conflits contemporains* **167** (1992).

'From war to war. A few myths, 1914–1942', in Valerie Holman and Debra Kelly (eds.), *France at War in the Twentieth Century. Propaganda, Myth and Metaphor* (Oxford, 2000).

Becker, Annette (ed.), *Journaux de combattants et civils de la France du Nord dans la Grande Guerre* (Lille, 1998).

Becker, Jean-Jacques, 'La fleur au fusil: retour sur un mythe', in Christophe Prochasson and Anne Rasmussen (eds.), *Vrai et faux dans la Grande Guerre* (Paris, 2004).

Bédarida, François, 'L'armée et la République', *Revue historique* **88** (1964).

Bell, David, *The Cult of the Nation in France. Inventing Nationalism, 1680–1800* (Cambridge, Mass., 2001).

Ben-Amos, Avner, *Funerals, Politics, and Memory in Modern France, 1789–1996* (Oxford, 2000).

'The Marseillaise as myth and metaphor', in Valerie Holman and Debra Kelly (eds.), *France at War in the Twentieth Century. Propaganda, Myth and Metaphor* (Oxford, 2000).

Bergès, Louis, *Résister à la conscription, 1798–1814. Le cas des départements aquitains* (Paris, 2002).

Bertaud, Jean-Paul (ed.), *Valmy, la démocratie en armes* (Paris, 1970).

La Révolution armée. Les soldats-citoyens et la Révolution Française (Paris, 1979).

Guerre et société en France de Louis XIV à Napoléon Ier (Paris, 1998).

La presse et le pouvoir de Louis XIII à Napoléon (Paris, 2000).

Bertaud, Jean-Paul and Reichel, Daniel, *Atlas de la Révolution Française. 3: L'armée et la guerre* (Paris, 1989).

Bezucha, Robert J., *The Lyon Uprising of 1834. Social and Political Conflict in the Early July Monarchy* (Cambridge, Mass., 1974).

Bianchi, Serge and Dupuy, Roger (eds.), *La Garde nationale entre nation et peuple en armes. Mythes et réalités, 1789–1871* (Rennes, 2006).

Bigard, L., 'Le Saint-Napoléon à Rueil et les évènements de 1814', *Revue Historique de Versailles* **27** (1925).

Birnbaum, Pierre, *Les fous de la République. Histoire politique des Juifs d'Etat de Gambetta à Vichy* (Paris, 1992).

Biver, Marie-Louise, *Fêtes révolutionnaires à Paris* (Paris, 1979).

Blanning, T.C.W., *The French Revolutionary Wars, 1787–1802* (London, 1996).

Blaufarb, Rafe, *Bonapartists in the Borderlands. French Exiles and Refugees of the Gulf Coast, 1815–1835* (Tuscaloosa, Ala., 2006).

Blom, Ida, Hagemann, Karen and Hall, Catherine (eds.), *Gendered Nations. Nationalisms and Gender Order in the Long Nineteenth Century* (Oxford, 2000).

Bois, Jean-Pierre, *Histoire des 14 juillet, 1789–1919* (Rennes, 1991).

Bordes, Philippe and Michel, Régis (eds.), *Aux armes et aux arts! Les arts de la Révolution, 1789–99* (Paris, 1988).

Boudon, Jacques-Olivier (ed.), *Brumaire. La prise de pouvoir de Bonaparte* (Paris, 2001).

Bouhet, Patrick, 'Les femmes et les armées de la Révolution à l'Empire', *Guerres mondiales et conflits contemporains* **198** (2000).

Boullenger, Eric, 'L'image de l'armée à travers la peinture du Consulat et du Premier Empire' (mémoire de maîtrise, Université de Paris-I, 1988).

Bourdin, Philippe and Loubinoux, Gérard (eds.), *Les arts de la scène et la Révolution Française* (Clermont-Ferrand, 2004).

Boursier, Jean-Yves (ed.), *Résistants et Résistance* (Paris, 1997).

Bozon, Michel, 'Conscrits et fêtes de conscrits à Villefranche-sur-Saône', *Ethnologie française*, nouvelle série **9**, numéro **1** (1979).

Les conscrits (Paris, 1981).

Brault, Yoann, Jiméno, Frédéric and Rabreau, Daniel (eds.), *L'Ecole Militaire, et l'axe Breteuil-Trocadéro* (Paris, 2002).
Bret, Patrice (ed.), *L'Expédition d'Égypte, une entreprise des Lumières, 1798–1801* (Paris, 1999).
Brochon, Pierre, *La chanson sociale de Béranger à Brassens* (Paris, 1961).
Broers, Michael, *The Politics of Religion in Napoleonic Italy. The War against God, 1801–14* (London, 2002).
Brower, Daniel, *The New Jacobins. The French Communist Party and the Popular Front* (Ithaca, N.Y., 1968).
Buffotot, Patrice, *Le socialisme français et la guerre. Du soldat-citoyen à l'armée professionnelle, 1871–1998* (Brussels, 1998).
Burke, Peter, *The Fabrication of Louis XIV* (New Haven, Conn., 1992).
Calvet, Stéphane, 'Les officiers de l'armée impériale et le pouvoir royal: tensions et conflits en Charente, 1814–32', in Natalie Petiteau (ed.), *Conflits d'Empire: Les Cahiers du GERHICO 9* (Poitiers, 2006).
Cambon, Pierre, 'Francs-tireurs et corps francs en 1870–1871: mythe et réalité' (mémoire de maîtrise, Université de Paris-I, 1976).
Carlson, Marvin, *The Theatre of the French Revolution* (Ithaca, N.Y., 1966).
Carrot, Georges, 'Une institution de la nation: la Garde Nationale, 1789–1871' (thèse de doctorat de 3e cycle, Université de Nice, 1979).
La Garde Nationale, 1789–1871. Une force publique ambiguë (Paris, 2001).
Castel, J.-A., 'L'application de la Loi Jourdan dans l'Hérault' (mémoire de maîtrise, Université de Montpellier, 1970).
Cavalier, Vincent, 'La représentation de la Révolution française à travers les manuels scolaires de 1870 à 1914' (mémoire de maîtrise, Université de Provence, 1996).
Chaline, Jean-Pierre, *La Restauration* (Paris, 1998).
Challener, Richard D, *The French Theory of the Nation in Arms, 1866–1939* (New York, 1955).
Chandler, David, *Dictionary of the Napoleonic Wars* (New York, 1993).
Chanet, Jean-François, *L'école républicaine et les petites patries* (Paris, 1996).
Vers l'armée nouvelle. République conservatrice et réforme militaire, 1871–1879 (Rennes, 2006).
Chapman, Guy, *The Dreyfus Trials* (London, 1972).
Chevalier, Jean-Michel, *Souvenirs des guerres napoléoniennes* (Paris, 1970).
Cholvy, Gérard and Hilaire, Yves-Marie, *Histoire religieuse de la France contemporaine* (2 vols., Toulouse 1985).
Clausewitz, Karl von, *On War*, trans. Michael Howard and Peter Paret (Princeton, 1976).
Cobban, Alfred, *Aspects of the French Revolution* (New York, 1968).
Cochet, Anick, 'L'opinion et le moral des soldats en 1916, d'après les archives du Contrôle Postal' (thèse de doctorat, Université de Paris-X, 1986).
Coignet, Jean-Roch, *Les cahiers du Capitaine Coignet* (Paris, 1968).
Colson, Bruno, *Le général Rogniat ingénieur et critique de Napoléon* (Paris, 2006).
Coste, Commandant E., *L'officier dans la Nation* (Paris, 1903).
Cox, Gary P., *The Halt in the Mud: French Strategic Planning from Waterloo to Sedan* (Boulder, Colo., 1994).

Crépin, Annie, *La conscription en débat, ou le triple apprentissage de la nation, de la citoyenneté, de la République, 1798–1889* (Arras, 1998).

Défendre la France: Les Français, la guerre et le service militaire, de la Guerre de Sept Ans à Verdun (Rennes, 2005).

Croisille, Christian and Ehrard, Jean (eds.), *La légende de la Révolution. Actes du colloque international de Clermont-Ferrand, juin 1986* (Clermont-Ferrand, 1988).

Cubells, Monique (ed.), *La Révolution Française: la guerre et la frontière* (Paris, 2000).

Dalisson, Rémi, *Les trois couleurs, Marianne et l'Empereur: Fêtes libérales et politiques symboliques en France, 1815–1870* (Paris, 2004).

Darriulat, Philippe, *Les Patriotes. La gauche républicaine et la Nation, 1830–70* (Paris, 2001).

Datta, Venita, '"L'appel au soldat": visions of the Napoleonic legend in popular culture of the belle epoque', *French Historical Studies* **28** (2005).

Demartial, Georges, *La guerre de 1914. La mobilisation des consciences* (Paris, 1927).

Documentation Française, La, *Le Centenaire de la Révolution, 1889* (Paris, 1989).

Doumenc, A., 'L'armée et les journées de juin', in *Actes du Congrès historique du Centenaire de la Révolution de 1848* (Paris, 1948).

Driskel, Michael Paul, *As Befits a Legend. Building a Tomb for Napoleon, 1840–61* (Kent, Ohio, 1993).

Dufay, Pierre, *Les sociétés populaires et l'armée, 1791–1794* (Paris, 1913).

Dumont, Jean-Marie, *La vie et l'oeuvre de Jean-Charles Pellerin, 1756–1836* (Epinal, 1956).

Les maîtres-graveurs populaires, 1800–50 (Epinal, 1965).

Dupâquier, Jacques, 'Problèmes démographiques de la France napoléonienne', *Revue d'histoire moderne et contemporaine* **17** (1970).

(ed.), *Histoire de la population française* (4 vols., Paris, 1988).

Dupuy, Roger, *La Garde Nationale et les débuts de la Révolution en Ille-et-Vilaine, 1789 – mars 1793* (Paris, 1972).

De la Révolution à la chouannerie. Paysans en Bretagne, 1788–94 (Paris, 1988).

Duquet, Alfred, *Les derniers jours de l'Armée du Rhin* (Paris, 1888).

Dwyer, Philip G., *Charles-Maurice de Talleyrand, 1754–1838. A Bibliography* (Westport, Conn., 1996).

'Napoleon Bonaparte as hero and saviour: image, rhetoric and behaviour in the construction of a legend', *French History* **18** (2004).

Ehrenberg, Alain, *Le corps militaire. Politique et pédagogie en démocratie* (Paris, 1983).

Elting, John R., *Swords around a Throne. Napoleon's Grande Armée* (London, 1989).

Emsley, Clive, *Gendarmes and the State in Nineteenth-Century Europe* (Oxford, 1999).

Englund, Steven, *Napoleon. A Political Life* (New York, 2004).

Esdaile, Charles, *The Wars of Napoleon* (London, 1995).

Evans, Martin, *The Memory of Resistance. French Opposition to the Algerian War, 1954–1962* (Oxford, 1997).

Ferguson, Priscilla Parkhurst, *Paris as Revolution. Writing the Nineteenth-century City* (Berkeley, Calif., 1994).

Fierro, Alfred, *Bibliographie critique des mémoires sur la Révolution écrits ou traduits en français* (Paris, 1988).

Forrest, Alan, *Conscripts and Deserters. The Army and French Society during the Revolution and Empire* (Oxford, 1989).

The Soldiers of the French Revolution (Durham, N.C., 1990).

Napoleon's Men. The Soldiers of the Revolution and Empire (London, 2002).

'La perspective de la paix dans l'opinion publique et la société militaire', *Bulletin de la Société des Antiquaires de Picardie* **166** (2002), pp. 251–62.

'Propaganda and the legitimation of power in Napoleonic France', *French History* **18** (2004).

'L'armée de l'an II: la levée en masse et la création d'un mythe républicain', *Annales historiques de la Révolution Française* **335** (2004), pp. 111–30.

Fortescue, William, *The Third Republic in France, 1870–1940. Conflicts and Continuities* (London, 2000).

Forth, Christopher E. and Taithe, Bertrand (eds.), *French Masculinities. History, Culture and Politics* (London, 2007).

Foucart, Bruno, 'La grande alliance de Napoléon et des peintres de son histoire', in *Napoléon, images et histoires. Peintures du Château de Versailles, 1789–1815* (Paris, 2001).

Freyssinet-Dominjon, Jacqueline, *Les manuels d'histoire de l'école libre, 1882–1959* (Paris, 1969).

Furet, François, *Revolutionary France, 1770–1880* (Oxford, 1993).

Furet, François and Ozouf, Mona (eds.), *La Gironde et les Girondins* (Paris, 1991).

Gaillard, Jeanne, *Paris, la ville 1852–1870: L'urbanisation parisienne à l'heure d'Haussman* (Paris, 1977).

Gallaher, John G., *Napoleon's Irish Legion* (Carbondale, Ill., 1993).

Garnier, Nicole, *Catalogue de l'imagerie populaire française. 2- Images d'Epinal gravées sur bois* (Paris, 1996).

Gates, David, *The Napoleonic Wars, 1803–1815* (London, 1997).

Gautier, Georges-Ferdinand, *Les Francs-tireurs de la Commune* (Paris, 1971).

Geffroy, Annie, 'Le mot *nation* chez Robespierre', in Jean-Pierre Jessenne, Gilles Deregnaucourt, Jean-Pierre Hirsch and Hervé Leuwers (eds.), *Robespierre: De la nation artésienne à la République et aux nations* (Lille, 1994).

Gellner, Ernest, *Nations and Nationalism* (London, 1983).

Gendron, François, *La Jeunesse dorée. Episodes de la Révolution Française* (Montréal, 1979).

Le général Marceau, figure emblématique du héros révolutionnaire, catalogue d'exposition, Musée des Beaux-Arts de Chartres (Chartres, 1996).

George, Henri, *Conscription, tirage au sort et imagerie populaire* (Paris, 1981).

Gérard, Alice, *La Révolution française, mythes et interprétations* (Paris, 1970).

Gerbod, Paul, 'La Révolution enseignée à la jeunesse française dans la première moitié du dix-neuvième siècle', *Revue historique* (1988).

Gervereau, Laurent and Prochasson, Christophe (eds.), *Images de 1917* (Paris, 1987).

Gildea, Robert, *The Past in French History* (New Haven, Conn., 1994).

Marianne in Chains. In Search of the German Occupation, 1940–1945 (London, 2002).

Girard, Louis, *La garde nationale, 1814–71* (Paris, 1964).

La Deuxième République, 1848–51 (Paris, 1968).

Girardet, Raoul, *La société militaire de 1815 à nos jours* (Paris, 1998).

Godechot, Jacques, *Un jury pour la Révolution* (Paris, 1974).

Gossez, Rémi (ed.), *Un ouvrier en 1820. Manuscrit inédit de Jacques-Etienne Bédé* (Paris, 1984).

Griffith, Paddy, *Military Thought in the French Army, 1815–51* (Manchester, 1989).

Gullickson, Gay L., *Unruly Women of Paris. Images of the Commune* (Ithaca, N.Y., 1996).

Hagemann, Karen, 'German heroes: the cult of the death for the fatherland in nineteenth-century Germany', in Stefan Dudink, Karen Hagemenn and John Tosh (eds.), *Masculinities in Politics and War. Gendering Modern History* (Manchester, 2004).

Hampson, Norman, 'The French Revolution and its historians', in Geoffrey Best (ed.), *The Permanent Revolution* (London, 1989).

Hantraye, Jacques, *Les Cosaques aux Champs-Élysées. L'occupation de la France après la chute de Napoléon* (Paris, 2005).

Harbi, Mohammed and Meynier, Gilbert (eds.), *Le FLN. Documents et histoire, 1954–1962* (Paris, 2004).

Hardier, Thierry and Jagielski, Jean-François, *Combattre et mourir pendant la Grande Guerre, 1914–25* (Paris, 2004).

Harel, Véronique (ed.), *Les affiches de la Grande Guerre* (Péronne, 1998).

Hargrove, June, *Les statues de Paris: la représentation des Grands Hommes dans les rues et sur les places de Paris* (Paris, 1989).

Haydon, Colin, and Doyle, William (eds.), *Robespierre* (Cambridge, 1999).

Hazareesingh, Sudhir (ed.), *The Jacobin Legacy in Modern France. Essays in Honour of Vincent Wright* (Oxford, 2002).

The Legend of Napoleon (London, 2004).

The Saint-Napoleon. Celebrations of Sovereignty in Nineteenth-century France (Cambridge, Mass., 2004).

Heim, Jean-François, Béraud, Claire and Heim, Philippe, *Les salons de peinture de la Révolution Française, 1789–99* (Paris, 1989).

Hélias, Yves, 'Les monuments aux morts: essai de sémiologie du politique' (mémoire dactylographié, Université de Rennes, 1977).

Herlaut (General), Le général rouge Ronsin, 1751–1894 (Paris, 1956).

Hippler, Thomas, 'Conscription in the French Restoration: the 1818 debate on military service', *War in History* **13** (2006).

Citizens, Soldiers and National Armies. Military Service in France and Germany, 1789–1830 (London, 2008).

Hollander, Paul d', 'Les gardes nationales en Limousin, juillet 1789 – juillet 1790', *Annales historiques de la Révolution Française* **190** (1992).

Holman, Valerie and Kelly, Debra (eds.), *France at War in the Twentieth Century. Propaganda, Myth and Metaphor* (Oxford, 2000).

Holt, Richard, *Sport and Society in Modern France* (London, 1981).

Hopkin, David, *Soldier and Peasant in French Popular Culture, 1766–1870* (London, 2003).

Horne, John, '"L'Impôt de sang". Republican rhetoric and industrial warfare in France, 1914–18', *Social History* **14** (1989).

'From *levée en masse* to total war: France and the revolutionary legacy, 1870–1945', in Robert Aldrich and Martyn Lyons (eds.), *The Sphinx in the Tuileries, and Other Essays in Modern French History* (Sydney, 1999).

'Defining the enemy. War, law and the levée en masse from 1870 to 1945', in Daniel Moran and Arthur Waldron (eds.), *The People in Arms. Military Myth and National Mobilization since the French Revolution* (Cambridge, 2003).

Horne, John and Kramer, Alan, *German Atrocities, 1914. A History of Denial* (New Haven, Conn., 2001).

Houdaille, Jacques, 'Pertes de l'armée de terre sous le Premier Empire, d'après les registres matricules', *Population* **27** (1972).

Howard, Michael, *The Franco-Prussian War. The German Invasion of France, 1870–71* (London, 1961).

Hublot, Emmanuel, *Valmy ou la défense de la nation par les armes* (Paris, 1987).

Hucker, Daniel, 'French public attitudes towards the prospect of war in 1938–1939: "pacifism" or "war anxiety"?', *French History* **21** (2007).

Humbert, Jean-Marcel, *Napoléon aux Invalides. 1840, le Retour des Cendres* (Paris, 1990).

Hynes, Samuel, *The Soldiers' Tale. Bearing Witness to Modern War* (London, 1997).

Ingrand, Henri, *Libération de l'Auvergne* (Paris, 1974).

Irvine, William D., *The Boulanger Affair Reconsidered. Royalism, Boulangism, and the Origins of the Radical Right in France* (Oxford, 1989).

Jauffret, Jean-Charles, *Soldats en Algérie, 1954–1962. Expériences contrastées des hommes du contingent* (Paris, 2000).

Jauffret, Jean-Claude, *Parlement, Gouvernement, Commandement. L'armée de métier sous la Troisième République, 1871–1914* (2 vols., Vincennes, 1987).

Jellinek, Frank, *The Paris Commune of 1871* (London, 1937).

Jourdan, Annie, 'Du sacre du philosophe au sacre du militaire', *Revue d'histoire moderne et contemporaine* **34** (1992).

'Les monuments de la Révolution française. Le discours des images dans l'espace parisien, 1789–1804' (doctoral thesis, University of Amsterdam, 1993).

Kanter, Sanford, 'Exposing the myth of the Franco-Prussian War', *War and Society* **4** (1986).

Kaplan, Steven L., *Adieu 89* (Paris, 1993).

Kriegel, Annie and Becker, Jean-Jacques (eds.), *1914. La guerre et le mouvement ouvrier français* (Paris, 1964).

Lagrave, Henri, Mazouer, Charles and Regaldo, Marc, *Le théâtre à Bordeaux des origines à nos jours* (Paris, 1985).

Lanier, Jean-François, *Le général Joseph Servan de Gerbey (Romans, 1741 – Paris, 1808). Pour une armée au service de l'homme* (Valence, 2001).

Largeaud, Jean-Marc, 'Waterloo dans la mémoire des Français, 1815–1914' (thèse de doctorat, Université de Lyon-II, 2000).

Leclercq, Jean-Yves, 'Le mythe de Bonaparte sous le Directoire, 1796–1799' (*mémoire de maîtrise*, Université de Paris-I, 1991).

Le Cour Grandmaison, Olivier, *Les citoyennetés en révolution, 1789–94* (Paris, 1992).

Le Gall, Didier, 'Etude léximétrique de la prose napoléonienne à travers les proclamations, les allocutions et les ordres du jour' (mémoire de maîtrise, Université de Paris-I, 1991).

Napoléon et le Mémorial de Sainte-Hélène. Analyse d'un discours (Paris, 2003).

Lehning, James R., *To Be a Citizen. The Political Culture of the Early Third Republic* (Ithaca, N.Y., 2001).

Leith, James A. (ed.), *Images of the Commune/Images de la Commune* (Montreal, 1978).

Lemalet, Martine, *Lettres d'Algérie, 1954–1962. La guerre des appelés, la mémoire d'une génération* (Paris, 1992).

Le Naour, Jean-Yves, *Misères et tourments de la chair durant la Grande Guerre. Les moeurs sexuelles des Français, 1914–18* (Paris, 2002).

Léonard, E. G., *L'armée et ses problèmes au dix-huitième siècle* (Paris, 1958).

Leveque, Guillaume, 'L'image des héros dans la presse photographique française de la Première Guerre Mondiale' (mémoire de DEA, Université de Paris-I, 1989).

Levi, M., *Consent, Dissent and Patriotism* (Cambridge, 1997).

Lewis, Gwynne, *The Second Vendée. The Continuity of Counter-revolution in the Department of the Gard, 1789–1815* (Oxford, 1978).

Lincoln, Margarette (ed.), *Nelson and Napoléon* (London, 2005).

Lucas-Dubreton, Jean, *Le culte de Napoléon, 1815–48* (Paris, 1960).

Luirard, Monique, *La France et ses morts. Les monuments commémoratifs dans la Loire* (Saint-Etienne, 1977).

Lüsebrink, Hans-Jürgen and Reichardt, Rolf, *The Bastille. A History of a Symbol of Despotism and Freedom* (Durham, N.C., 1997).

Luxardo, Hervé, *Histoire de la Marseillaise* (Paris, 1989).

Luzzatto, Sergio, *Mémoire de la Terreur* (Lyon, 1991).

Lynn, John, 'Toward an army of honor: the moral evolution of the French army, 1789–1815', *French Historical Studies* **16** (1989).

Lyons, Martyn, *Napoleon Bonaparte and the Legacy of the French Revolution* (London, 1994).

Macleod, Jenny, *Reconsidering Gallipoli* (Manchester, 2004).

McMillan, James F., *Napoleon III* (London, 1991).

Marnier, Jean, *Souvenirs de guerre en temps de paix, 1793–1806–1823–1862* (Paris, 1867).

Martin, Jean-Clément, *La Vendée de la mémoire, 1800–1980* (Paris, 1989).

'Travestissements, impostures, et la communauté historienne. A propos des femmes soldats de la Révolution et de l'Empire', *Politix* **74** (2006), pp. 31–48.

Martin, Marc, *Les origines de la presse militaire en France à la fin de l'Ancien Régime et sous la Révolution, 1770–99* (Vincennes, 1975).

Mason, Laura, *Singing the French Revolution. Popular Culture and Politics, 1787–99* (Ithaca, N.Y., 1996).

Ménager, Bernard, *Les Napoléon du peuple* (Paris, 1988).

Mézières, Alfred, *Récits de l'invasion. Alsace et Lorraine* (Paris, 1913).

Michaud, Stéphane, Mollier, Jean-Yves and Savy, Nicole (eds.), *Usages de l'image au dix-neuvième siècle* (Paris, 1992).

Michelet, Jules, *Les soldats de la Révolution* (Paris, 1898).

'Nos armées républicaines', in Paul Viallaneix (ed), *Oeuvres complètes de Michelet* (21 vols., Paris, 1980).

Miller, Paul B., *From Revolutionaries to Citizens. Anti-militarism in France, 1870–1914* (Raleigh, N.C., 2002).

Miquel, Pierre, *La guerre d'Algérie* (Paris, 1993).

Mjøset, Lars and Van Holde, Stephen (eds.), *The Comparative Study of Conscription in the Armed Forces (Comparative Social Research, vol. XX)* (Amsterdam, 2002).

Molis, Robert, *Les Francs-tireurs et les Garibaldi: soldats de la République, 1870–1871, en Bourgogne* (Paris, 1995).

Monteilhet, J., *Les institutions militaires de la France, 1814–1932. De la paix armée à la paix désarmée* (Paris, 1926).

Moran, Daniel and Waldron, Arthur (eds.), *The People in Arms. Military Myth and National Mobilization since the French Revolution* (Cambridge, 2003).

Morgan, Kevin, 'Une toute petite différence entre la Marseillaise et God Save the King: la gauche britannique et le problème de la nation dans les années trente', in Serge Wolikow and Annie Bleton-Ruget (eds.), *Antifascisme et Nation. Les gauches européennes au temps du Front Populaire* (Dijon, 1998).

Mosse, George L., *Fallen Soldiers: Reshaping the Memory of the World Wars* (New York, 1990).

Muir, Rory, *Tactics and the Experience of Battle in the Age of Napoleon* (New Haven, Conn., 1998).

Mukerji, Chandra, *Territorial Ambitions and the Gardens of Versailles* (Cambridge, 1997).

Namer, Gérard, *Batailles pour la mémoire: la commémoration en France de 1945 à nos jours* (Paris, 1983).

Neiberg, Michael S., *Soldiers' Lives Through History: The Nineteenth Century* (Westport, Conn., 2006).

Nelms, Brenda, *The Third Republic and the Centennial of 1789* (New York, 1987).

Nieto, Philippe, *Le centenaire de la Révolution dauphinoise. Vizille, un mythe républicain* (Grenoble, 1988).

Nora, Pierre, 'Lavisse, instituteur national', in Pierre Nora (ed.), *Les lieux de mémoire: 1 – La République* (Paris, 1984).

Nord, Philip, *The Republican Moment. Struggles for Democracy in Nineteenth-century France* (Cambridge, Mass., 1995).

O'Brien, David, 'Antoine-Jean Gros in Italy', *Burlington Magazine* **137** (1995), pp. 651–60.

Ory, Pascal, 'La commémoration révolutionnaire en 1939', in René Rémond and Janine Bourdin (eds.), *La France et les Français en 1938 et 1939* (Paris, 1978).

'Le centenaire de la Révolution Française. La preuve par 89', in Pierre Nora (ed.), *Les lieux de mémoire. 1 – La République (Paris, 1984)*, p. 531.

Une nation pour mémoire. 1889, 1939, 1989, trois jubilés révolutionnaires (Paris, 1992).

Ozouf, Jacques and Ozouf, Mona, 'Le thème du patriotisme dans les manuels primaires', *Mouvement social* **49** (1964).

'Le tour de la France par deux enfants. Le petit livre rouge de la République', in Pierre Nora (ed.), *Les lieux de mémoire: 1 – La République* (Paris, 1984).

La fête révolutionnaire (Paris, 1976).

L'école de la France. Essais sur la Révolution, l'utopie et l'enseignement (Paris, 1984).

Palmer, Robert R., *From Jacobin to Liberal. Marc-Antoine Jullien, 1775–1848* (Princeton, N.J., 1993).

Paret, Peter, Lewis, Beth Irwin and Paret, Paul, *Persuasive Images: Posters of War and Revolution* (Princeton, N.J., 1992).

Perrot, Danielle, 'La thématique politique des manuels d'histoire du cours élementaire de l'enseignement public' (mémoire pour le diplôme d'études supérieure de science politique, Université de Rennes, 1973).

Perrout, René, *Trésors des images d'Épinal* (Paris, 1985).

Pervillé, Guy, 'La génération de la Résistance face à la guerre d'Algérie', in François Marcot (ed.), *La Résistance et les Français. Lutte armée et maquis* (Paris, 1996).

Petiteau, Natalie, *Lendemains d'Empire. Les soldats de Napoléon dans la France du dix-neuvième siècle* (Paris, 2003).

(ed.), *Voies nouvelles pour l'histoire du Premier Empire. Territoires, Pouvoirs, Identités* (Paris, 2003).

Planchais, Jean, *Adieu Valmy. La fin de la nation en armes* (Paris, 2003).

Porch, Douglas, *Army and Revolution in France, 1815–1848* (London, 1974).

Prendergast, Christopher, *Napoleon and History Painting. Antoine-Jean Gros's 'La Bataille d'Eylau'* (Oxford, 1997).

Price, Roger (ed.), *1848 in France* (London, 1975).

Prochasson, Christophe and Rasmussen, Anne (eds.), *Au nom de la Patrie. Les intellectuels et la Première Guerre Mondiale, 1910–1919* (Paris, 1996).

Vrai et faux dans la Grande Guerre (Paris, 2004).

Prost, Antoine, 'Verdun: the life of a site of memory', in idem., *Republican Identities in War and Peace: Representations of France in the Nineteenth and Twentieth Centuries* (Oxford, 2002).

Puymège, Gérard de, *Chauvin, le soldat-laboureur. Contribution à l'étude des nationalismes* (Paris, 1993).

Raybaut, Paul, *Correspondance de guerre d'un rural, 1914–17* (Paris, 1974).

Régent, Frédéric, 'L'expédition d'Égypte de Bonaparte vue par la presse parisienne, 1798–99' (mémoire de maîtrise, Université de Paris-I, 1992).

Reinhard, Marcel, 'Nostalgie et service militaire pendant la Révolution', *Annales historiques de la Révolution Française* **30** (1958).

'Observations sur le rôle révolutionnaire de l'armée dans la Révolution française', *Annales historiques de la Révolution française* (1962).

(ed.), *Contributions à l'histoire démographique de la Révolution Française, 3e série – Etudes sur la population parisienne* (Paris, 1970).

Ridel, Charles, *Les embusqués* (Paris, 2007).

Rioux, Jean-Pierre, *La France perd la mémoire. Comment un pays démissionne de son histoire* (Paris, 2006).

Robert, Frédéric, *La Marseillaise* (Paris, 1989).

Roberts, J. M., *The Paris Commune from the Right* (London, 1973).

Rosanvallon, Pierre, *Le sacre du citoyen* (Paris, 1992).

Le peuple introuvable (Paris, 1998).

La démocratie inachevée (Paris, 2000).

Le modèle politique français. La société civile contre le jacobinisme de 1789 à nos jours (Paris, 2004).

Rossel, André, *1870. La première guerre, par l'affiche et l'image* (Paris, 1970).

Roth, François, *La guerre de 1870* (Paris, 1990).

Rouquet, François, Virgili, Fabrice and Voldman, Danièle (eds.), *Amours, guerres et sexualité, 1914–45* (Paris, 2007).

Rowe, Michael (ed.), *Collaboration and Resistance in Napoleonic Europe. State-Formation in an Age of Upheaval, c.1800–1815* (London, 2003).

Roynette, Odile, 'L'armée dans la bataille sociale: maintien de l'ordre et grèves ouvrières dans le Nord de la France, 1871–1906', *Mouvement Social* **179** (1997).

'Bons pour le service'. L'expérience de la caserne en France à la fin du dix-neuvième siècle (Paris, 2000).

Rutkoff, Peter M., *Revanche and Revision. The Ligue des Patriotes and the Origins of the Radical Right in France, 1882–1900* (Athens, Ohio, 1981).

Sansboeuf, Joseph, 'Les sociétés de gymnastique en France', in Philippe Tissié (ed.), *L'éducation physique* (Paris, 1901).

Savigear, P., 'Carbonarism and the French Army, 1815–24', *History* **54** (1969), pp. 198–211.

Schnapper, Bernard, *Le remplacement militaire en France. Quelques aspects politiques, économiques et sociaux du recrutement au dix-neuvième siècle* (Paris, 1968).

Scott, Samuel F., *The Response of the Royal Army to the French Revolution. The Role and Development of the Line Army, 1787–93* (Oxford, 1978).

Secher, Reynald, *Le génocide franco-français. La Vendée-vengé* (Paris, 1986).

Secrétariat d'Etat aux Anciens Combattants et Victimes de Guerre, *Monuments de mémoire. Monuments aux morts de la Grande Guerre*, eds. Philippe Rive, Annette Becker, Olivier Pelletier, Dominique Renoux and Christophe Thomas (Paris, 1991).

Serman, William, 'Le corps des officiers français sous la Deuxième République et le Second Empire', 3 vols., thèse de doctorat, Université de Paris-IV, 1976 (Lille, 1978).

Serman, William and Bertaud, Jean-Paul, *Nouvelle histoire militaire de la France, 1789–1919* (Paris, 1998).

Shafer, David A., *The Paris Commune. French Politics, Culture and Society at the Crossroads of the Revolutionary Tradition and Revolutionary Socialism* (London, 2005).

Sibalis, Michael, 'Arbitrary detention, human rights and the Napoleonic senate', in Howard G. Brown and Judith A. Miller (eds.), *Taking Liberties. Problems of a New Order from the French Revolution to Napoleon* (Manchester, 2002).

Slater, Catherine, *Defeatists and their Enemies. Political Invective in France, 1914–18* (Oxford, 1981).

Smith, Leonard V., *Between Mutiny and Obedience* (Princeton, 1994).

Soboul, Albert, *Les soldats de l'an II* (Paris, 1959).

Comprendre la Révolution. Problèmes politiques de la Révolution Française, 1789–99 (Paris, 1981).

Spitzer, Alan, *Old Hatreds and Young Hopes. The French Carbonari against the Bourbon Restoration* (Cambridge, Mass., 1971).

Stewart, John Hall, *A Documentary Survey of the French Revolution* (New York, 1951).

Stewart-McDougall, Mary Lynn, *The Artisan Republic. Revolution, Reaction and Resistance in Lyon, 1848–51* (Kingston, Ontario, 1984).

Strachan, John, 'Romance, religion and the Republic: Bruno's *Le Tour de la France par deux enfants*', *French History* **18** (2004).

Strieter, Terry W., 'The impact of the Franco-Prussian War on veterans. The company-level career patterns of the French army, 1870–1895', *War and Society* 7 (1989).

Sweets, John F., *Choices in Vichy France. The French under Nazi Occupation* (New York, 1986).

Citizenship and Wars. France in Turmoil, 1870–71 (London, 2001).

Thibaudet, Albert, *La république des professeurs* (Paris, 1927).

Thiesse, Anne-Marie, *Écrire la France. Le mouvement littéraire régionaliste de langue française entre la Belle Époque et la Libération* (Paris, 1991).

Thomson, Alistair, 'A past you can live with: digger memories and the Anzac legend', in Alan Seymour and Richard Nile (eds.), *Anzac: Meaning, Memory and Myth* (London, 1991).

Thomson, Richard, *The Troubled Republic. Visual Culture and Social Debate in France, 1889–1900* (New Haven, Conn., 2004).

Tint, Herbert, *The Decline of French Patriotism, 1870–1940* (London, 1964).

Tombs, Robert, *The Paris Commune, 1871* (London, 1999).

'Making memories of war: images of heroism and turpitude, 1870–1871', in *French History in the Antipodes. Proceedings of the Twelfth George Rudé Seminar on French History and Civilisation* (Wellington, New Zealand, 2001).

Tomiche, Nada, *Napoléon écrivain* (Paris, 1952).

Tomlinson, Matthew, 'Rebuilding Albert: reconstruction and remembrance on the Western Front, 1914–1932' (PhD thesis, University of York, 2005).

Trélat, Ulysse, 'La charbonnerie', in *Paris révolutionnaire*, vol. II (Paris, 1833).

Le Triomphe des mairies. Grands décors républicains à Paris, 1870–1914 (Catalogue d'exposition, Musée du Petit Palais, Paris, 1986).

Tuffrau, Paul, *1914–1918: Quatre années sur le front. Carnets d'un combattant* (Paris, 1998).

Tulard, Jean, *Nouvelle bibliographie critique des mémoires sur l'époque napoléonienne écrits ou traduits en français* (Geneva, 1991).

(ed.), *Napoléon: le Sacre* (Paris, 1993).

Utley, R. E., *The French Defence Debate. Consensus and Continuity in the Mitterrand Era* (London, 2000).

Vidal-Naquet, Pierre, *Face à la raison d'état, un historien dans la guerre d'Algérie* (Paris, 1989).

Vidalenc, Jean, *Les demi-solde. Etude d'une catégorie sociale* (Paris, 1955).

Vigarello, Georges, 'Le gymnaste et la nation armée', in Alain Corbin, Jean-Jacques Courtine and Georges Vigarello (eds.), *Histoire du corps* (3 vols., Paris, 2005), vol. II.

Viola, Paolo, 'Napoléon, chef de la révolution patriotique', in Jean-Clément Martin (ed.), *Napoléon et l'Europe* (Rennes, 2002).

Vittori, Jean-Pierre, *Nous, les appelés d'Algérie* (Paris, 1983).

Vogüé, Marie-Eugène-Melchior de, *Remarques sur l'Exposition du Centenaire* (Paris, 1889).

Voisin, André-Roger, *L'école des poilus. L'enseignement de la guerre dans les écoles primaires de 1870 à 1914* (Paris, 2007).

Vovelle, Michel, 'La Marseillaise. La guerre ou la paix', in Pierre Nora (ed.), *Les lieux de mémoire: 1 – La République* (Paris, 1984).

La Révolution Française: images et récit (5 vols., Paris, 1986).

(ed.), *L'image de la Révolution Française* (4 vols., Paris, 1989).

'Fortunes et infortunes de Marceau', in *Le Général Marceau. Figure emblématique du héros révolutionnaire* (exhibition catalogue, Chartres, 1996).

Walter, François, *Les figures paysagères de la nation. Territoire et paysage en Europe, 16e au 20e siècle* (Paris, 2004).

Waquet, Jean, 'La société civile devant l'insoumission et la désertion à l'époque de la conscription militaire', *Bibliothèque de l'Ecole des Chartes* **126** (1968).

Wardhaugh, Jessica, 'Fighting for the unknown soldier: the contested territory of the French nation in 1934–1938', *Modern and Contemporary France* **15** (2007).

Wartelle, François, 'Le thème de l'enfance héroïque dans les manuels scolaires de la Troisième République', in *Joseph Bara, 1779–1793: pour le deuxième centenaire de sa naissance* (Paris, 1981).

Weber, Eugen, *Peasants into Frenchmen. The Modernisation of Rural France, 1870–1914* (London, 1977).

France, fin de siècle (Cambridge, Mass., 1986).

Werth, Alexander, *De Gaulle* (London, 1965).

Wessells, Michael, 'Recruitment of children as soldiers in sub-Saharan Africa: an ecological analysis', in Lars Mjøset and Stephen Van Holde (eds.), *The Comparative Study of Conscription in the Armed Forces (Comparative Social Research, vol. XX)* (Amsterdam, 2002).

Wilson-Smith, Timothy, *Napoleon and his Artists* (London, 1996).

Woloch, Isser, *Jacobin Legacy. The Democratic Movement under the Directory* (Princeton, N.J., 1970).

The French Veteran from the Revolution to the Restoration (Chapel Hill, 1979).
Wright, Gordon, editor's introduction to Jules Michelet, *History of the French Revolution* (Chicago, 1967).
Wright, Julian, *The Regionalist Movement in France, 1890–1914. Jean Charles-Brun and French Political Thought* (Oxford, 2003).
Zeller, André, *Soldats perdus. Des armées de Napoléon aux garnisons de Louis XVIII* (Paris, 1977).

Index

Studies in the Social and Cultural History of Modern Warfare

Titles in the series:

1 *Sites of Memory, Sites of Mourning: The Great War in European Cultural History*
Jay Winter

2 *Capital Cities at War: Paris, London, Berlin 1914–1919*
Jay Winter and Jean-Louis Robert

3 *State, Society and Mobilization in Europe during the First World War*
Edited by John Horne

4 *A Time of Silence: Civil War and the Culture of Repression in Franco's Spain, 1936–1945*
Michael Richards

5 *War and Remembrance in the Twentieth Century*
Edited by Jay Winter and Emmanuel Sivan

6 *European Culture in the Great War: The Arts, Entertainment and Propaganda, 1914–1918*
Edited by Aviel Roshwald and Richard Stites

7 *The Labour of Loss: Mourning, Memory and Wartime Bereavement in Australia*
Joy Damousi

8 *The Legacy of Nazi Occupation: Patriotic Memory and National Recovery in Western Europe, 1945–1965*
Pieter Lagrou

9 *War Land on the Eastern Front: Culture, National Identity and German Occupation in World War I*
Vejas Gabriel Liulevicius

10 *The Spirit of 1914: Militarism, Myth and Mobilization in Germany*
Jeffrey Verhey

11 *German Anglophobia and the Great War, 1914–1918*
Matthew Stibbe

12 *Life between Memory and Hope: The Survivors of the Holocaust in Occupied Germany*
Zee W. Mankowitz

13 *Commemorating the Irish Civil War: History and Memory, 1923–2000*
Anne Dolan

14 *Jews and Gender in Liberation France*
Karen H. Adler

15 *America and the Armenian Genocide of 1915*
Edited by Jay Winter

16 *Fighting Different Wars: Experience, Memory and the First World War in Britain*
Janet S.K. Watson

17 *Vienna and the Fall of the Habsburg Empire: Total War and Everyday Life in World War I*
Maureen Healy

18 *The Moral Disarmament of France: Education, Pacifism, and Patriotism, 1914–1940*
Mona L. Siegel

19 *National Cleansing: Retribution against Nazi Collaborators in Post-War Czechoslovakia*
Benjamin Frommer

20 *China and the Great War: China's Pursuit of a New National Identity and Internationalization*
Xu Guoqi

21 *The Great War: Historical Debates, 1914 to the Present*
Antoine Prost and Jay Winter

22 *Citizen Soldiers: The Liverpool Territorials in the First World War*
Helen B. McCartney

23 *The Great War and Medieval Memory: War, Remembrance and Medievalism in Britain and Germany, 1914–1940*
Stefan Goebel

24 *The Great War and Urban Life in Germany: Freiburg, 1914–1918*
Roger Chickering

25 *Capital Cities at War: Paris, London, Berlin 1914–1919. Volume 2: A Cultural History*
Jay Winter and Jean-Louis Robert

26 *The Great Naval Game: Britain and Germany in the Age of Empire*
Jan Rüger

27 *Ghosts of War in Vietnam*
Heonik Kwon

28 *Japanese Society at War: Death, Memory and the Russo-Japanese War*
Naoko Shimazu

29 *The Legacy of the French Revolutionary Wars: The Nation-in-Arms in French Republican Memory*
Alan Forrest